Quantitative Semantics and Soft Computing Methods for the Web:

Perspectives and Applications

Ramon F. Brena
Tecnologico de Monterrey, Mexico

Adolfo Guzman–Arenas
Instituto Politécnico Nacional, Mexico

Information Science
REFERENCE

Managing Director:	Lindsay Johnston
Book Production Manager:	Sean Woznicki
Development Manager:	Joel Gamon
Development Editor:	Myla Harty
Acquisitions Editor:	Erika Carter
Typesetters:	Lisandro Gonzalez, Chris Shearer
Print Coordinator:	Jamie Snavely
Cover Design:	Nick Newcomer

Published in the United States of America by
Information Science Reference (an imprint of IGI Global)
701 E. Chocolate Avenue
Hershey PA 17033
Tel: 717-533-8845
Fax: 717-533-8661
E-mail: cust@igi-global.com
Web site: http://www.igi-global.com

Library of Congress Cataloging-in-Publication Data

Quantitative semantics and soft computing methods for the Web: perspectives and applications / Ramon F. Brena and Adolfo Guzman-Arenas, editors.
    p. cm.
 Includes bibliographical references and index.
  ISBN 978-1-60960-881-1 (hardcover) -- ISBN 978-1-60960-882-8 (ebook) -- ISBN 978-1-60960-883-5 (print & perpetual access) 1. Soft computing. 2. Semantic Web. I. Brena, Ramon F., 1954- II. Guzman, Adolfo.
 QA76.9.S63Q36 2011
 006.3--dc23
                              2011027134

British Cataloguing in Publication Data
A Cataloguing in Publication record for this book is available from the British Library.

All work contributed to this book is new, previously-unpublished material. The views expressed in this book are those of the authors, but not necessarily of the publisher.

Table of Contents

Detailed Table of Contents

Chapter 1

Adolfo Guzman-Arenas, Instituto Politécnico Nacional, México
Alma-Delia Cuevas, Instituto Politécnico Nacional, México

Recently, using confusion, the authors computed the centroid ("consensus value") and the inconsistency of a set (a bag, in fact) of qualitative assertions about the same property or variable (say, John's pet), reported by several observers. A bag of dissimilar assertions will have a large inconsistency, which could diminish if the problem at hand allows several centroids to be selected. John could have two pets, and the inconsistency of these two "consensus values" with all observations will be much better (much smaller): one part of the observers will feel little discomfort with one of the centroids; the remaining part will feel little discomfort with the second centroid. This chapter finds the set of centroids of a bag of qualitative values that minimizes the inconsistency of the bag; that is, the total discomfort of all members of the bag will be smallest. These centroids define clusters of the bag. All observers are equally credible, so differences in their findings arise from perception errors.

Chapter 2

Davide Magatti, Università degli Studi di Milano-Bicocca, Italy
Fabio Stella, Università degli Studi di Milano-Bicocca, Italy

A software system for topic discovery and document tagging is described. The system discovers the topics hidden in a given document collection, labels them according to user supplied taxonomy and tags new documents. It implements an information processing pipeline which consists of document preprocessing, topic extraction, automatic labeling of topics, and multi-label document classification. The preprocessing module allows importing of several kinds of documents and offers different document representations: binary, term frequency and term frequency inverse document frequency. The topic extraction module is implemented through a proprietary version of the Latent Dirichlet Allocation model. The optimal number of topics is selected through hierarchical clustering. The topic labeling module optimizes a set of similarity measures defined over the user supplied taxonomy. It is implemented through an algorithm over a topic tree. The document tagging module solves a multi-label classification problem through multi-net Naïve Bayes without the need to perform any learning tasks.

Chapter 3

Zhihua Wei, Tongji University, China
Duoqian Miao, Tongji University, China
Ruizhi Wang, Tongji University, China
Zhifei Zhang, Tongji University, China

Text representation is the prerequisite of various document processing tasks, such as information retrieval, text classification, text clustering, etc. It has been studied intensively for the past few years, and many excellent models have been designed as well. However, the performance of these models is affected by the problem of data sparseness. Existing smoothing techniques usually make use of statistic theory or linguistic information to assign a uniform distribution to absent words. They do not concern the real word distribution or distinguish between words. In this chapter, a method based on a kind of soft computing theory, Tolerance Rough Set theory, which makes use of upper approximation and lower approximation theory in Rough Set to assign different values for absent words in different approximation regions, is proposed. Theoretically, the authors' algorithms can estimate smoothing value for absent words according to their relation with respect to existing words. Text classification experiments by using Vector Space Model (VSM) and Latent Dirichlet Allocation (LDA) model on public corpora have shown that our algorithms greatly improve the performance of text representation model, especially for the performance of unbalanced corpus.

Chapter 4

Eduardo H. Ramírez, Tecnológico de Monterrey, México
Ramón F. Brena, Tecnológico de Monterrey, México

In this work the authors propose an alternative collection-modeling paradigm based on a simpler representation of topics as freely overlapping clusters of semantically similar documents, thus being able to take advantage of highly-scalable clustering algorithms. Then, they propose the Query-based Topic Modeling framework (QTM), an information-theoretic method that assumes the existence of a "golden" set of queries that can capture most of the semantic information of the collection and produce models with maximum semantic coherence. The QTM method uses information-theoretic heuristics to find a set of "topical-queries" which are then co-clustered along with the documents of the collection and transformed to produce overlapping document clusters. The QTM framework was designed with scalability in mind and is able to be executed in parallel over commodity-class machines using the Map-Reduce approach.

Chapter 5

Anna Lisa Gentile, University of Sheffield, UK
Ziqi Zhang, University of Sheffield, UK
Fabio Ciravegna, University of Sheffield, UK

This chapter proposes a novel Semantic Relatedness (SR) measure that exploits diverse features extracted from a knowledge resource. Computing SR is a crucial technique for many complex Natural Language Processing (NLP) as well as Semantic Web related tasks. Typically, semantic relatedness measures only make use of limited number of features without considering diverse feature sets or understanding the different contributions of features to the accuracy of a method. This chapter proposes a random graph walk model based method that naturally combines diverse features extracted from a knowledge resource in a balanced way in the task of computing semantic relatedness. A set of experiments is carefully designed to investigate the effects of choosing different features and altering their weights on the accuracy of the system. Next, using the derived feature sets and feature weights we evaluate the proposed method against the state-of-the-art semantic relatedness measures, and show that it obtains higher accuracy on many benchmarking datasets. Additionally, we justify the usefulness of the proposed method in a practical NLP task, i.e. Named Entity Disambiguation.

Chapter 6

    Gloria Bordogna, CNR-IDPA, Italy
    Alessandro Campi, Politecnico di Milano, Italy
    Giuseppe Psaila, Università di Bergamo, Italy
    Stefania Ronchi, Politecnico di Milano, Italy

In this chapter, the authors propose a novel multi-granular framework for visualization and exploration of the results of a complex search process, performed by a user by submitting several queries to possibly distinct search engines. The primary aim of the approach is to supply users with summaries, with distinct levels of details, of the results for a search process. It applies dynamic clustering to the results in each ordered list retrieved by a search engine evaluating a user's query. The single retrieved items, the clusters so identified, and the single retrieved lists, are considered as dealing with topics at distinct levels of granularity, from the finest level to the coarsest one, respectively. Implicit topics are revealed by associating labels with the retrieved items, the clusters, and the retrieved lists. Then, some manipulation operators, defined in this chapter, are applied to each pair of retrieved lists, clusters, and single items, to reveal their implicit relationships. These relationships have a semantic nature, since they are labeled to approximately represent the shared documents and the shared sub-topics between each pair of combined elements. Finally, both the topics retrieved by the distinct searches and their relationships are represented through multi-granular graphs, that represent the retrieved topics at three distinct levels of granularity. The exploration of the results can be performed by expanding the graphs nodes to see their contents, and by expanding the edges to see their shared contents and their common sub-topics.

Chapter 7

    Hiram Calvo, Nara Inst. of Science & Technology, Japan
    Kentaro Inui, Tohoku University, Japan
    Yuji Matsumoto, Nara Inst. of Science & Technology, Japan

Learning verb argument preferences has been approached as a verb and argument problem, or at most as a tri-nary relationship between subject, verb and object. However, the simultaneous correlation of all arguments in a sentence has not been explored thoroughly for sentence plausibility mensuration because of the increased number of potential combinations and data sparseness. In this work the authors present a review of some common methods for learning argument preferences beginning with the simplest case of considering binary co-relations, then they compare with tri-nary co-relations, and finally they consider all arguments. For this latter, the authors use an ensemble model for machine learning using discriminative and generative models, using co-occurrence features, and semantic features in different arrangements. The authors seek to answer questions about the number of optimal topics required for PLSI and LDA models, as well as the number of co-occurrences that should be required for improving performance. They explore the implications of using different ways of projecting co-relations, i.e., into a word space, or directly into a co-occurrence features space. We conducted tests using a pseudo-disambiguation task learning from large corpora extracted from Internet.

Chapter 8

Ana G. Maguitman, Universidad Nacional del Sur, Argentina
Carlos M. Lorenzetti, Universidad Nacional del Sur, Argentina
Rocío L. Cecchini, Universidad Nacional del Sur, Argentina

Performance evaluation plays a crucial role in the development and improvement of search systems in general and context-based systems in particular. In order to evaluate search systems, test collections are needed. These test collections typically involve a corpus of documents, a set of queries and a series of relevance assessments. In traditional approaches users or hired evaluators provide manual assessments of relevance. However this is difficult and expensive, and does not scale with the complexity and heterogeneity of available digital information. This chapter proposes a semantic evaluation framework that takes advantages of topic ontologies and semantic similarity data derived from these ontologies. The structure and content of the Open Directory Project topic ontology is used to derive semantic relations among a massive number of topics and to implement classical and ad hoc retrieval performance evaluation metrics. In addition, this chapter describes an incremental method for context-based retrieval, which is based on the notions of topic descriptors and topic discriminators. The incremental context-based retrieval method is used to illustrate the application of the proposed semantic evaluation framework. Finally, the chapter discusses the advantages of applying the proposed framework.

Chapter 9

Pavel Makagonov, Mixtec Technological University, Mexico
Celia Bertha Reyes Espinoza, Mixtec Technological University, Mexico
Grigori Sidorov, National Polytechnic Institute, Mexico

The main idea of the authors' research is to perform quantitative analysis of a text collection during the process of its preparation and transformation into a digital library for a website. They use as a case study the digital library of the website on Mixtec culture that we maintain. They propose using the concept of the text document search image (TSDI). For creating TSDIs the authors make analysis of word frequencies in the documents and distinguish between the Zipf's distribution that is typical for meaningful words and distributions approximated by an ellipse typical for auxiliary words. The authors also describe some analogies of these distributions in architecture and in urban planning. They describe a toolkit DDL that allows for TDSI creation and show its application for the mentioned website and for the corpus of dialogs with railway office information system.

Chapter 10

René Arnulfo García-Hernández, Autonomous University of the State of Mexico, Mexico
J. Fco. Martínez-Trinidad, National Institute of Astrophysics, Mexico
J. Ariel Carrasco-Ochoa, National Institute of Astrophysics, Mexico

This chapter introduces maximal sequential patterns, how to extract them, and some applications of maximal sequential patterns for document processing and web content mining. The main objective of this chapter is showing that maximal sequential patterns preserve document semantic, and therefore they could be a good alternative to the word and n-gram models. First, this chapter introduces the problem of maximal sequential pattern mining when the data are sequential chains of words. After, it defines several basic concepts and the problem of maximal sequential pattern mining in text documents. Then, it presents two algorithms proposed by the authors of this chapter for efficiently finding maximal sequential patterns in text documents. Additionally, it describes the use of maximal sequential patterns as a quantitative semantic tool for solving different problems related to document processing and web content mining. Finally, it shows some future research directions and conclusions.

Chapter 11

This chapter presents an approach for discovering and describing thematically related document groups (topics) by means of graph clustering; this approach responds to the need of organizing information in massive Web collections. Because a Web collection is hyperlinked, the authors can view it as a directed graph, whose vertices represent its pages and whose arcs represent links among these pages. Being this the case, we assume that topics will be graph clusters, where a graph cluster is a group of vertices with numerous arcs to the inside of the group and few arcs to the outside of it. In that sense, their topic mining task is mainly focused on clustering the document graph; to cope with scalability issues and enable the discovery of overlapping clusters, we particularly use a local approach, which maximizes a density-based fitness value over the neighborhoods of different starting points. Moreover, with the intent of enriching the discovered clusters, we include the calculation of semantic descriptors. Their approach was tested over the Wikipedia collection and we observed—by different means—that the resulting clusters in fact correspond to cohesive topical document groups, which leads us to conclude that topic mining can be treated as a graph clustering problem. An extensive review of existing literature on clustering and topic mining is given throughout the chapter as well.

Preface

APPROXIMATE METHODS IN SEMANTICS FOR THE INTERNET: AN INTRODUCTORY MAP TO QUANTITATIVE SEMANTICS

This preface offers a conceptual framework for putting in context the extensive work that has been done in areas related to semantic similarity measuring, approximate semantic methods, document clustering and grouping, and many others that we call generically "Quantitative Semantics". We present some of the most relevant works in these areas, classifying them so that a kind of map emerges, allowing a reader to understand the bigger picture of this tremendously relevant area in many text-processing tasks.

As part of this framework, we provide a brief explanation for the works herein exposed, giving to the reader a scaffolding structure where the works in this book can be conceptually attached.

INTRODUCTION

The Internet has been acknowledged as one of the recent technological revolutions due to its large impact on the whole society. Nevertheless, precisely due to its impact, limitations of the Internet have become apparent; in particular, its inability to take into account in an automatic way the meaning of online documents.

There are initiatives aiming to enhance the Internet, by introducing new languages, which are capable of expressing in a self-contained way the meaning of online documents. They have been called the "Semantic Web" (SW) (Antoniou, Van Harmelen 2004), and have delivered an impressive set of standards, like RDF, OWL and more, which are the base for writing "ontologies", as a way to encapsulate semantic units.

Nevertheless, several practical problems have hindered the Semantic Web from becoming mainstream. Today, some 10 year after been proposed in a manifesto, the SW-enabled web pages do not represent even a small fraction of the whole online available content; they are roughly a quarter of one percent of the whole web. Even duplicating its volume each year, SW would barely reach 1% of the web in two years, which is an overly optimistic estimation.

Many reasons have been argued for SW limited growth (Marshall, Shipman 2003), like SW technological sophistication requirements on users, the quantity of work required to rebuild the web on SW terms, or even (circularly) blaming the SW marginality for its little usability –which makes it marginal.

This book is inspired by the desire to find and extract useful information in Web-based documents, which are a wealth of readily-available information. Instead of waiting for the SW to become mainstream, we can analyze and process the actual content of today's Inter-net. At the least, extracting meaning from the actual Internet could complement and pave the way to SW future developments.

We wish to access the meaning residing in the documents, not just to find out if they contain certain key words or are sitting in highly popular web sites. So we try to answer the question of how to model the semantics of a document, and how to extract (useful) knowledge from one of them. Or, put in other way, how to model the semantic of words, how to extract (useful) knowledge from their appearance in actual documents?

One of the backbone concepts we will use in this chapter for presenting and comparing the different works included in this book, is the notion of "semantic similarity", which tries to give specific measures for the idea that two or more words or texts could refer to the same or similar topic. This concept is introduced in the next section, and then, in the following subsections we delve into three forms of semantic similarity, for documents, words, and concepts. After that, we will discuss the use of semantic similarity in information retrieval tasks such as search.

While discussing the above, we will present specific works for each of the items, using a label of the form "W.x" for a number x, -"W" standing for "work"- including of course the chapters of this book.

So, in this introductory chapter, our goal is to place the chapters of the book in the map of current literature of semantic similarity, not being exhaustive, but citing some relevant works for each topic.

SEMANTIC SIMILARITY

The semantic similarity between documents and terms has been studied in the fields of at least information retrieval and machine learning, and there is a whole body of literature on measuring the semantic similarity (Resnik, 1995; Landauer, Dumais 1997; Lin, 1998; Hatzivassiloglou et al. 1999; Turney, 2001; Maguitman et al. 2005; Ramirez, Brena, 2006; Sahami et al. 2006; Bollegala, 2007). These methods can be roughly classified into two major categories: knowledge-based approaches (§1.1.1) and corpus-based approaches (§1.1.2).

Before answering the questions asked in the preceding paragraphs, we must query again: What for? What is the goal of these models, of the intended extraction? Or, in equivalent form, how will I know if the constructed models are adequate, are appropriate? Do the models match the modeled documents, regarding the information in them contained? How will I know if the correct conclusions were obtained from the accessed documents (or from those reported as "relevant")? We can recognize four important goals:

- Finding similarity among documents (§1.1);
- Finding similarity among words or symbolic values (§1.2);
- Finding similarity among *concepts* (not words) (§1.3);

Semantic Similarity among Documents

Automatic methods to compute similarity between texts have applications in many information retrieval related areas, including natural language processing and image retrieval from the Web, where the text surrounding the image can be automatically augmented to convey a better sense of the topic of the image.

Here we place the efforts to group documents in collections of "semantically similar" documents. This grouping or clustering can be done by either

- Attaching them a specific label or tag –or using a predefined taxonomy or collection of such tags (§1.1.1); or by
- Grouping or clustering the documents, but without use of predefined labels or taxonomies (§1.1.2).

These two alternatives correspond to the classification of semantic similarity into two main approaches that we mentioned before: Knowledge-based methods and corpus-based methods.

Knowledge-Based Methods

Knowledge-based approaches are based on the use of predefined directories or ontologies to identify semantic relations. Measures of semantic similarity between documents take as a starting point the structure of a directory or document classification scheme where the entities have been previously sorted. Examples of such classifications include WordNet (See W.19) for the case of terms, and Dmoz, the Wikipedia's List of Academic Disciplines or the Yahoo directory, for the case of documents.

These methods attach to the documents a specific label or tag: the theme or topic they cover, the "name" of the collection. When the methods use human-defined categories for topics (Among them, W.3, W.4, W.6, W.7, W.8) they become prone to problems of disagreement, difficulty to update, etc.

Keeping up-to-date the ontologies used by the knowledge-based approaches is expensive. For example, the semantic similarity between terms changes across different contexts. Take for instance the term java, which is frequently associated with the java programming language among computer scientist. However, this sense of java is not the only one possible as the term may be referring to the java coffee, the java island or the java Russian cigarettes, among other possibilities. New words are constantly being created as well as new senses are assigned to existing words. As a consequence, the use of knowledge-based approaches has disadvantages because they require that the ontologies be manually maintained. Alternatively, methods that disambiguate words into meanings (See W.2) can be used.

W.1. Some organizations have tried to organize pages in a predefined classification, and have manually built large directories of topics (e.g. Dmoz or the Yahoo! directory). But given the huge size and the dynamic nature of the Web, keeping track of pages and their topic manually is a daunting task. There is also the problem of agreeing on a standard classification, and this has proved to be a formidable problem, as different individuals and organizations tend to classify things differently.

W.2. Automatic methods to identify the topic of a piece of text. Clasitex (Guzman 1998) finds the main topics that a document talks about. When visiting in a left-to-right one pass each word of the document, counters are incremented. But Clasitex does not count the words, but the *concepts* to which they refer. Since words are ambiguous, a word usually increments several counters (one for each concept the word denotes). Thus, without really disambiguating, concept counting is achieved (instead of word counting as in Support Vectors (See W.10)).

W.3. Automatic methods to identify the topic of a piece of text have also been used in text summarization (Erkan and Radev 2004),

W.4. Automatic methods to identify the topic of a piece of text have also been used in text categorization (Ko et al. 2004),

W.5. A method that automatically assigns labels to clusters of retrieved documents (using keywords and perhaps several search engines) is described in (Bordogna *et al*, *this book*). It accomplishes this task by using labels at different levels of granularity. Implicit topics are revealed by associating labels with the retrieved items, the clusters, and the retrieved lists. Then, some manipulation operators are applied to each pair of retrieved lists, clusters, and single items, to reveal their implicit relationships. The outcome is represented as multi-granular graphs, at three granularity levels. The algorithm uses Latent Semantic Analysis (see W.11).

W.6. Automatic methods to identify the topic of a piece of text have also been used in word sense disambiguation (Manning, Schutze 1999).

W.7. Automatic methods for identifying the topic of a text have been used in evaluation of text coherence (Lapata and Barzilay 2005)

W.8. Automatic methods to identify the topic of a piece of text have also been used in automatic translation (Liu and Zong 2004),

W.9. If we retrieve documents using some form of contextual search, how do we evaluate the semantic similarity of the retrieved documents with respect to the contextual search specified? How well was the retrieval achieved? (Maguitman, Lorenzetti and Cecchini, *this book*) propose a way to evaluate contextual search using a framework that takes advantage of semantic similarity data. For this purpose, they first review the graph-based measures of semantic similarity. They use an incremental algorithm that uses topic descriptors and discriminators for evaluating the described semantic similarity (Lorenzetti & Maguitman, 2009).

One common method for measuring relatedness of two classified entities is to measure the distance between them when traveling in the hierarchy from one to the other (Budanitsky, Hirst 2006). For example, let us consider the Wikipedia hierarchy of Academic Disciplines. Consider the "Machine learning" and "Functional programming" articles; by examining the list of disciplines, a path for each one can be extracted (in our case, to facilitate distance measuring when two pages fall into completely different disciplines, a root element called Areas has been included). They both belong to the area of Computer Science; so, in order to get to Functional Programming one would have to go 1) from Machine Learning to Cognitive Science, 2) from Cognitive Science to Artificial Intelligence, 3) from Artificial Intelligence to Computer Science, 4) from Computer Science to Programming Languages, and finally 5) from Programming languages to Functional Programming. The number of hops was five. It is possible to refine this kind of metrics by weighting the distance according to the depth in the hierarchy, in order to give more importance to branching occurring high in the hierarchy. It has also been proposed to define the "familial distance" $d_f(s, d)$ from a source document s to another document d in a class hierarchy be the distance from s's class to the most specific class dominating both s and d (Haveliwala et al., 2002); the problem with this last metric is that it is not symmetric, that is, $d_f(s, d)$ is not always the same as $d_f(d, s)$. This problem has been studied in the context of words (symbolic values) placed in a hierarchy (see W.25).

However, measuring semantic proximity based on hierarchies has several drawbacks. First, it is necessary to incorporate to the hierarchy all and every one of the documents to be considered. But the coverage of any extensive directory is known to be rather small; less than 4 million pages are in any directory, out from billions indexed by Google alone. Next, keeping hierarchies up-to-date manually is difficult, as the growing pace of the Internet is of at least 25 millions of websites per year. Automated approaches have been proposed for automatic incorporation of new web pages (Pierrakos et al., 2003), using some of the methods we discuss later.

Corpus-Based Methods

These methods work without a hierarchy of terms, of without specifying the topic that groups the documents in a collection. That is, these documents are semantically similar since they talk about certain topic, but the topic is not specified, so the similarity is more of a "statistical" nature, as the documents in a class contain the same proportion of words, or the same groups of words.

W.10. Support vectors (Joachims 2002). Words of a given language can be lexicographically ordered along an axis. Counting the words appearing in a document maps this axis into a long sparse vector that represents the document. Support vector machines allow to classify the points in this multidimensional space by drawing a hyperplane separating two categories. Document similarity can also be improved by mapping each word into the concept it represents (See W.2), so that the vector now contains concepts appearing in the document.

W.11. Latent semantic analysis. A well-known approach of corpora-based method is latent semantic analysis (Landauer, Dumais 1997), which applies singular value decomposition to reduce the dimensions of the term-document space, harvesting the latent relations existing between documents and between terms in large text corpora. Less computationally expensive techniques are based on mapping documents to a kernel space where documents that do not share any term can still be close to each other (Joachims et. al 2001; Liu et al. 2004). Another corpus-based technique that has been applied to estimate semantic similarity is PMI-IR (Turney, 2001). This information retrieval method is based on pointwise mutual information, which measures the strength of association between two elements (e.g., terms) by contrasting their observed frequency against their expected frequency.

W.12. As an evolution of Latent Semantic analysis, Latent Dirichlet Allocation (LDA) (Blei et al. 2003) proposes a generative approach, where each document is supposed to be "generated" as a *combination* of a given set of topics, in varying proportions. Further, each topic is considered as a probability distribution over words, and each word occurrence in a specific document is supposed to be attributable to a particular topic. Of course the problem is to find out, given a collection of documents, to find out the set of topics, for each topic its associated word probabilities, the topic responsible of generating each word, and the topic mixture for each document. This process is computationally costly, as it involves cycles through each and every word appearing in each document.

W.13. Frequently, topics of a collection of documents are computed by analyzing probabilistic distributions of terms (see, for instance, W.26) and in this way the topic model (a taxonomy, say) of the collection is obtained. (Ramírez and Brena, *this book*) observe that this approach is costly in computation time, and propose that a set of semantically similar documents be identified (as the answer to a *query*) as a semantic cluster, so that a collection of documents can be modeled as several of these semantic clusters, with overlaps. Their Query-based Topic Modeling framework (QTM) assumes the existence of a "preferred" set of queries, that cover most of the information in the set of documents and are somehow orthogonal (maximum semantic coherence). Two advantages of the QTM approach are 1) that it uses highly scalable clustering algorithms, and that 2) they can be executed using Map-Reduce parallelizing techniques.

W.14. (Zhihua Wei et al, *this book*) attack the problem found in a document: many words do not appear in such text (data sparseness). Therefore, it is useful to smooth the information, for instance to make use of statistic theory or linguistic information to assign a uniform distribution to absent words. Instead of doing this, the authors of this interesting chapter use Rough Sets to assign different values for absent words in different approximation regions.

W.15. (Makagonov and Reyes, *this book*) compare the similarity of two documents by reducing them to their *text document search image* (TDSI), which contains only words belonging to the domain of the text collection. The chapter defines: "A word belongs to the domain of a specific text collection if its relative frequency is higher – at least three times higher – than the frequency of the same word in the word frequency list of common language." In addition to finding similar documents, this chapter exploits the fact that the words in a document follow Zipf's law, in order to find restrictions and peculiar shapes on the plot (at the bi-logarithm scale) of the frequency of words for the collection under study. For instance, see its Figure 3.

W.16. (Garza and Brena, *this book*) use graph analysis to identify clusters of hyperlinks-connected documents, like the ones in the Wikipedia. The idea behind this method is to assume that in general a link could relate this document to another one with a similar topic (this is of course not the case of links to years in the Wikipedia). So they try to maximize the proportion of links that point to another document in the same cluster, and the resulting cluster is supposed to belong to a common topic. In order to avoid scalability problems, they make use of local analysis methods in the document graph.

Finding Similarity among Words or Symbolic Values

Instead of grouping documents, a basic approach is to group *words* into "semantically similar" if they represent or denote the same concept, or nearby concepts. This grouping can be carried out considering the words themselves (unattached to documents), considering the words contained in a group of documents (and the words in each document), or considering an a priori organization of words (a tree, say). Thus, we have two divisions:

- Grouping words using only word information (§1.2.1);
- Grouping words using a predefined taxonomy or arrangement of words (§1.2.2);
- Grouping words using a collection of documents (§1.2.3).

Intrinsic Relationship between Words

These methods group words using only word information.

W.17. Lemmatizers. Nouns, verbs and other types of words have declinations that express gender, tenses, number, etc. All these variations can be considered "similar" since they basically convey the same meaning (eat, ate, eaten), so it is useful to consider them as an equivalence class, and to select one of them (usually the verb in infinitive form, or the noun in singular) as their representative or *lemma*. Reducing derivatives to a single word is usually taken into consideration as preprocessing step, prior to the application of some of the methods we are presenting here (see for instance W.13).

W.18. Long sentences frequently appearing in a text are found ("maximal sequential patterns") using standard and new data mining algorithms by (García-Hernández *et al*, *this book*). Two algorithms are proposed, one for finding long sentences in a document, the other for finding them in a collection of documents. Both start with the Apriori algorithm (Agrawal & Srikant, 1994), and avoid frequent passes to the database by using a data structure residing in memory. They propose several uses of the maximal sequential patterns: document clustering, authorship attribution, question answering, mining hyponyms from the web, automatic text summarization.

W.19. Synonyms. WordNet is the classical example (Miller 1995), putting together words in groups of synonyms (Synsets), and then organizing these into a taxonomy.

W.20. An interesting variant is presented by (Hiram Calvo et al, *this book*). It analyzes the forms in which a verb and a subject can be related. They consider subject and object of a phrase as arguments to the verb, and answer the question of what arguments prefer which verbs. Is this a binary relation, one between three participants, or even more? One of the goals of this work is to identify situations where a verb argument is ill-chosen, like in "density *has brought me to you*", or in "*It looks like a* tattoo *subject*", by analyzing the plausibility of arguments.

Similarity of Words with Respect to a Given Taxonomy

These methods, known as "knowledge-based methods," group words using a previous arrangement or taxonomy of words.

W.21. Measuring the amount of information contained. (Resnik, 1995; Lin, 1998). In an information theoretic approach, the semantic similarity between two entities is related to their commonality and to their differences. Given a set of entities in a hierarchical taxonomy, the commonality of two entities can be estimated by the extent to which they share information, indicated by the most specific class in the hierarchy that subsumes both. Once this common classification is identified, the meaning shared by two entities can be measured by the amount of information needed to state the commonality of the two objects. Generalizations of the information theoretic notion of semantic similarity for the case of general ontologies (i.e., taxonomies that include both hierarchical and non-hierarchical components) have been proposed by Maguitman et al. (2005).

W.22. Distances in a concept network or taxonomy (Rada et al. 1989).

W.23. Taking into account both the distance (between words) in a taxonomy as well as the contained information (Jiang, Conrath 1997).

W.24. The semantic relatedness of two words could be assessed either by co-occurrence statistics over a large corpus, or by "knowledge-based methods" that rest upon known or given taxonomies or arrangements (WordNet, see 19, Wikipedia). Surely the features of two given words (as represented in the arrangement) contribute to ascertain their semantic similarity. But, how much each features contributes, and how? (Gentile, Zhang and Ciravegna, *this book*) find answers to these questions, using a random walk model on the (combined) features of the words. Weights are attached to these features.

W.25. Resting upon the concepts of abstraction and specialization (animal is more abstract than vertebrate; a specialization of vertebrate is mammal; mammal specializes into rodent, equines and other specializations), (Levachkine, Guzman 2007) organize words (they call them symbolic values) of a given topic in a hierarchy: a tree where each node is a word or, if it is a set, then the subsets of this set form a partition of it. The root denotes the most abstract concept; the leaves contain values that denote the most concrete items. On a hierarchy, it can be defined the function conf(r, s) that measures the confusion of using symbolic value *r* instead of the correct or intended symbolic value (word) *s*. In a chapter in this book, (Cuevas and Guzman), using *conf*, can compare the similarity of a collection of these values. The *inconsistency* of the set is found –it is large if the symbolic values are quite disparate, and is small if the values are quite similar. The *centroid* of the set is also found, it is their most likely representative, or *consensus value,* akin to the *lemma* of lemmatized words (See W.17). According to the context, a collection of values can have *several centroids,* and the chapter tells how to find them.

Grouping Words Guided by a Corpus of Documents

W.26. Using a proprietary version of the Latent Dirichlet Allocation method (Blei et al., 2003), (Magatti and Stella, *this book*) find topics in a document, and tag such documents according to a user-supplied taxonomy. Hierarchical clustering is used to select the optimal number of topics. The user needs to supply a set of similarity measures. The algorithm uses them for the topic labeling task. It also reviews several similarity measures between vectors (representing documents).

Finding Similarity among Concepts

An approach similar to §1.1.2 but more semantic in spirit consists in grouping the *concepts* (not the words) as "semantically similar" if they represent or denote the same objects in the real world, or near-by objects. Researchers have found out that a word can denote several concepts, according to the context or theme being described. (Wittgenstein used to say, humorously: "if words are ambiguous and concepts are unique, why don't we stop using words to communicate, and do it solely by concepts?"). Then, instead of grouping words similar to *java,* now we will group concepts similar to java1 (the programming language), Java2 (the island of Java) and java3 (a kind of coffee).

W.27. Formal Concept Analysis (Ganter, Wille 2004). Assume there are *n* properties that an object may or may not have (i. e., binary properties). A given object may have none, all, or more frequently, some of the *n* properties. These objects form a lattice, the top element represents the object(s) having *all n* properties, the bottom element is the object having *none* of these properties. Objects having one property (objects having "large"; objects having "red", …) lie near the bottom. A *concept* is any node in this lattice, for instance, node "red and heavy". Formally, a concept is a predicate of one variable, p(x), which is true if object x has property p (if it is red and heavy, say). The theory develops nicely, but the lattice is quite large. Even more, most of the nodes are useless, are chimeras (things that do not exist in the real world), for instance, object "flies and has scales and breathes air and has four legs."

W.28. (Kalfoglou, Schorlemmer 2002) uses FCA to establish a logical infomorphism between two local ontologies (ontologies of two different cultures –two islands, say; formally, a *local logic*). The mapping (the infomorphism) tries to preserve the relations (restrictions) found in each local ontology, and guarantees to preserve them for *normal instances*. It may be said that two concepts, one from ontology A, another from B, are equivalent if the infomorphism maps one into the other. It is a theoretical approach that perhaps has not yet found application.

W.29. (Olivares, Guzman 2004) develops a method (called COM) to compare concepts sitting in different ontologies (independently created) about the same or similar topic. His algorithm finds in an ontology the concept most similar to a given concept that belongs to another ontology. COM compares not only the names associated to both concepts, but their properties, their relations, their ascendants, etc.

CONCLUSION

We have reviewed in this introductory chapter some of the main proposals in this relatively new discipline of approximate, quantitative and "soft" methods for taking into account the meaning of pieces of text. So the main contribution of this book is to make a point about what is the current "state of affaires" in this novel area, and to present some of the methods in the voice of their authors.

It is our hope that in the next years, the advancement in the semantic analysis would be reflected in the creation of computer-based sophisticated systems for serving millions of users everyday goals, improving thus their lives in a meaningful way.

Ramon F. Brena
Tecnologico de Monterrey, Mexico

Adolfo Guzman-Arenas
Instituto Politécnico Nacional, Mexico

REFERENCES

Agrawal, R., & Srikant, R. (1994). Fast algorithms for mining association rules. In J. B. Bocca, M. Jarke, & C. Zaniolo (Eds.), *Int. Conf. Very Large Databases* (pp.487-499). San Francisco: Morgan Kaufmann.

Antoniou, G., & Van Harmelen, F. (2004). *A semantic web primer*. Cambridge, MA: The MIT Press.

Blei, D. M., Andrew, N., & Jordan, M. I. (2003). Latent Dirichlet Allocation. *Journal of Machine Learning Research, 3*, 993–1022.

Bollegala, D. (2007). Measuring Semantic Similarity Between Words using Web Search Engines. In *Proceedings of the Sixteenth International Conference on World Wide Web (WWW 07)*. (pp. 757-766). New York: ACM Press.

Budanitsky, A., & Hirst, G. (2006). Evaluating wordnet-based measures of lexical semantic relatedness. [Cambridge, MA: MIT Press.]. *Computational Linguistics, 32*(1), 13–47. doi:10.1162/coli.2006.32.1.13

Cuevas, A. D., & Guzman, A. (2008). A language and algorithm for automatic merging of ontologies . In Rittgen, P. (Ed.), *Handbook of Ontologies for Business Interaction* (pp. 381–404). Hershey, PA: IGI Global.

Erkan, G., & Radev, D. R. (2004). LexRank: Graph-based lexical central-ity as salience in text summarization. *Journal of Artificial Intelligence Research, 22*(1), 457–479.

Furnas, G. W., Landauer, T. K., Gomez, L. M., & Dumais, S. T. (1987). The vocabulary problem in human-system communication. *Communications of the ACM, 30*(11), 964–971. doi:10.1145/32206.32212

Ganter, B., & Wille, R. (2004). *Formal Concept Analysis*. Springer-Verlag.

Guzmán, A. (1998). Finding the main themes in a Spanish document. [Elsevier.]. *Journal Expert Systems with Applications, 14*(1/2), 139–148. doi:10.1016/S0957-4174(97)00055-9

Guzman, A., & Olivares, J. (2004). Finding the Most Similar Concepts in two Different Ontologies. [Springer-Verlag.]. *Lecture Notes in Artificial Intelligence LNAI, 2972,* 129–138.

Hatzivassiloglou, V., Klavans, J., & Eskin, E. (1999). Detecting Text Similarity over Short Passages: Exploring Linguistic Feature Combinations via Machine Learning. In *Proceedings of the Joint SIGDAT Conference on Empirical Methods in Natural Language Processing and Very Large Corpora (EMNLP 99),* pp. 203-212.

Haveliwala, T. H., Gionis, A., Klein, D., & Indyk, P. (2002). Evaluating strategies for similarity search on the web. In *Proceedings of the 11th international conference on World Wide Web,* pp.432-442. New York: ACM.

Jiang, J. J., & Conrath, D. W. (1997). Semantic similarity based on corpus statistics and lexical taxonomy, In *Proceedings of International Conference on Research in Computational Linguistics (ROCLING X),* Taiwan, pp. 19–33.

Joachims, T. (2002). Learning to classify text using support vector machines: Methods, theory, and algorithms. *Computational Linguistics, 29*(4), 656–664.

Joachims, T., Cristianini, N., & Shawe-Taylor, J. (2001). *Composite kernels for hypertext categorization* (pp. 250–257). MACHINE LEARNING-INTERNATIONAL WORKSHOP.

Kalfoglou, Y., & Schorlemmer, M. (2002). Information-Flow-based Ontology Mapping. In *Proceedings of the 1st International Conference on Ontologies, Databases and Application of Semantics (ODBASE'02),* Irvine, CA, USA.

Ko, Y., Park, J., & Seo, J. (2004). Improving text categorization using the importance of sentences. [New York: Elsevier.]. *Information Processing & Management, 40*(1), 65–79. doi:10.1016/S0306-4573(02)00056-0

Landauer, T. K., & Dumais, S. T. (1997). A Solution to Plato's Problem: The Latent Semantic Analysis Theory of the Acquisition, Induction, and Representation of Knowledge. *Psychological Review, 104*(2), 211–240. doi:10.1037/0033-295X.104.2.211

Lapata, M., & Barzilay, R. (2005). *Automatic evaluation of text coherence: Models and representations.* IJCAI 2005 Proceedings, pp. 1085.

Levachkine, S., & Guzman-Arenas, A. (2007). Hierarchy as a new data type for qualitative variables. [Elsevier.]. *Expert Systems with Applications, 32*(3), 899–910. doi:10.1016/j.eswa.2006.01.024

Lin, D. (1998). An Information-theoretic Definition of Similarity. In *Proceedings of the Fifteenth International Conference on Machine Learning (ICML 98)*, pp. 296-304, San Francisco, CA.

Liu, Y., & Zong, C. (2004). Example-based chinese-english MT, Systems, Man and Cybernetics, 2004 *IEEE International Conference on, 7*, pp.6093-6096. Washington, DC: IEEE Press.

Lorenzetti, C. M., & Maguitman, A. G. (2009). A semi-supervised incremental algorithm to automatically formulate topical queries. [Elsevier.]. *Information Sciences, 179*(12), 1881–1892. doi:10.1016/j.ins.2009.01.029

Maguitman, A., Menczer, F., Roinestad, H., & Vespignani, A. (2005). Algorithmic Detection of Semantic Similarity. In *Proceedings 14th International World Wide Web Conference (WWW 05)*, pp. 107 - 116, New York: ACM Press.

Manning, C., & Schutze, H. (1999). Word Sense Disambiguation . In *Foundations of Statistical Natural Language Processing* (pp. 229–261). Cambridge, MA: MIT Press.

Marshall, C. C., & Shipman, F. M. (2003). Which semantic web? In *Proceedings of the fourteenth ACM conference on Hypertext and hypermedia*, pp. 57-66. New York: ACM Press.

Miller, G. A. (1995). WordNet: a lexical database for English. [New York: ACM Press.]. *Communications of the ACM, 38*(11), 39–41. doi:10.1145/219717.219748

Olivares-Ceja, J. M., & Guzman-Arenas, A. (2004). Concept similarity measures the understanding between two agents. In *Natural Language Processing and Information Systems*. Lecture Notes in Computer Science, LNCS 3136, pp. 366-376, Springer.

Pierrakos, D., Paliouras, G., Papatheodorou, C., Karkaletsis, V., & Dikaiakos, M. (2003). *Construction of Web community directories using document clustering and Web usage mining*. In ECML/PKDD 2003: First European Web Mining Forum proceedings.

Rada, R., Mili, H., Bicknell, E., & Blettner, M. (1989). Development and application of a metric on semantic nets. [Washington, DC: IEEE.]. *IEEE Transactions on Systems, Man, and Cybernetics, 9*(1), 17–30. doi:10.1109/21.24528

Resnik, P. (1995). Using Information Content to Evaluate Semantic Similarity in a Taxonomy. In *Proceedings of the Fourteenth International Joint Conference on Artificial Intelligence (IJCAI 95)*, pp. 448-453.

Sahami, M., & Heilman, T. (2006). A Web-Based Kernel Function for Measuring the Similarity of Short Text Snippets. In: *Proceedings of the Fifteenth Inter-national World Wide Web Conference (WWW 06)*, pp.377-386. New York:ACM Press.

Turney, P. (2001). Mining the Web for Synonyms: PMI-IR versus LSA on TOEFL. In *Proceedings of the Twelfth European Conference on Machine Learning (ECML 01)*, pp.491-502. San Francisco: Morgan Kaufmann.

Yates, R. B., & Neto, B. R. (1999). *Modern information retrieval*. New York: Addition Wesley.

KEY TERMS AND DEFINITIONS

Clustering: Action of grouping together related items in a collection; it is considered as a non-supervised form of learning.

Corpus-Based: Any method relying entirely on the actual contents of a collection of documents.

Infomorphism: Mapping among information structures.

Knowledge-Based: Any method supported by knowledge previously acquired by humans.

Quantitative: Related to measures, as opposed to qualitative.

Semantics: Related to the meaning of languages, phrases, etc.

Taxonomy: Tree-like classification.

Chapter 1
Clustering Via Centroids a Bag of Qualitative Values and Measuring its Inconsistency

Adolfo Guzman-Arenas
Instituto Politécnico Nacional, México

Alma-Delia Cuevas
Instituto Politécnico Nacional, México

ABSTRACT

Recently, using confusion, we computed the centroid ("consensus value") and the inconsistency of a set (a bag, in fact) of qualitative assertions about the same property or variable (say, John's pet), reported by several observers.

A bag of dissimilar assertions will have a large inconsistency, which could diminish if the problem at hand allows several centroids to be selected. John could have two pets, and the inconsistency of these two "consensus values" with all observations will be much better (much smaller): one part of the observers will feel little discomfort with one of the centroids; the remaining part will feel little discomfort with the second centroid. This chapter finds the set of centroids of a bag of qualitative values that minimizes the inconsistency of the bag; that is, the total discomfort of all members of the bag will be smallest. These centroids define clusters of the bag.

All observers are equally credible, so differences in their findings arise from perception errors.

DOI: 10.4018/978-1-60960-881-1.ch001

INTRODUCTION

It is well understood how to compute the average of a set of numeric values; thus, handling inconsistent measurements is possible. Recently, using *confusion,* we showed a way to compute the "average," consensus or centroid of a bag of assertions (made by *observers*) about a non-numeric property, such as John's pet. The values of those assertions lie in a hierarchy. Intuitively, such consensus minimizes the discomfort of all observers (of the pet) when they know which of the animals of the bag was selected as the consensus pet. The *inconsistency* of the bag is such total discomfort divided by the bag's size. It is a number that tells how far apart the values of the bag are. It should be emphasized that an asserted value obtained by an observer (such as *Schnauzer* in "the pet was a Schnauzer") represents not only itself, but all the values from it up to the root of the hierarchy: Schnauzer, dog, mammal, animal, living creature.

A bag of dissimilar assertions will have a large inconsistency, which could diminish if the problem at hand allows *several centroids* to be selected. John could have two pets, and the inconsistency of these two "consensus values" with all observations will be much better (much smaller): one part of the observers will feel little discomfort with one of the centroids; the remaining part will feel little discomfort with the second centroid. This chapter finds the set of centroids of a bag of qualitative values that minimizes the inconsistency of the bag; that is, the total discomfort of all members of the bag will be smallest. These centroids define clusters, that is, subsets of the bag.

All observers are equally credible, so differences in their findings arise from perception errors, and from the limited accuracy of their individual findings.

1. PREVIOUS WORK AND PROBLEM STATEMENT

Our work is in the general area of extracting useful properties (such as "centers" and "clusters") from a set of non-numeric values.

1.1 Problem Statement

Assume several measurements are performed on the same property (for instance, the length of a table). One measurer took a quick look and asserted "3m." Another person with the help of a meter said "3.13m". A lady with a micrometer reported "3.1427m." The problem of finding the average of a set of quantitative values (to be called "Problem 0") can be solved simply by computing the average ($\mu=3.09$m, the average length) as well as the dispersion of these measurements (σ, the variance), perhaps disregarding some outliers. For quantitative measurements we know how to take into account contradicting facts, and we do not regard them necessarily as inconsistent. We just assume that the observers' gauges have different precisions or accuracies.

It could also be that observers have a propensity to lie, and in this case we apply the Theory of Evidence (Dempster, A. (1968); Shafer, G. (1976)). Or we could use Fuzzy Logic, selecting some sets as possible answers and assigning a degree of membership to each measurement for each set.

Problem 1 statement (informal). Similar to Problem 0, we want to solve the problem of finding the "average," most plausible value, or centroid of several non-numeric or symbolic values.[1] This is "Problem 1," solved elsewhere (Guzman-Arenas, A., & Jimenez, A. (2010)) and briefly exposed in §1.4. There we find that the centroid is the value that minimizes the *total confusion* in the bag, a number that tells us how "comfortable" the elements of the bag with the chosen centroid are. Nevertheless, according to the problem at hand, it may be possible to have more than one "average." A bag, thus, may have several centroids, each of them representing or being "the center" of a cluster.[2] Several symbolic values in a bag could be better represented (in the sense of a smaller *total confusion* for the bag) by more than one centroid. Thus, we would like to cluster a bag of values into several centroids. This is "Problem 2" and its formal statement and solution (in Section 2) is the subject of this chapter.

1.2 Related Work

Many clustering methods that are used for objects represented by numbers (points in an n-dimensional space) can also be applied to symbolic values, if a numeric similarity function $sim(x, y)$ is defined for each pair of those values. See, for instance, (Ruiz-Shulclóper, J., Guzman-Arenas, A. and Martinez-Trinidad, F. (1999)). The great majority of them assumes that *sim* is a distance function. A recent work (Luo, P., Xiong, H., Zhan, G., Wu, J., & Shi, Z. (2009)) classifies these distances using information theory.

Yin *et al* (Yin, X., Han, J. & Fu, P. (2008)) provide a manner to find the most likely "truth" among a set of qualitative information obtained from "information providers" in the Web. The information is an assertion about a qualitative value, a "fact" as found in the Web. This work resorts to the "trustworthiness" of each informant (resembling Dempster-Schafer), as well as a measure of the similarity among two of these non-numeric values (resembling our *confusion*, as defined in §1.3).

A recent paper (Guzman-Arenas, A., & Jimenez, A. (2010)) finds the centroid or most likely value of a bag of qualitative values, such as {Afghanistan; Beirut; Iraq; Kabul; Middle East; Afghanistan; Syria}. The answer is not necessarily the most popular value or mode (Afghanistan), or the lowest common ancestor (Middle East). The answer is not based on the probability that informants lie [like in the theory of Dempster-Schafer (Dempster, A. (1968); Shafer, G. (1976))], nor it contains fuzzy values. The answer assumes that all informants are equally credible, and the discrepancy of their findings arises from the way or method used when obtaining their observations. This work relies on the confusion *conf* (§1.3) of using a value r instead of the real or intended value s.

As an example, let us assume we want to find the ethnicity of Emille. We pose this question to her friends. One of them, from the sound of the name, assumes she is French. Other friend, knowing the Roman origin of the name, tells us that she is Italian. Another acquaintance tells us "she is white," still another says "she is European." Assume that the values are {French, Roman, Italian, White, European, American}. Given that information, one of these values is her most likely ethnicity. If "Italian" is selected, reporter 3 ("Italian") is happy (shows no discomfort, since our selection agrees with his report). Reporter 2 ("Roman") is somewhat displaced, since she reported a girl from Rome, not just from Italy. Reporter 1 ("French") is somewhat displeased, but reporter 6 ("American") is even more displeased with our selection. If we select "American" as Emille's ethnicity, only reporter 6 is at comfort, while the others show different degrees of dissatisfaction. If we could measure these discomforts, we could select as her most likely ethnicity (consensus value) *the value that minimizes the sum of disagreements* or discomforts for all the observers when they learn of the value chosen as the consensus value. *It is the best value for her ethnicity, given that all we know is the information in the bag.*

It should be emphasized that an asserted value obtained by an observer (such as *Doberman* in "John's pet was a Doberman") represents not only itself, but all the values from it up to the root of the hierarchy: Doberman, dog, mammal, vertebrate, and animal. This is because the observer, having all these values to select when reporting his observation, reports the most precise value.

The "discomfort" or disagreement when value r is reported instead of the "true" value s (as found by the observer) is called the *confusion* in using r

Figure 1. A hierarchy of symbolic values is a tree where every node is either a symbolic value or, if it is a set, then its immediate descendants form a partition. Hierarchies make possible to compute the confusion conf(r, s) that results when value r is used instead of s, the true or intended value. The confusion (§1.3) is the number of descending links in the path from r to s, divided by the height of the hierarchy. For instance, conf(dog, Doberman) = 1/4, conf(Doberman, dog) = 0, conf (Doberman, German Shepherd) = 1/4, conf (Doberman, iguana) = 2/4, conf(iguana, Doberman) = 3/4. Observe that conf ∈ [0, 1]. Refer to Section 1.3. The values marked ×, □ and • are used in examples 3, 5 and 6 of sections 1.3 and 1.4.

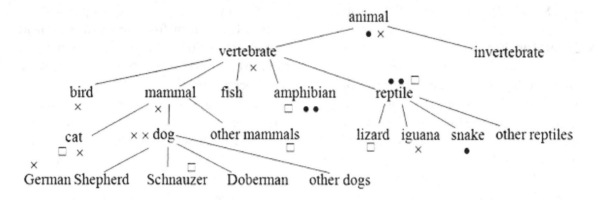

instead of *s* (Levachkine, S, Guzman-Arenas, A. & de Gyves, V.P. (2005); for a brief introduction see Section 1.3). To measure this, it is necessary to give all observers the same *context*, that is, the same set of possible qualitative answers as well as how these are related by specificity or generality. This set is called a *hierarchy* (Figure 1); it is a tree where each node is a qualitative value or, if it is a set, then its immediate descendants form a *partition* of it.

Using hierarchies, next section (§1.3) tells how to compute the confusion among two qualitative values, while section 1.4 explains how to find the consensus or most likely value of a bag of qualitative values.

Sections 1.3 and 1.4 report some of our previous work, necessary to understand this article. Our contributions appear in section 2, where several centroids of a bag of qualitative values are found, both in an exact manner (§2.2) and in an approximate algorithm (§2.5). §2.6 tells us how many centroids (clusters) are good to have. Clusters are derived for each centroid found. Also, the *inconsistency* of each cluster (degree of fitting

of the centroids to the cluster) is also computed. Results and comparisons against similar methods should wait for a comprehensive test of experiments. Conclusions and discussion are in section 3.

1.3 Comparing Values: The Confusion Between Two Qualitative Values

The *confusion* between qualitative values is dealt elsewhere (Guzman-Arenas, A., & Levachkine, S. (2004a); Guzman-Arenas, A., & Levachkine, S. (2004b); Levachkine, S, Guzman-Arenas, A. & de Gyves, V.P. (2005)0; Levachkine, S., & Guzman-Arenas, A. (2007)); this section is placed here for completeness. How close are two numeric values v_1 and v_2? The answer is $|v_2 - v_1|$. How close are two symbolic values such as *cat* and *dog*? The answer comes in a variety of similarity measures and distances. Hierarchies (introduced in Figure 1) allow us to define the confusion conf(r, s) between two symbolic values. The function conf will open the way to evaluate in Section 1.4 the inconsistency of a bag of symbolic observations. We assume that the observers of a given fact (such as *the killer is…*) share a set of common vocabulary, best arranged in a hierarchy. A hierarchy can be regarded as the "common terminology"[3] for the observers of a bag: their *context*. Observers reporting in other bag may share a different context, that is, another hierarchy.

What is the capital of Germany? *Berlin* is the right answer; *Frankfurt* is a close miss, *Madrid* a fair error, and *sausage* a gross error. What is closer to a *cat*, a *dog* or an *orange*? Can we measure these errors and similarities? Can we retrieve objects in a database that are close to a desired item? Yes, because qualitative variables take symbolic values such as *cat, orange, California,* which can be organized in a hierarchy *H*, a mathematical construct among these values. Over *H*, we can define the function *confusion* resulting when using a symbolic value instead of another.

Definition. For *r, s* ∈ *H*, the *absolute confusion* in using *r* instead of *s,* is

$$CONF(r,r) = CONF(r, \text{ any ascendant of } r) = 0$$

$$CONF(r,s) = 1 + CONF(r, \text{ father of}(s))$$

To measure CONF, count the descending links from *r* (the replacing value) to *s* (the intended or real value) in *H*. CONF is not a distance, nor an ultradistance.

We can normalize CONF by dividing it into *h*, the height of *H* (the number of links from the root of *H* to the farthest element of *H*), yielding the following

Definition. The *confusion* in using *r* instead of *s* is

$$conf(r,s) = CONF(r,s) \,/\, h$$

Notice that $0 \le conf(r, s) \le 1$. It is not symmetric: $conf(r, s) \ne conf(s, r)$, in general. The function conf is not a distance, but it obeys the

triangle inequality (Guzman-Arenas, A., & Jimenez, A. (2010)). Also, conf(*r, s*) = 0 does not mean necessarily that *r=s*.

The relation of a hierarchy with an ontology is:

A. A hierarchy can be regarded as a simplified ontology, where only the relations "subset" and "member" are used.
B. In an ontology, a concept may have several ancestors; in a hierarchy, only one.

Example 1. For the hierarchy of Figure 1, CONF(cat, mammal) =0; if I ask for a mammal and I am given a cat instead, I am happy, and CONF=0. But CONF(mammal, cat) =1; if I ask for a cat and I get a mammal, I am somewhat unhappy, and CONF=1. For the same reason, CONF(vertebrate, cat) =2. Being given a vertebrate when I ask for a cat makes me unhappier than when I was handed a mammal.

Example 2. In the hierarchy of Figure 1, conf(cat, dog) =1/4; conf(cat, Schnauzer) =1/2.

Example 3. The confusion among values marked with □ in Figure 1 is given in Table 1.

The type of hierarchy of Figure 1 is the most common type, and it is called a *normal* hierarchy, as opposed to ordered [(B) in Figure 3] or percentage hierarchies (Levachkine, S, Guzman-Arenas, A. & de Gyves, V.P. (2005)).

1.4 The Consensus and Inconsistency of a Bag of Qualitative Values

The consensus or *centroid* of a bag is dealt in (Guzman-Arenas, A., & Jimenez, A. (2010); Jimenez, A. (in press)); this section is placed here for completeness.

The setting is that several observers report (qualitative) values about a given property of an object they were asked to observe. Two observers may report the same value, thus a bag (and not a set) is used to collect them. These values are usually different, but our observers are not

Table 1. The confusion conf (r, s) of using value r instead of the intended value s is found at the intersection of row r and column s. For instance, conf(lizard, reptile) = 0, while conf(reptile, lizard) = ¼, and conf(reptile, Schnauzer) = ¾ [If I want a Schnauzer and they give me a reptile, my confusion is large = ¾, close to 1, the highest]. The last column (explained in §2.2) gives the total confusion provoked in the bag {Schnauzer, cat, other mammals, amphibian, reptile, lizard} by the corresponding row. For instance, the total confusion that "cat" provokes in the bag is ½ + 0 + ¼ + ¼ + ¼ + 1/2 =1.75.

	Schnauzer	Cat	Other Mammals	Amphibian	Reptile	Lizard	Total Confusion
Schnauzer	0	¼	¼	¼	¼	½	1.5
Cat	½	0	¼	¼	¼	½	1.75
Other Mammals	½	¼	0	¼	¼	½	1.75
Amphibian	¾	½	½	0	¼	½	2.5
Reptile	¾	½	½	¼	0	¼	2.25
Lizard	¾	½	½	¼	0	0	2

Remark. Since symbolic values lie in a hierarchy, it is not possible for a value to have two immediate ascendants, to have more than one path from it towards the root. That is, *rabbit* may not be both a mammal and a bird.

liars (the Dempster-Schafer's theory of evidence does not apply). Their reported values are crisp (no fuzzy values are reported –no fuzzy logic is needed). The explanation for not all reporting the same value is that the way they observed (assessed, "measured" or gauged) the property was different –their methods of observation had different precision; accuracy varies. Granularities were not the same.

Problem 1. Given a bag of n observations reporting non-numeric values, how can we measure its inconsistency? What is the value in the bag that minimizes this inconsistency? We shall call $r*$ this value and σ the inconsistency that $r*$ produces. Notice that *inconsistency* is a property of a bag of values, not of a single value.

Restrictions to the solution to Problem 1:

A. All the reported values are about the same *fact* or property. One observer can not report about the identity of the killer, while another observer tells us about the weather in London.

B. The fact or feature that the observers are gauging, has a single value. There is only one killer.[4] The weather in London (for a

particular date and corner of the city) is unique.

C. All reporters use the same *context* expressed in a vocabulary arranged in a hierarchy –the same hierarchy for all observations in a bag. It contains all possible answers. It is clear that for observers with other conceptions about the animals of Figure 1 and their differences, the consensus $r*$ will differ. Thus, $r*$ and σ are a function of the bag and the hierarchy.

Intuitively, $r*$ is the value *in the bag*[5] most likely to be true, given the available information, and taking into account observation errors. One of the values of the bag must be the most plausible value, the consensus, its "centroid". Since all observers are equally believable, we could find the confusion of any given observer with respect to a selected value r --a kind of "discomfort" measured by conf(r, s) when value r is preferred or selected (as the centroid), instead of the value s reported by him. Adding these confusions for all observers, we find the total confusion (total "discomfort") that such value r produced (if it were selected as the "consensus") in all n observers. There must be a value $r*$ that produces the lowest total confusion.

Such $r*$ is the consensus or centroid of the bag. The inconsistency of the bag, called σ, is such minimum divided by the number of elements of the bag. Thus, we have

Solution. The *centroid* or *consensus* $r*$ of a bag *B* of *n* observations reporting qualitative values $\{s_1, s_2, \ldots s_n\}$ is the value $r_j \in B$ that minimizes

$$\sum_{i=1}^{n} conf(r, s) \qquad \text{for } j = 1 \qquad n$$

For each r_j, this sum is the total confusion that r_j produces among all elements of the bag. The *inconsistency* σ of *B* is the minimum that such $r*$ produces, divided by *n*:

$$\sigma = (1 / n) \min_{j} \sum_{i=1}^{n} conf(r_i, s_i) = (1 / n) \sum_{i=1}^{n} conf(r*, s_i)$$

Example 4. Assume bag_3 is {air, airplane, land, road, subway, subway, motorcycle}. Bag_3 is marked with × in Figure 2. Since the bag contains the set of observations made by different observers, some of their findings may coincide. In this example, two observers found "subway". For bag_3, the total confusion for air is $(0+1+1+2+3+3+3)/3$ $=4.333$; for airplane, is $(0+0+1+2+3+3+3)/3 =4$;

for land, it is 3.333; for road is 2.666; for subway is 2; for motorcycle is 2.333. Thus, its consensus is subway, and its inconsistency is 2/7. *Example 5.* For bag_1 = {animal, vertebrate, bird, mammal, cat, dog, dog, iguana, German Shepherd} (marked with × in Figure 1), the consensus or centroid $r*$ is German Shepherd, and the inconsistency of bag_1 is $[(0+0+1+0+1+0+0+2+0)/4]/9 =1/9$. *Example 6.* For bag_2 = {animal, amphibian, amphibian, reptile, reptile, snake} marked with • in Figure 1, $r*$ = snake, σ = 1/12. *Example 7.* For observations in Figure 1 with □, $r*$ = Schnauzer, σ = $(6/4)/6 = ¼$.

Remarks. [More at (Guzman-Arenas, A., & Jimenez, A. (2010))].

- $r*$ and σ are properties of the bag, and depend on the context of use –represented by the hierarchy employed. The role of the hierarchy in the solution to Problem 1 is to provide a *common vocabulary* for all observations. See restriction 1.4.(C).
- The inconsistency $\sigma \in [0, 1)$. In fact, for a bag *B* of size *n*, $0 \le \sigma \le (n\text{-}1)/n$.
- There may be more than one value $r*$ that minimizes the total confusion.
- To compute the inconsistency of a bag, we resort to finding $r*$ first. In other words, the inconsistency of a bag is the average

Figure 2. A hierarchy of types of transportation. The observations of bag_3 (see Example 4) are shown with ×. conf(airplane, transport) =0; conf(transport, airplane) =2/3; conf(U-boat, ROV) =conf(U-boat, canoe) =1/3; conf(U-boat, motorcycle)=1

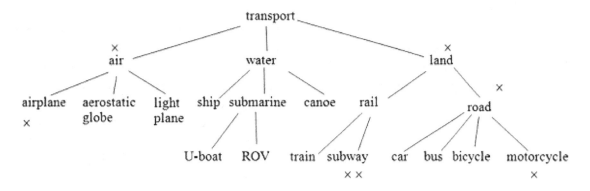

Figure 3. Hierarchies for places to live (A), a normal hierarchy, and height of persons (B), an ordered hierarchy. conf(Mexico, North America) =0; conf(North America, Mexico) =1/3; conf(Mexico, South America) =2/3; conf(South America, Mexico)=1. Ordered hierarchies have height 1 always, and all the values hanging from the root are totally ordered. In (Guzman-Arenas, A., and Levachkine, S., 2004) we find that, for an ordered hierarchy with a root and n children, the confusion between children i and j is |i − j| / (n -1). Thus, conf(short, medium) =conf(medium, tall)=1/2; conf(short, tall) =1; conf(short, unknown) = 0; conf(unknown, short) = conf(unknown, medium) =1.

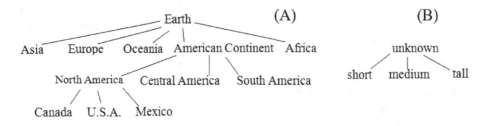

total discomfort (average total confusion) produced by r^*. This is the lowest discomfort attainable; any other element different from r^* will give a larger or equal total confusion (by definition of r^*).

- The consensus r^* is not inevitably the most popular value (the mode), which is dog in Example 5 for the elements marked with (×), while r^* =German Shepherd.

- The *lowest common ancestor* (vertebrate in example 7) produces a total confusion larger or at best equal than the total confusion produced by r^* = Schnauzer. It is "too general" for many of the observers.

- Given the consensus r^* of B, there is no $r' \in B$ such that r' is a descendant of r^*. This implies that, if an element r of the bag has a descendant r' in the bag, then that r can not be the consensus.

Notice that we have found a way of adding (and averaging) apples and oranges, and a quantity (σ) to quantify how disperse or divergent a bag of symbolic values is.

1.5 Is The Centroid the Condorcet Winner?

The Condorcet winner of an election is the candidate who, when compared with every other candidate, is preferred by more voters *in each comparison*. Informally, the Condorcet winner is the person who would win a two-candidate election against each of the other candidates. A Condorcet winner will not always exist in a given set of votes.

If we consider the selection of the centroid of a bag as an election held by the members of such bag, then its centroid is the Condorcet winner. This is so because r^* has the lowest total confusion (the criteria to select the winner), thus beating (or tying) any other candidate.

A voting system satisfies the Condorcet criterion if it chooses the Condorcet winner when one exists. Our method for "electing" the centroid (using total confusion) satisfies the Condorcet criterion. In fact, the total confusion induces a total ordering among the qualitative values of the bag. They can be ordered $s_1 \leq s_2 \leq ... \leq s_k$, where s_1 is the centroid (or Condorcet winner), and s_k is the Condorcet loser -- a candidate who can be defeated (or tied) in a head-to-head competition against every other candidate.

2. WHEN A BAG CAN HAVE SEVERAL CENTROIDS

According to the problem at hand, it may be meaningful or desirable to find more than one "consensus" for a bag of qualitative values. For a bag reporting intelligence findings about the place where Osama Bin Laden may be hiding, it makes sense to find the two or three most likely places, and go and search for him there. Thus, an algorithm that computes more than one centroid is desirable, especially if the inconsistency provoked by a single centroid (§1.4) is high.

In the solution to Problem 1 (§ 1.4), the centroid $r*$ produces the lowest total confusion. The inconsistency is that lowest total confusion divided by n, the size of the bag.

Intuitively, to find more than one centroid, we could ask every element e of the bag to select *the best* candidate for such e, and we will select two or three of these "best" candidates to be the centroids. Unfortunately, this approach will not work –every e will select *itself*, since $conf(e, e)$ =0, and we will end up with a large number of "best" candidates.

If we want to select two centroids, we could present sequentially every pair of candidates (c_i, c_j) to each element e of the bag. For each pair, e will select c_i as its preferred centroid if $conf(c_i, e)$ < $conf(c_j, e)$, select c_j if $conf(c_i, e)$ > $conf(c_j, e)$, or select one of c_i, c_j arbitrarily if $conf(c_i, e)$ = $conf(c_j, e)$. The smaller of these confusions will accumulate so as to obtain the total confusion provoked by the pair of candidates in all elements of the bag. Having done that with all possible pairs of candidates, the pair with the smallest total confusion will be the winner –they are the two centroids. Each of these two centroids induces a cluster (a subset of the bag), formed by those elements that selected that centroid as their best candidate (its "core constituency"). There may be a few elements of the bags whose best candidate was a tie between the two winning centroids; those elements could

be considered outside the two clusters, or could be included in either.

2.1 Finding the *K* Centroids of a Bag

A bag may have not just one or two centroids, but *k* of them. Thus, we state formally

Problem 2. Given a bag of n values, what are its k centroids? What is the inconsistency of such bag?
Solution.
To find the two (the pair of) *centroids* (Algorithm 1 of §2.3 formalizes this):
The total confusion (tc) provoked by two candidates c_i, c_j in a bag $\{c_1, c_2, ..., c_n\}$ is

$$tc(c_i, c_j) = \min(conf(c_i, c_1), conf(c_j, c_1)) + \min(conf(c_i, c_2), conf(c_j, c_2)) + ... + \min(conf(c_i, c_n), conf(c_j, c_n))$$

and the *pair of centroids* r_1*, r_2* is the pair c_i, c_j that minimizes the above tc. The *inconsistency* of the bag is such smallest tc divided by n. The bag is broken in two clusters: one of them holds those elements that preferred r_1* to r_2*; the other cluster holds those elements that preferred r_2* to r_1*. The elements e having $conf(r_1*, e)$ = $conf(r_2*, e)$ could be left as a residue, or could assigned to either cluster.

Remark. There may be more than one pair of centroids; for instance, two pairs (r_1*, r_2*) and (r_3*, r_4*) may provoke the same lowest total confusion in the bag.

To find the three (the trio of) *centroids:*

The total confusion provoked by three candidates c_i, c_j, c_m in a bag $\{c_1, c_2, ..., c_n\}$ is

$$tc(c_i, c_j, c_m) = \min(conf(c_i, c_1), conf(c_j, c_1), conf(c_m, c_1)) + \min(conf(c_i, c_2), conf(c_j, c_2), conf(c_m, c_2)) + ... + \min(conf(c_i, c_n), conf(c_j, c_n), conf(c_m, c_n))$$

and the trio of centroids r_1^*, r_2^*, r_3^* is the trio c_i, c_j, c_m that minimizes the above tc. The inconsistency of the bag is such smallest tc divided by n. The three clusters are formed by the elements that preferred r_1^*, r_2^* or r_3^*, respectively. An "undecided" element c_i showed the same lowest confusion for more than one centroid: either $conf(r_1^*,c_i)=conf(r_2^*,c_i)$, or $conf(r_1^*,c_i)=conf(r_3^*,c_i)$ or $conf(r_2^*,c_i)=conf(r_3^*,c_i)$ or $conf(r_1^*,c_i)=conf(r_2^*,c_i)=conf(r_3^*,c_i)$. That c_i can be assigned to either of its preferred clusters, or it can be left in a residue bag.

To find the k centroids:
The total confusion provoked by k candidates c_i, c_j,... c_k in a bag $\{c_1,c_2,...,c_n\}$ of n elements is

$tc(c_i,c_j, ... c_k) = min(conf(c_i,c_1), conf(c_j,c_1), ... conf(c_k,c_1)) + min(conf(c_i,c_2), conf(c_j,c_2), ... conf(c_k,c_2)) +...+ min(conf(c_i,c_n), conf(c_j,c_n), ... conf(c_k,c_n))$

and the solution r_1^*, r_2^*,... r_k^* is the k-tuple c_i, c_j,...c_k that minimizes the above tc. The inconsistency of the bag is such smallest tc divided by n. The k clusters are formed by the elements that preferred r_1^*, r_2^*,... or r_k^*, respectively. "Undecided" elements are handled as before. There may be more than one k-tuples of centroids that minimize tc. If "residue" bags are allowed, there may be several of them.

As the number of allowed centroids increases, the inconsistency of the bag decreases, since each element of the bag can find better candidates (lower confusion) when there are more of them.

Remarks.

1. The above solution is slow –it is an exhaustive search. The number of distinct sets of k candidates is $n!/[(n\text{-}k)!k!]$ and the amount of *conf*'s needed to compute tc for each of these sets of candidates is nk, so that the total number of *conf*'s needed is $nkn!/[(n\text{-}k)!k!]$; thus, the complexity of the solution is $O(n)\times O(n^n)/O(n^{n\text{-}k}) = O(n^{k+1})$, since k is constant.

2. Up to this point, we still do not know how to set k, the appropriate number of centroids to have. A low number of centroids is desirable, but it is also desirable to have a small inconsistency.

3. We see that the inconsistency of a bag is a monotonic function, starting at some value $\sigma \geq 0$ for 1 centroid, and reaching 0 for n centroids. In fact, if there are repeated elements in the bag, it reaches 0 for less than n centroids. See Figure 4.

We could try to minimize a linear combination of the number k of centroids and the inconsistency σ caused by them, such as $\alpha k + (1-\alpha)\sigma$ for $0 \leq \alpha \leq 1$. Small values of α will favor many centroids, while a large α will favor few. Empiricism will dictate which α is "best" or "appropriate." We follow instead another (empirical) solution: to search for a large drop in the inconsistency (§2.6) as we add more centroids; that drop sets k.

2.2 Finding the K Centroids of a Bag of Qualitative Values –Exact Solution

We explain the algorithm with an example, and then formalize it in *Algorithm 1* of §2.3 for k=2. Let us compute the centroids of bag {Schnauzer, cat, other mammals, amphibian, reptile, lizard} which is marked with □ in Figure 1.

One Centroid: If we were going to select one centroid for the bag {Schnauzer, cat, other mammals, amphibian, reptile, lizard}, it will be Schnauzer, with an inconsistency σ =1.5/6 =0.25 (See Table 1). That is, to find one centroid of a bag we apply the formula of §1.4.

Two Centroids: For selecting two centroids, we have the following choices: (Schnauzer, cat); (Schnauzer, other mammals), (Schnauzer, amphibian), (Schnauzer, lizard)[6], (cat, other mammals), (cat, amphibian), (cat, lizard), (other mammals, amphibian), (other mammals, lizard), and (amphibian, lizard). We compute the total confusions caused by each of these pairs. As an example, let us compute the confusion caused by the pair (cat, lizard). Considering the rows of Table 1 corresponding to cat and lizard, we construct Table 2. Each element (each "voter") of the bag selects one of these two candidates –the best for it, the candidate provoking in the candidate the smaller confusion. For instance, voter Schnauzer selects candidate cat, voter cat selects candidate cat, voter "other mammals" selects candidate cat, voter amphibian selects either, voter reptile selects lizard… The results appear in the last row of Table 2. Thus, the pair (cat, lizard) provokes a total confusion of 1.

Computing the total confusion for all pairs, the values are: (Schnauzer, cat) =1.25; (Schnauzer, other mammals) =1.25, (Schnauzer, amphibian) =1.25, (Schnauzer, lizard) =0.75, (cat, other mammals) =1.5, (cat, amphibian) =1.5, (cat, lizard) =1, (other mammals, amphibian) =1.5, (other mammals, lizard) =1, and (amphibian, lizard) =1.75. Thus, the best pair is (Schnauzer, lizard) with an inconsistency of 0.75/6 =0.125. §02.3 gives a detailed description of this algorithm.

Three Centroids: Computing the total confusion for all trios, the values are: (Schnauzer, cat, other mammals) =1; (Schnauzer, cat, amphibian) =1; (Schnauzer, cat, lizard) =0.5; (Schnauzer, other mammals, amphibian) =1; (Schnauzer, other mammals, lizard) =0.5; (Schnauzer, amphibian, lizard) =0.5; (cat, other mammals, amphibian) =1.25; (cat, other mammals, lizard) =0.75; (cat, amphibian, lizard) =1; (other mammals, amphibian, lizard) =0.75. Thus, we have a triple tie, the winners of the best three centroids are (Schnauzer, cat, lizard), (Schnauzer, other

mammals, lizard), and (Schnauzer, amphibian, lizard), each with an inconsistency of 0.5/6 = 0.083.

Four Centroids: Computing the total confusion for all quartets, these are: (Schnauzer, cat, other mammals, amphibian) =0.75; (Schnauzer, cat, other mammals, lizard) =0.25; (Schnauzer, cat, amphibian, lizard) =0.25; (Schnauzer, other mammals, amphibian, lizard) =0.25; and (cat, other mammals, amphibian, lizard) =0.5. There are three winners, the quartets (Schnauzer, cat, other mammals, lizard), (Schnauzer, cat, amphibian, lizard), and (Schnauzer, other mammals, amphibian, lizard), with an inconsistency of 0.25/6 =0.041.

Five Centroids: Finally, we see that the quintet (Schnauzer, cat, other mammals, amphibian, lizard) has total confusion =0. That is the solution if we insist in five centroids. See Figure 4.

Notice that, once the pair wise confusions among the values (Table 1) are found, there are no more tedious calculations to make. For finding the best pair of centroids, it is enough to select every two rows of Table 1, finding the max of each column, and add these values. Table 2 seeks to explain this procedure. Notice that Table 2 is a subset of Table 1. Similarly, for finding the best trio of centroids, it is enough to select every three rows of Table 1, find the max of each column, and add these values. And so on.

The above algorithm is exact (it will select the best pair, the best trio…) but it will be too slow for large bags. We present in §2.5 an approximate algorithm that is much faster.

2.2.1 Repeated Centroids are Unnecessary

If a bag has repeated elements, could it be that in its k centroids exist repeated elements, too? For instance, let us consider bag {Schnauzer,

Table 2. To compute the total confusion caused by the pair (cat, lizard) in each element (each "voter") of the bag, we select for each column the smallest confusion (results shown in last row) and add these values. For instance, for column "Schnauzer" we select the smallest of ½ and ¾, and place that value (1/2) in the third row of that column. The result of adding the values of the third row is ½ + 0 + ¼ + ¼ + 0 + 0 =1 (which is placed in the last row, last column). This table is part of Table 1, hence, a practical algorithm will use Table 1 and ignore or select appropriate rows of it.

	Schnauzer	Cat	Other Mammal	Amphibian	Reptile	Lizard	Total Confusion
Cat	½	0	¼	¼	¼	½	
Lizard	¾	½	½	¼	0	0	
Smaller Value	½	0	¼	¼	0	0	1

Schnauzer, cat, other mammals, amphibian, reptile, lizard}. Its two centroids are (Schnauzer, lizard). Could it be that its three centroids are (Schnauzer, Schnauzer, lizard)? That can not be, for the following reason. Replacing one of the Schnauzers (of the trio of centroids) by any other value in the bag not already in the set of centroids (say, by cat) will lower (or at least will not increase) the total confusion provoked by the new trio (Schnauzer, cat, lizard), since elements that selected the eliminated Schnauzer can still vote *for the other Schnauzer* and not increase the total confusion. And the new inserted candidate, cat, will now vote for itself with confusion 0, which may lower the total confusion, since 0 is not larger that conf(cat, Schnauzer) or conf(cat, lizard). Thus, replacing a duplicated candidate by some other candidate will not increase the total confusion, and may lower it. Likewise, expunging the duplicate candidate from the set of candidates will lower the number of candidates, but will not lower the total confusion provoked by them.

2.3 Finding the Two Centroids of a Bag: Exact Solution

The algorithm outlined in §2.2 for finding the two centroids of a bag –that is, for clustering the bag in two clusters, is described here in detail.

We find the total confusion produced in the bag by each pair (c_i, c_j) of candidates, and select the pair with the lowest total confusion. If there is a tie (more than one pair achieves the lowest total confusion) we use some breaking rules, later explained. Let us call "voters" the elements of the bag (a single voter will be denoted by v), since they will select or "vote" for one of the two candidates c_i or c_j. The algorithm is the following.

Algorithm 1. Finding the two centroids of bag B of n>1 elements (qualitative values).

Input: B, a bag with at least two values.

Output: Two elements of B, its two centroids.

1. For every pair p of candidates (c_i, c_j) such that i=1,… $n, j>i, c_i \neq c_j$, compute:

toti(p) = total confusion caused by voters v for which conf(c_i, v) < conf(c_j, v)

= Σ conf(c_i, v) where the sum is over all $v \square B$ such that conf(c_i, v) < conf(c_j, v));

totj(p) = total confusion caused by voters v for which conf(c_i, v) > conf(c_j, v));

totd(p) = total confusion caused by voters v for which conf$(c_i v)$ = conf(c_j, v));

tc(p) = toti(p) +totj(p) +totd(p) /* tc(p) is the total confusion caused in B by pair p, as defined in § 2.1 */

2.A. Find those p's which minimize tc(p). Usually there is one; there may be more than one.

If p is unique, return that pair as the answer. Otherwise,

    2.B. Eliminating one p. If there is more than one p, then take a couple of these pairs, in order to eliminate one of them. Say the chosen pairs are $p_1 = (c_1, c_2)$ and $p_2 = (c_3, c_4)$.

        i.   It could be that one of the candidates in one pair appears in both pairs. Without loss of generality, we can assume that $c_1 = c_3$. Then, that candidate will surely be one of the two centroids of the surviving pair. The other surviving centroid, c_2 or c_4, will be that with the lowest total confusion toti or totj. (Notice that tc is not used here.) If there is a tie, select either as the second survivor.

        ii.   If none of the candidates of one pair appears in the other pair, select as survivor the pair containing the candidate with the lowest total confusion. In a tie, select either pair.

    2.C. Eliminate the other pair. Go to 2.B unless one pair remains.

    2.D. Return the surviving pair as the answer. *End of Algorithm 1.*

Notice that step 2.A finds the pair(s) p that minimizes the total confusion, tc(p). If several p are attained, only then toti(p) and totj(p) are used (steps 2.B and C) to discriminate among them.

Example 8. For bag {Schnauzer, cat, other mammals, amphibian, reptile, lizard}, Step 1 of Algorithm 1 produces:

For candidates (Schnnauzer, cat): toti(Schnauzer) =0;[7] totj(cat) =0;[8] totd =1.25;[9] tc(Schnauzer, cat) =1.25;

For candidates (Schnnauzer, other mammals): toti(Schnauzer) =0;[10] totj(other mammals) =0;[10] totd =1.25;[10] tc(Schnauzer, other mammals) =1.25;

For candidates (Schnnauzer, amphibian): toti(Schnauzer) =0.5; totj(amphibian) =0; totd =0.75; tc(Schnauzer, amphibian)=1.25;

For candidates (Schnnauzer, lizard): toti(Schnauzer) =0.5; totj(lizard) =0; totd =0.25; tc(Schnauzer, lizard) =0.75;

For candidates (cat, other mammals): toti(cat)=0; totj(other mammals) =0; totd =1.5; tc(cat, other mammals) =1.5;

For candidates (cat. amphibian): toti(cat) =0.75; totj(amphibian) =0; totd =0.75; tc(cat, amphibian) =1.5;

For candidates (cat, lizard): toti(cat) =0.75; totj(lizard) =0; totd =0.25; tc(cat, lizard) =1 (see also Table 2);

For candidates (other mammals, amphibian): toti(other mammals)=0.75; totj(amphibian) =0; totd =0.75; tc(other mammals, amphibian) =1.5;

For candidates (other mammals, lizard): toti(other mammals)=0.75; totj(lizard) =0; totd =0.25; tc(other mammals, lizard) =1, and

For candidates (amphibian, lizard): toti(amphibian) =0; totj(lizard)=0; totd =1.75; tc(amphibian, lizard) =1.75.

In step 2.A, we find that the lowest total confusion (tc) is 0.75, and it is reached only by (Schnauzer, lizard). Therefore, the accumulators toti() and totj() were not used to disambiguate any tie among best pairs.

Thus, the two centroids are (Schnauzer, lizard) with an inconsistency of 0.75/6 =0.125. The clusters (according to Table 1) are {Schnauzer, cat, other mammals}, {lizard, amphibian, reptile}. The only indifferent value was amphibian, who selected equally Schnauzer or lizard, since conf(Schnauzer, amphibian) =conf(lizard, amphibian) = ¼.

2.3.1 Is the Pair of Centroids a Condorcet Winner?

The Condorcet winner, when it exists, is a single individual –not two of them. But we could imagine a country which always elects two co-presidents, so that voters manifest their preference about couples of candidates –each candidate appears in every possible pair. In that country, competition at elections is among pairs of candidates, not among candidates. In that case, our method of "electing" the best pair is a Condorcet method (Cf. §1.5), and the victorious pair (r_1^*, r_2^*) is the Condorcet winner, since it beats (or draws) all other pairs. The cluster "around" r_1^* [formed by those elements e where $\text{conf}(r_1^*, e) < \text{conf}(r_2^*, e)$] is the constituency or supporters of r_1^*; the cluster "around" r_2^* is the constituency of r_2^*; the elements e for which $\text{conf}(r_1^*, e) = \text{conf}(r_2^*, e)$ are the undecided voters (swing voters, floating voters –their vote can go to r_1^* or to r_2), they can cluster around r_1^*, around r_2^*, or be split into the two clusters. These swing voters swung only between r_1^* and r_2^*; any other candidate was less preferred.

2.4 Finding One More Centroid of a Bag That Already Has K

If by some means we already found k centroids or consensus for a bag, and still we want to find $k+1$ of them, this section provides an algorithm that does this in an approximate manner. This algorithm avoids the exhaustive search of §2.2, but the $k+1$ "centroids" it delivers may not be the true centroids.

The idea is to replace the worst of the k centroids, by two new found. This replacement is straightforward, if we accumulate for each centroid the total confusion caused by it (Step D below). The algorithm follows.

Algorithm 2. Find one more centroid of bag B with k centroids $(c_1, c_2, ..., c_k)$
Input: B, a bag of size at least $k+1$; k, the number of centroids; and the k centroids $(c_1, c_2, ..., c_k)$

Output: The $k+1$ centroids $c_1', c_2', ..., c_k', c_{k+1}'$.
   A.   If $k=0$, apply formula of §1.4 to find one centroid, and return that as output.
   B.   If $k=1$, apply Algorithm 1 of §2.3 to find two centroids; return that as output.
   C.   Otherwise, find which of the centroids $c_1, c_2, ..., c_k$ is the worst – has the largest total confusion. To achieve that, let each value v of the bag select the centroid which provokes in that v the lowest confusion; that is, the centroid c_j that minimizes $\text{conf}(c_j, v)$ is selected by v.
      a.   Thus, for each v in the bag,
   1.   If precisely one centroid c_j is selected by v (as that minimizing $\text{conf}(c_j, v)$), then accumulate the confusion $\text{conf}(c_j, v)$ in a counter totconf(j) for that jth centroid.
Also, keep the list (v, c_j) meaning "value v voted for c_j."
   2.   If several centroids $c_i, c_j, ... c_m$ are selected (that is, $\text{conf}(c_i,v) = \text{conf}(c_j,v) = ... = \text{conf}(c_m,v)$ --several centroids provoked the same minimum in the confusion of using that centroid instead of v), accumulate the confusion $\text{conf}(c_i,v)$ in a counter totconfindif –here we accumulate the confusion provoked in v if v is an *indifferent* voter.
Also, keep the candidates selected by v in the list (v, c_i, c_j, c_m) meaning "value v voted indifferently for c_i or c_j or ... or c_m".
      b.   After all elements of the bag have made their selection in step a, find which of these centroids has the largest (worst) total confusion totconf(). In this, totconfindif is not used. Call w this worst centroid. If there is a tie, select any.
      c.   Discard that worst centroid w found in step b, but first find which voters voted for it, including the voters which voted for w indifferently (that is, voters who voted for w and for somebody else). Let $B' =$ those voters. Remark: $B' \subset B$.

D. At this point, k-1 centroids remain (one was discarded). Using Algorithm 1, find the best two centroids for bag B'. Return those two best centroids together with the remaining k-1 centroids as the desired k+1 centroids of bag B. *End of Algorithm 2.*

Remarks.

- In step C, we compute again the total confusion totconf(j) that centroid c_j provokes. We do not use totj(p) of Algorithm 1, because totj(p) was computed when only two centroids were contending (for the vote of v), whereas in Algorithm 2 we have k centroids contending.
- In step C, all k centroids are eligible for removal.
- In step D, the two centroids for bag B' should belong, of course, to B'.[11]
- The centroid discarded in step C.c could be selected again when step D returns two additional centroids; that is, the discarded

centroid could reappear and be one of these two.

- Algorithm 2 converges quickly because at each step, the best k-1 centroids are kept, and in the new election only the voters (B') who voted for the discarded centroid are going to select two by voting again –a voting population smaller than B.

Example 9. Let us ask Algorithm 2 to find one more centroid of bag {Schnauzer, cat, other mammals, amphibian, reptile, lizard} for k = 2 and centroids (Schnauzer, lizard) as already found in Example 8. Inputs for Algorithm 2 are: B ={Schnauzer, cat, other mammals, amphibian, reptile, lizard}, n=2, centroids =(Schnauzer, lizard).

Step C computes, for every v in B, conf(Schnauzer, v), conf(lizard, v) and accumulates conf(Schnauzer, v) into totconf(Schnauzer) if conf(Schnauzer, v) < conf(lizard, v), into totconf(lizard) if conf(Schnauzer, v)>conf(lizard, v), or into totconfindif if conf(Schnauzer, v) =conf(lizard, v). These accumulations are shown in Table 3, which was built from left to right. The last column shows the final contents of accumula-

Table 3. Step C.a of example 9. Columns show voters. They vote for Schnauzer or for lizard. The first two rows show their confusions. The selection of each voter (the smallest of the two confusions) accumulates in either totconf(Schnauzer) or totconf(lizard). If both confusions are the same, it gets accumulated into totconfindif. For instance, first voter (column Schnauzer) selects to vote for Schnauzer, so it adds 0 to the accumulator totconf(Schnauzer), shown in the same Schnauzer column. Second voter (cat) selects to vote for Schnauzer, so adds ¼ to totconf(Schnauzer). Other mammals, our third voter, votes for Schnauzer, so ¼ is added to totconf(Schnaunzer), which now is ½. Fourth voter (column amphibian) is an indifferent voter, so adds its confusion (1/4) to totconfindif. Reptile votes for lizard and adds 0 to totconf(lizard); the same happens to lizard. In the last column we find the final value of accumulators totconf(Schnauzer)=1/2, totconf(lizard)=0 and totconfindif=1/4: the final values when the vote of lizard, the last voter, is taken.

	Schnauzer	Cat	Other Mammals	Amphibian	Reptile	Lizard
Schnauzer	0	¼	¼	¼	¼	½
Lizard	¾	½	½	¼	0	0
totconf(Schnauzer)	0	¼	½	½ ·	½	½
totconf(Lizard)	0	0	0	0	0	0
totconfindif	0	0	0	¼	¼	¼

tors totconf(Schnauzer) =1/2, totconf(lizard) =0, totconfindif =1/4 when step C.a finishes.

Now step C.b selects the worst of the two centroids: Schnauzer. Step C.c discards Schnauzer and finds who voted for Schnauzer (including indifferent voters). They are {Schnauzer, cat, other mammals, amphibian}. *They will be given another chance to vote.* Thus, B' is set to {Schnauzer, cat, other mammals, amphibian}.

Step D calls Algorithm 1 to find two centroids for B'. They are (Schnauzer, cat). Then, (lizard, Schnauzer, cat) is returned as the best three centroids of bag {Schnauzer, cat, other mammals, amphibian, reptile, lizard}. Note that the centroid Schnauzer, discarded in step C.b, reappeared again in step D. See Figure 4. This solution agrees with the exact solution found in §2.2. The three clusters are {lizard, reptile, amphibian}, {Schnauzer}, {cat, other mammals}. The indifferent values (see Table 1) were "other mammals" (selecting either Schnauzer or cat as its preferred centroid)[12]

and amphibian (selecting as its preferred centroid Schnauzer, cat or lizard).

2.5 Finding (Approximately) The Centroids of a Bag of Values –Two by Two

Up to this point, we can find k centroids of a bag B. But, who sets the value k? How many centroids is it "best" to have? Let us call κ this "best" k.

We now give an algorithm for finding the κ centroids of a bag of qualitative values. Rigorously, they should be called "quasi-centroids," since they are not guaranteed to be the *real* centroids. The idea is to find one centroid for B (using §1.4), then two centroids (using §2.3), then the three centroids (using §2.4), and so on, at each time using §2.4 to find one more centroid, but to stop as soon as the condition of §2.6 is met: a sharp drop in the inconsistency. Notice that this algorithm (Algorithm 3) finds κ as well as the κ centroids of B.

Figure 4. The inconsistency of bag {Schnauzer, cat, other mammals, amphibian, reptile, lizard} as a function of the number of centroids it is allowed to have. The centroid Schnauzer gives an inconsistency of 0.25. If the bag is allowed to have two centroids, these are (Schnauzer, lizard) and σ drops to 0.125. The three centroids are (Schnauzer, cat, lizard) with σ =0.083. Another trio of centroids is (Schnauzer, other mammals, lizard); still another trio is (Schnauzer, amphibian, lizard). The four centroids of the bag are (Schnauzer, cat, other mammals, lizard) with σ =0.042. There are other quartets of centroids (see text). Finally, the quintet (Schnauzer, cat, other mammals, amphibian, lizard) yields the lowest value, 0, for the bag's inconsistency.

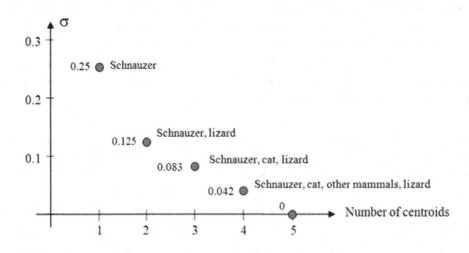

Algorithm 3. Find the (approximate) centroids of a bag of qualitative values.

1. Find the centroid of B, with the help of §1.4. One centroid.
2. Find the two centroids of B, with the help of Algorithm 1 of §2.3.
3. Apply the test of §2.6 to see whether the inconsistency of the larger number of centroids is significantly inferior to the inconsistency of the smaller number of centroids.
    a. If that is the case, return the larger number of centroids as the answer. Stop.
    b. Otherwise, find the worst centroid and replace it with two new ones, using Algorithm 2 of §2.4.
4. Go to step 3. End of Algorithm 3.

2.6 How to Select the Appropriate Number κ of Centroids

In clustering or unsupervised pattern classification, there is often no good way to select an appropriate number of clusters, since frequently it is desired to minimize some similarity function inside each cluster, and simultaneously not to have too many clusters. That is our case. In these situations, an empirical choice is made. One of them is already mentioned in §2.1: minimize a linear combination of k (the number of centroids) and σ (the inconsistency). In this section we provide another empirical selection: stop adding centroids when a sharp decrease in inconsistency happens. Other selection criteria could be used.

The inconsistency of a bag decreases monotonically (Figure 4) as the number of centroids grows. We look for sharp descents in the inconsistency (say, a drop of at least 20%), and we select the number of centroids that contains the first sharp descent. In other words, adding more centroids will give only slight decreases in inconsistency.

In Figure 4, when we go from 1 centroid to 2, the inconsistency drops from 0.25 to 0.125, or a drop of 50%. Thus, we have found the first sharp drop and we keep these two centroids. Therefore, we say that bag {Green lizard, German Shepherd, other dogs, Green lizard, cat, dog} has two centroids and an inconsistency of 0.125, and $\kappa = 2$.

3. CONCLUSION AND DISCUSSION

3.1 Conclusions

Our paper (Guzman-Arenas, A., & Jimenez, A. (2010)), summarized in §1.4, provides a way, using conf, to obtain the centroid (r^*) and inconsistency (σ) of a bag of symbolic values reported (by several observers) for the same observed property of the same object. r^* and σ are crisp, not fuzzy, values. In addition, σ is a number, not a qualitative assessment. The observers are equally credible, so that their dissimilar observations are due to the difference in their methods (or instruments) of observation. When methods are crude, the observed values have "limited precision" (are located close to the root of the hierarchy). Other observers could obtain more detailed measurements, positioned deeper in the hierarchy. The *inconsistency* of the bag measures how far apart the testimonies (the values) in the bag are; it is a number between 0 and 1, not just 0 or 1.

Work reported in this chapter solves the same problem when it is possible for the bag to have *several* centroids. Each of the centroids induces a *cluster* of the bag: those elements for which that centroid minimizes the confusion conf(centroid, element). In this way, we can cluster qualitative values in such a way to produce a small inconsistency. The method also shows *indifferent values*, which could belong to either of two (or more) clusters.

Chapter 2 describes (§2.3) an exact method for computing the two centroids of a bag. It also describes (§2.2) an exact method for computing the k centroids of a bag, and an approximate, but faster, method (§2.6) to do the same.

3.2 Discussion

Numeric values have a meaning "of their own," so it is easy to agree in the difference between, say, 7 and 13. Opposite to that, symbolic values (such as Mexico City or airplane) must have a *context* against which their closeness or difference can be gauged. This context is provided by hierarchies, over which the function conf is defined. The function conf(r, s) measures the confusion when symbolic value r is used instead of the real, or intended, value s. The function conf always has as a parameter a hierarchy of possible or likely symbolic values. This hierarchy can be regarded as a simplified ontology, where only the relations "subset" and "member" are used. In principle, all the relations in an ontology could be used by a (modified) function conf, but this issue remains unexplored.

The similarity function conf is not a distance. Many other similarity functions exist (for instance, the Jacquard coefficient), and which is better depends on its purpose, on its intended use. conf is useful when qualitative values have different precisions, so that some values are refinements or "extensions" of another values (Doberman and Schnauzer are "refinements" of dog), and there are levels or tiers of values having the same "granularity" (or "precision"). [Therefore, they can best be arranged in a *hierarchy*].

When several numeric measurements are performed over the same property of the same object, and a bag of different values is obtained, how can we measure the inconsistency of that bag?[13] What is the most likely value for the property? Ordinary Logic tells us that there is no such value, and the inconsistency of the bag is 1 (false), since the measurements are incompatible. Dempster-Schafer theory (Dempster, A. (1968); Shafer, G. (1976)) uses the likelihood of different measurers telling the truth (their credibility), to compute the most likely value. Fuzzy logic can also be used. Other researchers (Byrne, E., & Hunter, A. (2005); Hunter, A., & Konieczny, S.

(2008)) count how many predicates are violated by the bag of observations, and that count is the inconsistency of the bag. Still others try to remove assertions from an inconsistent set; the number of assertions removed until the remaining set becomes consistent tells how inconsistent the original set was. For most of us, the most likely value for that property, given a bag of measurements, is just the average or centroid of these values, and the inconsistency of the bag is just the variance σ of the observations.

Bags of values referring to a single-valued variable (such as "x is the father of Emille") can have just one centroid (a bag of opinions about who is the father of Emille), whereas other bags can have more than one centroid (a bag of opinions about who are the friends of Emille). When the problem allows the existence of several centroids, the exposed methods relying in confusion and total confusion easily express the preference of voters (elements of the bags) about candidates (possible centroids), so that the task of finding a reasonable number of centroids attains relevance. We solve it reasonably by a heuristic method: seeking a sharp drop in the inconsistency as the number of allowed centroids grows. The solution is quantitative and crisp.

It should be emphasized that an asserted value obtained by an observer (such as *Doberman* in "John's pet was a Doberman") represents not only itself, but all the values from it up to the root of the hierarchy: Doberman, dog, mammal, vertebrate, and animal. This is because the observer, having all these values to select when reporting his observation, reports the most precise value.

3.3 Different Manners to Deal with Inconsistency

If two observers or informants report different values for the same variable, say, $x=1$ and $x=0$, how to deal with the inconsistency or contradiction? This is an important question, since there are many sources of information, and not all of them agree. Some manners (one of which is our *inconsistency* approach) are:

1. Multivalued variables. It could be that x could have more than one value, for instance, friend_of_John=Mary and friend_of_John=Susan, since John can have several friends.

2. Contradiction. Logics tells that $a \wedge \bar{a}$ = F, and from here everything can be deduced.

   a. Inconsistency removal. An approach (Hunter, A. & Konieczny, S. (2008)) will be to remove enough formulas from the inconsistent set until consistency is attained. The smallest number of formulas to remove measures the inconsistency of the set.

3. Probability. Stochastic variable. Sometimes x=0, at other times (with probabilities p and 1-p) x=1.

4. Fuzzy logic. Fuzzy variable. x has a membership degree (say, 0.7) in the set of numbers equal to 0, and other membership degree (say, 0.5) in the set of numbers equal to 1. That is, x is closer to 0 than to 1.

5. Dempster-Shafer. Theory of evidence. (Dempster, A. (1968); Shafer, G. (1976)). If somebody says that x=0 and somebody else claims that x=1, pay attention to the degree of credibility (propensity to tell lies) of each informant, in order to determine the value of x.

6. Possibility and Necessity (Dubois, D., and Prade, H. (1988)). Given a universe Θ, let $P(\Theta)$ be the power set of Θ. A set function *Pos* is said to be a possibility measure if

   a) $Pos(\varnothing) = 0$ and $Pos(\Theta) = 1$;

   b) $Pos(\bigcup_l A_l) = \sup_l Pos(A_l) \forall A_l \in P(\Theta)$

   The triplet $(\Theta, P(\Theta), Pos)$ is called a possibility space, and the set A_l in $P(\Theta)$ is called a fuzzy event (Shen, Q., and Zhao, R. (2011)).

Also, a set function *Nec* is said to be a necessity measure if

a) $Nec(\varnothing) = 0$ and $Nec(\Theta) =$

b) $Nec(\bigcap_l A_l) = \inf_l Nec(A_l) \forall A_l \in P(\Theta)$

   It is obvious that $Nec(A) = 1 - Pos(A^C)$ $\forall A \in P(\Theta)$. That is, the necessity measure is the dual of the possibility measure.

7. Credibility. It is defined as the average of Possibility and Necessity. The credibility measure of a set A, Cr(A), is defined as Cr(A) = (Pos(A) + Nec(A))/2. The credibility has important properties:

   a. $Cr(\varnothing) = 0$ and cr $(\Theta) = 1$.

   b. Cr is monotonically increasing, i.e., $Cr(A) \le Cr(B)$ whenever $A \subseteq B$.

   c. $Nec(A) \le Cr(A) \le Pos(A) \forall A \in P(\Theta)$.

   d. Cr is sub-additivity, i.e., $Cr(A \cup B) \le Cr(A) + Cr(B)$.

   e. Cr is self-dual, i.e., $Cr(A) + Cr(A^C) = 1$ $\forall A \in P(\Theta)$

      Dubois (Dubois, D., and Prade, H. (1988)) defines a different measure also called "credibility", not used here. Points 6 and 7 are taken from (Shen, Q., and Zhao, R. (2011)).

8. Inconsistency using confusion (Guzman-Arenas, A., & Jimenez, A. (2010); Guzman-Arenas, A., Cuevas, A. and Jimenez, A. (2011)). If somebody says that x=0 and somebody else claims that x=1, it is because they used different gauges to measure the value, or used different methods to observe the (qualitative) value. Their precision differs, the granularity of the reported values is not the same –nevertheless, in the *confusion* sense, it is the *same* value (or, at least, a consensus can be achieved). In fact, this chapter deals with the case where *several* consensus are possible.

   a. How to measure the inconsistency of a bag of observations (a bag of qualitative values)? How to find the *centroid* or consensus of such bag? This we called *Problem 1,* and it is solved in (Guzman-Arenas, A., & Jimenez, A. (2010)).

b. If a bag can have several centroids, how to find them? And the inconsistency of the bag? This is *Problem 2,* solved in this chapter.

c. How to decrease the inconsistency of a bag. Finding the greatest outlier. This is *Problem 3,* is solved in (Guzman-Arenas, A., & Jimenez, A. (2010)).

d. Incremental computation of the inconsistency. Is there a way to incrementally compute the inconsistency of a large bag when a new observation arrives? This is *Problem 4*, and is solved in (Guzman-Arenas, A., & Jimenez, A. (2010)).

e. Negative assertions. If one observer says that "the pet of John is not a mammal", how to combine this affirmation with the other assertions? This is solved in (Guzman-Arenas, A., & Jimenez, A. (2010)).

f. How to measure the inconsistency of a bag of objects (each object being defined by several qualitative values)? How to find the *centroid* or consensus of such bag of objects (not of values)? This we called *Problem 5,* and is solved in (Guzman-Arenas, A., Cuevas, A. and Jimenez, A. (2011)).

g. When the values change. Imagine now that x changes with time, and that observer 1 reports a *stream* of values for x, while observer 2 reports a second stream of values. Additional observers may report additional streams. Each value in a stream is time-stamped, but not all the times coincide, nor all the streams have the same length. We are also given a set of models. For simplic-

ity, assume that these models are finite state machines, and that the values of x correspond to *states* in the machines, but they are reported "with confusion" (the observers have limited precision), so that state q may be reported as a more general value (as some ascendant of q in the hierarchy).[14] What is the model (machine) that best fits all the observed streams? That is, what is the "consensus model"? What is its inconsistency? This is *Problem 6,* which we may wish to tackle next. The real world produced just one stream of (real) states, while each reporter distorted by some degree (measured with limited accuracy) the values in the stream.

h. When several machines feed to a stream. Like in *Problem 6,* several observers watch the same stream of values, and each of them reports his own stream (of perceived values). Again, we have a set of finite state machines, each of them feeding their states (their events) to the stream, so that the stream is composed of a mixture of individual outputs of (several) machines. We want to determine what are the active machines that produce such a stream. That is, we want to decompose the observed stream in several substreams, such that each of them is produced by a machine. More than one copy of a machine can be feeding to the stream. This problem has been solved by (Cybenko, G., and Berk, V. H. (2007)), when all the values of the stream are reported perfectly (no inaccurate observations). We wish to solve the problem when there is "noise" caused by imperfect observations, but we have several observers that report somewhat different streams. This is *Problem 7*, not yet solved.

All these manners are valid approaches to handle inconsistency and contradiction. According to the problem at hand, some of them may be more appropriate than others.

3.4 Possible Applications of *Centroids* and *Inconsistency*

Approach (8) above is quite new; hence, no real life applications have been performed, to date. (de Gyves, V.P., Guzman, A., and Levachkine, S. (2005)) used confusion to extend SQL to queries with arbitrary confusion. It could also be used to solve *Problems 6* and *7,* cited above. We would like to extend (8) to handle arbitrary combinations of ANDs, ORs and NOTs (and perhaps, formulas with quantifiers). Some of this has been already done in (Guzman-Arenas, A., & Jimenez, A. (2010)). Why? Because we want to merge ontologies derived from different documents, and not all of the information is consistent. We want to have a resulting ontology with as much consistency as possible. This work (not done) falls under "belief updating", "belief revision" and "ontology merging."

ACKNOWLEDGMENT

Work was in part supported by CONACYT grant 43377 and by SNI. Comments by the reviewers increased the quality of this work.

REFERENCES

Byrne, E., & Hunter, A. (2005). Evaluating violations of expectations to find exceptional information. *Data & Knowledge Engineering, 54*(2), 97–120. doi:10.1016/j.datak.2004.09.003

Cuevas, A., & Guzman-Arenas, A. (2008). A language and algorithm for automatic merging of ontologies . In Rittgen, P. (Ed.), *Handbook of Ontologies for Business Interaction* (pp. 381–404). Hershey, PA: IGI Global.

Cybenko, G., & Berk, V. H. (2007). Process Query Systems. *IEEE Computer*, 62-70.

Dempster, A. (1968). A generalization of Bayesian inference. *Journal of the Royal Statistical Society. Series B. Methodological,* (30): 205–247.

Dubois, D., & Prade, H. (1988). *Possibility Theory*. New York: Plenum.

Guzman-Arenas, A., Cuevas, A., & Jimenez, A. (2011). The centroid or consensus of a set of objects with qualitative attributes. *Expert Systems with Applications, 38,* 4908–4919. doi:10.1016/j. eswa.2010.09.169

Guzman-Arenas, A., & Jimenez, A. (2010). Obtaining the consensus and inconsistency among a set of assertions on a qualitative attribute. *Journal Expert Systems with Applications (*37), 158-164.

Guzman-Arenas, A., & Levachkine, S. (2004a). Hierarchies Measuring Qualitative Variables. *Lecture Notes in Computer Science LNCS* (2945), 262-274.

Guzman-Arenas, A., & Levachkine, S. (2004b). Graduated errors in approximate queries using hierarchies and ordered sets. *Lecture Notes in Artificial Intelligence* LNAI (2972), 139-148.

Hunter, A., & Konieczny, S. (2008). Measuring inconsistency through minimal inconsistent sets. *Proceedings of the* 11th *International Conference on Knowledge Representation.* (pp. 358-366). Stratham, NH: AAI Press.

Jimenez, A. (in press). *Characterization and measurement of logical properties of qualitative values organized in hierarchies*. Mexico City, Mexico . *CIC-IPN.*

Levachkine, S., & Guzman-Arenas, A. (2007). Hierarchy as a new data type for qualitative variables. *Journal Expert Systems with Application, 32*(3), 139–148.

Levachkine, S., Guzman-Arenas, A., & de Gyves, V. P. (2005). The semantics of confusion in hierarchies: from theory to practice. ICCS 05 (Ed). *13ᵗʰ International Conference on Conceptual Structures: common semantics for sharing knowledge.* (pp. 94-107). Kassel, Germany.

Luo, P., Xiong, H., Zhan, G., Wu, J., & Shi, Z. (2009). Information-theoretic distances for cluster validation: generalization and normalization. *IEEE Transactions on Knowledge and Data Engineering, 21*(9), 1249–1262. doi:10.1109/TKDE.2008.200

Ruiz-Shulclóper, J., Guzman-Arenas, A., & Martinez-Trinidad, F. (1999). *Logical combinatorial approach to Pattern Recognition: supervised classification.* Valencia, Spain: Editorial Politécnica.

Shafer, G. (1976). *A Mathematical Theory of Evidence*. Princeton, NJ: Princeton University Press.

Shen, Q., & Zhao, R. (2011). A credibilistic approach to assumption-based truth maintenance. *IEEE Transactions on Systems, Man and Cybernetics . Part A, 41*(2), 85–95.

Yin, X., Han, J., & Fu, P. S. (2008). Truth Discovery with multiple conflicting information providers on the Web. *IEEE Trans. KDE, 20*(6), 796–808.

KEY TERMS AND DEFINITIONS

Centroid: (Similar to the centroid of a set of points in n-dimensional space). Most likely value of a bag of qualitative values. Consensus based on all evidence in the bag. Synonym: consensus, consensus value.

Clustering: Methods that are used to form subgroups of objects represented by a list of numeric values (points in an n-dimensional space). These methods can also be applied to symbolic values. More in Guzman-Arenas, A., Cuevas, A. and Jimenez, A. (2011).

Confusion: We define *conf(r, s)* as the confusion or error in using value r instead of s, the intended or correct value. These definitions agree with the human sense of estimation in closeness for several wrong but approximate answers to a given question; each is applicable to particular endeavors. More in Guzman-Arenas, A., & Levachkine, S. (2004a).

Consensus: The value that minimizes the sum of disagreements or discomforts for all the observers when they learn of the value chosen as the consensus value more in Guzman-Arenas, A., Cuevas, A. and Jimenez, A. (2011). Synonym: centroid.

Hierarchies: A tree of qualitative values, such that each node is either a qualitative value or, if it is a set, its descendants form a partition of such a set. A hierarchy can be regarded as the "common terminology" for several observers that are asked to inform about a particular value obtained by a symbolic variable. More in Guzman-Arenas, A., Cuevas, A. and Jimenez, A. (2011).

Inconsistency: The "dispersion" (variance), discrepancy or degree of disagreement of a bag of values. Guzman-Arenas, A., & Jimenez, A. (2010).

Knowledge Representation: A representation (of data, of facts) precise enough for a software to extract non trivial answers from it. Our knowledge representation is through ontologies, but in the examples of this chapter, we use hierarchies (for simplicity).

Qualitative Values: (As opposed to numeric or quantitative value). The value that a qualitative attribute may attain. Example: Afghanistan; Beirut; Iraq; Kabul; Middle East; Syria. Guzman-Arenas, Synonyms: Non numeric values, linguistic constants. A., Cuevas, A. and Jimenez, A. (2011).

Qualitative Attribute: (As opposed to numeric attribute). An aspect or feature of an object that is best described by a non numeric description.

Qualitative attributes (such as religion or color of hair) are also called symbolic or non-numeric properties, features, facets, attributes, symbolic variables or linguistic variables.

ENDNOTES

1   Qualitative attributes (such as religion or color of hair) are also called symbolic or non-numeric properties, features, facets, attributes, or linguistic variables. The values these attribute attain (such as Muslim or brown) are called qualitative values, non numeric values, or linguistic constants.

2   Each centroid has a cluster (a subset of the bag) associated with it: those elements that are most comfortable (lowest total confusion) with that centroid.

3   If the symbolic values become full *concepts,* it is best to use an *ontology* instead of a *hierarchy* to place them. (Cuevas, A & Guzman-Arenas, A. (2008)).

4   Problem 1 assumes just one centroid is possible. This chapter solves Problem 2 in Section 2, where the situation is such that several centroids are possible.

5   No values other than those in the bag are available for consensus; it will be a surprise to *all* observers to find out that the killer was Andrew, if *noboby* reported Andrew in his/her findings.

6   Due to remark VII of §1.4, the value reptile can never be a centroid.

7   Only value Schnauzer voted for candidate Schnauzer.

8   Only value cat voted for candidate cat.

9   Values "other mammals," amphibian, reptile and lizard voted indifferently (with the same confusion) for Schnauzer or cat.

10   Only value Schnauzer voted for candidate Schnauzer; only value "other mammals" voted for candidate "other mammals;" values cat, amphibian, reptile and lizard voted indifferently for Schnauzer and for "other mammals."

11   By definition of the centroid of a bag, in step D only members of B' participate in the election of the two centroids of B'.

12   conf(Schnauzer, other mammals) = conf(cat, other mammals) = ¼, as per Table 1.

13   I mean a bag of assertions, such as {the length is 7.2m; the length is 7.29m; the length is 6.85m; the length is 7m}.

14   For instance, if the state q corresponds to "John, the catcher, bought a Doberman", some informant may place in his stream the description "John bought a dog", while another informant may report the same event as "A base ball player bought a Doberman".

APPENDIX

Dealing with Confusion

Guzman-Arenas, A., & Levachkine, S. (2004a). Hierarchies Measuring Qualitative Variables. *Lecture Notes in Computer Science LNCS* (2945), 262-274.

Guzman-Arenas, A., & Levachkine, S. (2004b). Graduated errors in approximate queries using hierarchies and ordered sets. *Lecture Notes in Artificial Intelligence* LNAI (2972), 139-148.

de Gyves, V.P., Guzman, A., and Levachkine, S. (2005) Extending databases to precision-controlled retrieval of qualitative information. *Lecture Notes in Computer Science* 3563, 21-32.

Levachkine, S, Guzman-Arenas, A. & de Gyves, V.P. (2005) The semantics of confusion in hierarchies: from theory to practice. ICCS 05 (Ed). *13th International Conference on Conceptual Structures: common semantics for sharing knowledge.* (pp. 94-107). Kassel, Germany.

Levachkine, S., & Guzman-Arenas, A. (2007) Hierarchy as a new data type for qualitative variables. *Journal Expert Systems with Applications, 32*(3), 139-148

Dealing with Inconsistency

Adolfo Guzman-Arenas, Adriana Jimenez, (2010) Obtaining the consensus and inconsistency among a set of assertions on a qualitative attribute. *Journal Expert Systems with Applications*, 37, 158-164.

Adolfo Guzman-Arenas, Alma-Delia Cuevas, Adriana Jimenez. (2011) The centroid or consensus of a set of objects with qualitative attributes. *Expert Systems with Applications, 38* (2011) 4908-4919.

Chapter 2
Probabilistic Topic Discovery and Automatic Document Tagging

Davide Magatti
Università degli Studi di Milano-Bicocca, Italy

Fabio Stella
Università degli Studi di Milano-Bicocca, Italy

ABSTRACT

A software system for topic discovery and document tagging is described. The system discovers the topics hidden in a given document collection, labels them according to user supplied taxonomy and tags new documents. It implements an information processing pipeline which consists of document preprocessing, topic extraction, automatic labeling of topics, and multi-label document classification. The preprocessing module allows importing of several kinds of documents and offers different document representations: binary, term frequency and term frequency inverse document frequency. The topic extraction module is implemented through a proprietary version of the Latent Dirichlet Allocation model. The optimal number of topics is selected through hierarchical clustering. The topic labeling module optimizes a set of similarity measures defined over the user supplied taxonomy. It is implemented through an algorithm over a topic tree. The document tagging module solves a multi-label classification problem through multi-net Naïve Bayes without the need to perform any learning tasks.

1. INTRODUCTION

From 1990 to 2005 more than one billion people worldwide entered the middle class, get richer, become more literate and thus fueled the information market (The Economist, 2010). The effect of

such an economic and social revolution, together with the improvements achieved by information and communication technologies, is called the *information explosion*. Indeed, in the last five years the information created started to diverge from the storage capacity as reported by the International Data Corporation (2010). Data and information has gone from scarce to superabundant. While it

DOI: 10.4018/978-1-60960-881-1.ch002

is common opinion that this setting brings huge benefits it is also clear to everyone that it brings big headaches (The Economist, 2010). In the next ten years the data available on the WEB will amount to forty times the current size (International Data Corporation, 2010). The knowledge hidden in such a huge amount of data will heavily influence social behavior, political decisions, medicine and health care, company business models and strategies as well as financial investment opportunities. The overwhelming amount of available un-structured data has transformed the information from useful to troublesome. Indeed, it is becoming increasingly clear that our recording and processing capabilities are growing much slower than the amount of generated data and information. Search engines exacerbated this problem and although new paradigm of web-search are now being explored (Baeza-Yates & Raghavan, 2010), they normally provide users with huge amount of un-structured results, which need to be pruned and organized to become useful and valuable.

Halevy, Norvig and Pereira (2009) explain how *the unreasonable effectiveness of data* will be the pillar of the new WEB revolution. Their position originates from noticing that the biggest successes in natural language related machine learning have been statistical speech recognition and statistical machine translation. These tasks are much harder than document classification, while being routinely done every day for real human need. Therefore, a training set large enough, on the input/output behavior we want to automate, is available in the rough. In contrast, document classification, part-of-speech tagging, named-entity recognition, or parsing are not routine tasks, thus no large corpora are available in the wild. The corpora requires skilled human annotation which is slow, expensive and also difficult to agree on. Therefore, the first lesson of WEB-scale learning is to use the data available over the WEB rather than generating expensive annotated data. It is increasingly recognized that useful semantic relationships can be automatically learned from the statistics of search queries and the corresponding results, as well as from the accumulated evidence of WEB-based text patterns and formatted tables; in both cases no manually annotated data is required. A second lesson learnt from speech recognition and machine translation is that memorization offers a good strategy in the case where a lot of data is available. The statistical models used are based on huge databases, of probabilities associated with *n-grams*, i.e. short sequences of words, which have been built by exploiting billions or trillions of examples. A third lesson is the following; all the experimental evidence from the last decade in machine learning suggests that throwing away rare events is almost always a bad idea. Indeed, much WEB data consists of individually rare but collectively frequent events. Finally, the authors observed that for many tasks, words and word combinations provide all the representational machinery we need to learn from text. Halevy et al. (2009) conclude their manuscript with the following recommendation "Choose a representation that can use unsupervised learning on un-labeled data, which is so much more plentiful than labeled data." (p.12). This chapter follows the path suggested by Halevy et al. (2009) and exploits statistical methods together with un-labeled WEB documents to extract semantic knowledge to be used for organizing electronic archives and thus to achieve effective browsing and exploring. The knowledge extraction process is implemented through an information processing pipeline which transforms documents from plain to tagged. The tagging process exploits the semantic knowledge obtained by combining the topics extracted from a document corpus with user supplied taxonomy. The information processing pipeline relies on topic models (Blei, Ng & Jordan, 2003) to extract topics from the document corpus. Then, each topic is automatically labeled according to user supplied taxonomy through the ALOT algorithm (Magatti, Calegari, Ciucci & Stella, 2009). This algorithm automatically associates each topic with one or more labels from the user supplied taxonomy. Its main ingredients are a set of similarity measures and a set of topic labeling rules. The labeling rules are specifically designed to find the most agreed labels between the given topic and the user supplied taxonomy. Finally, the learnt topics together with their labels allow to automatically tag the document corpus as well as new documents. The document tagging task, which consists of multi-label document classification, is performed by using a multi-net Naïve Bayes model (Kim, Han, Rim & Myaeng, 2006). A formula mapping the output of the topic extraction process to the parameters of the multi-net Naïve Bayes model avoids the learning task to take place.

The chapter is organized as follows. The next section is devoted to introducing and describing the main ingredients of the information processing pipeline. In subsection 2.1 we describe the Latent Dirichlet Allocation (LDA) model and the available learning algorithms together with the illustration of the way in which the LDA posterior distribution can be used to explore the document corpus. Subsection 2.2 introduces the similarity measures which are used by the ALOT algorithm and discusses their main characteristics. The multi-label classification problem is introduced and described in subsection 2.3, together with the multi-net Naïve Bayes supervised classification model and the main performance measures used to evaluate supervised text classification. Section 3 is devoted to describe the information processing pipeline. The specific instance of the LDA model and the ALOT algorithm together with the formula mapping the topic learning output to the multi-net Naïve Bayes parameters are described. Numerical experiments illustrating the functionalities of the information processing pipeline are described in Section 4. This section shows how the information processing pipeline is used to organize a document corpus and to automatically tag previously unseen documents. Future research directions, emerging trends, paradigms and conclusions close the chapter.

2. BACKGROUND

Text mining (Feldman & Sanger, 2007; Berry & Castellanos, 2008), is an emerging research area which aims to solve the problem of information overload. Its typical tasks are: text categorization, document clustering and organization, and information extraction. Text mining exploits models and algorithms from data mining, machine learning, information retrieval and natural language processing to automatically extract knowledge from semi-structured and un-structured data. Among such methods, Support Vector Machines (SVMs) (Joachims, 2002) have been shown to be effective to solve the text categorization problem. However, SVMs are endowed by an implicit limitation: they rely on a set of labeled samples. This condition is extremely costly to be achieved and thus it is not easily met; whenever it is satisfied the result of the labeling process cannot be guaranteed to be coherent.

A lot of efforts have been oriented towards document clustering and organization: which do not require labeled samples and automatically group documents according to some similarity or distance measure. Classical algorithms like *K-means* (MacQueen, 1967) or Nearest Neighbor (Duda, Hart & Stork, 2000) represent documents as vectors in a metric space and compute pairwise distance to generate documents clusters. Hierarchical clustering algorithms have also been described in the specialized literature (Johnson, 1967; Duda, Hart & Stork, 2000). This class of algorithms returns a nested sequence of partitions in which higher clusters contain a set of similar documents obtained from couples of more specific partitions and recursively repeat this idea until the partitions consist of a single document. Drawbacks of classical clustering consist in the inability to capture the meaning of the different documents parts, forcing them inside a determined bin or subset of bins. Another problem is the labeling of clusters that often relies on humans.

Landauer, Foltz, and Laham, (1998) proposed Latent Semantic Analysis to document clustering and organization which has been later extended with a probabilistic model, based on mixture decomposition via a latent class model, by Hofmann (2001). These models capture the concept contained in a document and identified by set of related words (Blei et al., 2003).

This section gives basic definitions and tools required to understand the proposed approach to topic discovery and automatic document tagging. The reader familiar with latent Dirichlet allocation, similarity measures and multi-label text classification can skip this section to go to Section 3.

2.1. Latent Dirichlet Allocation

Latent Dirichlet Allocation (LDA) originates from the study of Latent Semantic Indexing (LSI) (Deerwester, Dumais, Landauer, Furnas & Harshman, 1990) and its probabilistic extension named probabilistic Latent Semantic Indexing (pLSI) (Hofmann, 1999).

The main idea of LDA can be summarized as follows; a document is a linear combination of multiple topics. A *topic* is a probability distribution over a given vocabulary. Figure 1 depicts two topics derived from the TASA corpus, a collection of over 37,000 text passages from educational materials (Griffiths & Steyvers, 2004). Each topic is associated with a specific argument, idea or theme. In the case where the two topics of Figure 1 are concerned, a document can be formed by assuming that each topic is associated with an urn whose content depends on the probability distribution associated with its topic (Figure 2).

A document is formed by first deciding its number of words, the mixing coefficients associated with the two topics and then by repeatedly choosing an urn, according to the mixing coefficients and finally by sampling a word from the selected urn. The choice of the urn to be sampled from and the subsequent sampling step are re-

Figure 1. Illustration of two (out of 300) topics extracted from the TASA corpus (language & arts, social studies, health, sciences). The ten most probable words (word) for each topic are listed together with the corresponding probability value (prob)

Topic 247		Topic 5	
word	*prob*	*word*	*Prob*
Drugs	.069	Red	.202
Drug	.060	Blue	.099
Medicine	.027	Green	.096
Effects	.026	Yellow	.073
Body	.023	White	.048
Medicines	.019	Color	.048
Pain	.016	Bright	.030
Person	.016	Colors	.029
Marijuana	.014	Orange	.027
Label	.012	Brown	.027

peated until the document consists of the specified number of words.

To clearly describe how the LDA model works, let $P(z)$ be the probability distribution over K topics z, i.e. the *topic distribution*, and $P(w \mid z)$ be the probability distribution over words w given topic z. The *topic-word distribution* $P(w \mid z)$ specifies the weight to thematically related words. A document is assumed to be formed as follows: its ith word w_i is generated by first extracting a sample from the topic distribution $P(z)$, then sampling a word from the topic-word distribution $P(w \mid z)$. Formally, we let $P(z_i = j)$ be the probability that the jth topic was sampled for the ith word token, while $P(w_i \mid z_i = j)$ is the probability of word w_i under topic j. Therefore, the LDA model induces the following probability distribution over words within a document:

$$P(w_i) = \sum_{j=1}^{K} P(w_i \mid z_i = j) P(z_i = j)$$

Figure 2. Two urns, Topic 247 and Topic 5, used to generate a document with mixing coefficient 0.7 for Topic 247 and 0.3 for Topic 5. The words in bold are sampled from the Topic 247

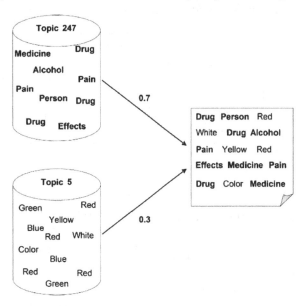

However, the available information consists of the words mentioned in each document, while the hidden components, i.e. the topic distribution and the topic-word distribution, are unknown and have to be learned from data. Given a document collection, the learning task associated with the LDA model consists of computing the posterior distribution of the hidden components given the observed documents. The posterior distribution is then used to perform tasks such as information retrieval and document browsing.

To better introduce and describe the interplay between the document collection and the structure of the hidden components, it is important to describe the generative nature of the LDA model. Let V be the size of the vocabulary, $\underline{\alpha}$ be a K-dimensional vector of non-negative elements, and η a scalar. Furthermore, let $Dir_V\left(\underline{\alpha}\right)$ and $Dir_K\left(\eta\right)$ be respectively a V-dimensional Dirichlet with parameter vector $\underline{\alpha}$ and a K-dimensional Dirichlet with parameter η. Furthermore, let $Mult\left(\underline{\beta}\right)$ be the multinomial distribution with parameter $\underline{\beta}$. The LDA generative model can be summarized through the following simple algorithm (Blei & Lafferty, 2009).

LDA generative model
For each topic k,
    (a) Draw a distribution over words $\underline{\beta}_k \sim Dir_K\left(\eta\right)$.
For each document d,
    (a) Draw a vector of topic proportions $\underline{\theta}_d \sim Dir_V\left(\underline{\alpha}\right)$.
    (b) For each word,
        i. Draw a topic assignment $Z_{d,n} \sim Mult\left(\underline{\theta}_d\right), Z_{d,n} \in \left\{1,...,K\right\}$.
        ii. Draw a word $W_{d,n} \sim Mult\left(\underline{\beta}_{z_{d,n}}\right)$, $W_{d,n} \in \left\{1,...,V\right\}$.

The LDA generative model can be conveniently represented as a directed graphical model through the thin plate notation (Figure 3).

In 2004, Griffiths and Steyvers introduced an extension of the original LDA model which associates a Dirichlet prior, with hyper-parameter,

Figure 3. A graphical representation of the LDA model according to the thin plate notation. The shaded node is associated with observed data while other nodes are associated with hidden components. Furthermore, rectangular boxes are called plate notation and are used to denote replication

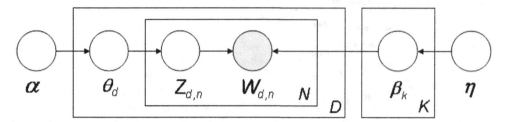

also to the topic-word distribution $P\left(w \mid z\right)$. The authors suggested the hyper-parameter to be interpreted as the prior observation count on the number of times words are sampled from a topic before any word from the corpus is observed. This choice can smooth the word distribution in every topic with the amount of smoothing determined by the value of the hyper-parameter. The authors showed that good choices for the hyper-parameters will depend on number of topics K and vocabulary size V.

Topic extraction, i.e. estimation of the topic-word distributions and topic distributions for each document, can be implemented through different algorithms. Hofmann (1999) used a direct estimation approach based on the Expectation-Maximization (EM) algorithm. However, such an approach suffers from problems involving local maxima of the likelihood function. A better alternative has been proposed by Blei et al. (2003), which directly estimates the posterior distribution over the topic given the observed words. However, many text collections contain millions of word tokens, and thus the estimation of the posterior over the topic requires the adoption of efficient procedures. Gibbs sampling, a form of Markov Chain Monte Carlo (MCMC), is easy to implement and provides a relatively efficient method of extracting a set of topics from a large corpus. It is worthwhile to mention that topic extraction can be performed when the number of topics K is given. However, in many cases this quantity

is unknown, and we have to resort to empirical procedures and/or to statistical measures such as perplexity to choose the optimal number of topics to be retained after the un-supervised learning task has been performed.

2.2. Similarity Measures

A central element of the algorithm for automatic labeling of topics is the similarity measure used for topics comparison. A large variety of similarity measures has been proposed in the specialized literature. Guadarrama and Garrido (2008) presented, analyzed, compared and partitioned into two groups a representative set of similarity measures. The first class consists of mutual similarity, dice similarity, overlap similarity, cosine similarity, P-similarity and S-similarity. Therefore, it contains all those similarity measures showing a coherent behavior with respect to the semantics of the compared concepts. The second class contains similarity measures which do not show a coherent behavior, i.e. Euclidean similarity, T-similarity, L-similarity and W-similarity. In this paper we consider a subset of the first class; namely cosine similarity, overlap similarity, mutual similarity and dice similarity. Moreover we adopted other two similarities, namely Tanimoto and Jaccard, which are commonly used in the information retrieval field for benchmarking (Manning et al., 2007). The definitions of the above similarity measures are provided for clarity.

Let $\underline{x}$ and $\underline{y}$ be two vectors while $\|\underline{x}\|$ be the Euclidean norm of vector $\underline{x}$, then the *cosine similarity* between vector $\underline{x}$ and vector $\underline{y}$ is defined as follows:

$$\text{Cosine}\left(\underline{x}, \underline{y}\right) := \frac{\underline{x}\,\underline{y}^{T}}{\|\underline{x}\| \cdot \|\underline{y}\|}. \qquad (1)$$

It measures the similarity of the argument vectors through the cosine of the angle between them. The smaller the angle the greater the similarity between the argument vectors is. It is worthwhile to mention that vectors $\underline{x}$ and $\underline{y}$ are binary representations respectively for set A and B. The dimensionality of $\underline{x}$ and $\underline{y}$ equals the cardinality of the union set $A \cup B$.

The *overlap similarity* measure is defined as follows:

$$Overlap\left(A, B\right) := \frac{|A \cap B|}{\min\left(|A|, |B|\right)} \qquad (2)$$

where A and B are sets, while $|A|$ represents the cardinality of the set A.

The *mutual similarity* uses the degree of inclusion of set A into set B and the degree of inclusion of set B into set A. It computes their average value as follows:

$$Mutual\left(A, B\right) := \frac{\dfrac{|A \cap B|}{|A|} + \dfrac{|A \cap B|}{|B|}}{2}. \qquad (3)$$

The *dice similarity* is defined as follows:

$$Dice\left(A, B\right) := \frac{2 \cdot |A \cap B|}{|A| + |B|}, \qquad (4)$$

and is related to the Jaccard coefficient, commonly used in information retrieval to measure the overlap between two sets.

The *Jaccard coefficient* is defined as follows:

$$Jaccard\left(A, B\right) := \frac{|A \cap B|}{|A \cup B|}. \qquad (5)$$

It ranges from zero to one as the cosine similarity measure. Finally, the *Tanimoto distance*, commonly used to compute the similarity between sets with different cardinalities is defined as follows:

$$Tanimoto\left(A, B\right) := 1 - \frac{|A| + |B| - 2 \cdot |A \cap B|}{|A| + |B| - |A \cap B|}. \qquad (6)$$

2.3. Multi-label Text Classification

The main scenarios in text classification are binary, multi-class and multi-label (Joachims, 2002). The *binary* scenario is the simplest and consists of learning a supervised classifier from two class data; *multi-class* is the straightforward generalization of binary classification. It consists of documents coming from more than two classes. However, most of the text classification problems belong to the *multi-label* scenario. In such a scenario, there is no one-to-one correspondence between class and document. Given a fixed number L of classes, each document can be in multiple, exactly one or no class at all. Classes are usually semantic topic identifiers used to tag documents, newswires, web pages, etc... (Figure 4).

The multi-label text classification setting is modeled with an L-dimensional class vector $\underline{y}$ where each component can take value on $\{-1, +1\}$. Formally, the class vector is defined as follows:

$$\underline{y} = \left\{-1, +1\right\}^{L}.$$

Joachims (2002) pointed out that in the multi-label setting it is not clear how classification errors have to be counted. Indeed, the 0/1 loss function does not allow to model *close misses* while a reasonable distance metric is offered by the Hamming distance which counts the number of mismatches between the *class vector y* and the *classifier output $\hat{y}$*. Therefore, whether the Hamming distance is used, the expected loss equals the sum of the error rates of L binary text classification tasks. This means that the multi-label text classification task can be conveniently split into L binary classification tasks. Joachims (2002) motivated this approach by making the

assumption that classes are independent, given the *document vector x* and thus using a Bayes argument concerning the optimality of the maximum posterior classification rule.

The documents are usually associated with a document vector x which is a V-dimensional vector where V represents the cardinality of the vocabulary of the document corpus. The document

vector can be represented in different ways; such representations usually play a central role on the generalization ability achieved by the learning algorithm. The main representation schemes are the following; binary or 0/1, term frequency and term frequency inverse document frequency. In *binary representation* each document is associated with a binary vector x whose i^{th} component equals 1, whether the document contains at least one instance of the ith word of the vocabulary and 0 otherwise. The *term frequency* representation counts the occurrence of each word of the vocabulary. Therefore, the ith component of the vector x contains the number of occurrences of the ith word in the considered document. The last representation scheme, namely the *term frequency inverse document frequency* (Salton, 1991), consists of two components; the term frequency and the inverse document frequency. The *term frequency* component for the ith word $tf(i)$ is the same as in the term frequency representation. The *inverse document frequency* component of the ith word is the reciprocal of the number of document $df(i)$ where it occurs. Thus, the Term Frequency Inverse Document Frequency (TF-IDF) for the ith word is defined as follows:

$$tf - idf\left(i\right) = tf\left(i\right) \cdot \log\left(\frac{1}{df\left(i\right)}\right). \qquad (7)$$

It is customary to normalize term frequency inverse document frequency (7) to account for different documents length.

Standard learning methods for text classification are: Naïve Bayes, Rocchio, K-nearest neighbors and decision trees. However, it has been recognized that Support Vector Machines (SVMs) are state of the art to solve the text classification problem (Joachims, 2002; Turchi, Mammone & Cristianini, 2009).

Methods and algorithms for binary text classification are usually compared on the basis of the following performance measures; accuracy, precision and recall. In such a setting each document is labeled as a *positive* sample (+1) or a *negative* sample (-1). Let y and $\hat{y}$ be respectively the true label and classifier forecasted label for the document described by vector $\underline{x}$. It is customary to define as *TruePositive* (*TrueNegative*) those documents where $y = \hat{y} = +1$ ($y = \hat{y} = -1$), while a document such that $y = +1$ and $\hat{y} = -1$ ($y = -1$ and $\hat{y} = +1$) is said to be a *FalseNegative* (*FalsePositive*). Then, given a document corpus consisting of N elements the *accuracy* of a classifier algorithm or method for binary text classification is defined as follows:

$$accuracy = \frac{TP + TN}{N} \qquad (8)$$

and measures the effectiveness of the classifier, i.e. its capability to provide reliable forecasts. *Precision* is defined as follows:

$$precision = \frac{TP}{TP + FP} \qquad (9)$$

and measures the reliability of the classifier to provide correct forecasts for the positive class. Finally, the *recall* measure is defined as follows:

$$recall = \frac{TP}{TP + FN} \qquad (10)$$

and measures the fraction of true positive documents which are recalled from the classifier.

Given a document corpus and a classification algorithm or method, the performance measures, accuracy, precision and recall, are usually estimated through *k-folds cross validation* (Stone, 1977) to control the risk of over-fitting, i.e. to reduce the risk to obtain an over-optimistic estimate of the performance of the classifier.

3. THE INFORMATION PROCESSING PIPELINE

This section will illustrate the modular architecture of the information processing pipeline. For each module we will describe all the tools and techniques that are used to manipulate and transform a variety of textual sources in a kind of information that enables users to dominate and organize their data and to make rational decisions upon them.

The pipeline is intended to satisfy the needs of business companies with a little impact on their internal procedures. The system is able to deal with the business company document collection and automatically extracts the relevant topics, labels them according to the company view and offers a reliable service that grants the labeling of new documents coherently with respect to the old ones.

The modules of the information processing pipeline, together with their interactions, are illustrated in Figure 5. The pipeline is inputted with a document collection and outputs an inducer that

Figure 5. Modules of the information processing pipeline together with their interactions

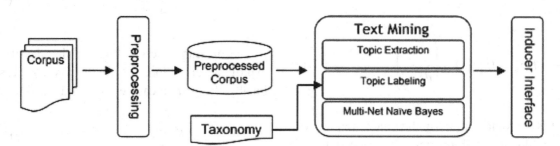

is able to classify new documents according to the topics hidden in the document collection. The first module of the pipeline, i.e. *Preprocessing*, is devoted to data manipulation and transformation to improve the effectiveness of the subsequent modules.

The *Text Mining* module is composed of three different sub-modules: the *Topic Extraction* sub-module is devoted to topic extraction and also includes the quality assessment procedure. The *Topic Labeling* submodule implements a labeling procedure that exploits user supplied taxonomy. The *Multi-Net Naïve Bayes* submodule is devoted to the creation of a Bayesian classifier that exploits the extracted topics; the output of this module is an inducer, the front-end of the pipeline. The inducer associates each document with a set of topics, i.e. it tags any input document.

3.1. Text Preprocessing

Given a textual source containing different types of documents (different formats, language registers, formatting) the first action that should be taken is standardization.

The *standardization* step consists in the conversion of the data in a common, shared and machine readable format. In the specialized literature the common destination formats are identified with eXtensible Markup Language (XML) that allows a structured representation of the documents (i.e. it is possible to identify different sections

in a document, like title, abstract, chapters, sections etc…) or TXT (ASCII or Unicode) that is preferred whenever the system needs a plain and straight format.

The proposed system is able to deal with documents in format like PDF, DOC, RTF, HTML, and the resulting *corpus* is a set of TXT documents. Once the corpus has been generated, the next step is *document preprocessing*, in which the system applies different filters to remove all the data that in the specific pipeline implementation are considered to be non informative. Hence the system applies a tokenization algorithm that identifies each word, removing the punctuation, numeric values and other standardization debris. Then, each token is matched against a *stop-word list*, containing articles, pronouns, common abbreviations that are considered to be non informative. The list is language dependent, and whenever the system has to deal with multi-language corpora, different stop word lists should be applied. If the size of the corpus is huge, the dimension of the relative *vocabulary* (i.e. the set of all the words appearing in the corpus) can become quite large. One possible solution to reduce the number of words and to speed up the computation with a minor loss of information is the removal of too frequent words that are normally language or corpus specific and the removal of less frequent words that usually are typos or some other kind of errors. The approach used by the pipeline consists in the computation of the empirical distribution of the words sorted by frequency that usually follows a *zipf law*. Then, the system selects two quantiles, upper and lower tails. The vocabulary is reduced to contain only those words with a frequency within the selected quantiles.

The last component of the text preprocessing module is *document representation*. Once the documents have been transformed and filtered out of all the useless information, the system should transform the un-structured text in a highly structured format. This format is problem dependent and could be the binary, the term frequency or the term frequency inverse document frequency representation. It is worthwhile to mention that for topic extraction the term frequency representation is used.

3.2. Topic Extraction and Selection

After the preprocessing of the document collection, the next module of the pipeline starts elaborating the structured version of the corpus.

The first step consists of multiple runs of the LDA algorithm with different parameters. The system exploits a customized version of the Gibbs Sampling procedure proposed by Griffiths and Steyvers (2004). The most important parameters of the algorithms are: the number of topics to be extracted (T), the number of iterations (I) and the value of the hyper-parameters for the topic-word distribution and for the topic mixing proportions for each document. After the burn-in period the algorithm starts to collect samples for the given number of iterations.

As stated in the previous section the choice of the value of the parameters is still an open problem. Wallach, Murray and Salakhutdinov (2009) proposed several different measures to evaluate the quality of extracted topics on held-out document sets; Boyd-Graber, Chang, Gerrish, Wang and Blei (2009) instead, show how a pure computational approach to topic evaluation gives controversial results compared to human judgment. The best results obtained according

to perplexity evaluation received lower score from human judges. The approach adopted by the pipeline exploits a technique based on the evaluation of an intra-topic similarity according to a *symmetrized Kullback-Leibler* measure. This measure is the main ingredient to compute a hierarchical clustering that describes topic similarities. Then the obtained dendrogram is cut at the height computed by the Mojena stopping rule (Mojena, 1977). *Kullback-Leibler divergence* (*KL*) (Lin, 1991) is a similarity function commonly used to compare different probability distributions with the same support and is defined as follows:

$$KL(t_i, t_j) = \sum_{k=1}^{W} t_i^k \log\left(\frac{t_i^k}{t_j^k}\right) \qquad (11)$$

where t_i^k is $P(w_k \mid z = i)$. The quantity is equal to zero when for all k, $t_i^k = t_j^k$. *KL* divergence (11) is asymmetric, but clustering algorithms require computing pair wise distance for each object pair, so it is convenient to use a symmetrized version defined as follows:

$$sKL(t_i, t_j) = \frac{1}{2}\Big(KL(t_i, t_j) + KL(t_j, t_i)\Big) .$$
$$(12)$$

Given the symmetric matrix generated from the distance computation (12), a *hierarchical clustering algorithm* starts creating clusters composed of pairs of objects that are close together. Then, the algorithm links each cluster to the others creating bigger clusters until all the objects of the original dataset are linked together in a hierarchical tree (i.e. the root of the tree is one single cluster containing all the initial data). The aggregation strategy computes a distance function between the content of each cluster. Such distance functions are problem dependent. The proposed pipeline utilizes the *average linkage function*:

$$Link_{avg}(X,Y) = \frac{1}{|X| \cdot |Y|} \sum_i^{|X|} \sum_j^{|Y|} d(x_i, y_j)$$

$$(13)$$

where $x_i \in X, y_j \in Y$, $|X|$ is the cardinality of cluster X while $d(x_i, y_j)$ is the distance between the argument objects.

The result of a hierarchical clustering is conveniently represented as a dendrogram. The vertical axis represents the distance at which successive clusters are joined. On the horizontal axis all the data points are represented. After the algorithm has computed the cluster tree, the system requires choosing the "optimal" height at which the tree should be cut. Mojena (1977) provides a stopping criterion based on the heights at which the clusters are joined. Formally the rule states that the cut height is computed as:

$$cut_{height} = \bar{h} + \alpha \sigma_h \qquad (14)$$

where $\bar{h}$ is the average of the heights for all the clusters, σ_h is the standard deviation of the heights and α is a specified constant. Mojena suggested to use the value of α in (14) which satisfies $2.5 < \alpha < 3.0$. Successive analysis by Milligan and Cooper (1985) suggested a value equal to 1.25.

3.3. Automatic Labeling of Topic

Topic labeling is an emerging problem. There are two possible approaches to solve the problem: *manual labeling* requires users to read and interpret the meaning of topics according to their background knowledge: this approach naturally biases the resulting classification. On the other hand, totally *automatic labeling* can take advantage of the document collection to extract candidate phrases represented by multinomial distributions and ranked according to *KL* divergence (Mei et al.,

2007) or by exploiting a co-occurrence analysis to extract significant *n-grams* used to label the topics (Blei & Laferty, 2009).

The proposed algorithm tries to conjugate and reconcile human judgment with computer discovered solutions. The idea originated from the observation of business companies best practice. Indeed, many business companies organize their document collections through the use of specialized document management systems. These systems require the user to associate each document against taxonomy or a given controlled vocabulary. Such taxonomies are built to exactly match the company needs and goals. They are context dependent and describe the full knowledge base of the business company. The proposed approach allocates the extracted topics inside the hierarchy, and finds the associated label and organization. The taxonomy (Hotho, Staab & Stumme, 2003) is encoded in a particular structure defined as *topic tree* and formally described by $\Psi = \langle O, E \rangle$ where O are the nodes indexed by non-negative integer values, while $E = O \times O$ are the edges between nodes. Each node j is associated with a topic $T_\Psi(j) = \langle$ *label*,words,info$\rangle$ where *label* is the label of the topic, *words* is the list of words describing the topic, and *info* is additional information. The *root node*, indexed by 0, is considered as *all-the-topics*. The edges describe how topics are related and express an *is-a* relation between topics.

The Automatic Labeling of Topic (ALOT) algorithm, inputted with the topic tree Ψ and extracted topic $T_e(i)$, finds topic $T_\Psi(j)$ nearest to $T_e(i)$ solving the optimization problem:

$$j_r^* = \underset{j}{\operatorname{argmax}} \ S_r(T_e(i), T_\Psi(j))$$

where j_r^* is the index of the topic $T_\Psi(j_r^*)$ which has the greatest similarity S_r with $T_e(i)$. This operation is repeated for all the similarity measures (1-6) (i.e. *Tanimoto, Cosine, Jaccard, Overlap, Dice and Mutual)* and returns for each extracted topic two vectors: $L(i) = \left\{ j_1^*, ..., j_6^* \right\}$ containing the node index and

$$\Delta(i) = \left\{ T_\Psi\left(j_1^* \right), ..., T_\Psi\left(j_6^* \right) \right\}$$

the corresponding topics labels. $L(i)$ and $\Delta(i)$ are mapped to the topic tree (shaded nodes). Given a topic $T_e(i)$, the following cases can occur:

- **Topic concordance (TC):** *All the similarity measures agree on which the nearest topic* $T_\Psi(j^*)$ *is.* ALOT labels the extracted topic with the label associated with node $T_\Psi(j^*)$.
- **Topic discordance (TD):** At least two similarity measures disagree on which the nearest topic is. The ALOT algorithm labels $T_e(i)$ according to:
  1. **SA (*Semantic Association*):** Topics belonging to $\Delta(i)$ share a predecessor, not the root. ALOT looks for a topic, not necessarily in $\Delta(i)$, that synthesizes all the topics in $\Delta(i)$:
     a) **Path:** All the topics in $\Delta(i)$ lie on the same path from the root node. ALOT labels the extracted topic with the label associated with the shallowest node in $\Delta(i)$ (Figure 6).
     b) **Subtree:** All the nodes belong to a common subtree. ALOT assigns the label to the common deepest predecessor of topic. Notice that the label can belong to a node in $\Delta(i)$ (Figure 7).
  2. **NSA (*Non Semantic Association*):** topics in $\Delta(i)$ do not share a predecessor except for the root node. ALOT uses a majority voting scheme to select the maximally

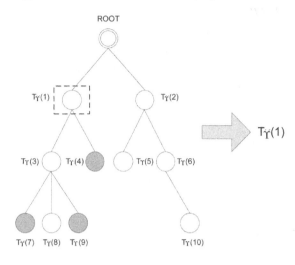

Figure 6. Semantic Association (SA) Subtree

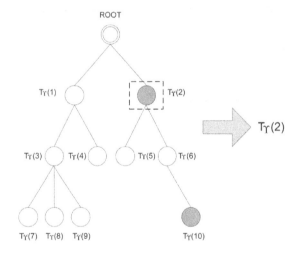

Figure 7. Semantic Association (SA) Path Subcase

agreed topics predecessor, i.e. the node $T_\Psi(j^{\max})$ such that $depth\left(j^{\max} \right)$ and $\left| successors\left(j^{\max} \right) \cap L(i) \right|$ are maximized.

a) **S-dmatp:** (*Single deepest maximally agreed topic predecessor*); a single topic is obtained and its label is associated with $T_e(i)$ (Figure 8).

Figure 8. Non Semantic Association (NSA) S-dmatp

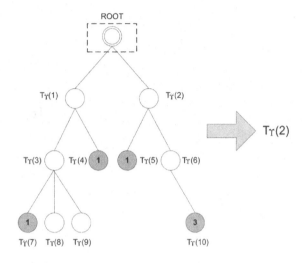

Figure 9. Non Semantic Association (NSA) M-dmatp

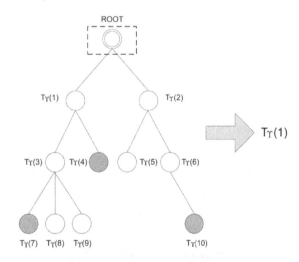

b) **M-dmatp:** (*Multiple deepest maximally agreed topic predecessor*); more than one topic is returned by the majority voting scheme. ALOT computes how many times each $T_\Psi(j_l^*)$ **is a descendant of all the** $T_\Psi(j^{\max})$, stores this information into the *info* field and finds the node with the maximum number of occurrences (Figure 9).

c) **R-dmatp:** (*Rooted deepest maximally not agreed topics predecessor*); the root node is returned by the majority voting scheme and the maximum number of occurrences $T_\Psi(j^{\max})$ **is** *the same for at least two descendants in* $\Delta(i)$. The root node is returned.

Algorithm: ALOT

Requires: a Topic Tree Ψ, a topic $T_e(i)$ to be labeled

Ensure: The label of $T_e(i)$

1. Compute
    $$j_r^* = \operatorname*{argmax}_j \ S_r(T_e(i), T_\Psi(j))$$

2. Set $L(i) = \left\{ j_1^*, j_2^*, ..., j_6^* \right\}$

3. **if** $j_1^* = j_2^* = ... = j_6^*$ **then** {*case***TC**}.

4. **else** {*case***TD**}

5. Case **Path:** Find j the most shallow topic in $\Delta(i)$.

6. Case **Subtree:** Find φ, the deepest predecessor of nodes belonging to $\Delta(i)$

7. **if** $T_\Psi(j) \neq ROOT$ **then** {*case***SA**}

8. **else**

9. compute $j^{\max}$ s.t. $depth\left(j^{\max}\right)$ and $\left| successors\left(j^{\max}\right) \cap L(i) \right|$ is maximized

10. **if** $j^{\max}$ is unique **then** {*case***S-dmatp**}

11. **else**

12. **if** $ROOT \notin j^{\max}$ **then** {*case***M-dmatp**}

13. **else** {*case***R-dmatp**}

Magatti et al. (2009b) shows that a taxonomy expansion, implemented through automatic synonym insertion, tends to worsen the performance of automatic labeling. Therefore, it is likely that a human taxonomy expansion will improve the labeling quality.

3.4. Document Tagging

The last module of the pipeline is devoted to the tagging of new documents, exploiting the extracted and labeled topics. The motivation of this module originates from the requirements of business companies models. Indeed, given a collection of available documents and a related taxonomy, a company wants to avoid its users the burden of manual labeling of the available documents and desires a reliable and powerful way to automatically label new documents. The topic extraction step offers a set of topics that project the document collection in a lower dimensional space, which represents the core arguments, while the ALOT algorithm associates each topic with reliable labeling and with an allocation inside the hierarchy. The key point of this module is that the Naïve Bayes learning, from document corpus, is avoided. Indeed, the conditional probability distributions, associated with the Multi Net Naïve Bayes model, are recoverd from the LDA learning process through a simple mathematical formula. The implemented classifier is a specific instance of the Multi-Net Naïve Bayes classifier (MNNB) (Kim et al., 2006) that despite its simplifying assumptions (i.e. the attributes are independent given the class variable) gives good performances (Magatti et al., 2009). The MNNB classifier is the obvious choice for the document classification step due to the Bayesian nature of LDA, although other algorithms like Support Vector Machines are known to have very good performance in binary and multi-class problems. In multi-label set-up they have long training phase and suffer of less good performance. Moreover, the linking of SVM with LDA models is more complex, not straightforward and implies the discarding of the Bayesian approach. The Naïve Bayes classifier computes the probability that a document d_j

represented as a vector $\underline{w}$ of words, belongs to a class z_i through the Bayes' theorem as follows:

$$P(z_i \mid \underline{w}) = \frac{P\left(\underline{w} \mid z_i\right) \cdot P\left(z_i\right)}{p\left(\underline{w}\right)} = \frac{e^{t_{ij}} \cdot P\left(z_i\right)}{e^{t_{ij}} \cdot P\left(z_i\right) + P\left(\overline{z_i}\right)}$$

where:

$$t_{ij} = \log \frac{P\left(\underline{w} \mid z_i\right)}{P\left(\underline{w} \mid \overline{z_i}\right)} \tag{15}$$

Exploiting this framework and arranging the derivation of t_{ij} (15) accordingly to different document representation it is possible to compute $P(z_i \mid d_j)$. The t_{ij} factor (15) for *binary* representation is defined as follows:

$$t_{ij}^{binary} = \sum_{w \in \underline{w}} 1_w \log \frac{P\left(w \mid z_i\right)}{P\left(w \mid \overline{z_i}\right)} \tag{16}$$

where w is a word of the vocabulary, 1_w is an indicator function equal to 1 if $w \in d_j$, and equal to 0 otherwise. The *term frequency* representation is as follows:

$$t_{ij}^{TF} = \sum_{w \in \underline{w}} tf(w) \log \frac{P\left(w \mid z_i\right)}{P\left(w \mid \overline{z_i}\right)} \tag{17}$$

where tf(w) is the term frequency of word w for the document d_j. The *term frequency inverse document frequency* representation is defined as follows:

$$t_{ij}^{TFIDF} = \sum_{w \in \underline{w}} \text{tf} - \text{idf(w)} \log \frac{P\left(w \mid z_i\right)}{P\left(w \mid \overline{z_i}\right)} \tag{18}$$

where tf-idf(w) is equal to the term TF-IDF of the word w in the document d_j.

The MNNB classifier exploits the values computed by the LDA model for the prior probability over the topics $P(z_i)$, *and the conditional probability* $P(w \mid z_i)$ *for each word in the vocabulary given the topic while the conditional probability* $P(w \mid \overline{z_i})$ *can be efficiently computed as follows:*

$$P(w \mid \overline{z_i}) = \frac{P(w) - P(w \mid z_i) \cdot P(z_i)}{P(\overline{z_i})} \quad (19)$$

It is worthwhile to notice that the information processing pipeline implements a specific instance of the MNNB in which each document is evaluated through several classifiers, each one associated with a given topic. Hence, each document will be associated with a vector whose i^{th} component is the probability that the document belongs to the class associated with the topic z_i.

3.5. Software Architecture

The pipeline is composed of different software components; the first two implement back-office functionalities and are performance oriented. Thus, they have been implemented in C++. The standardization step exploits open source tools for document conversion, while the preprocessing component is able to generate several document representations. The topic extraction is a C++ implementation of the LDA algorithm and it is also able to compute distance matrices to evaluate documents and topic similarities, moreover it is able to build the MNNB to be inputted to the classifier. The labeling step is performed through a C++ component that computes the similarities and applies the labeling. The MNNB classifier, instead, is a front-office component and has been implemented in C#. The MNNB classifier has two different front-ends, a standalone client that could be installed on the user personal computer (see Figure 10), or as a web-service with SOAP

Figure 10. The Multi-Net Naïve Bayes classifier standalone client

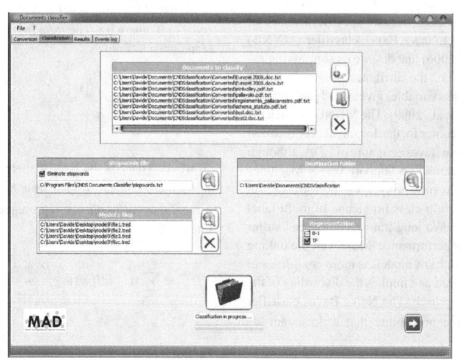

interface that allows clients to query the service for document tagging.

4. NUMERICAL EXPERIMENTS

The quality of the information processing pipeline is measured through a document corpus and an associated taxonomy. However, common literature corpora like Reuters-21875 satisfy the first prerequisite, but usually lack an associated taxonomy. Taxonomy, are typically used in the business world or in very specific sectors where the taxonomy is tailored for the specific needs. Possible examples are represented by Medical Subjects Headings, Criminal Law – Lawyer Sources and the Google Directory that requires the related corpus to be harvested and mined. In the proposed experimental set-up, we choose as reference taxonomy the Google Directory (gDir), which is part of the Open Directory Project. This project manages the largest human-edited directory available on the web. Editors guarantee fairness and correctness of the directory.

4.1. Document Corpus and Taxonomy

The Google Directory (Figure 11) is a hierarchical structure that organizes web-sites according to 16 macro categories, and for each category offers a classification subtree of variable depth. The experimental setup used all the 16 macro-categories, but discarded the implicit category ADULT that is a mere replication of the hierarchy including adult suggested pages. The tree has been cut to depth 5.

The *topic tree* (Figure 12) has been built as follows: each node of the directory is a topic and its children are the words that specify the topic, this structure is repeated recursively. The topic tree contains 4,516 nodes.

The corpus has been generated by submitting a set consisting of 960 queries to the Google search engine through the Google Ajax API. Each query is formed by a couple of words randomly selected from the union of word lists associated with the topic tree.

Some examples of random queries are *"Music Environment"*, *"News and Media Current Events"*, *"Holidays Ukrainian'*. For matters of simplicity, the results are filtered, and only PDF files written in the English language have been retained. The performed query process retrieved 46,480 documents.

Figure 11. The Google directory

Figure 12. The topic tree

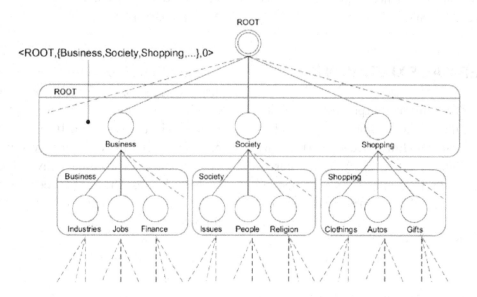

4.2. Preprocessing

The document corpus has been standardized to plain text. The preprocessing step consisted of stop-words removal. To regularize the document lengths, we applied a size-based filtering: only documents with a size between 2 and 400 KB have been retained, thus almost empty documents and too long or garbage documents are discarded. The filtered document corpus consisted of 33,801 documents, while the global vocabulary has been reduced by removing the distribution tails: words mentioned in less than 10 or in more than 2,551 documents are removed: the resulting vocabulary consists of 111,795 words.

4.3. Topic Extraction and Labeling

The topic extraction step has been performed with the following hyper-parameter values: $\alpha=50/T$ and $\eta=0.01$. The number of iterations has been set to 700. Each run had a burn-in period of 200 iterations. Each run has been repeated to assure the topic stability according to sKL divergence (12). In order to assess the correct number of topics, we started by computing a large number

of topics, computing infra-topic similarities according to sKL distance (12) and computing a hierarchical clustering (13). Then, we applied the Mojena rule (14): the value of the parameter has been adjusted to the particularities of topic models and the related distances. We extracted two different topic models with number of topics T=250 and T=500. The dendrogram in Figure 13 shows topic similarities according to sKL divergence (12): shallow joins indicate higher similarities between topics. According to the Mojena stopping rule (14), the optimal number of clusters is 100. Then we run the LDA model setting the number of topics to 100 while keeping constant the other parameter values. Some of the extracted topics are shown in Figure 14. Then, the ALOT algorithm is applied (Figure 15) and the labels assigned. The *Topic_66* is a *Topic Concordance* (TC) case and it is easy to label. The Topic_0 and *Topic_15* are associated with a *Topic Discordance* (TD) case and a *Semantic Association* (SA) subcase: the former contains labels on the same path while the latter contains labels of the same sub-tree. The *Topic_24* instead, is a *Non Semantic Association* subcase (NSA), and the labeling is resolved by

Figure 13. Dendrogram and tree cut

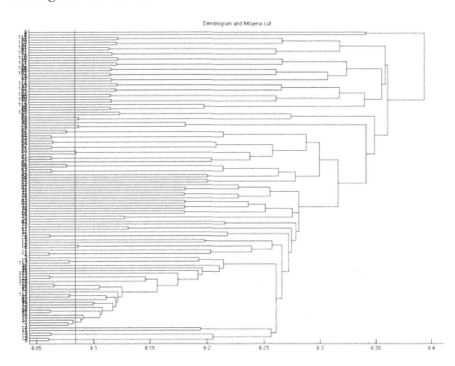

Figure 14. A subset of the extracted topics

computing the maximally agreed topic predecessor (M-dmatp).

4.4. Document Tagging

The last module of the pipeline is devoted to document tagging. Once the topics have been labeled (Figure 16) the system generates the inducer.

The system requires the user to specify the model and the number of words used for each topic: this information will generate the global vocabulary associated with the inducer. After the inducer has been built, the user is requested to choose the document representation to use and a probability threshold associated with class labels. These parameters are particularly important whenever the system is used as a component in a bigger system, e.g. document management systems, where for each document a meaningful labeling is requested: a unique labeling with high probability.

Topic_66	.008
encyclopedia	.023
atlas	.023
bibliography	.017
directories	.016
dictionary	.015
catalog	.014
periodicals	.012
genealogy	.012
abstracts	.012
librarians	.012

Topic_0	.013
cells	.025
protein	.010
genetic	.008
gene	.007
samples	.006
acid	.006
proteins	.005
bone	.005
genes	.005
tissue	.005

Topic_15	.011
firms	.037
suppliers	.012
enterprises	.012
venture	.009
entrepreneurs	.008
productivity	.008
procurement	.007
logistics	.007
supplier	.006
incentives	.006

Topic_38	.013
assets	.022
loan	.018
banks	.018
loans	.017
debt	.014
investments	.013
equity	.012
securities	.011
banking	.011
expenses	.010

Figure 15. Candidate labels according to similarities measures. For each label, the full path is displayed

Topic_66	
Tanimoto	root-**Reference**
Jaccard	root-**Reference**
Dice	root-**Reference**
Cosine	root-**Reference**
Overlap	root-**Reference**
Mutual	root-**Reference**

Topic_0	
Tanimoto	root-Science-**Biology**
Jaccard	root-Science-**Biology**
Dice	root-Science-**Biology**
Cosine	root-Science-**Biology**-Bioinformatics-Online_Services
Overlap	root-Science-**Biology**-Bioinformatics-Online_Services
Mutual	root-Science-**Biology**-Bioinformatics-Online_Services

Topic_15	
Tanimoto	root-**Business**-Financial_Services
Jaccard	root-**Business**-Financial_Services
Dice	root-**Business**-Financial_Services
Cosine	root-**Business**-Financial_Services
Overlap	root-**Business**-Business_Services-Consulting
Mutual	root-**Business**-Business_Services-Consulting

Topic_38	
Tanimoto	root-Business-**Financial_Services**
Jaccard	root-Business-**Financial_Services**
Dice	root-Business-**Financial_Services**
Cosine	root-Business-**Financial_Services**
Overlap	root-Computers-Software-Industry_Specific-Insurance
Mutual	root-Computers-Software-Industry_Specific-Insurance

Figure 16. Labeling rules and resulting labels

Topic_0	SA	Path	**Biology**
Topic_15	SA	Subtree	**Business**
Topic_38	NSA	M-dmatp	**Financial Services**
Topic_66	TC	Concordance	**Reference**

To evaluate the performance of the proposed system we downloaded 189 new documents using the same methodology used for the corpus generation, these documents have been manually labeled as: Biology, Business, Financial Services or Reference. They were inputted to the MNNB inducer with the term frequency representation (17) and threshold value set to 0.5.

The performance measures; accuracy (8), precision (9), and recall (10), are summarized in Table 1.

The precision of the topics *Biology, Business* and *Financial Services* is nearly perfect due to the high specificity of the word lists. The test set is composed of many technical papers which are easily labeled. On the other hand the achieved recall value is consistently lower than precision. A possible explanation to this behavior is as fol-

Table 1. Classification performances.

	Precision	Recall	Accuracy
Biology	1.00	0.45	0.71
Business	1.00	0.35	0.80
Financial Services	0.96	0.69	0.83
Reference	0.88	0.13	0.61

lows; the manual labeling procedure is both complex and ambiguous; it could label documents by using a broader meaning for each topic. Therefore, it is expected that automatic document classification would not achieve excellent performance with respect to both precision and recall.

However, it is important to keep in mind the difficulty of the considered labeling task, together with the fact that human labeling of documents can result in ambiguous and contradictory label assignment. The Reference topic has sensibly lower performances due to its particular nature. Indeed, it is not easily captured by the human labeling who tends to assign this topic to many generic documents, and moreover, the documents matching the topic semantics in the test set are too few.

It is worthwhile to notice, that topic models are language independent (as long the language is based on latin alphabets) and are able to extract topics for each language without mixing them. Therefore, the pipeline is able to deal with multi-language corpora as long as a multi-language taxonomy is inputted. Nonetheless a semantic analysis of the documents is expected to improve the performance achieved by the pipeline which can fruitfully exploit the information that comes with the use of language.

5. FUTURE RESEARCH DIRECTIONS

Capturing document meaning will be the gold standard in the next few years. Nowadays search engines are very efficient in document retrieving but they still lack the ability to capture the meaning of the retrieved documents according to the user query. The Semantic Web is becoming the corner stone of the future of the web search. However, it is still unable to deal with the enormous amount of existing data and still relies on human intervention for the creation and maintenance of knowledge repositories. The specialized literature has spent a great deal of effort to develop new automatic ways to capture and aggregate bits of information and to create knowledge bases that can be used to satisfy users information needs (Chakrabarti, Sarawagi & Sudarshan, 2010; Weikum & Theobald, 2010).

Topic extraction models offer an efficient and effective answer to capturing the meaning of document collections. They are particularly useful whenever we have to deal with mid-sized document repositories and when we need an overview on what the documents are about. Further developments of topics models have shown their capability to associate entities with topics, to follow topic evolution over time or to extract and organize topic according to hidden hierarchies. The most recent development is described by Chang and Blei (2010). The authors proposed a model to capture document networks, while Chang, Boyd-Graber and Blei, (2009) proposed a model that infers the description of related entities. Future research in topic models will be more and more focused on the integration of topics with network data, like social networks with the aim to help users to identify sub-networks that meet their interest and vision.

6. CONCLUSION

In this chapter we proposed an information processing pipeline that exploits probabilistic topic models, an automatic labeling procedure and a document tagging service that helps users to efficiently manage and organize their documents.

We presented results of applying the pipeline to a real world corpus automatically generated by retrieving documents through random queries. The extracted topics show a high quality and semantic significance.

Topic labeling has been performed by exploiting the Google directory, a real and hand crafted taxonomy that tries to classify web pages according to predefined categories.

The performances of the document tagger have been evaluated against a set of manually labeled documents and show interesting and promising results.

The probabilistic models behind the pipeline exploits Latent Dirichlet Allocation for topic extraction and the classifier implements a particular instance of a Multi-Net Naïve Bayes model through automatic mapping of the extracted topics which do not require any learning step to take place.

The pipeline offers many application scenarios: it can be used for document management, implemented in a vertical information retrieval application, for press coverage management service and many others.

Recent models can also be applied to improve or characterize the particular application: hierarchical topic models, relational models or author-topic models can offer interesting developments and improved applicability.

A software prototype of the described information processing pipeline, specialized for the Italian legal domain, is available at the following URL: http://dedalus.cnds.disco.unimib.it:8080/sideinformer/.

REFERENCES

Baeza-Yates, R. A., & Raghavan, P. (2010). Next Generation Web Search. In Ceri, S., & Brambilla, M. (Eds.), *Search Computing* (pp. 11–23). Berlin, Heidelberg: Springer. doi:10.1007/978-3-642-12310-8_2

Berry, M. W., & Castellanos, M. (2008). *Survey of Text Mining II clustering, classification and retrieval*. London: Springer.

Blei, D. & Lafferty, J., (2009). Visualizing topics with multi-word expressions. Retrieved from http//arxiv.org/abs/0907.1013.

Blei, D., Ng, A., & Jordan, M. I. (2003). Latent Dirichlet allocation. *Journal of Machine Learning Research*, 3, 993–1022.

Boyd-Graber, J., Chang, J. J., Gerrish, S., Wang, C., & Blei, D. (2009). Reading tea leaves How humans interpret topic models. In Bengio, Y., Schuurmans, D., Lafferty, J., Williams, C. K. I., & Culotta, A. (Eds.), *Advances in Neural Information Processing Systems* (pp. 288–296).

Chakrabarti, S., Sarawagi, S., & Sudarshan, S. (2010). Enhancing Search with Structure. *A Quarterly Bulletin of the Computer Society of the IEEE Technical Committee on Data Engineering*, *33*(1), 1–13.

Chang, J., & Blei, D. M. (2010). Hierarchical relational models for document networks. *The Annals of Applied Statistics*, *4*(1), 124–150. doi:10.1214/09-AOAS309

Chang, J., Boyd-Graber, J., & Blei, D. (2009). Connections between the lines: augmenting social networks with text. In *Proceedings of the 15th ACM SIGKDD international conference on Knowledge discovery and data mining* (p. 169–178). ACM.

Deerwester, S., Dumais, S. T., Furnas, G. W., Landauer, T. K., & Harshman, R. (1990). Indexing by Latent Semantic Analysis. *Journal of the American Society for Information Science American Society for Information Science*, *41*, 391–407. doi:10.1002/(SICI)1097-4571(199009)41:6<391::AID-ASI1>3.0.CO;2-9

Duda, R. O., Hart, P. E., & Stork, D. G. (2000). *Pattern Classification* (2nd ed.). New York: Wiley-Interscience.

Feldman, R., & Sanger, J. (2007). *The text mining handbook*. New York: Cambridge University Press.

Griffiths, T. L., & Steyvers, M. (2004). Probabilistic Topic Models, Finding scientific topics. [Palo Alto, CA: Stanford University.]. *Proceedings of the National Academy of Sciences of the United States of America*, *101*, 5228–5235. doi:10.1073/pnas.0307752101

Guadarrama, S., & Garrido, M. (2008). Concept-Analizer A tool for analyzing fuzzy concepts. In Magdalena, L., Ojeda-Aciego, M., & Verdegay, J. L. (Eds.), *Proceedings of the Information Processing and Management of Uncertainty in Knowledge-Based Systems, IPMU08.* (pp. 1084-1089). Torremolinos, Malaga, Spain.

Halevy, A., Norvig, P., & Pereira, F. (2009). The unreasonable effectiveness of data . *IEEE Intelligent Systems*, *24*(2), 8–12. doi:10.1109/MIS.2009.36

Hofmann, T. (1999). Probabilistic Latent Semantic Analysis. [Stockholm.]. *Proceedings of Uncertainty in Artificial Intelligence, UAI*, *99*, 289–296.

Hofmann, T. (2001). Unsupervised learning by probabilistic latent semantic analysis. *Machine Learning*, *42*(1-2), 177–196. doi:10.1023/A:1007617005950

Hotho, A., Staab, S., & Stumme, G. (2003). Ontologies improve text document clustering. In *Third IEEE International Conference on Data Mining (ICDM'03)* (pp. 541-545). Published by the IEEE Computer Society.

International Data Corporation. (2010). *The Digital Universe Decade, Are You Ready?* http//www.emc.com/collateral/demos/microsites/idc-digital-universe/iview.htm.

Joachims, T. (2002). *Learning to classify text using support vector machines Methods, theory, and algorithms*. London: Springer.

Johnson, S. C. (1967). Hierarchical Clustering Schemes. *Psychometrika*, *32*(3), 241–254. doi:10.1007/BF02289588

Kim, S. B., Han, S., Rim, H. C., & Myaeng, S. H. (2006). Some effective techniques for naive bayes text classification . *IEEE Transactions on Knowledge and Data Engineering*, *18*(11), 1457–1466. doi:10.1109/TKDE.2006.180

Landauer, T. K., Foltz, P. W., & Laham, D. (1998). An Introduction to Latent Semantic Analysis. *Discourse Processes*, *25*, 259–284. doi:10.1080/01638539809545028

Lin, J. (1991). Divergence Measures Based on the Shannon Entropy. *IEEE Transactions on Information Theory*, *37*(I), 145–151. doi:10.1109/18.61115

MacQueen, J. (1967). Some methods for classification and analysis of multivariate observations. In LeCam, L. & Neyman, J. (Eds.), *Proceedings of the Fifth Berkeley Symposium on Mathematical Statistics and Probability Vol. 1* (pp. 281-297). University of California Press, Berkeley.

Magatti, D., Calegari, S., Ciucci, D., & Stella, F. (2009b). Automatic labeling of topics. ISDA09 *Proceedings of the 2009 Ninth International Conference on Intelligent Systems Design and Applications* (pp. 1227-1232). IEEE Computer Society, Washington, DC, USA.

Magatti, D., Stella, F., & Faini, M. (2009). A Software System for Topic Extraction and Document Classification. *Proceeding of 2009 IEEE/WIC/ACM International Joint Conference on Web Intelligence and Intelligent Agent Technology Vol. 1* (pp. 283-286). IEEE Computer Society, Los Alamitos, CA, USA.

Manning, C. D., Raghavan, P., & Schtze, H. (2008). *Introduction to Information Retrieval*. New York: Cambridge University Press.

Mei, Q., Shen, X., & Zhai, C. (2007). Automatic labeling of multinomial topic models. KDD07 *Proceedings of the 13th ACM SIGKDD international conference on Knowledge discovery and data mining*. (pp. 490-499). San Jose, CA: ACM.

Milligan, G. W., & Cooper, M. C. (1985). An examination procedures for determining the number of clusters in a data set. *Psychometrika*, *50*(2), 159–179. doi:10.1007/BF02294245

Mojena, R. (1977). Hierarchical grouping methods and stopping rules an evaluation. *The Computer Journal*, *20*(4), 359–363. doi:10.1093/comjnl/20.4.359

Salton, G. (1991). Developments in automatic text retrieval. *Science*, *253*, 974–979. doi:10.1126/science.253.5023.974

Stone, M. (1977). Asymptotics for and against cross-validation. *Biometrika*, *64*(1), 29–35. doi:10.1093/biomet/64.1.29

The Economist. (2010). *A special report on managing information Data, data everywhere*. http//www.economist.com/opinion/displaystory.cfm?story_id=15557443.

Turchi, M., Mammone, A., & Cristianini, N. (2009). Anallysis of text patterns using kernel methods . In Srivastava, A. N., & Sahami, M. (Eds.), *Text Mining Theory and Applications* (pp. 1–25). Taylor and Francis Publisher.

Wallach, H., Murray, I., Salakhutdinov, R., & D. (2009). Evaluation methods for topic models. In *Proceedings of the 26th Annual International Conference on Machine Learning ICML 09* (pp. 1-8).

Weikum, G., & Theobald, M. (2010). From information to knowledge: harvesting entities and relationships from web sources. *In Proceedings of the twenty-ninth ACM SIGMOD-SIGACT-SIGART symposium on Principles of database systems of data* (p. 65–76). ACM.

ADDITIONAL READING

Applications for Topic Models. Text and Beyond. *NIPS2009Workshop*. http://nips2009.topicmodels.net

Blei, D. (2004). Probabilistic models of text and images. *PhD Thesis*

Blei, D., Griffiths, T., & Jordan, M. (2010). The nested Chinese restaurant process and Bayesian nonparametric inference of topic hierarchies. [JACM]. *Journal of the ACM*, *57*(2), 1–30. doi:10.1145/1667053.1667056

Blei, D. M., & Lafferty, J. D. (2009). Topic models . In *Text Mining: Theory and Applications*. London: Taylor and Francis.

Gelman, A. (2004). *Bayesian data analysis* (p. 668). Chapman & Hall/CRC.

Griffiths, T. L., Steyvers, M., & Tenenbaum, J. B. (2007). Topics in Semantic Representation. *Psychological Review*, *114*(2), 211–244. doi:10.1037/0033-295X.114.2.211

Gruber, A., Rosen-Zvi, M., & Weiss, Y. (2007). Hidden topic Markov models . In *Artificial Intelligence and Statistics*. AISTATS.

Landauer, T., & Dumais, S. (1997). Solution to Plato's Problem: The Latent Semantic Analysis Theory of Acquisition, Induction and Representation of Knowledge. *Psychological Review*, (104): 211–240. doi:10.1037/0033-295X.104.2.211

Landauer, T. K. (2007). *Handbook of latent semantic analysis* (p. 532).

Li, W., Blei, D., & Mccallum, A. (2007). Nonparametric Bayes pachinko allocation. In *Proceedings of Conference on Uncertainty in Artificial Intelligence*.

Mccallum, A., & Nigam, K. (1998). A comparison of event models for naive bayes text classification. *AAAI98 Workshop on Learning for Text Categorization (1998), 752*, 41-48.

Mimno, D., & McCallum, A. (2007). Organizing the OCA: Learning faceted subjects from a library of digital books. In *Proceedings of the 7th ACM/IEEE-CS joint conference on Digital libraries* (pp. 376-385).

Rosen-Zvi, M., Chemudugunta, C., Griffiths, T., Smyth, P., & Steyvers, M. (2010). Learning author-topic models from text corpora. [TOIS]. *ACM Transactions on Information Systems, 28*(1), 1–38. doi:10.1145/1658377.1658381

Wang, W., Barnaghi, P. M., & Bargiela, A. (2010). Probabilistic topic models for learning terminological ontologies. *IEEE Transactions on Knowledge and Data Engineering, 22*(7), 1028–1040. doi:10.1109/TKDE.2009.122

Wang, X., McCallum, A., & Wei, X. (2007). Topical n-grams: Phrase and topic discovery, with an application to information retrieval. *Proceedings of the 7th IEEE International Conference on Data Mining, 0*, 697-702.

ENDNOTE

The document corpus, as well as the set of extracted topics, together with their labels and the labeled test-set are accessible at the Davide Magatti's homepage at the Model and Algorithms for Data and Text Mining laboratory (MAD Lab), (http://www.mad.disco.unimib.it).

Chapter 3
Smoothing Text Representation Models Based on Rough Set

Zhihua Wei
Tongji University, China

Duoqian Miao
Tongji University, China

Ruizhi Wang
Tongji University, China

Zhifei Zhang
Tongji University, China

ABSTRACT

Text representation is the prerequisite of various document processing tasks, such as information retrieval, text classification, text clustering, etc. It has been studied intensively for the past few years, and many excellent models have been designed as well. However, the performance of these models is affected by the problem of data sparseness. Existing smoothing techniques usually make use of statistic theory or linguistic information to assign a uniform distribution to absent words. They do not concern the real word distribution or distinguish between words. In this chapter, a method based on a kind of soft computing theory, Tolerance Rough Set theory, which makes use of upper approximation and lower approximation theory in Rough Set to assign different values for absent words in different approximation regions, is proposed. Theoretically, our algorithms can estimate smoothing value for absent words according to their relation with respect to existing words. Text classification experiments by using Vector Space Model (VSM) and Latent Dirichlet Allocation (LDA) model on public corpora have shown that our algorithms greatly improve the performance of text representation model, especially for the performance of unbalanced corpus.

DOI: 10.4018/978-1-60960-881-1.ch003

INTRODUCTION

Representation of texts is critical in text information processing tasks like retrieval, classification, clustering, summarization etc. Text representation is the prerequisite of document processing mainly because it determines the coding ways of text which directly affect processing performance. Effective representing form enables efficient processing on large amount of documents while preserving as much as possible semantic information that is useful to certain tasks.

Many excellent text representation models are designed based on intensive mathematic theories, including Vector Space Model (VSM) which is proposed by G. Salton et al. (1975) and some statistical topic models. VSM, a predominant method used for the present, represents a document as a vector where each dimension corresponds to a separate term. If a term occurs in the document, its value in the vector is non-zero. Several different ways of computing these values and also known as (term) weights, have been developed. In recent years, statistical topic models have been successfully applied in many text processing tasks. These models can capture the word correlations in the corpus with a low-dimensional set of multinomial distribution, called "topics", and can find a relatively short description of the documents. Latent Dirichlet Allocation (LDA) model which is proposed by D. Blei et al. (2003) is a widely used statistical topic model. Its basic idea is that documents are represented as random mixtures over latent topics, where each topic is characterized by a distribution over words.

However, most of these models suffer from the data sparseness problem. Taking text classification task as an example, there is a variety of sparseness which is resulted from the difference of vocabularies of different classes. In a corpus, vocabulary of each class is a subset of whole vocabulary. Consequently, when a document is represented with a model constructed on global vocabulary, it is not likely to contain the weight information of words that did not appear on its own. This phenomenon affects classification performance greatly. In fact, "absence" is not actually "not exist". If the corpus is large enough, these words should present themselves. In order to simulate the reality and the improved classification performance, it is necessary to conduct some smoothing strategies. In this chapter, we focus on the smoothing problem of VSM and LDA.

The name "smoothing" comes from the fact that these techniques tend to make distributions more uniform. Discounting seen words and assigning reasonable counts to unseen words are two exact goals of text model smoothing. S. Chen & J. Goodman (1998) regarded that not only do smoothing methods generally prevent zero probabilities, but they also attempt to improve the accuracy of the model as a whole. Previous researches on smoothing problem mainly follow two ways: smoothing based on statistical theory and smoothing based on semantic information. Statistical based smoothing method includes Laplace smoothing, Jelinek-Mercer smoothing, absolute discount and so on. While semantic based smoothing methods mainly consider semantic similarity from many views. Although the former is effective to prevent zero probability in many cases, it treats all terms as the same and cannot emphasis the class-specific terms. The later consider this problem and has proposed some effective solutions. In this way, linguistic information is supposed to be combined for smoothing purpose. This chapter proposes a new smoothing strategy from the view of soft computing. It regards the smoothing problem as a kind of imprecision problem. Tolerance Rough Set theory is adopted to describe different imprecision degrees according to co-occurrence which is a kind of statistical semantic information.

Rough Set (RS) theory, which is put forward by Poland mathematician Z. Pawlak (1991), is a mathematical tool that can effectively analyze and process incomplete, inconsistent, inaccurate data. The classical RS theory is based on equivalence relation that divides the universe of objects into disjoint classes. However, for some applications, the requirement for equivalence relation has shown to be too strict. For example, let us consider a collection of scientific documents and keywords describing those documents. It is clear that each document could have several keywords and a set of keywords could be associated with many documents. Thus, in the universe of documents, keywords can form overlapping classes. By relaxing an equivalence relation to a tolerance relation, where transitivity property is not required, Tolerance Rough Set (TRS) is introduced. This flexibility allows a blurring of the boundaries of the former rough or crisp equivalence classes and objects may now belong to more than one tolerance class.

The advantage of TRS is that it could divide different semantic similarity degree according to upper approximation and lower approximation. Consequently, proper smoothing weight strategies could be adopted in corresponding region. It effectively avoids uniform distribution in smoothing process and emphasizes the terms which have much more similarity with some class. This chapter will propose smoothing algorithm based on TRS for VSM and LDA model separately.

In VSM, the weights of those terms which do not occur in the document are assigned zero value. Document vector is characteristic of high dimension and sparseness. It results in zero-valued similarity problem between vectors frequently, which decreases classification performance. In order to solve this problem, a smoothing text representation model based on TRS is proposed. The absence of terms in a document is considered as missing information. According to TRS, tolerance classes in both term space and document space are generated. The missing information of document can be complemented by incorporating the corresponding weights of terms in tolerance classes and thus the zero-valued similarity problem can be avoided. The experiment results indicate the proposed algorithm improves classification performance effectively.

The same as VSM, the difference of the vocabularies of each class results in sparseness problem in LDA model. LDA model learned from documents of a certain class could only compute generative probability of a new document according to the vocabulary of this class. Unknown word in object documents will bring zero probability; as a result, the model is invalid. Blei designed a direct smoothing method that set an exchangeable prior Dirichlet distribution on variable. In a view of the disadvantage of this method, arbitrarily revising the variable in smooth process, a smoothing strategy based on Tolerance Rough Set is put forward. It constructs tolerance class in global vocabulary database firstly and then assigns value for unknown words in each class according to tolerance class. Experiments on both Chinese and English corpus indicate that the algorithm can enhance the classification performance obviously both for balance and for unbalanced dataset.

The chapter is organized as follows. The first section is an introduction of the chapter. The second section represents related research works in text representation model smoothing. The third section represents related definitions and concepts. The fourth section represents text model smoothing algorithm based on TRS and two examples: a smoothing Vector Space Model (VSM) and a smoothing Latent Dirichlet Allocation (LDA) model. Related experiments are also presented. The fifth section represents the future research direction and conclusions.

BACKGROUND

With the rapidly development of Internet, Web information brings more and more convenience to people. However, the limitations of the Internet have become obvious, in particular, the inability to take an automatic way the meaning of online documents into account. Many researchers attempt to develop effective text representation models which can uncover much semantic information hidden in documents. However, the data sparseness problems of these models greatly degrade their performance. A lot of research work paid much attention to smoothing models which approximately modeled the meaning of absent words in documents.

Zhou et al. (2008) referred that smoothing text representation model can be implemented in two ways: background smoothing and semantic smoothing. The former refers to the smoothing approaches based on the statistics from the whole collection such as Laplace smoothing, Jelinek-Mercer, Dirichlet, absolute discount, two-stage smoothing, etc. These models have been empirically proved effective upon text representation in IR application (C. Zhai & J. Lafferty, 2001a&2002). The latter refers to the smoothing approach that incorporates context and sense information into text representation model. Many semantic smoothing methods have been proposed for text representation model aimed at the applications such as information retrieval, text classification and text clustering, etc.

Laplacian smoothing, which simply add one count to all terms in the vocabulary, is frequently used for Bayesian model smoothing. But it proves to be not effective in many applications (F. Jelinek, 1990). The probability mass of a term given in a document is calculated as follows.

$$P(t \mid d) = \frac{tf_{t,d} + 1}{L_d}$$

C. Zhai and J. Lafferty (2001a&2002) have proposed several effective smoothing techniques that interpolate the document model with the background collection model, including Jelinek-Mercer (JM), Dirichlet, absolute discount and two-stage smoothing to smooth text representation models.

JM smoothing usages a mixture between a document-specific and entire collection-specific multinomial distribution:

$$P(t \mid d) = \lambda P_{mle}(t \mid M_d) + (1 - \lambda) P_{mle}(t \mid M_c)$$

Where, $0 < \lambda < 1$ is the smoothing parameter and M_d and M_c are the text models derived from a document and from the entire document collection, respectively.

Bayesian smoothing using Dirichlet priors is an alternative of JM smoothing which is to use a text model built from the whole collection as a prior Bayesian distribution in a Bayesian updating process. This is written as:

$$P(t \mid d) = \frac{tf_{t,d} + \mu P_{mle}(t \mid M)}{L_d + \mu}$$

Where, μ is the smoothing parameter. The larger the value of μ, the more smoothing the model is.

Absolute discounting is another smoothing method used in text representation. The idea is similar to the interpolation method. It works by discounting the probability of seen terms by subtracting a constant instead of multiplying it.

Lafferty and Zhai (2001b) introduce another more generic and flexible language model called KL-divergence retrieval model as a special case of their risk minimization retrieval framework. KL-divergence retrieval estimates the query model as well as the document model.

An improved smoothing method is the Good-Turing smoothing (S.F. Chen & J. Goodman, 1996) which re-estimates the frequency of the term that occurs tf times as:

$$tf_t^* = (tf_t + 1) \frac{n_{tf_t} + 1}{n_{tf_t}}$$

Where, n_{tf_t} is the number of terms that occur exactly tf_t times in the training data. Good-Turing is often used in combination with the back-off and interpolation algorithms rather than using it itself.

Some smoothing strategies for Latent Dirichlet Allocation (LDA) model are also proposed based on statistic theory. The model proposed by D. Blei et al. (2003) applies variation inference methods to the extended model that is Dirichlet smoothing on the multinomial parameter. Data-driven smoothing strategy is provided by W. Li et al. (2008) in which probability mass is allocated from smoothing-data to latent variables by the intrinsic inference procedure of LDA. Following this data-driven strategy, two concrete methods, Laplacian smoothing and Jelinek-Mercer smoothing, are employed in LDA model. A feature-enhanced smoothing method is brought by D.X. Liu et al. (2009) in the idea that words not appeared in the training corpus can help to improve the classification performance.

Although these simple smoothing methods are effective way to prevent zero probabilities, researchers think that it may not be so effective as to guess an appropriate redistribution of probability mass over the set of possible words. To solve this problem, some researchers propose semantic smoothing methods which emphasize on "discount" general words and "emphasize" more significantly on core words in a document.

A general idea of semantic smoothing method is similarity-based text representation approaches which employ the heuristic $TF * IDF$ scheme to discount the effect of "general" words (M. Steinbach & al., 2000).

Berger and Lafferty (2006) proposed a kind of semantic smoothing approach referred to as the statistical translation language model which statistically mapped document terms onto query terms.

$$p(q \mid d) = \sum_{w} t(q \mid w) p(w \mid d)$$

Where, $t(q \mid w)$ is the probability of translating the document term w to the query term q and $p(w \mid d)$ is the maximum likelihood estimator of the document model. With term translations, a document containing "star" may be returned to the query "movie" because two words have strong association on the topic of entertainment. However, this approach suffers from the context-insensitivity problem, i.e., it is unable to incorporate contextual and sense information into the model. Thus, the resulting translation may be fairly general and contain mixed topics.

Some researchers adopt smoothing method based on topic signature approach which statistically maps topic signatures in all training documents of a class into single-word features. However, the mere use of topic signature semantic mapping may lead to the fact that information loss (X. Wei et al., 2006 & X. Zhou, et al., 2006). X. Zhou et al. (2008) interpolate the semantic mapping component with statistic language model as described in following formula:

$$p_s(w \mid c_i) = (1 - \lambda) p_b(w \mid c_i) + \lambda \sum_{k} p(w \mid t_k) p(t_k \mid c_i)$$

Where, $p_s(w \mid c_i)$ stands for the unigram class model with semantic smoothing and t_k denotes the k-th topic signature and $p(t_k \mid c_i)$ is the distribution of topic signatures in training documents of a given class.

X. Zhang et al. (2006) proposed a context-sensitive semantic smoothing method based on topic signature language model for document clustering application. The basic idea of the smoothing method is to identify multiword phrases and then statistically map multiword phrases into individual document terms. For example, a document containing word "Israel" may be merged into the same cluster with a document containing phrase "Arab country" because "Arab country" is highly associated with "Israel" in the corpus.

In this chapter, a smoothing method based on an extended Rough Set Theory (RST), Tolerance Rough Set Theory (TRST), is proposed. RST is put forward by Poland mathematician Z. Pawlak (1991). As a kind of soft computing method, it can effectively analyze and process incomplete, inconsistent, inaccurate data (D. Miao & al., 2007). It gets widespread international concern as it has been successfully applied in areas such as Knowledge Discovery (KD) in recent years. The classical RST is based on equivalence relation that divides the universe of objects into disjoint classes. Tolerance Rough Set Theory which is put forward by W. Ziarko (1993) extends the equivalence relation in classic RST to tolerance relation. This kind of relaxation is more suitable for some practical applications.

PRELIMINARIES

In this section, we will introduce some preliminaries of two kinds of text representation model, Vector Space Model and Latent Dirichlet Allocation model, and Tolerance Rough Set (TRS) theory for the purpose of text model smoothing.

Vector Space Model

Vector Space Model (VSM), which is proposed by Salton et al. (1975), is an algebraic model for representing text documents as vectors of identifiers such as index terms. It is used in Text Classification, Information Filtering, Information Retrieval, etc.

In VSM, each Web document is viewed as a bag of terms and represented by a term vector. $TF * IDF$ (Term Frequency Times Inverse Document Frequency) weighting is the most often used scheme to assign weight values for document's vector. The standard $TF * IDF$ is defined as follows.

$$w_{ij} = tf_{ij} \times \log(N / df_i)$$

Where, tf_{ij} is the frequency of the term t_i in Web document d_j; df_i is number of Web documents in which term t_i occurs; N is the total number of Web documents. Normalization by vector's length is applied to all vectors as follows.

$$w_{ij}^* = w_{ij} / \sqrt{\sum_{t_k \in d_i} (w_{ik})^2}$$

Assuming that there are N Web documents and n different terms in a set of Web document, using $TF * IDF$, and each Web document is represented by an n-dimensional term vector. The N Web documents in the set can be represented by an $N \times n$ matrix $DW = [w_{ij}']$, where $w_{ij}' = w_{ij}^*$, if the term t_i occurs in the document d_j, otherwise, $w_{ij}' = 0$. Together with decision attributes, i.e., the class label of Web documents, the matrix can be considered as a decision table. According to the weight computation, if the term t_j is absent in the Web document d_i, w_{ij}' is equal to zero. This way of assigning the weights to absent terms brings zero-valued similarity problem among vectors.

Latent Dirichlet Allocation Model

Formally, we define the following terms (D. Blei & al., 2003).

A word, which is an item of the vocabulary indexed by $\{1, \ldots, V\}$, is the basic unit of discrete data. We represent words using unit-basis vectors that have a single component equal to one and all other components equal to zero. Thus, using superscripts to denote components, the v th word in the vocabulary is represented by a V-vector w such as $w^v = 1$ and $w^u = 0$ for u $\neq$ v.

A ***document*** is a sequence of N words denoted by $w = \{w_1; w_2; ...; w_N\}$, where w_n is the n th word in the sequence.

A ***corpus*** is a collection of M documents denoted by $D = \{w_1; w_2; ...; w_M\}$.

Latent Dirichlet Allocation (LDA) model is a generative probabilistic model of a corpus. The basic idea is that documents are represented as random mixtures of latent topics, where each topic is characterized by a distribution over words.

LDA assumes the following generative process for each document w in a corpus D:

1. Choose $N \sim Poisson(\xi)$.
2. Choose $\theta \sim Dir(\alpha)$.
3. For each of the N words w_n:
    a) Choose a topic $z_n \sim$ Multinomial (θ).
    b) Choose a word w_n from $p(w_n \mid z_n, \beta)$, a multinomial probability conditioned on the topic z_n.

Several simplifying assumptions are made in this basic model. Here, we just introduce most important facets. First of all, the dimensionality k of the Dirichlet distribution (and thus the dimensionality of the topic variable z) is assumed to be known and fixed. What's more, the word probabilities are parameterized by a $K \times V$ matrix β where $\beta_{ij} = p(w_j = 1 \mid z_i = 1)$, which now we treat as a fixed quantity that is going to be estimated. In addition, the Poisson assumption is not critical to anything that follows and more realistic document length distributions can be necessary. Furthermore, noting that N is independent of all the other data generating variables (θ and z). Thus, it is an ancillary variable and we will generally ignore its randomness in the subsequent development.

A k-dimensional Dirichlet random variable θ can take values in the $k - 1$-simplex (a k-vector θ lies in the $k - 1$-simplex if

$\theta_i \geq 0, \sum_{i=1}^{k} \theta_i = 1$, and has the following probability density on this simplex:

$$p(\theta \mid \alpha) = \frac{\Gamma(\sum_{i=1}^{k} \alpha_i)}{\prod_{i=1}^{k} \Gamma(\alpha)} \theta_1^{\alpha_1 - 1} ... \theta_k^{\alpha_k - 1}$$

Where, the parameter α is a k-vector with components $\alpha_i > 0$ and $\Gamma(x)$ is the Gamma function. The Dirichlet is a convenient distribution on the simplex—it is in the exponential family, has finite dimensional sufficient statistics, and is conjugate to the multinomial distribution.

Given the parameters α and β, the joint distribution of a topic mixture θ, a set of N topics z, and a set of N words w is given by:

$$p(\theta, z, w \mid \alpha, \beta) = p(\theta \mid \alpha) \prod_{n=1}^{N} p(z_n \mid \theta) p(w_n \mid z_n, \beta)$$

Where $p(z_n \mid \theta)$ is simply θ_i for the unique i such as $z_n^t = 1$. Integrating over θ and summing over z, we obtain the marginal distribution of a document as follows.

$$p(w \mid \alpha, \beta) = \int p(\theta \mid \alpha) \left(\prod_{n=1}^{N} \sum_{z} p(z_n \mid \theta) p(w_n \mid z_n, \beta) \right) d\theta$$

Therefore, taking the product of the marginal probabilities of single documents, we obtain the formula as follows.

$$p(D \mid \alpha, \beta) = \prod_{d=1}^{M} \int p(\theta_d \mid \alpha) \left(\prod_{n=1}^{N_d} \sum_{z_{dn}} p(z_{dn} \mid \theta_d) p(w_{dn} \mid z_{dn}, \beta) \right) d\theta_d$$

The LDA model is represented as a probabilistic graphical model. There are three levels to the LDA representation. The parameters α and β are corpus level parameters, assumed to be sampled once in the process of generating a corpus. The variables θ_d are document-level variables, sampled once per document. Finally, the variables z_{dn} and w_{dn} are word-level variables and are sampled once for each word in each document.

Tolerance Rough Set

Let $S = (U, A, V, f)$ be an information system, where U is a nonempty finite set of objects called universe of discourse, A is a nonempty finite set of conditional attributes; and for every $a \in A$, such as $f : U \rightarrow V_a$, where V_a is called the value set of attribute a.

Definition 1: If some of the precise attribute values in an information system are not known, i.e., missing or known partially, then such a system is called an incomplete information system. Otherwise the system is called a complete information system.

Definition 2: Let $S = (U, A, V, f)$ be an information system and the sign * denote null value, a tolerance relation T is defined as:

$$T(B) = \{(x, y) \in U \times U \mid \forall b \in B, b(x)$$
$$= b(y) \vee b(x) = * \vee b(y) = *\}.$$

Where, $B \subseteq A$. Obviously, T is reflexive and symmetric, but not transferable. Let $I_B(x) = \{y \in U \mid (x, y) \in T(B)\}$, and then $I_B(x)$ is called the tolerance class of the object x with respect to the set $B \subseteq A$.

Definition 3: Let $S = (U, A, V, f)$ be an information system, $X \subseteq U$, $B \subseteq A$, the upper approximation and lower approximation of X with regards to attribute set B under the tolerance relation T can be defined as:

$$U_B(X) = \{x \in U \mid I_B(x) \cap X \neq \varnothing\}$$

$$L_B(X) = \{x \in U \mid I_B(x) \subseteq X\}$$

SMOOTHING METHOD BASED ON TOLERANCE ROUGH SET THEORY

In this section, a kind of extended RST, Tolerance Rough Set (TRS), will be used to construct two algorithms: a smoothing Vector Space Model and a smoothing Latent Dirichlet Allocation model.

Text Representation Based on Tolerance Rough Set

Taking document classification domain as an example, we define the corresponding concepts.

An incomplete information system for a document set is represented as:

$$WS = (U, TS \cup \{class\}, f),$$

where U is the set of documents, each document is an object $d \in U$; TS is the set of total terms which occur in the document set, *class* is the decision attribute, i.e., the class label of the documents. The weights of those terms which do not occur in a Web document are considered missing information and denoted by sign * instead of zero.

In Web document space, the tolerance relation and tolerance class of Web document are defined as (Q. Duan & al., 2007):

Definition 4. For a subset of TS, $B \subseteq TS$, a tolerance relation $T(B)$ on U is defined as:

$$T(B) = \{(d_x, d_y) \in U \times U \mid \forall b \in B, \mid b(d_x)$$
$$-d(d_y) \mid \leq \delta \vee b(d_x) = * \vee b(d_y) = *\}.$$

Because weights are real values, the requirement $b(d_x) = b(d_y)$ is too strict. Here it is replaced by $\mid b(d_x) - b(d_y) \mid \leq \delta$, where, $\delta \in [0, 1]$. Consequently, tolerance class of a document d_x with respect to $B \subseteq TS$, $I_B(d_x)$ is the set of documents which are indiscernible to d_x, i.e., $I_B(d_x) = \{d_y \in U \mid (d_x, d_y) \in T(B)\}$.

Table 1. Sample document-term frequency array

	t_1	t_2	t_3	t_4	t_5	Class
d_1	0	0	6	8	0	C_1
d_2	1	3	12	0	9	C_1
d_3	2	3	0	12	14	C_1
d_4	0	0	5	4	2	C_2
d_5	10	9	4	0	3	C_2
d_6	12	14	2	2	0	C_2
d_7	11	12	0	4	2	C_2

On the other hand, correlation between terms is valuable for complementing missing information. Thus, the tolerance class of term is also defined in term space. Let $U = \{d_1, ..., d_M\}$ be a set of documents and $TS = \{t_1, ..., t_N\}$ set of terms for U. The tolerance space of term is defined over a universe of all terms for U.

Definition 5. Let $f_D(t_i, t_j)$ denotes the number of documents in U in which both term t_i and t_j occurs. The uncertainty function I with regards to co-occurrence threshold θ is defined as:

$$I_\theta(t_i) = \{t_j \mid f_D(t_i, t_j) \geq \theta\} \cup \{t_i\}$$

Clearly, the above function satisfies conditions of being reflexive: $t_i \in I_\theta(t_i)$ and symmetric: $t_j \in I_\theta(t_i) \Leftrightarrow t_i \in I_\theta(t_j)$ for any $t_i, t_j \in T$. Thus, $I_\theta(t_i)$ is the tolerance class of term t_i. Tolerance class of terms is generated to capture conceptually related terms into classes. The degree of correlation of terms in tolerance classes can be controlled by varying the threshold θ.

In tolerance space of term, an expanded representation of document can be acquired by representing document as set of tolerance classes of terms it contains. This can be achieved by simply representing document with its upper approximation, e.g., the Web document $d_i \in U$ is represented by:

$$U_R(d_i) = \{t_i \in T \mid I_\theta(t_i) \cap d_i \neq \varnothing\}$$

This approach to Web document representation takes not only terms actually occurring document but also other related terms with similar meanings into consideration.

To demonstrate the use of the smoothed model, we detail an example as follows.

Example 1: Let document set be $U = \{d_1, d_2, d_3, d_4, d_5, d_6, d_7\}$, term set be $TS = \{t_1, t_2, t_3, t_4, t_5\}$, $B = TS$, the class label set be $class = \{C_1, C_2\}$. The frequency data is listed in Table 1.

Let co-occurrence threshold $\theta = 4$, tolerance class of each term t_i ($i = 1, 2, \cdots, 5$) and upper approximations of the document d_i ($i = 1, 2, \cdots, 7$) can be computed as below:

$$I_\theta(t_1) = I_\theta(t_2) = \{t_1, t_2\}$$

$$I_\theta(t_3) = \{t_3\}$$

$$I_\theta(t_4) = I_\theta(t_5) = \{t_4, t_5\}$$

$$U_B(d_1) = U_B(d_4) = \{t_3, t_4, t_5\}$$

$$U_B(d_2) = \{t_1, t_2, t_3\}$$

$$U_B(d_3) = U_B(d_7) = \{t_1, t_2, t_4, t_5\}$$

$$U_B(d_5) = U_B(d_6) = \{t_1, t_2, t_3, t_4, t_5\}$$

A Smoothing Vector Space Model Based on Tolerance Rough Set

For Vector Space Model, the best values of these missing weights are determined by incorporating two parts, i.e., weights of terms in term's tolerance class and corresponding term weight of the most similar vector, which has the same class label in tolerance class of the Web document. Here, the similarity measure between vectors is computed based on the distance $Sim(d_x, d_y)$.

$$Sim(d_x, d_y) = \frac{1}{1 + \sum_{k=1}^{M} |w_{ik} - w_{jk}|}.$$

After the tolerance classes for both term and Web document are generated, the essential information (i.e., the similarity between Web documents and the correlation between terms) is identified. To complement the missing weights of terms in the Web document's vectors, we produce an improved $TF * IDF$ weighting scheme based on the traditional $TF * IDF$. The weighting scheme is defined as below.

$$w_{ij} = \begin{cases} 1 + \log(f_{d_i}(t_j)) \times \log \frac{N}{f_D(t_j)} & \text{if } t_j \in d_i, \\ \alpha \times w_{kj} & \text{if } t_j \notin U_R(d_i), \\ \alpha \times w_{kj} + \beta \times (\min_{t_n \in d_i \wedge t_n \in I_\theta(t_j)} w_{in}) & \text{if } t_j \in U_R(d_i) \wedge t_j \notin d_i \end{cases}$$

In the above formula, w_{kj} is the weight value of corresponding term of the most similarity vector with the same class label in Web document tolerance class; $\alpha, \beta \in [0,1]$, they adjust the rela-tive impact of relevant terms and Web documents respectively. Here, let parameters α and β be 0.2.

According to the above algorithm, the text classification process based on VSM can be described as follows. Firstly, terms are extracted from training set of Web documents, and then tolerance classes of Web documents and terms are computed. Secondly, the missing weights of incomplete vectors are complemented. Thirdly, the classifier is constructed. Finally, the new Web document is classified into the category where the similarity measure is the highest among all other categories. The similarities are computed between the new Web document and each category centroid, in which the similarity formula is defined as follows.

$$Dis(d_i, c_j) = \frac{\sum_{k=1}^{M} W_{ik} \times W_{jk}}{\sqrt{(\sum_{K=1}^{M} W_{ik}^2) \times (\sum_{K=1}^{M} W_{jk}^2)}}$$

Where, d_i is the new Web document, c_j is the j th category centroid, M is the term dimension.

To evaluate the proposed approach, we use two popular data collections in our experiments. The first one is the WebKB data set 1, which contains 8,282 Web documents collected from computer science departments of various universities. The pages were manually classified into the following categories: student, faculty, staff, department, course, project, other (respectively abbreviated here as St, Fa, Sta, De, Co, Pr, Ot). In our experiments, each category is employed. The second collection is the Reuters-21578, which has 21,578 documents collected from the Reuters newswire. Of the 135 categories, only the most populous eight categories are used, i.e, acq, corn, crude, earn, grain, interest, money and trade (respectively abbreviated here as Ac, Co, Cr, Ea, Gr, In, Mo, Tr). The construction of each data set

Table 2. Comparison of classification performance on WebKB

	St	Fa	Sta	De	Co	Pr	Ot	Avg
VSM	0.671	0.613	0.437	0.468	0.635	0.554	0.725	0.586
VSM_{TRS}	0.756	0.734	0.633	0.630	0.691	0.712	0.787	0.710

for our experiments is done as follows. Firstly, we randomly select 30% of the Web documents from the each category, and put them into test set to evaluate the performance of classifier. Secondly, the rest are used to create training sets. We extract and select the 100 most frequently occurred keywords from each category. For WebKB data set and Reuters-21578, the total numbers of all distinct keywords are 463 and 689 respectively.

To analyze the performance of classification, we adopt the popular $F1$ measure. $F1$ measure is a combination of $recall(re)$ and $precision(pr)$, $F1 = 2 * re * pr / (re + pr)$. Pr $ecision$ means the rate of documents classified correctly among the result of classifier and $recall$ signifies the rate of correct classified documents among them to be classified correctly. The $F1$ measure which is the harmonic mean of precision and recall is used in this study since it takes into account effects of both quantities (C. J. van Rijsbergen, 1979).

The results of WebKB data set are summarized in Table 2. Our approach yields a higher performance compared to the normal VSM for all categories. For example, in student category, our approach yields the $F1$ values of 75.6%, whereas the normal VSM yields the $F1$ values of 67.1%.

In Table 2, *avg* shows summarized result which is calculated by averaging the $F1$ values over all

categories. Our approach yields higher average classification performance of 12.4% over the normal VSM. We perform the same experiments on the Reuters-21578. The results are shown in Table 3, in which *avg* also shows summarized result. Our approach yields higher average classification performance of 8.5% over the normal VSM for Reuters-21578.

A Smoothing Latent Dirichlet Allocation Model Based on Tolerance Rough Set

As analyzed in the former, the difference of the vocabularies of each class results in sparseness. In this case, LDA model (α^i, β^i) learned from documents of class i could only compute generative probability of a new document according to the vocabulary of class i. Unknown word in object documents will bring zero probability, as a result, the model is invalid.

LDA model (α^i, β^i) learned from documents of class i has two parameters α^i and β^i. The initial value of α^i could be manually assigned. However, β^i which is related to vocabulary should be smoothed.

Table 3. Comparison of classification performance on Reuters-21578

	Ac	Co	Cr	Ea	Gr	In	Mo	Tr	Avg
VSM	0.710	0.575	0.644	0.723	0.681	0.637	0.625	0.612	0.651
VSM_{TRS}	0.736	0.673	0.727	0.780	0.769	0.740	0.768	0.694	0.736

Definition 6. Assuming that v_i is vocabulary of class c_i, the out-of-vocabulary (oov) words of class c_i is represented as follows.

$$oov_i = \cup_{j=1}^{c} v_j - v_i$$

For the application of text classification, unknown words will increase greatly due to the growth of the number of class. This may degrade the performance of model, especially for an unbalanced corpus.

D. Blei (2003) designed a direct smoothing method which sets an exchangeable prior Dirichlet distribution $Dir(\eta)$ for β. Bayes inference is performed on this smoothed model and the estimation of parameter β' is as follows.

$$\beta'_{ij} = \eta + \beta_{ij}$$

In fact, this process only adds a positive value on original estimate. Obviously, every word in β^i is not zero, as a result, zero probability is avoided in LDA model. Whereas, there are some disadvantages in this smoothing strategy.

It is likely to modify latent parameter β arbitrarily. β is related to latent variation (θ, z) and α. Directly modifying the β may neglect its effect on other parameters. The selection of exchangeable Dirichlet prior is in consideration of the conductible of LDA model. It confines the distribution of smoothing method. The assignment of parameter η is derived from experience. There is no principle for its assignment.

To avoid the above problems in classic LDA model, a strategy based on TRS, named TRS-LDA, is proposed in this chapter. Its main idea is compensating the out-of-vocabulary (oov) word list for class i and assigning corresponding value according to the information coming from its tolerance class. In this case, the zero probability could be reduced (Z. Wei, 2010).

Firstly, the oov word list is added to class i and LDA model could be trained with an extended vocabulary. The inference mechanism in LDA could be maturely applied. That is, parameter (θ, z) and α could be served in smoothing process with the changing of w. This strategy avoids the arbitrariness in modification parameters in model.

Secondly, we could adjust the scale of tolerance class to meet different situations. As it is different from the classic smoothing strategy, it could adopt various prior distributions more flexibly.

We make use of the idea of Laplacian transform to add virtual vocabulary to each class and assign its value as follows.

$$P\left(w_t | c_i\right) = \frac{n_i\left(w_t\right) + \lambda}{n_i\left(c_i\right) + \lambda \, | V |}$$

$$\lambda = \begin{cases} tf_{ij} + 1 & if \ t_j \in d_i, \\ \varphi + \rho min_{t_k \in d_i} TF_{ik} & if \ t_j \notin U_R(d_i), \\ \varphi & if \ t_j \in U_R(d_i) \wedge t_j \notin d_i \end{cases}$$

Where, tf_{ij} is the frequency of term t_j in document d_i, $\varphi, \rho \in [0,1]$. In this chapter, we assign the paprameter $\varphi = \rho = 0.2$ based on experience. That is, for an unknown word, we assign its prior value according to three cases: appearing in d_i, being absent in d_i, yet appearing in $U_R(d_i)$ and being absent in $U_R(d_i)$.

The smoothing strategy has different effects on big classes and small classes. Normally, there is much more vocabulary in big class. As a result, the virtual vocabulary added has little change on its original one, vice verse, for a small class. Consequently, a perfect smoothing algorithm could effectively improve the classification performance on small classes.

Experiments are performed on both English corpus 20Newsgroup and Chinese corpus Tan-

Corp-12. 20Newsgroup was collected by Ken Lang for text classification research. All documents are distributed across 20 categories evenly (balanced), altogether 20,000 texts. TanCorp-12 which is collected by Dr. S. Tan includes 14,150 texts, distributing in 12 categories (unbalanced).

For both corpora, we extracted 70% texts in each class as the training set and the rest 30% as the testing set. We repeated our experiments five times and got the average results of each experiment setting.

In our experiments, the Micro-F1 and the Macro-F1 measures are used to evaluate the synthesis classification performance. Macro-F1 can be achieved by computing the average of recall $\bar{r}$ and the average of precision $\bar{p}$ firstly is showed in the following formulas (C. J. van Rijsbergen, 1979).

$$\bar{r} = \left(\sum\nolimits_{\infty C} r_c\right) \Big/ |C|$$

$$\bar{p} = \left(\sum\nolimits_{\infty C} P_c\right) \Big/ |C|$$

Micro-F1 can be achieved based on multi-class confusion matrix, as showed in following formulas.

$$\bar{r} = \frac{\sum\limits_{\infty C} d}{\sum\limits_{\infty C} d + \sum\limits_{\infty C} c}$$

$$\bar{p} = \frac{\sum\limits_{\infty C} d}{\sum\limits_{\infty C} d + \sum\limits_{\infty C} b}$$

We perform the comparison between our algorithm TRS-LDA and traditional LDA model. For LDA model, the number of latent topics is an important factor which defines the granularity of the model. So we evaluate models on different topic numbers: 5, 10, 20, 50, 100.

1. Experiments on Analysis Synthesis Performance on 20Newsgroup.

   Firstly, we use English corpus 20Newsgroup to testify our algorithm. There are 700 texts used for training classifier in each class and the other (300 texts) for the testing process. The results are shown in Figure 1. Some phenomena could be observed as follows.

   a. On the whole, TRS-LDA model has an evident higher performance of about 6%~7% absolutely than LDA model both on Micro-F1 and Macro-F1. This occurs across all values of topic number.

Figure 1. Comparing Classification results on 20Newsgroup between TRS-LDA and LDA

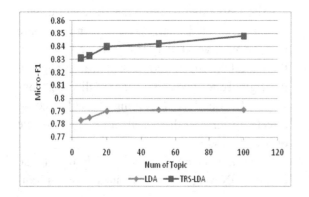
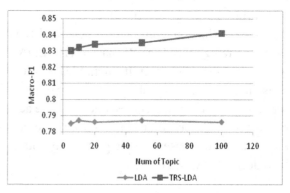

b. When different latent topic number is selected, the behaviors of the two models are different. With the increase of topic number, the performance of LDA model changes little. However, the TRS-LDA model improves little by little.

c. Micro-F1 and Macro-F1 have the very consistent results.

2. Experiments on Analysis Synthesis Performance on TanCorp-12:

    We also use Chinese corpus TanCorp-12 to testify our algorithm. There are 70% texts used for training classifier in each class and the other (30% texts) for the testing process. The results are shown in Figure 2. Some phenomena can be observed as follows.

    a. TRS-LDA model has an evident higher performance of about 7% absolutely than LDA model on Micro-F1 across all values of topic number.

    b. TRS-LDA model has an evident higher performance of nearly 20% absolutely than LDA model on Macro-F1 across all values of topic number.

    c. When different latent topic number is selected, the behaviors of the two models are different. With the increase of topic number, the Micro-F1 value of LDA model changes a little. However,

that of TRS-LDA model improves little by little.

d. Micro-F1 and Macro-F1 have inconsistent results. The possible reason is that TanCorp-12 is an unbalanced corpus.

From the experiments, we could find that TRS-LDA model could improve the classification performance obviously on unbalanced corpus. For an unbalanced text classification task, the classification performance on small classes are usually not satisfied because there are too few training documents in small classes. TRS-LDA algorithm could improve the classification performance on small classes to some extent.

3. Analysis on performance of each class on unbalanced corpus

Let us observe the effectiveness of TRS-LDA from the more refined granularity. From the distribution of TanCorp-12, we could find that the largest class includes nearly 3,000 documents while the smallest one includes only 150 documents.

We still adopt F1 metrics to observe the classification performance on each class. Figure 3. shows the distribution of TanCorp-12 and the F1 performance on each class on this corpus. The class sequence in the right of Figure 3. is consistent with that in the left. That is, the classes are ordered ascending according to the number of documents in class.

Figure 2. Comparing Classification results on TanCorp-12 between TRS-LDA and LDA

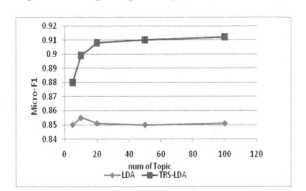 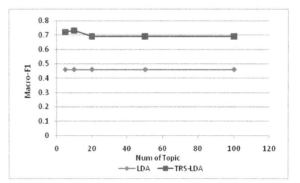

Figure 3. Relation between class size and classification performance

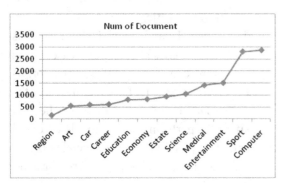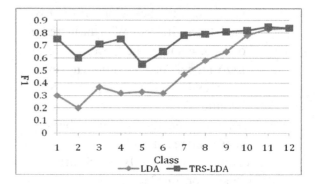

From Figure 3., we could find that F1 values of TRS-LDA model are always higher than those of LDA model. The increase of F1 values on big classes are less than those on small classes. It indicates that the contribution of TRS-LDA algorithm lies in improving the classification effectiveness on small classes, in the same time, not degrading the performance on big classes. The effect of this smoothing algorithm lies in relieving the over-fitting on small class.

FUTURE RESEARCH DIRECTIONS

Soft computing differs from conventional (hard) computing in the fact that it is tolerant of imprecision, uncertainty, partial truth, and approximation. Rough Set, as a kind of soft computing method, have been applied in many applications. In this chapter, two smoothing algorithms based on RST are constructed for the application of text classification. However, the text representation model for different application is distinct. Taking document clustering as an example, there is no category information in clustering process while the category information could be a kind of guide in training classifier. Thus, further research should focus on developing smoothing text representation model based on RST for other applications such as document clustering, information retrieval and

so on. Other soft computing theories should also be adopted for this purpose.

Algorithms proposed in this chapter only make use of the co-occurrence information for the purpose of smoothing. It is only a kind of statistic semantic information which does not consider the word semantic relations in dictionary. We expect that linguistic semantic information could be incorporated into constructing tolerance class to enhance text representation models.

Observed from experiments, we could find that the smoothing algorithms based on TRS improve the classification performance greatly when the distribution of classes is unbalanced. However, we do not know the effect of smoothing algorithm with the change of scale of corpus. That is, when the unbalanced degree of a corpus is increasing or decreasing, how does the performance of smoothing algorithms change?

CONCLUSION

Text representation is a prerequisite of text processing applications. However, data sparseness problem limits the performance of existing text representation models. This chapter reviews two kinds of prevalent smoothing ways, background smoothing based on statistic theory and semantic-based smoothing. From the viewpoint of soft computing, a smoothing method based on

Tolerance Rough Set theory is proposed, which consider term co-occurrence semantic information combining with statistic smoothing theory.

The basic idea of the algorithm is constructing term tolerance class according to term co-occurrence and compensating the weight or probability of unknown words based on tolerance class information. Corresponding smoothing algorithms on both Vector Space Model and Latent Dirichlet Allocation model for classification application have been constructed. Experiments on public corpora show that the algorithms could improve classification performance greatly, especially when the corpus is unbalanced.

REFERENCES

Bai, J., Nie, J. Y., & Cao, G. (2005). Integrating Compound Terms in Bayesian Text Classification. In A. Skowron et al. (Ed.), *IEEE / WIC / ACM International Conference on Web Intelligence (WI 2005)*. 19-22, September 2005, Compiegne, France.

Berger, A., & Lafferty, J. (1999). Information Retrieval as Statistical Translation. *In Proceedings of the 22nd ACM SIGIR Conference on Research and Development in Information Retrieval*. 222-229. Berkeley, CA, USA.

Blei, D., Ng, A., & Jordan, M. (2003). Latent Dirichlet Allocation. *Journal of Machine Learning Research, 3*, 993–1022.

Chen, S. F., & Goodman, J. T. (1999). An Empirical Study of Smoothing Techniques for Language Modeling. *Computer Speech & Language, 13*(4), 359–393. doi:10.1006/csla.1999.0128

Duan, Q., Miao, D., & Chen, M. (2007). Web Document Classification Based on Rough Set. In A. An, et al. (Ed.), *Lecture Notes in Computer Science 4482, Rough Sets, Fuzzy Sets, Data Mining and Granular Computing, 11th International Conference, RSFDGrC 2007*. 240-247, May 2007, Toronto, Canada.

Jelinek, F. (1990). Self-Organized Language Modeling for Speech Recognition, In B. A. Wei & K. F. Lee (Ed.), *Readings in Speech Recognition* (pp. 450-505). Los Altos, CA: Morgan Kaufmann publishing.

Li, W. B., Sun, L., Feng, Y. Y., & Zhang, D. K. (2008). Smoothing LDA Model for Text Categorization. In H. Li et al. (Ed.), *Lecture Notes in Computer Science, Volume 4993/2008, 4th Asia Information Retrieval Symposium, AIRS 2008*, 83-94, January, 2008, Harbin, China.

Liu, D. X., Xu, W. R., & Hu, J. N. (2009). A feature-enhanced smoothing method for LDA model applied to text classification. In: International Conference on Natural Language Processing and Knowledge Engineering (NLP-KE). 1- 7, September 2009, Dalian, China.

Miao, D., Wang, G., & Liu, Q. (2007). *Granular Computing: Past, Present and future*. Beijing, China: Science Publisher.

Pawlak, Z. (1991). *Rough Sets: Theoretical Aspects of Reasoning about Data*. Dordrecht: Kluwer Academic publisher.

Salton, G., Wong, A., & Yang, C. S. (1975). A Vector Space Model for Automatic Indexing . *Communications of the ACM, 18*(11), 613–620. doi:10.1145/361219.361220

Steinbach, M., Karypis, G., & Kumar, V. (2000). *A Comparison of document clustering techniques. Technical Report #00-034*. Dept. of Computer Science and Engineering, University of Minnesota, USA.

Van Rijsbergen, C. J. (1979). *Information Retrieval*. London: Butterworths.

Wei, X., & Croft, W. B. (2006). LDA-based document models for ad-hoc retrieval. In E. N. Efthimiadis (Ed.), *Proceedings of the 29th ACM SIGIR Conference on Research and Development in IR*. 178-185, August 2006, Seattle, Washington, USA.

Wei, Z. (2010). *The research on Chinese text multi-label classification*. Unpublished doctoral dissertation, University of Tongji, China.

Zhai, C., & Lafferty, J. (2001a). A Study of Smoothing Methods for Language Models Applied to Ad hoc Information Retrieval. In W. B. Croft et al. (Ed.), *Proceedings of the 24th ACM SIGIR Conference on Research and Development in IR*. 334-342, September 2001, New Orleans, Louisiana, USA.

Zhai, C., & Lafferty, J. (2001b). Model-based feedback in the KL-divergence retrieval model. *In 10th International Conference on Information and Knowledge Management, CIKM2001*. 403-410, November, 2001, Atlanta, Georgia, USA.

Zhai, C., & Lafferty, J. (2002). Two-Stage Language Models for Information Retrieval, In M. Beaulieu (Ed.), *Proceeding of ACM SIGIR2002 Conference on Research and Development in Information Retrieval*. 49-56, August 2002, Tampere, Finland.

Zhang, X., Zhou, X., & Hu, X. (2006). Semantic Smoothing for Model-based Document Clustering. *In Proceedings of the 6th IEEE International Conference on Data Mining (ICDM2006)*. 1193-1198, December 2006, Hong Kong, China.

Zhou, X., Hu, X., Zhang, X., Lin, X., & Song, I. Y. Context-sensitive Semantic Smoothing for Language Modeling Approach to Genomic Information Retrieval, In E. N. Efthimiadis (Ed.), *Proceedings of the 29th ACM SIGIR Conference on Research and Development in IR*. 170-177, August 2006, Seattle, Washington, USA.

Zhou, X., Zhang, X., & Hu, X. (2008). Semantic Smoothing for Bayesian Text Classification with Small Training Data. In M. J. Zaki & K. Wang (Ed.), *Proceedings of the SIAM International Conference on Data Mining, SDM2008*. 289-300, April 2008, Atlanta, Georgia, USA.

Ziarko, W. (1993). Variable precision rough set model. *Journal of Computer and System Sciences, 46*(1), 39–59. doi:10.1016/0022-0000(93)90048-2

ADDITIONAL READING

Bai, J., Nie, J. Y., & Cao, G. (2005). Integrating Compound Terms in Bayesian Text Classification. In A. Skowron et al. (Ed.), *IEEE / WIC / ACM International Conference on Web Intelligence (WI 2005)*. 19-22, September 2005, Compiegne, France.

Berger, A., & Lafferty, J. (1999). Information Retrieval as Statistical Translation. *In Proceedings of the 22nd ACM SIGIR Conference on Research and Development in Information Retrieval*. 222-229. Berkeley, CA, USA.

Blei, D., Ng, A., & Jordan, M. (2003). Latent Dirichlet Allocation. *Journal of Machine Learning Research, 3*, 993–1022.

Chen, S. F., & Goodman, J. T. (1999). An Empirical Study of Smoothing Techniques for Language Modeling. *Computer Speech & Language, 13*(4), 359–393. doi:10.1006/csla.1999.0128

Duan, Q., Miao, D., & Chen, M. (2007). Web Document Classification Based on Rough Set. In A. An, et al. (Ed.), *Lecture Notes in Computer Science 4482, Rough Sets, Fuzzy Sets, Data Mining and Granular Computing, 11th International Conference, RSFDGrC 2007*. 240-247, May 2007, Toronto, Canada.

Ho, T. B., & Nguyen, N. B. (2002). Nonhierarchical Document Clustering based on A Tolerance Tough Set Model. *International Journal of Intelligent Systems, 17*, 199–212. doi:10.1002/int.10016

Jelinek, F. (1990). Self-Organized Language Modeling for Speech Recognition, In B. A. Wei and K. F. Lee (Ed.), *Readings in Speech Recognition* (pp. 450-505). Los Altos, CA: Morgan Kaufmann publishing.

Kryszkiewicz, M. (1998). Rough set approach to incomplete information system. *Information Sciences, 112*, 39–49. doi:10.1016/S0020-0255(98)10019-1

Lang, N. C. (2003). *A tolerance rough set approach to clustering Web search results*. Master Thesis of Warsaw University, Poland.

Lewis, D. D., Li, F., Rose, T., & Yang, Y. (2004). RCV1: A new benchmark collection for text categorization research. *Journal of Machine Learning Research, 5*(3), 361–397.

Li, W. B., Sun, L., Feng, Y. Y., & Zhang, D. K. (2008). Smoothing LDA Model for Text Categorization. In H. Li et al. (Ed.), *Lecture Notes in Computer Science, Volume 4993/2008, 4th Asia Information Retrieval Symposium, AIRS 2008*, 83-94, January, 2008, Harbin, China.

Lidstone, G. J. (1920). Note on the general case of the Bayes-Laplace formala for inductive or a posteriori probabilities. *Transactions of the Faculty of Actuaries, 1920(8)*. 182-192.

Liu, D. X., Xu, W. R., & Hu, J. N. (2009). A feature-enhanced smoothing method for LDA model applied to text classification, In: *International Conference on Natural Language Processing and Knowledge Engineering (NLP-KE)*. 1- 7, September 2009, Dalian, China.

Liu, Q. (2003). *Rough set and Rough Reasoning*. Beijing, China: Science Publisher.

Miao, D., Wang, G., & Liu, Q. (2007). *Granular Computing: Past, Present and future*. Beijing, China: Science Publisher.

Ngo, C. L., & Nguyen, H. S. (2004). A Tolerance Rough Set Approach to Clustering Web Search Results. In: J. F. Boulicaut et al. (Ed.), *Lecture Notes in Computer Science 3202, Knowledge Discovery in Databases: PKDD 2004, 8th European Conference on Principles and Practice of Knowledge Discovery in Databases*. 515-517, September 2004, Pisa, Italy.

Pawlak, Z. (1991). *Rough Sets: Theoretical Aspects of Reasoning about Data*. Dordrecht: Kluwer Academic publisher.

Salton, G., Wong, A., & Yang, C. S. (1975). A Vector Space Model for Automatic Indexing . *Communications of the ACM, 18*(11), 613–620. doi:10.1145/361219.361220

Sebastiani, F. (2002). Machine learning in automated text categorization. *ACM Computing Surveys, 34*(1), 1–47. doi:10.1145/505282.505283

Skowron, A., & Stepaniuk, J. (1996). Tolerance approximation spaces. *Fundamenta Informaticae, 27*(2-3), 245–253.

Van Rijsbergen, C. J. (1979). *Information Retrieval*. London: Butterworths.

Wei, X., & Croft, W. B. (2006). LDA-based document models for ad-hoc retrieval. In E. N. Efthimiadis (Ed.), *Proceedings of the 29th ACM SIGIR Conference on Research and Development in IR*. 178-185, August 2006, Seattle, Washington, USA.

Wei, Z. (2010). *The research on Chinese text multi-label classification*. Unpublished doctoral dissertation, University of Tongji, China.

Yao, Y. Y., Wong, S. K. M., & Lin, T. Y. (1997). A Review of Rough Set Models . In Lin, T. Y., & Cercone, N. (Eds.), *Rough Sets and Data Mining: Analysis for Imprecise Data* (pp. 47–75). Boston: Kluwer Academic Publishers.

Zhai, C., & Lafferty, J. (2001a). A Study of Smoothing Methods for Language Models Applied to Ad hoc Information Retrieval, In W. B. Croft et al. (Ed.), *Proceedings of the 24th ACM SIGIR Conference on Research and Development in IR*. 334-342, September 2001, New Orleans, Louisiana, USA.

Zhai, C., & Lafferty, J. (2001b). Model-based feedback in the KL-divergence retrieval model. *In 10th International Conference on Information and Knowledge Management, CIKM2001*. 403-410, November, 2001, Atlanta, Georgia, USA.

Zhai, C., & Lafferty, J. (2002). Two-Stage Language Models for Information Retrieval, In M. Beaulieu (Ed.), *Proceeding of ACM SIGIR2002 Conference on Research and Development in Information Retrieval*. 49-56, August 2002, Tampere, Finland.

Zhang, X., Zhou, X., & Hu, X. (2006). Semantic Smoothing for Model-based Document Clustering. *In Proceedings of the 6th IEEE International Conference on Data Mining (ICDM 2006)*. 1193-1198, December 2006, Hong Kong, China.

Zhou, X., Hu, X., Zhang, X., Lin, X., & Song, I. Y. Context-sensitive Semantic Smoothing for Language Modeling Approach to Genomic Information Retrieval, In E. N. Efthimiadis (Ed.), *Proceedings of the 29th ACM SIGIR Conference on Research and Development in IR*. 170-177, August 2006, Seattle, Washington, USA.

Zhou, X., Zhang, X., & Hu, X. (2008). Semantic Smoothing for Bayesian Text Classification with Small Training Data. In M. J. Zaki and K. Wang (Ed.), *Proceedings of the SIAM International Conference on Data Mining, SDM2008*. 289-300, April 2008, Atlanta, Georgia, USA.

Ziarko, W. (1993). Variable precision rough set model. *Journal of Computer and System Sciences, 46*(1), 39–59. doi:10.1016/0022-0000(93)90048-2

KEY TERMS AND DEFINITIONS

Data Sparseness: In text representation model or language model, the zero-value probability problem of terms resulted from the vocabulary difference between classes.

Latent Dirichlet Allocation (LDA): A widely used statistical topic model whose basic idea is that documents are represented as random mixtures over latent topics, where each topic is characterized by a distribution over words.

Model Smoothing: In text processing applications, it is a technique to prevent zero probabilities by estimating an appropriate redistribution of probability mass over the set of absent words.

Text classification: As a kind of application of text processing, it assign an electronic document to one or more categories, based on its contents.

Text Representation: text coding ways for special text processing application such as information retrieval, text classification, document clustering and so on.

Tolerance Rough Set (TRS): A kind of extended Rough Set which is a kind of soft computing method.

Vector Space Model (VSM): A predominant text representation method for the present, which represents a document as a vector where each dimension corresponds to a separate term.

Chapter 4
Query Based Topic Modeling:
An Information–Theoretic Framework for Semantic Analysis in Large–Scale Collections

Eduardo H. Ramírez
Tecnológico de Monterrey, México

Ramón F. Brena
Tecnológico de Monterrey, México

ABSTRACT

Creating topic models of text collections is an important step towards more adaptive information access and retrieval applications. Such models encode knowledge of the topics discussed on a collection, the documents that belong to each topic and the semantic similarity of a given pair of topics. So far, the dominant paradigm to topic modeling has been the Probabilistic Topic Modeling approach in which topics are represented as probability distributions of terms. Although such models are theoretically sound, their high computational complexity makes them difficult to use in very large-scale collections.

In this work the authors propose an alternative collection-modeling paradigm based on a simpler representation of topics as freely overlapping clusters of semantically similar documents, thus being able to take advantage of highly-scalable clustering algorithms. Then, the authors propose the Query-based Topic Modeling framework (QTM), an information-theoretic method that assumes the existence of a "golden" set of queries that can capture most of the semantic information of the collection and produce models with maximum semantic coherence. The QTM method uses information-theoretic heuristics to find a set of "topical-queries" which are then co-clustered along with the documents of the collection and transformed to produce overlapping document clusters. The QTM framework was designed with scalability in mind and is able to be executed in parallel over commodity-class machines using the Map-Reduce approach.

DOI: 10.4018/978-1-60960-881-1.ch004

Finally, in order to compare the QTM results with models generated by other methods we have developed probabilistic metrics that formalize the notion of semantic coherence using probabilistic concepts and can be used to validate overlapping and incomplete clustering using multi-labeled corpora. They show that the proposed method can produce models of comparable, or even superior quality, than those produced with state of the art probabilistic methods.

INTRODUCTION

Now more than ever, many activities of life, work and business depend on the information stored on massive, fast-growing document collections like the World-Wide Web. However, despite the impressive advances in Web retrieval technologies, searching the web or browsing extensive repositories are not simple tasks for many users. Very often users pose ineffective queries and need to reformulate them to better express their intent, unfortunately, producing effective query reformulations to achieve an information goal is not always a straightforward task (Broder, 2002),(Jansen, Booth, & Spink, 2009).

On the other hand, when queries get longer or users lack enough domain knowledge, it turns more likely that query terms may differ from the terms in the documents, thus making relevant documents less likely to be retrieved. This problem has been characterized by Furnas et. al (1987), as the "vocabulary problem" or the "term mismatch problem" and is a consequence of *synonymy* in language. Currently, in order to deal with synonymy, the most skilled search users need to infer the words that may appear on their relevant documents and try different query variations using equivalent terms and expressions.

A number of solutions to the "term-mismatch" and the ambiguity problems have been reported in the literature since the late 80's. One of the ultimate motivations and long-term goal of many of such developments, including the one presented in this work, is to evolve retrieval technologies from lexical matching towards semantic matching, that is, being able to retrieve documents that do

not necessarily include the query terms but solve the information need.

One of the first solutions that were proposed under this line of thought was *Latent Semantic Indexing* (Deerwester, Dumais, Landauer, Furnas, & Harshman, 1990) (LSI). They proposed a vectorial representation of words and documents and used linear algebra to create a spatial representation in which documents with similar terms appear close to each other. As LSI was criticized for lacking a theoretical foundation, Hofmann (1999) proposed a probabilistic version of LSI, namely *Probabilistic Latent Semantic Indexing* (PLSI). PLSI and all subsequent methods like *Latent Dirichlet Allocation* (Blei, Ng, & Jordan, 2003) (LDA), work under the assumption that a document can be modeled as a mixture of hidden topics, and that those topics can be modeled as probability distributions over words. Then, some sort of parameter estimation algorithm (e.g. maximum likelihood estimation) is applied to the observed data to learn the parameters of the hidden topics. Authors like Griffiths and Steyvers have characterized this family of works as *Probabilistic Topic Models* (Griffiths, Steyvers, & Tenenbaum, 2007).

The idea of modeling collections based on its topics and representing each topic as a probability distribution of terms is central to state of the art approaches; besides, it provides additional benefits versus spatial representations. Also, it has been shown to be a good idea; by using probabilistic topic modeling methods it is possible to improve access to information in collections in different application scenarios, such as retrieval (R. M. Li, Kaptein, Hiemstra, & Kamps, 2008), (Wei & Croft, 2006), or collection browsing (Blei & Lafferty, 2007). So, on the basis of such evidence, we may confidently state that creating a topic model of the collection is a necessary step towards more adaptive search engines and applications. However, due to its high computational complexity the applicability of probabilistic topic modeling methods remains limited on large corpus.

Therefore, in the aim of making semantic modeling feasible on large-scale collections, in this work we propose the Query-Based Topic Modeling framework (QTM), an alternative topic modeling method based on a simplified representation of topics as freely overlapping sets or clusters of semantically similar documents. By simplifying the notion of topic, the problem of Probabilistic Topic Modeling can be reformulated as one of *"Discrete Topic Modeling"* and essentially transforming it into an overlapping clustering problem, thus making possible to take advantage of a broad array of clustering techniques existing in the literature.

In this regard, a fairly recent innovation has been found to be a very natural match for the goals of this research on virtue of its information-theoretic nature and algorithmic properties. The Co-Clustering method, proposed by Dhillon et. al (2003) is a distributional clustering algorithm that simultaneously clusters data over a two-dimensional matrix while maximizing the preserved mutual information between the original and the clustered data. In addition, the Co-Clustering algorithm also exhibits great scalability and its computational complexity is not polynomial with respect to the input size, as it happens to be the case in LDA. Co-Clustering has been used successfully to process very large collections (Puppin, Silvestri, & Laforenza, 2006) and parallel implementations exist (Papadimitriou & Sun, 2008).

However, when approaching the clustering problem from the collection modeling perspective we found that the evaluation of the quality of the models was still a challenging task. Validation of probabilistic topic models was done typically by user studies, which are costly and hard to reproduce (Chang, Boyd-Graber, Gerrish, Wang, &

Blei, 2009). On the other hand, the metrics used to validate traditional, non-overlapping, hard clusters are not well suited to validate an overlapping and potentially incomplete clustering (Wu, Xiong, & Chen, 2009), (Denoeud & Guénoche, 2006).

Therefore, we have defined a novel set of metrics inspired on the notion of "semantic coherence" interpreted as the probability of randomly sampling two documents from the same topic or class after having randomly selected a cluster. The proposed metrics use multi-labeled corpora to measure the quality of overlapping and incomplete topic models in an inexpensive and repeatable way.

The key idea behind our approach to collection modeling is the assumption of the existence of a "golden" set of highly informative queries, defined as the "topical-queries", such that when co-clustered along with the documents, they result in a model with maximum semantic coherence. We provide experimental evidence to show that a set of queries generated and selected using simple information-theoretic heuristics are superior to the collection vocabulary in terms of the semantic coherence of the resulting clusters. For that reason, we place a special emphasis on the analysis of the heuristics that can be used to generate, evaluate, and select this set of "topical-queries", and efficiently build collection models.

The proposed Query-Based Topic Modeling (QTM) framework is a scalable, information-theoretic, discrete topic modeling method that uses search queries to incorporate semantic information into the modeling process. Generally speaking, the QTM method comprises two phases. In the first phase, the collection is processed and heuristics are used to generate and select a set of candidate topical queries. Then, using the query-vector document model, the queries and documents are co-clustered. The resulting clusters can be used to produce two kinds of collection models: a) non-overlapping models, that are essentially "hard" document clusters and b) overlapping topic models, similar to those produced with LDA, that rely on an estimation of document-topic probabilities.

In terms of model quality, we will also show experimentally that using the QTM approach is possible to produce models of comparable quality to those produced by state of the art methods such as LDA. However, in contrast to other topic modeling methods, the QTM framework can produce the models with very high scalability through parallel execution, as QTM was designed using the Map-Reduce architectural style on each of its components.

BACKGROUND: IDENTIFYING AND MODELING TOPICS IN COLLECTIONS

Broadly speaking, the abstract problem that concerns us is that of identifying the latent topic structure of a document collection in such a way that may be used to solve other computational problems such as classification, filtering, translation or retrieval.

The methods greatly vary in their computational strategy that depends on the initial assumptions of what a topic is how topics relate to documents and how topics relate to each other. However, all the referred methods, including ours, share the baseline assumption that corpus statistics contain enough information to produce useful results without requirements of expert knowledge.

The former requirement mostly complies with the "statistical semantics" paradigm, defined by G. Furnas et. al (1984) as the study of "how the statistical patterns of human word usage can be used to figure out what people mean, at least to a level sufficient for information access". In contrast to lexicon approaches, the statistical semantics philosophy pushes towards the development of fully automated cross-language corpus-based algorithms.

Latent Semantic Indexing

The Latent Semantic Indexing (LSI) method was presented in (Dumais, Furnas, Landauer, Deerwester, & Harshman, 1988), (Deerwester et al., 1990), (Berry, Dumais, & O'Brien, 1995) as a linear algebra based solution to the "term mismatch" problem in retrieval. The LSI method leverages the term co-occurrence in the term-document matrix and applies Singular Value Decomposition in order to create a reduced matrix, in which semantically related documents appear closer. This reduced matrix is usually referred as the *latent semantic space*.

The method begins by creating a term-document matrix A of i terms by j documents, in which each $a(i,j)$ cell contains the frequency of term i in document j. The SVD factorization of A may be expressed as: $A=U\cdot\Sigma\cdot V^t$. For the sake of efficiency, the SVD is usually truncated to a k number of dimensions. The values of Σ (singular values) are sorted by magnitude and the top k are used as the latent semantic representation of A, all other values are set to 0. After defining k the top k columns in a new matrix U_k are kept and the top k rows in the matrix V^t. Terms may be compared by computing the inner product of the rows in U_k and documents may be compared comparing the columns in V^t_k.

Some concerns regarding the LSI method are the lack of theoretical foundations (Blei et al., 2003), (Hofmann, 1999) and the computational costs involved in the SVD computation, which is in the order of $O(N^2k^3)$ where N is the number of documents in a collection and k the number of terms, in addition, the LSI computations cannot be optimized by using inverted indexes, which are the base of current web retrieval systems.

In conclusion, the LSI technique is not well suited to be applied on large web collections, although it has been used to semantically cluster the top result pages in order to improve user interface. However, the LSI method provided strong evidence towards the development of semantic capabilities using frequency based metrics.

Probabilistic Topic Modeling

In the following years Hofmann (1999) proposed a probabilistic version of LSI, namely *Probabilistic Latent Semantic Indexing* (PLSI). PLSI and all the methods that followed its approach work under the assumption that a document can be modeled as mixture of a number of hidden topics, and that those topics can be represented as probability distributions over words. Then, some sort of parameter estimation algorithm is applied to the observed data to estimate the parameters of the hidden topics. In the case of PLSI, the kind of estimation performed is a maximum likelihood estimation (MLE).

Later on, Blei et. al (2003) proposed the *Latent Dirichlet Allocation* (LDA) which was shown to be a generalization of PLSI by Girolami and Kabán (2003). The key innovation in LDA was the introduction of fully generative semantics into the model formulation and thus allowing the problem to be treated by Markov Chain Monte Carlo (MCMC) methods such as Gibbs sampling. In LDA each topic is represented as a multinomial distribution over words and each document is represented as a random mixture of topics, sampled from a Dirichlet distribution. In order to learn the model a topic mixture is sampled from a Dirichlet distribution, then a topic is sampled from this distribution and samples a word from that topic. The process is repeated for every word of every document until the full collection is generated. It is assumed that the words are generated based on the mixture of topic proportions. The reported complexity of the LDA procedure using variational inference is on the order of $O(N^2k)$.

The generative modeling approach introduced by LDA quickly became very popular and several models have been based on it. In these new models, topics are "first-class citizens" because they are now explicitly represented using a probability distribution and the task is not only to estimate its parameters, but also to learn the correlations between topics or to learn a structure that may be hierarchical, such as in hLDA (Blei, Gri, Jordan, & Tenenbaum, 2004) and non-parametric. Also of particular interest is in *Pachinko Allocation* (W. Li & McCallum, 2006) PAM, which can learn arbitrary topic correlations using a Directed Acyclical Graph. The PAM model also presents algorithmic improvements into the sampling procedure by challenging the assumption of the randomness of the mixing proportions and extending the topic representation schema.

Previously discussed models extract latent classes or aspects from the documents, however the number of classes is usually predefined and the resulting topic structure is a predefined parameter of the system, so that neither the nature of the underlying topic structure nor their hierarchical or semantic proximity relations were major concerns. Recently Blei & Lafferty (2007) applied variants of the LDA model to obtain correlated topic models of the *Science* magazine archives, and Griffiths and Steyvers (2004) applied a similar method to the PNAS database. In both cases, they usually predefine a fixed number of topics (say 100), so if they run the analysis truncating the database in time, they could analyze the relative topic "hotness" in time.

Distributional Clustering

The concept of distributional clustering was first introduced by Pereira et. al (1993) and was motivated by the word-sense disambiguation problem. The goal of the original algorithm proposed was to cluster words depending on their different "senses". One of the key ideas that define this family of methods was to represent each individual to cluster as a conditional probability distribution and then, assign each individual to the most likely cluster using existing information-theoretic distribution similarity measures such as the Kullback-Leibler divergence (Cover & Thomas, 1991). Conceptually, an important contribution of distributional clustering algorithms is that they replace the usage of arbitrary distance or similarity functions in favor of more objective information preservation criteria.

The Information Bottleneck (IB) family of methods counts among the best-known distributional clustering algorithms. Tishby, et. al (1999) generalized the original distributional clustering problem presented in (Pereira et al., 1993) as the problem of self-organizing the members of a set X, based on the similarity of their conditional distributions over the members of another set, namely $p(y|x)$. That is, every element $x_i \in X$ is represented by a vector of real numbers that contains the conditional probability distribution of x_i over another random variable Y that is $x_i = \{ p(y_1|x_i), p(y_2|x_i) \dots p(y_i|x_i)\}$

So, they reformulated the distributional clustering problem as a compression problem of finding the relevant information that a signal X provides about another signal Y. In simpler terms, and considering the document-clustering problem, the IB method finds a partition of the documents that preserves as much as possible the mutual information about the words, each document represented by a conditional probability distribution over the words of the collection. The authors found that the IB problem had an exact analytical solution, and proposed a greedy, locally optimal, agglomerative clustering algorithm, namely the *Agglomerative Information Bottleneck*, (aIB)(Slonim & Tishby, 1999). The aIB method had the advantage of being non-parametric with respect of the number of clusters but it came at very high computational cost, specifically its time complexity was in the order of $O(|X^3|)$. Such high complexity of the aIB was due to the fact that it required pair-wise comparisons between elements in order to perform the best possible merge at every step.

Thus, in later works, Slonim et. al (2002) presented a remarkably more efficient algorithm, the *Sequential Information Bottleneck* (sIB) and showed that it outperformed aIB in both clustering

performance and computational complexity. In contrast to aIB, the sIB method required a number of clusters to be found and then starting from an initial random partition, at each step one element was re-assigned to the best possible cluster until no further improvements were possible.

Finally, with respect to the document clustering application, the same authors proposed the *Double Information Bottleneck* method (dIB) (Slonim & Tishby, 2000). Notably, the dIB algorithm introduced the idea of clustering both dimensions X and Y to improve the overall result. In the dIB method, first the words Y are clustered and a set of word clusters $Y*$ that preserve information about the documents is found. Then, documents were clustered in relation to the discovered word clusters. A very relevant finding of this work is that by clustering the two dimensions the results improved and the dimensionality of the problem could be reduced. The dIB method however was based on aIB and thus it suffered from the same performance drawbacks.

Co-Clustering

The authors of the dIB method described above were aware that a natural generalization of their work consisted of achieving a simultaneous compression of both dimensions of the co-ocurrence matrix, however, such generalization was proposed by Dhillon, et. al. (2003) although under slightly different settings. The Co-Clustering algorithm benefited from a fresh perspective and approached the problem of simultaneously clustering rows and columns from an input matrix representing the joint probability distribution of the variables $p(X,Y)$ while maximizing the preserved mutual information (or minimizing the mutual information loss) along both dimensions.

In contrast to the IB methods, the Co-Clustering algorithm required the number of rows and column clusters to be specified beforehand. By doing so, it decoupled the clustering problem from the model selection problem and thus it created opportunities for achieving greater efficiency than preceding techniques. In that sense, co-clustering avoided the double-optimization issue present in IB methods and worked towards optimizing a unique global criteria, defined as the minimum loss of mutual information between the original joint probability distribution $p(X, Y)$ and the joint probability distribution of the clustered variables $p(X^*, Y^*)$ So, the optimal co-clustering solution is the one that minimizes $I(X, Y) - I(X^*, Y^*)$. The co-clustering algorithm is guaranteed to converge to a local minimum after a fixed number of steps.

The co-clustering algorithm reassigns a row and a column to a different cluster on each step. However, instead of performing element-to-element comparisons, it compares the evaluated element against the cluster-prototypes, which can be thought of as "centroids" in the context of k-means. As a matter of fact, the ability of algorithms such as k-means or co-clustering that only require to perform comparisons against a cluster representative, is a defining feature to achieve good scalability. The computational complexity of co-clustering is given by $O(n_z \cdot \tau \cdot (k+l))$, where n_z is the number of non-zeros in the joint distribution $p(X, Y)$; τ is the number of iterations; k and l the number of row and column clusters respectively.

Recently, alternative versions of the co-clustering algorithm have been proposed in order to produce soft-clusters. Among the methods that address such problem we can name the Bayesian Co-Clustering (Shan & Banerjee, 2008) and the Latent Dirichlet Bayesian Co-Clustering method (Wang, Domeniconi, & Laskey, 2009).

Discussion

Probabilistic topic models are a flexible and theoretically sound approach to learn topics in collections, however in relation to our area of concern which is (very) large scale collection analysis, the main limitation of the approach is the computational complexity as it is heavily dependent on the number of topics in the model.

Although there have been proposals on how to improve the efficiency of the sampling (Porteous et al., 2008) or performing distributed inference (Newman, Asuncion, Smyth, & Welling, 2007), achieving greater scalability for very large corpora seems to imply a trade-offs in the quality of the estimations by limiting the number of topics below the optimal values and reducing the sampling iterations before the convergence zone. So, we conclude that there exists a need for an alternative approach to the general topic-modeling problem, designed to work well in the scenarios where the size of the collection is in the order of billions of documents of variable length and the number of topics is unknown and presumably very large.

PROBLEM STATEMENT

Preliminary definitions

- Let $D=\{d_1, d_2 ... d_n\}$ be the document corpus of size N,
- Let $W=\{w_1, w_2 ... w_M\}$ the vocabulary of all terms in the corpus and Q be the set of all boolean queries that may be defined over the vocabulary W that will match at least one document from D. Also, given that each $w_i \in W$ is a query itself, then $W \subset Q$.
- Let $L(d_i) = \{l_{i1}, l_{i2} ... l_{ik}\}$ be the set of topic labels assigned to document by a human judge. We say that two documents, are *semantically similar* they have at least one label in common, that is, if $\{L(d_1) \cap L(d_2)\} \neq \emptyset$.
- A *topic* is $T_i \subset D$ is defined as a *set of documents*. From the practical point of view, it is desirable but not essential, that such sets are comprised of semantically similar documents in accordance to human judgement.
- A *topical-query* denoted by $q_i \in Q^*$, $Q^* \subset Q$ is a query that retrieves semantically similar documents, therefore, according to

previous definition is a query that retrieves documents containing the same labels.

Discrete Topic Modeling Task

We define the general *discrete topic modeling task* (DTM) as the problem of finding a clustering of D in K clusters: $U=\{u_1,...,u_K\}$ with maximum semantic coherence with respect to human judgment. As naturally occurring, topics may overlap across documents and a single document may belong to several topics, so, the clusters in U that model the "real" topics are also allowed to overlap each other. For the purposes of this work, semantic coherence is defined as the harmonic mean of two quantities:

- The probability of randomly selecting two documents from the same topic taken from a randomly sampled cluster, denoted by P_{PM}.
- The probability that a randomly selected document is included in at least one cluster, denoted by R_U.

Which can be expressed as:

$$F_o(U) = \frac{2P_{PM}R_U}{P_{PM} + R_U} \qquad (1)$$

The metric described in formula (1) is a form of the well-known F-score and as such, it accounts both for the completeness and for the coherence of the clustering under consideration. As simple as it may sound, the computation of the "coherence" probabilities is not trivial and a more detailed discussion will be offered. However, the discrete topic modeling task along with the semantic coherence metric serve as the foundations to compare probabilistic topic modeling approaches with alternative soft-clustering and overlapping clustering algorithms such as the one presented in this work.

Query-Based Topic Modeling Task

The Query-Based Topic Modeling (QTM) problem is a particular instance of the Discrete Topic Modeling task and it can be defined as follows: Given a text document collection represented as a query-document co-occurrence matrix, where the rows of the matrix can be any subset of Q, find:

1. A set of topical queries Q^* that maximizes the coherence of the clustering
2. A semantically coherent clustering of D in K potentially overlapping clusters,

Notice that in this case the rows of the matrix can be the vocabulary W (given that $W \subset Q$) or any other query set that contains information about the documents. For instance, in Puppin et. al (2006) a set of popular search queries from a search engine has been selected, then the set was co-clustered along with documents to group together the documents that will likely be retrieved by similar queries.

From the collection modeling perspective, we acknowledge that both the vocabulary and a set of popular search queries are subsets of Q that define all the valid queries that could be constructed using the vocabulary terms. However, it is presumable that not every query set is equally useful for the purpose of modeling the collection topics. For instance, speaking of the extreme cases, if the query set is very small and does not retrieve all the documents of the collection, the missing documents will result in a recall penalization. On the other extreme, is a very large subset of Q is selected, it will quickly become unpractical to process.

So, the fundamental problem of QTM could be summarized as that of finding a set of topical queries Q^* and use it to build a semantically coherent clustering of D efficiently using the computational resources at hand. As we will show later, the resource constraints could play a role in the different QTM strategies used.

Figure 1. Map/Reduce version of the topic identification algorithm

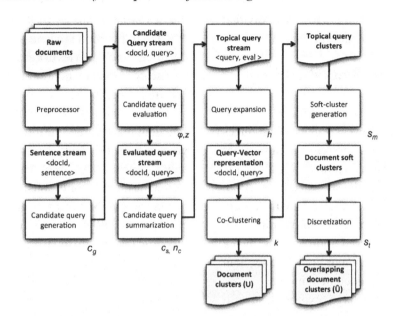

THE QUERY-BASED TOPIC MODELING FRAMEWORK

In this section we describe the Query-Based Topic Modeling (QTM) framework, an information-theoretic approach to build semantic models of large text collections. In contrast to Probabilistic Topic Modeling (PTM) methods like LDA, QTM models topics as overlapping sets of semantically similar documents associated to "topical-queries". A simpler notion of topic drives computational advantages, for instance, in QTM a mixture of topic probabilities is estimated for each document, however, the estimation of term-topic probabilities is not performed at all. In addition, the QTM framework follows the map/reduce style of design, relying as much as possible in stream-oriented operations, which significantly decreases the amount of memory required to run the algorithm and allows operations to be performed in parallel.

The QTM Process

The query-based topic modeling framework (QTM) illustrated in figure 1 summarizes our approach to collection semantic modeling. Given a raw document collection, the QTM process can generate two kinds of models. The simplest is a traditional clustering, with non-overlapping partitions where every document is guaranteed to belong to exactly one partition. The second type of model is an overlapping clustering, where a document may belong to zero or more partitions. Depending on the type of model that is to be generated the process could take 3 to 4 phases, described as follows.

Pre-Processing

The pre-processing phase takes the raw documents of the corpus. The first process that is performed is the document indexation into an inverted index. Stop-words were not removed during the indexing process, as they are important to the evaluation. The second operation in pre-processing involves the tokenization of the documents to create a stream of sentences. Each document is divided into sentences and a new line is produced for each.

Candidate Query Generation

The candidate query generator takes as input the sentence stream and for every sentence it produces candidate queries. Thus, implicitly assuming that the topics discussed in a document will affect the term co-occurrences at the sentence level. Also, it implies that the generated queries will capture some of the influence of lexical proximity. As a consequence, the proposed approach assumes a "bag-of-sentences" document model rather than a pure "bag-of-words" document model.

In this regard, we have explored several methods to generate candidate queries, such as creating term combinations and computing the sentence n-grams. One method that has produced good results is based on a technique developed by Theobald et. al (2008). Interestingly, the technique was designed as a method to find duplicated documents by generating its semantic signatures or spot-sigs. For the purposes of this work, the SpotSigs candidate generation method consists on splitting the sentences using a short list of stop-words or function words as markers or separators and extracting the resulting sets of contiguous remaining words as candidates. In our final method, we first split the list using the stop-words, and then generate additional 2-element combinations of the resulting units and keep all the queries that contain 2, 3 and 4 words. In our implementation, resulting units longer than 4 words were splitted into shorter units of 2 or 3 words.

Candidate Query Evaluation using Semantic Force

In general, the evaluator component could be any program that reads the candidate query stream, line by line, evaluates each query and writes to the evaluated query stream. The evaluation results are used to rank and select a subset of the candidate queries in latter phases of the process, thus, the evaluation function is a heuristic that should help deciding which queries to keep and which queries to discard. Good evaluation functions should be "cheap" to compute.

In the course of this research, we have explored functions that leverage the information-theoretical properties of the query terms to infer properties about the retrieved documents *without* actually retrieving them, by only considering the hit counts of some alterations of the original query. The discussed approach based on the usage of information theoretic function to measure semantic force was initially presented in Ramirez & Brena (2009). Some of the explored semantic force functions are:

Kullback-Lleibler Divergence. Let q_i be a Boolean query defined over a set of k words of the vocabulary and $W(q_i)$ the set of its terms, $W(q_i) = \{w_1, w_2, ..., w_k\}$. Now, we define two events for the experiment of selecting a random document of the corpus.

Let y be the event of observing "all" the terms of the set $W(q_i)$. So, its probability $P(y)$ would be computed as the probability of selecting a document retrieved by a conjunctive query with all the terms of $W(q_i)$, like $a_i = \{w_1 \wedge w_2 .. \wedge w_k\}$.

As x and y are not independent events, we may notice that there exist the conditional event of observing *all* the query terms after having observed *any* of them with probability distribution $P(Y|x)$ So, we propose to compute the Kullback-Leibler divergence (Cover & Thomas, 1991) or *information gain* over this two events as follows:

$$K(P(Y \mid x) \parallel P(Y)) = \sum_{y_j \in Y} p(y_j \mid x) log \frac{p(y_j \mid x)}{p(y_j)} \quad (2)$$

Where $P(Y)$ is the probability distribution defined over the discrete random variable $Y = \{y, \neg y\}$. And $p(y_j)$ is the individual probability value for the event y_j as defined by the distribution $P(Y)$.

In analogous way, $P(Y|x)$ is a discrete probability distribution that assigns probability values $p(y_j|x)$ to the conditional events $\{y \wedge x, \neg y \wedge x\}$. The KL-divergence can be directly interpreted as how much more certain we are about the fact that our randomly selected document will contain all the words of the query (y), given that it has any of them (x).

Query mutual information (MI). This function is similar in nature to the described in eq. 2 as it uses the mentioned events $P(Y)$ to denote the probability of occurrence of all the terms of the query and and $P(x)$ to denote the probability of any of them. The mutual information is a measure of the dependence of both quantities and is also interpreted as the expected information gain.

$$QMI(X,Y) = \sum_{x_i \in X} p(x_i) KL(P(Y \mid x_i) \| P(Y))$$

(3)

As it can be observed, the mutual information function holds a strong relation to the presented KL divergence function but it incorporates more clearly the frequency of the terms of the query by using $P(X)$.

Query Frequency (QF). For a given query q_i the frequency of a query is simply defined as the number of documents that match q_i.

In some of the presented functions and evaluation could require sending queries to an index-server. Depending on the size of the collection, the index may be located on a single machine, distributed to the nodes in the map/reduce cluster or accessed remotely from an index-serving cluster. Each deployment has different implications that need to be further researched.

Candidate Query Summarization

The summarization phase consist in determining the final query set of topical queries to be included into the model. Among the many candidate query selection strategies are possible we have analyzed two:

- **By-document selection.** Consists on selecting the maximum s_c evaluated queries of each document, where $s_c > 0$. Then duplicates are removed. This method guarantees that every document will be retrieved by at least one query in the final topical query set.
- **Global selection.** Consists on selecting the maximum s_c evaluated queries of any document. This method doesn't guarantee that every document is retrieved by a query in the final topical query set, however it can include queries with higher evaluations than the previously described method.

Query Expansion and Co-Clustering

At the beginning of this phase, we have a set of topical-queries that ideally should capture most of the semantic information of the collection. As this set is too large to be useful for human analysis, queries and documents should be clustered to obtain a smaller number of broader topics. Among several algorithms co-clustering, proposed by Dillon, et. al. (2003) turned out to be a natural match to the QTM problem given that: a) we need to cluster bi-dimensional data, b) it is guided by information-theoretic principles and b) it has been shown to be scalable.

However, before running the co-clustering algorithm, the collection has to be represented as a contingency matrix where each row is a query q_i and each column a document d_j. So, we transformed our collection representation using a variant of the Query-Vector document model (QV), originally proposed by Puppin and Silvestri (2006). In the QV document model, each document is represented as a weighted vector of queries that retrieve it. Then those query-document vectors are used to create a contingency matrix that can be interpreted as a joint probability distribution of documents and queries.

It is important to notice that in Puppin's original model, the weights of the vector terms representing d_j were assigned based on the rank of the document d_j for each query q_i, whereas in our case an equal weight was assigned to every document ranked below a specified cut value h. We decided to assign an equal weight to each retrieved document in order to better control the effects of the ranking function on the final model. Documents are ranked using the Apache Lucene's default scoring function, which essentially uses the *tf-idf* term weighting over a vector-space document model. We will show experimentally that our strategy preserves enough information to build the model, however, the effects of the ranking function and its potential to provide additional value by incorporating information such as linkage or term prominence is a problem that remains to be explored.

Finally, in our implementation, the co-clustering algorithm requires a single parameter k, to specify the number of row (queries) and column (document) clusters to be produced. If the application under consideration can work using non-overlapping partitions, the results of this phase can be considered the final output of the QTM process.

Soft-Clustering Generation and Discretization

The final steps of QTM process deal with the problem of generating an overlapping partition of the document collection taking as input the non-overlapping query and document partitions generated by the co-clustering algorithm. The resulting overlapping partition of the corpus, identified by $\hat{U}$ will be considered the final representation of the topic structure.

In general, the strategy employed to generate the overlapping clusters is to first to generate a "soft" clustering based on an estimation of docu-

ment-topic probabilities and then discretize the document-topic probabilities to create "hard" document-topic associations using a threshold value s_t.

The probability of the document d_j belonging to a given topic $\hat{U}m$ is estimated by the number of queries matching d_j that belong to query cluster Q_m divided by the total number of queries that match d_j.

$$p(d_j \in \hat{U}_m) = \frac{\sum_i (q_{ij} \in Q_m)}{\sum_i q_{ij}} \qquad (4)$$

Where $\{q_{1j}, q_{2j} \ldots q_{nj}\}$ is the list of queries that match document d_j.

PROBABILISTIC METRICS FOR TOPIC MODEL EVALUATION

Introduction and Notation

Evaluating the performance of techniques such as LDA, LSI or any other unsupervised modeling algorithm including QTM is a non-trivial problem, especially when it comes to drawing strong conclusions about the quality of the models. In this chapter we present a novel set of metrics that can be used to perform external validation of the semantic coherence of topic modeling and soft clustering methods using multi-labeled corpora such as Reuters-21578 or 20-Newsgroups.

The proposed topic modeling validation approach is based on transforming the topic model under analysis into a "hard" overlapping partition by discretizing the "soft" document-topic associations. The proposed metrics, presented in detail by Ramirez, et. al, (2010) are based on alternative interpretations of widely accepted concepts such as "precision" and "recall". In addition, the presented validation approach has among its advantages:

1. An intuitive and explicit probabilistic interpretation.
2. Applicability to validate overlapping and incomplete partitions.

After the soft-clustering solution of a multi-labeled corpus is discretized to obtain a corresponding hard clustering, the problem to be faced with consists of correctly evaluating the quality of the resulting overlapping partitions. Let us first introduce the terminology and the notation that will be used in the rest of the paper. Every "hard-clustering" problem applied to a multi labeled document corpus involves the following elements:

- A dataset $D=\{d_1, d_2..d_n\}$ consisting of n documents;
- a partition of D in K clusters: $U =\{u_1, ... u_K\}$;
- a partition of D in S classes: $C =\{c_1, ... c_S\}$;.

Most of the existing validation metrics (Wu et al., 2009) can be expressed in terms of a $|U|\times|C|$ contingency (Table 1) where the content of each cell n_{ij} represents the number of documents belonging to cluster u_i and class c_j.

In the special case where clusters do not overlap and the document corpus is uni-labeled, the following properties hold:

1. $\bigcap_0^K u_i = D$
2. $u_i \cap u_j = \varnothing \ \forall i, j=1,...,K$ with $i \neq j$: there is no "overlap" between the elements of the cluster partition;

3. $c_i \cap c_j = \varnothing \ \forall i, j = 1, ..., S$ with $i \neq j$: there is no "overlap" between the elements of the class partition.

In this work we consider the case where the aforementioned properties cannot be assumed to hold. Indeed, in a realistic setting:

- the tresholding procedure used to move from soft to hard clustering, may result in some documents being unassigned;
- a document can be assigned to more than one cluster;
- the document corpus is multi-label and thus in principle every document can be assigned to one or more classes.

Metrics for Overlapping Partitions

As previously stated, our goal is to measure the semantic coherence of an overlapping clustering, by computing the harmonic mean of two probabilities: a) The probability of randomly selecting two documents from the same topic taken from a randomly sampled cluster, denoted by P_{PM}, and, b) the probability that a randomly selected document is included in at least one cluster, denoted by R_U.

Partial Class Match Precision (P_{PM})

The Partial Class Match Precision (P_{PM}) measures the probability of randomly selecting two documents from the same class taken from a randomly sampled cluster and is inspired on the

Table 1. Cluster-class contingency matrix

		Classes				
		c_1	c_2	...	c_s	Σ
	u_1	n_{11}	$n_{1,2}$	...	n_{1s}	n_{1*}
Cluster	u_2	n_{21}	$n_{2,2}$	...	n_{2s}	n_{2*}
	...	...	...	...	...	...
	u_k	n_{k1}	n_{k2}	...	n_{ks}	n_{k*}
	Σ	n_{*1}	n_{*2}	...	n_{*s}	n_{**}

notion of precision utilized in the IR field. The metric requires first randomly sampling a cluster and then randomly sampling two documents from the sampled cluster. In order to clearly differentiate both random events, we use $\tilde{S}_{c*}$ to denote the event of selecting two documents belonging to the same class sampled from a given cluster. Formally, the P_{PM} metric is defined as follows:

$$P_{PM} = P(\tilde{S}_{c*}) = \sum_i P(\tilde{S}_{c*} \mid u_i)P(u_i) \qquad (1)$$

Where the prior probability of selecting the cluster u_i is given by $P(u_i) = n_i / n_{**}$.

P_{PM} measures the probability of the event $\tilde{S}_{c*}$, i.e. to sample two documents from the same class, *after* having randomly selected a cluster. However, the computation of each individual $P(\tilde{S}_{c*} \mid u_i)$ needs to be generalized for the case of classes overlapping.

Therefore, we need to add up the probability of selecting two documents from each class comprised within the cluster $P(\tilde{S}_{c*} \mid u_i)$ under the general rule of the addition for non-independent events, that requires discounting the probability of a success in two classes simultaneously. So, each individual $P(\tilde{S}_{c*} \mid u_i)$ would be given by:

$$P(\tilde{S}_{c_*} \mid u_i) = \sum_j P(\tilde{S}_{c_j} \mid u_i) - J(u_i) \qquad (2)$$

Where $J(u_i)$, which represents the probability to sample two elements from two or more classes when selecting documents d_1 and d_2 which belong to cluster u_i, is given by:

$$J(u_i) = \sum_j \sum_{j'>j} P(\{S_{u_i c_j} \cap S_{u_i c_{j'}}\} \mid u_i) \qquad (3)$$

The previous equation requires computing a half-matrix of class overlaps, and then computing the probabilities of selecting two from each "bin".

$$J(u_i) = \sum_j \sum_{j'>j} h(|u_i|, \{S_{u_i c_j} \cap S_{u_i c_{j'}}\}, 2, 2) \qquad (4)$$

This metric is designed to work well with multi-labeled documents corpus. The name *"Partial"* comes from the fact that in a multi-label setting the two randomly sampled elements d_1 and d_2 can be associated with many classes. As long as one of their classes matches we will consider the result to be semantically coherent, thus as success. We consider that this property of the metric is a valuable feature to focus on measuring semantic coherence rather than mere partitions similarity. For instance, there is not a unique way to achieve the maximum evaluation. In fact, we can visualize two solutions that will obtain the maximum evaluation under this setting.

1. Creating one cluster for every class, and assigning all the elements in c_j to u_i, so that $k=|C|$.
2. Creating clusters of elements that share exactly the same class labels.

Before wrapping up, we should notice that the above-presented metric has some problems under very high overlapping conditions; however, in realistic settings we have shown that this does not represent an issue. However, if it were the case, the probabilities can be computed by performing a full enumeration of the sample space or via Monte Carlo simulation.

Recall Metrics

In the IR field the "recall" measure represents the probability that a relevant document is retrieved. Therefore, for the clustering scenarios under consideration, when the completeness of the partition cannot be assumed, it is critical to provide clear ways to measure the completeness of the clustering. Let N_c be the total number of class assignments, given by the sum of the sizes of every class:

$$N_c = \sum_j \left| c_j \right|$$

In overlapping and incomplete clustering we must not to rely on the values of the contingency matrix to compute recall values, given that they can account for duplicates and that they do not consider elements not included in clusters. If we are interested in measuring which classes are better captured by the clustering, then it is straightforward to compute a by-class recall value. We define this "class recall" as the probability that a document d, randomly sampled from the class c_j, is included in any cluster.

$$R(c_j) = P([x \in \cup_i^k u_i] \mid c_j) = \frac{\left| \bigcap_i^k \{u_i \cap c_j\} \right|}{\left| c_j \right|}$$

(5)

In other words, equation (9) means dividing the number of documents of class c_j that were recalled by any cluster u_i by the total number of documents belonging to class c_j. Then, considering that the probability of selecting a class would be given by $P(c_j) = |c_j|/N_c$ it is possible to derive an unconditional expression to measure the recall of the whole clustering.

$$R_U = P(x \in \cup_i^k u_i) = \sum_j P(x \in \cup_i^k u_i \mid c_j) P(c_j)$$

(6)

The probability of selecting any class would be given by $|c_j|/N_c$. So, it can be conveniently expressed as:

$$R_U = \frac{1}{N_c} \sum_j R(c_j) \left| c_j \right|$$

EXPERIMENTAL RESULTS

We will present a quantitative analysis of the QTM framework; the presented evidence will be helpful to gain insights into issues like:

- The effects of the different heuristics and settings in performance, including candidate selection method, and evaluation function,
- Determining how the method stands against other alternatives such as LDA.
- The efficiency of the different strategies in terms of computational resource usage.

Model Description Notation

As previously stated, there are two kinds of QTM models under consideration:

1. Models for non-overlapping partitions denoted by: $U \sim Q_{TM}(c_g, \phi, z, c_s, n_c, k, h)$ and,
2. Models for overlapping partitions denoted by: $\hat{U} \sim Q_{TM}(c_g, \phi, z, c_s, n_c, k, h, s_m, s_t)$,

Where the model parameters are defined as follows:

- c_g: Candidate query generation method.
- φ: Candidate query evaluation function.
- z: Minimum query results allowed.
- c_s: Candidate query selection method.
- n_c: Number of selected queries.
- k: Number of topics to construct.
- h: Number of hits per query to include in the query-vector representation.
- s_m: Soft-clustering generation method.
- s_t: Soft-clustering inclusion threshold

Experimental Framework

As QTM models are subject to a number of choices that determine their performance an experimental framework was built in order to perform a semi-automated exploration of the parameter space. In total we produced 17,984 different models with unique parameters combinations, from which we have created 3 consistent and standardized experiments subsets.

For every combination of the values of parameters $\{c_g, \phi, z, c_s, n_c, h\}$, the value of k was automatically varied within $10, 30, 50, 70, 90$ and 117. In the same way, for overlapping models, the parameter s_t was varied within $0.05, 0.10, 0.15, 0.25, 0.30$ and 0.35. Finally, the value of Fo was averaged for every group of (k, s_c), assuming that the proper selection of k and s_t are more properly implementation concerns.

The main experiment set, herein labeled "ST", which will be referred as contained information of 15,617 models based on the valid combinations of the above described parameters. The goal of this data set is to perform comparative analyses of the main evaluation functions, candidate generation methods and candidate selection methods as well as the measuring the impact of the numeric parameters n_c and h that determine the problem size. The models included in the set have the following properties:

- Two candidate selection methods: Global $c_s = G$, and by document $c_s = D$.
- For $c_s = G$, two generation methods: spotsigs, $c_g = S$ and n-grams $c_s = N$.
- For $c_s = G$, selecting $n_c = \{5000, 15000, 20000, 25000\}$ total queries.
- For $c_s = D$, selecting $n_c = \{1, 3, 5, 10\}$ queries per document.
- By-document candidates were only generated using spotsigs, $c_g = S$
- Three evaluation functions $\phi = \{KL, QMI, QF\}$.
- For the functions KL and QMI, the value of $z = \{2, 10\}$.
- All the models were run for $h = \{10, 100, 500\}$.

Model Efficiency

As stated in our research goals, the resource usage efficiency is an important dimension of quality. So, in order to measure the efficiency of the models we have decided to observe the size of the last phase of the process, which is the co-clustering phase. Certainly it is not the only cost metric, but it is a variable that clearly provides a hint about the size of the problem being solved.

So, we are measuring efficiency as the performance obtained in relation to the size of the co-clustering contingency matrix, measured in number of non-empty cells. The concrete measurement performed is defined as the number of *f-score percentage points obtained by thousand of matrix cells* and it is computed as:

$$E_f(Q_{TM}) = \frac{100 F_o(U)}{1000 C} = \frac{10^5 F_o}{C} \tag{7}$$

Where U is the set of partitions obtained by model Q_{TM} and C is the number of non-empty cells in the co-clustering contingency matrix.

Comparing Candidate Selection Methods

For this analysis we use the ST experiment set and we're interested in comparing two candidate query selection strategies:

- *By-document Candidates* (D). Using $n_c = \{1, 3, 5, 10\}$ queries per document.
- *Global candidates* (G). Using $n_c = \{5000, 15000, 20000, 25000\}$ total queries.

In figure 2 we report the average and maximum performance for the two strategies combined with the type of model generated, using the literal U to represent non-overlapping models and O to represent overlapping models. Given that the setting of n_c is somehow arbitrary, the obtained

Figure 2. Performance by candidate selection method, evaluation function and model type

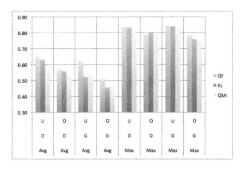

(a) Fo by candidate selection method, evaluation function and model type

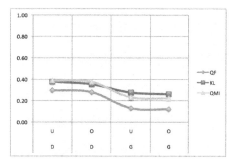

(b) Efficiency by selection method, evaluation function, model type

averages cannot be assumed to represent the efficiency of the method. Also, a different average and maximum was computed for the 3 evaluation functions listed in previous section.

In general, from this experiment we can observe that the by-document selection method $c_s = D$ is in general helpful to obtain better average performance, especially when creating overlapping models, given that:

- For overlapping clusterings, the by-document selection $c_s = D$ showed better performance than $c_s = G$. Average performance of group O,D was: 0.57, 0.56, 0.53, while for group O,G was 0.51, 0.46, 0.47, for functions QF, KL and QMI respectively.
- In terms of maximum performance, both strategies produced very similar models. The apparent differences can be perceived only between U and O groups, where the non-overlapping model (U) is usually superior to the overlapping by 3 to 5 points.

Good performance could be obtained using any of the strategies, however, the average performance and the efficiency results on figure 3 show that it is somehow easier to find a good and more efficient model using by-document selection in combination with F or KL functions. Interestingly, the best function for $c_s = D$ under the current settings was clearly the pure query frequency QF. In terms of efficiency, $c_s = D$ nearly doubles $c_s = G$.

Hits and By-Document Candidates

Previous results are encouraging to analyze a bit deeper the behavior of the by-document selection method, this time in combination with the number of hits selected for the final clustering phase. The results of the experiment are summarized in figures 3 and 4. In order to obtain the previous results, we used dataset ST, now grouping by the value of $h=\{10,100,500\}$.

In figure 3(a) is evident that using $h=10$ hurts the average performance dramatically. On the other hand, increasing h from 100 to 500 does not improve the performance, moreover, it seems slightly reduced and the efficiency drops from the mid 30's to the 10's. The QMI evaluation function exhibits a greater sensitivity to the value of n_c. This is very noticeable for the $h=100$ series. In 3(b) we can observe that QMI could be more efficient than alternatives, however it is usually the case when the performance is the least satisfactory.

The best results were obtained by using the KL and QF functions, however, the difference between KL and QF was usually very small. An important fact is that KL function can and should be tuned in order to obtain good performance whereas F

Figure 3. Performance by hits and number of by-document candidates

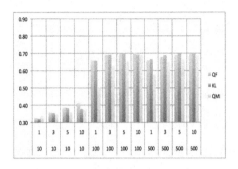

(a) Average Fo by number of by-document candidates and number of hits

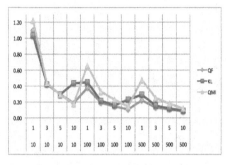

(b) Efficiency by number of by-document candidates and number of hits

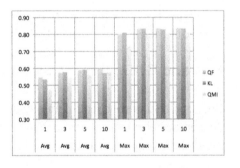

(c) Fo by number of by-document candidates

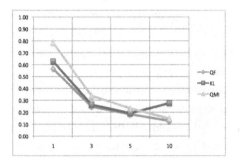

(d) Efficiency by number of candidates per document

Figure 4. Performance by number of global candidates

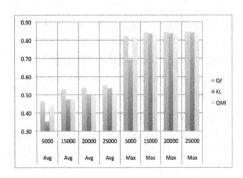

(a) Fo by number of global candidates and evaluation function

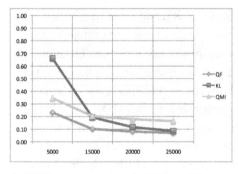

(b) Efficiency by number of global candidates and evaluation function

does not require any parameterization. This factor should be properly weighted when selecting a candidate query evaluation function. Regarding the setting of h, the previous experiments clearly indicate that it should be increased gradually until no performance benefits are observed.

Figures 3(a) and 3(c) aim to answer the question of how many candidates per document should be selected. From the results we can notice that increasing the number of candidates does not substantially result on a performance increase but it does result in a notorious efficiency decrease going from $(0.57, 0.63, 0.79)$ to $(0.18, 0.19, 0.23)$ when increasing from 1 to 5. So, the conclusion is to keep as small as possible, especially when using QF or KL.

Number of Global Candidates

Although it has been shown that by-document candidate is a more elegant option in terms of performance versus efficiency trade-off, it requires more careful tuning of the n_c parameter and evaluation function. So, the global candidate selection strategy is still worth analyzing, as it is simpler to implement and tune.

In figure 4(a) we can observe how by gradually increasing the number of global candidates the performance is improved until adding more candidates results in no-improvement, which happens

around $n_c = 20,000$. On the other hand, it is also worth to notice that the KL function is the only one that appears to be more sensitive to the lack of information, as it dramatically underperform the alternatives when $n_c = 5,000$.

Alternative Candidate Query Generation Methods

In this section we are concerned with analyzing alternative query generation methods. We are interested in comparing the spotsigs ($c_g=S$), n-grams ($c_g=N$) and two of its subsets, namely: Unigrams ($c_g=U$) and Bigrams ($c_g=B$) The rest of inclusion criteria were:

- The evaluation function for all the cases was $\varphi=QF$.
- Candidate selection was $c_s=G$ for all the cases.
- Number of selected queries was $n_c = \{5000, 15000, 20000, 25000\}$ total queries.
- All the models were run for $h=\{10, 100\}$.

All the performance results of this section were evaluated using the frequency function.

Figure 5. Performance by model type and query generation method

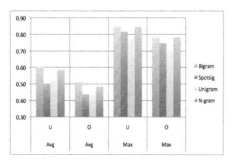

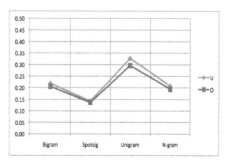

(a) Fo by model type and candidate query generation method

(b) Efficiency by model type and candidate query generation method

Performance by Model Type and Query Generation Method

Figure 5(a) shows average performance and efficiency of the models grouped by model type and candidate generation method. The most interesting result of this set is that Bigrams perform better on average than n-grams, from which they are a subset. So, the inclusion of the Unigrams (the most frequent words) does not add value to the model, moreover, it can decrease it. Notice that the usage of Unigrams makes the model comparable to a traditional term-by-document clustering algorithm. The performance of the SpotSigs heuristic is lower on average although it is possible to find good models.

This experiment supports a key conclusion of this work: *selecting a good set of candidate queries is important to create good models and is better than selecting only the vocabulary (unigrams) of the collection.* From the theoretical standpoint, the result clearly shows how different subset of queries, produced by different rules can contain different amounts of semantic information. This fact contrasts with pure term-by-document clustering approaches that do not provide a mechanism to leverage the term proximity or sentence co-occurrence information.

Candidate Generation Method and Number of Selected Candidates

A more detailed analysis on the effects of the candidate generation method together with the number of global candidates is shown on figure 6. Two key facts can be observed from charts:

- Spotsigs perform dramatically bad if n_c is low.
- Performance of Bigrams is consistently better than N-Grams as n_c increases.
- Performance of Unigrams drops sharply after increasing the number of selected candidates to 25,000, which suggests that the inclusion of unfrequent terms is the cause of the performance penalty for $c_g=U$, $c_g=N$.

In summary, the SpotSigs candidate generation method should be avoided particularly if the number of selected candidates is required to remain low. So far, the best global candidate generation heuristic to use in combination with the frequency evaluation function was the use of corpus bigrams. This result suggests that more experimentation is required to determine the performance of several other orders of n-grams in combination with other selection and evaluation heuristics.

Figure 6. Performance by alternative query generation method and number of selected candidates

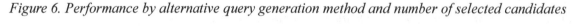

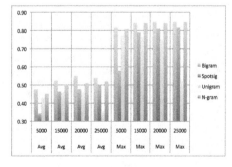

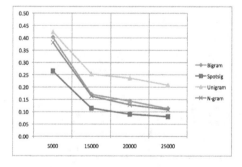

(a) Fo by candidate query generation method and number of selected global candidates

(b) Efficiency by candidate query generation method and number of selected global candidates

Alternative Evaluation Functions

For the following experiments, the experimental setup contained 3,456 instances and was designed to benchmark the previously introduced functions KL, QMI and QF against a hypothetical term-document mutual information function (MI). The experiment was motivated after observing the rather decent performance of QF, which led to the hypotheses that QF works well because it is an approximation of a "wiser" mutual information function. The inclusion criteria for this dataset were:

- Four evaluation functions $\varphi=\{KL,QMI,QF,MI\}$.
- Candidate selection was c_s=G for all the cases.
- Candidate generation was c_g=N for all the cases.
- Number of selected queries was n_c = $\{5000,15000,20000,25000\}$ total queries.
- All the models were run for $h=\{10,100,500\}$

Semantic Force as Query Contribution to MI

One of the most intriguing results was the superior performance of the frequency function in contrast to more complex functions, such as KL and QMI. The evidence led us to revise the underlying working hypotheses and go back to the information-theoretic fundamentals. As a result, the new working hypothesis proposed was that the good performance of the QF function was due to its ability to capture mutual information between queries and documents, resembling the principles of the Information Bottleneck (IB) method.

In the IB method, the documents of the collection are modeled as a probability distribution of terms. In our case, the model was adapted to let each document be represented by its conditional probability distribution of candidate topical-queries, defined by:

$$p(q \mid d) = \frac{n(q \mid d)}{\sum_{q' \in Q} n(q' \mid d)} \qquad (8)$$

Where $n(q|d)$ is the number of occurrences of the query q in the document d. So, we could define a candidate query evaluation criteria based on those queries in Q that contribute the most to the mutual information (MI) about documents, a quantity that may be expressed as follows:

$$MI = I(q; D) = p(q) \sum_{d \in D} p(d \mid q) log \frac{p(d \mid q)}{p(d)} \qquad (9)$$

Where the probabilities in equation (13) were estimated using the full set of generated candidate queries Q_c that includes as many occurrences of every query as the number of times it was generated during the query generation process. So, the probability of selecting a document given a query was given by $p(d|q)=n(q|d)/n(q)$. The prior probability of a query: $p(q) = n(q)/|Q_c|$. The prior probability of randomly selecting a document: $p(d) = \sum_{q' \in Q_c} n(q' \mid d) / |Q_c|$. The denominator $|Q_c|$ represents the total number of candidate queries generated, which may include several occurrences of each query associated to different documents. In our case, $|Q_c|$ was simply the number of lines of the file emitted by the candidate query generator component (1,647,773).

Discussion

The experiments in figures 7(a) and 7(c) resume our findings concerning the relation of function QF and MI. In general, from what we can observe is that QF and MI in general exhibit very similar behavior, with QF being slightly superior to MI for a low value of h and MI being slightly superior to MI in any other case. We believe however that the results were so similar to make any strong conclusion, however, such similarity opens a

Figure 7: Performance of alternative evaluation functions

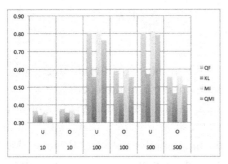

(a) Average Fo by evaluation function, model type and hits

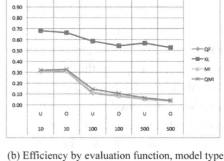

(b) Efficiency by evaluation function, model type and hits

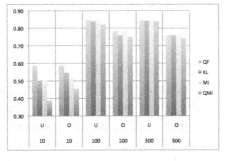

(c) Maximum Fo by evaluation function, model type and hits

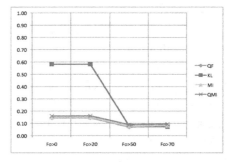

(d) Efficiency at minimum performance level

promising line of improvements over the baseline results. So far, the best model we could produce resulted from the MI function described above.

In terms of efficiency, these last results also serve to establish some basic conclusions. First of all, from 7(b) we can observe that the efficiency of the KL function was substantially higher than alternatives. Such efficiency was not translated to performance, moreover, in figure 7(d) we measured efficiency grouping by performance levels, to our surprise finding that the efficiency of KL drops sharply when the performance requirements raise, resulting in no advantage versus the alternatives.

Overall QTM Performance

Finally, in this section we show some of the best results achieved by the QTM versus LDA. The presented results only attempt to show that in terms of semantic coherence, QTM can produce models of comparable quality than established topic modeling methods like LDA. The best results for non-overlapping and overlapping models are presented in tables 2 and 3 respectively. The best combination of k and s_t found is shown, along with the average for the group. For the LDA method, the best k and threshold s_t was also selected.

From the analysis of the presented tables, some interesting facts can be observed and deserve further consideration. Although, those statements cannot be considered conclusive given that the presented table contains data from multiple data sets. So far, our most relevant findings can be summarized as follows:

- *Model type should determine the candidate selection strategy.* Both of the candidate

Table 2. Best non-overlapping QTM models and LDA performance

Model	k	s_t	z	c_g	eval	c_s	n_c	h	n	Fo(avg)	Fo(max)
1	117	*	2	N	MI	G	20,000	100	6	0.8147	0.8517
2	117	*	2	N	MI	G	25,000	100	6	0.8122	0.8480
3	90	*	2	N	MI	G	25,000	500	6	0.8188	0.8474
4	90	*	2	B	QF	G	25,000	100	6	0.8012	0.8472
5	90	*	2	B	QF	G	20,000	100	6	0.8142	0.8469
6	117	*	10	N	KL	G	10,000	500	6	0.8144	0.8465
7	117	*	2	N	MI	G	20,000	500	6	0.8140	0.8461
8	117	*	2	N	QF	G	25,000	100	6	0.8157	0.8461
9	90	*	2	N	MI	G	15,000	100	6	0.8131	0.8459
10	117	*	2	N	QF	G	20,000	500	6	0.8121	0.8454
LDA	30	0.2	0	*	*	*	*	*	30	0.6711	0.7728

selection strategies proposed can achieve good results. However global-candidate selection performed better when producing non-overlapping models, and by-document candidates resulted more useful to produce overlapping models. Both kinds of models perform well in comparison to LDA in terms of semantic coherence.

- *More queries do not guarantee more performance.* In terms of candidate generation, the usage of bigrams outperformed the unigrams and the extended n-grams set, defined as the union of bigrams and unigrams. The striking finding was that the inclusion of unigrams in the model hurts performance. This result indirectly supports a key assumption of the QTM approach: That more information exists in a good set of candidate queries than in the vocabulary of the collection, thus, finding a good set of candidate topical-queries is a challenging problem.

- *Query contribution to MI was established as the baseline evaluation function.* All the

Table 3. Best overlapping models and LDA performance

Model	k	s_t	z	c_g	eval	c_s	n_c	h	n	Fo(avg)	Fo(max)
1	70	0.15	2	S	KL	D	10	100	42	0.7008	0.7978
2	117	0.1	2	N	MI	G	20,000	100	42	0.6012	0.7918
3	117	0.1	2	N	MI	G	25,000	100	42	0.6021	0.7910
4	70	0.15	10	S	KL	D	5	100	42	0.6957	0.7909
5	70	0.15	100	S	KL	D	10	100	42	0.6928	0.7897
6	50	0.2	50	S	QMI	D	10	500	42	0.6883	0.7896
7	70	0.15	2	S	QF	D	10	100	42	0.6938	0.7875
8	117	0.15	2	S	QF	D	10	500	42	0.6878	0.7861
9	70	0.15	10	S	QF	D	10	100	42	0.6899	0.7860
10	70	0.15	100	S	QMI	D	10	100	42	0.6859	0.7854
LDA	30	0.2	*	*	*	*	*	*	30	0.6711	0.7728

analyzed evaluation functions were found to be sensitive to basic model parameters such as the number of candidates n_c and number of query hits h, but not all of them were sensitive in the same degree to the minimum frequency threshold z or the number of selected candidates n_c. In particular, functions such as QF and contribution to MI, were found to be less sensitive to parameterization, which is an important practical aspect, given that less tuning is required to find good models.

CONCLUSION AND FUTURE WORK

In this work we have proposed an alternative approach to the problem on constructing semantic models of text collections, formally defined as Discrete Topic Modeling (DTM). The DTM approach takes advantage of a simplified notion of topic, interpreted as a set of semantically similar documents, to essentially transform the Probabilistic Topic Modeling problem, which requires the usage of sampling methods, into an overlapping clustering problem.

Then, based on the hypothesis that there exist a set of search queries that can capture a great deal of the semantic information about the documents of the collection in the form of co-occurrence and proximity relations, we have proposed the Query-Based Topic Modeling framework, a discrete, information-theoretic method based on heuristics to generate, select and evaluate a set of candidate topical-queries which are then co-clustered along with the documents of the collection and finally used to estimate topic-document probabilities and overlapping clusters. All the steps of the QTM process have been designed following the map-reduce style and thus can be executed in parallel over clusters of commodity class machines.

We have shown that queries selected using information-theoretic heuristics can produce better models than the set of vocabulary terms, and as a consequence, the heuristics that can be used to generate and select those queries were studied, with an emphasis on the functions that measure the mutual information between queries and documents.

A key enabler of many of the results produced over this research was the set of proposed probabilistic, semantic-coherence metrics inspired on the familiar concepts of recall and precision that were designed to inexpensively validate overlapping and incomplete topic models using multi-labeled corpora, and resulted in an ideal tool to compare the QTM results to those produced using LDA. As a result of the benchmarks, we conclude that QTM can produce models of comparable and in many cases superior performance, with the added benefit of an algorithmic design that offers greater scalability.

After our experimental results concerning the query-evaluation functions, we found that one of the most promising lines of research is to explore new candidate query generation heuristics. In general, try to provide richer and better answers to the question on what is the query generation method that can lead to produce the best models. For instance, we have shown that a query set generated using bi-grams was superior to the collection unigrams (or vocabulary terms), and in fact was superior to the union of both sets. Also, we have shown that signature-calculation methods like Spotsigs (Theobald et al., 2008), offered promising performance in combination with other heuristics.

Among the aspects of model building that we consider worth of further research we can name the effects of different ranking functions when constructing the query-vector document model of the collection. The issue can be especially critical when clustering web documents as the ranking could be used to introduce additional information such as the linkage structure of the collection. The effects of the document ranking when produced query-based topic models was in general omitted in the current scope. Also, the effect of introducing usage-based queries is still to be explored.

The last phase of the QTM process, which involves producing an overlapping document clustering from a hard partition, is subject to many improvements. Recently, some "soft" versions of the co-clustering have been presented which propose alternative ways to define probabilistic document-cluster associations, like the Bayesian Co-Clustering technique (Shan & Banerjee, 2008) and the Latent Dirichlet Bayesian Co-Clustering technique (Wang et al., 2009). Being theoretically sound, those alternative co-clustering methods lead us to hypothesize that they may convey performance improvements in the construction of overlapping-clusters, however, the potential improvements should be evaluated in terms of their computational costs and their parallel processing ability.

The work on metrics presented here and in related publications is still in progress. Among the major aspects that require further analysis is the full generalization of the metrics to work under any degree of inter-class overlap, avoiding the need to fall back to enumerative computations that could quickly become impractical. Also, the applications of the Full-class match precision metric needs to be further explored so as to determine the circumstances under which of the proposed metric provides better information.

Finally, as this research was motivated by the potential that semantic modeling offers to improve retrieval and other machine learning tasks, we believe that a necessary step in that direction is the construction of effective retrieval models and classifiers based on the generated query-based topic models. During that process, it would be very valuable to assess the predictive power of the probabilistic metrics on the task performance, for which specific benchmarks usually exist. In this regard, it would be critical to explore and understand the relation of the semantic-coherence of the model and task specific performance.

REFERENCES

Berry, M. W., Dumais, S. T., & O'Brien, G. W. (1995). Using linear algebra for intelligent information retrieval. *SIAM Review*, *37*(4), 573–595. doi:10.1137/1037127

Blei, D., Gri, T., Jordan, M., & Tenenbaum, J. (2004). Hierarchical topic models and the nested chinese restaurant process. *Advances in Neural Information Processing Systems*, 16.

Blei, D., & Lafferty, J. (2007). A correlated topic model of science. *1*(1), 17-35.

Blei, D., Ng, A., & Jordan, M. (2003). Latent dirichlet allocation. *Journal of Machine Learning Research*, *3*, 993–1022.

Broder, A. (2002). A taxonomy of web search. *SIGIR Forum*, *36*(2), 3–10. doi:10.1145/792550.792552

Chang, J., Boyd-Graber, J., Gerrish, S., Wang, C., & Blei, D. (2009). Reading tea leaves: How humans interpret topic models . In *Neural information processing systems*. NIPS.

Chu, H. (2003). *Information representation and retrieval in the digital age*. Information Today Inc.

Cover, T. M., & Thomas, J. (1991). *Elements of information theory*. Wiley. doi:10.1002/0471200611

Deerwester, S. C., Dumais, S. T., Landauer, T. K., Furnas, G. W., & Harshman, R. A. (1990). Indexing by latent semantic analysis. *Journal of the American Society for Information Science American Society for Information Science*, *41*(6), 391–407. doi:10.1002/(SICI)1097-4571(199009)41:6<391::AID-ASI1>3.0.CO;2-9

Denoeud, L., & Guénoche, A. (2006). Comparison of distance indices between partitions. *Studies in Classification, Data Analysis, and Knowledge Organization*, 21-28.

Dhillon, I. S., Mallela, S., & Modha, D. S. (2003). Information-theoretic co-clustering. In *Kdd '03: Proceedings of the ninth acm sigkdd international conference on knowledge discovery and data mining* (pp. 89–98). New York: ACM.

Dumais, S. T., Furnas, G. W., Landauer, T. K., Deerwester, S., & Harshman, R. (1988). Using latent semantic analysis to improve access to textual information. In *Chi '88: Proceedings of the sigchi conference on human factors in computing systems* (pp. 281–285). New York: ACM.

Fowlkes, E. B., & Mallows, C. L. (1983). A method for comparing two hierarchical clusterings. *Journal of the American Statistical Association, 78*(383), 553–569. doi:10.2307/2288117

Furnas, G. W., Landauer, T. K., Gomez, L. M., & Dumais, S. T. (1984). Statistical semantics: analysis of the potential performance of keyword information systems. 187–242.

Furnas, G. W., Landauer, T. K., Gomez, L. M., & Dumais, S. T. (1987). The vocabulary problem in human-system communication. *Communications of the ACM, 30*(11), 964–971. doi:10.1145/32206.32212

Girolami, M., & Kabán, A. (2003). *On an equivalence between plsi and lda* (pp. 433–434). SIGIR.

Griffiths, T. L., & Steyvers, M. (2004, April). Finding scientific topics. *Proceedings of the National Academy of Sciences of the United States of America, 101*(Suppl 1), 5228–5235. doi:10.1073/pnas.0307752101

Griffiths, T. L., Steyvers, M., & Tenenbaum, J. B. (2007). Topics in semantic representation. *Psychological Review, 114*, 211–244. doi:10.1037/0033-295X.114.2.211

Hofmann, T. (1999). Probabilistic latent semantic indexing. In *Sigir '99: Proceedings of the 22nd annual international acm sigir conference on research and development in information retrieval* (pp. 50–57). New York: ACM.

Jansen, B. J., Booth, D. L., & Spink, A. (2009). Patterns of query reformulation during web searching. *Journal of the American Society for Information Science and Technology, 60*(7), 1358–1371. doi:10.1002/asi.21071

Li, R. M., Kaptein, R., Hiemstra, D., & Kamps, J. (2008, April). Exploring topic-based language models for effective web information retrieval. In E. Hoenkamp, M. de Cock, & V. Hoste (Eds.), *Proceedings of the dutch-belgian information retrieval workshop* (*dir 2008*), *maastricht, the netherlands* (pp. 65–71). Enschede: Neslia Paniculata. http://eprints.eemcs.utwente.nl/12277/.

Li, W., & McCallum, A. (2006). Pachinko allocation: Dag-structured mixture models of topic correlations. In *Icml '06: Proceedings of the 23rd international conference on machine learning* (pp. 577–584). New York: ACM.

Newman, D., Asuncion, A., Smyth, P., & Welling, M. (2007). Distributed inference for latent dirichlet allocation. In *Advances in neural information processing systems* (Vol. 20).

Papadimitriou, S., & Sun, J. (2008). Disco: Distributed co-clustering with map-reduce: A case study towards petabyte-scale end-to-end mining. In *ICDM '08: Proceedings of the 2008 eighth ieee international conference on data mining* (pp. 512–521). Washington, DC: IEEE Computer Society.

Pereira, F., Tishby, N., & Lee, L. (1993). Distributional clustering of english words. In *In proceedings of the 31st annual meeting of the association for computational linguistics* (pp. 183–190).

Porteous, I., Newman, D., Ihler, A., Asuncion, A., Smyth, P., & Welling, M. (2008). Fast collapsed gibbs sampling for latent dirichlet allocation. In *Kdd '08: Proceeding of the 14th acm sigkdd international conference on knowledge discovery and data mining* (pp. 569–577). New York: ACM.

Puppin, D., & Silvestri, F. (2006). The query-vector document model. In *Cikm '06: Proceedings of the 15th acm international conference on information and knowledge management* (pp. 880–881). New York: ACM.

Puppin, D., Silvestri, F., & Laforenza, D. (2006). Query-driven document partitioning and collection selection. In *Infoscale '06: Proceedings of the 1st international conference on scalable information systems* (p. 34). New York: ACM.

Ramirez, E. H., & Brena, R. (2009). An Information-Theoretic Approach for Unsupervised Topic Mining in Large Text Collections. In *Proceedings of the 2009 IEEE/WIC/ACM International Joint Conference on Web Intelligence and Intelligent Agent Technology.* (pp. 331 – 334). Milan, Italy

Ramirez, E. H., Brena, R., Magatti, D., & Stella, F. (2010). Probabilistic Metrics for Soft-Clustering and Topic Model Validation. In *Proceedings of the 2010 IEEE/WIC/ACM International Joint Conference on Web Intelligence and Intelligent Agent Technology.* (pp. 406 – 412). Toronto, Ontario.

Shan, H., & Banerjee, A. (2008). Bayesian co-clustering. In *ICDM '08: Proceedings of the 2008 eighth ieee international conference on data mining* (pp. 530–539). Washington, DC: IEEE Computer Society.

Slonim, N., Friedman, N., & Tishby, N. (2002). Unsupervised document classification using sequential information maximization. In *Sigir '02: Proceedings of the 25th annual international acm sigir conference on research and development in information retrieval* (pp. 129–136). New York: ACM.

Slonim, N., & Tishby, N. (1999). *Agglomerative information bottleneck* (pp. 617–623). Cambridge, MA: MIT Press.

Slonim, N., & Tishby, N. (2000). Document clustering using word clusters via the information bottleneck method. In *In acm sigir 2000* (pp. 208–215). ACM press. doi:10.1145/345508.345578

Steyvers, M., & Griffiths, T. (2007). Probabilistic topic models. In Landauer, T., Mcnamara, D., Dennis, S., & Kintsch, W. (Eds.), *Handbook of latent semantic analysis*. Mahwah, NJ: Lawrence Erlbaum Associates.

Theobald, M., Siddharth, J., & Paepcke, A. (2008). Spotsigs: robust and efficient near duplicate detection in large web collections. In *Sigir '08: Proceedings of the 31st annual international acm sigir conference on research and development in information retrieval* (pp. 563–570). New York: ACM.

Tishby, N., Pereira, F. C., & Bialek, W. (1999). The information bottleneck method. In (pp. 368–377).

Wang, P., Domeniconi, C., & Laskey, K. B. (2009). Latent dirichlet bayesian co-clustering. In *Ecml pkdd '09: Proceedings of the european conference on machine learning and knowledge discovery in databases* (pp. 522–537). Berlin, Heidelberg: Springer-Verlag.

Wu, J., Xiong, H., & Chen, J. (2009). Adapting the right measures for k-means clustering. In *Kdd '09: Proceedings of the 15th acm sigkdd international conference on knowledge discovery and data mining* (pp. 877–886). New York: ACM.

Chapter 5

Combining Diverse Knowledge Based Features for Semantic Relatedness Measures

Anna Lisa Gentile
University of Sheffield, UK

Ziqi Zhang
University of Sheffield, UK

Fabio Ciravegna
University of Sheffield, UK

ABSTRACT

This chapter proposes a novel Semantic Relatedness (SR) measure that exploits diverse features extracted from a knowledge resource. Computing SR is a crucial technique for many complex Natural Language Processing (NLP) as well as Semantic Web related tasks. Typically, semantic relatedness measures only make use of limited number of features without considering diverse feature sets or understanding the different contributions of features to the accuracy of a method. This chapter proposes a random graph walk model based method that naturally combines diverse features extracted from a knowledge resource in a balanced way in the task of computing semantic relatedness. A set of experiments is carefully designed to investigate the effects of choosing different features and altering their weights on the accuracy of the system. Next, using the derived feature sets and feature weights we evaluate the proposed method against the state-of-the-art semantic relatedness measures, and show that it obtains higher accuracy on many benchmarking datasets. Additionally, the authors justify the usefulness of the proposed method in a practical NLP task, i.e. Named Entity Disambiguation.

DOI: 10.4018/978-1-60960-881-1.ch005

INTRODUCTION

Semantic relatedness quantifies how much two terms or concepts are related by encompassing all kinds of relations between them, such as hypernymy, hyponymy, antonymy and functional relations. State-of-the-art semantic relatedness measures can be roughly divided into two mainstreams. The first makes use of distribution of terms or co-occurrence statistics observed in a large corpus (Bollegala, et al., 2007; R. Cilibrasi & Vitányi, 2007; Matsuo, et al., 2006; Sahami & Heilman, 2006). These methods are usually referred to as "statistic-based". The second mainstream is constituted by "knowledge-based" methods, which employ structural and lexical features extracted from certain knowledge resources, such as WordNet, Wiktionary and Wikipedia. Among these, WordNet has been extensively used in this field (Banerjee & Pedersen, 2003; Hughes & Ramage, 2007; Leacock & Chodorow, 1998; Resnik, 1995a) but also criticized by its lack of coverage for named entities and specialized concepts which are crucial to domain-specific problems (Bollegala, et al., 2007; Strube & Ponzetto, 2006). With the increasing popularity of using collaborative knowledge resources (Zesch, et al., 2008a) in NLP, Wiktionary has been proposed as an alternative to WordNet, often achieving better results (Müller & Gurevych, 2009; Weale, et al., 2009; Zesch, et al., 2008b). Unfortunately, being a similar word-based knowledge resource to WordNet, Wiktionary does not overcome the limitation that it has little or no coverage of specialized concepts or named entities, which may hinder its application to domain-specific NLP tasks. In contrast, a major alternative collaborative knowledge source such as Wikipedia contains rich structural and lexical knowledge about entities and concepts (Kazama & Torisawa, 2007). Such knowledge has proved useful features for computing semantic relatedness. For this reason, it has attracted increasing attention from researchers of SR (Gabrilovich &

Markovitch, 2007; Hassan & Mihalcea, 2009; Strube & Ponzetto, 2006; Zesch, et al., 2008b).

However, state-of-the-art methods typically employ one or two types of structural elements and information content extracted from the knowledge resources. Although this reduces the level of complication in the methods, experiences from other information extraction tasks such as Named Entity Recognition (Grishman & Sundheim, 1996) and relation extraction (Giuliano, et al., 2006) suggest that combining multiple and mutually exclusive features can lead to improved performance. With this motivation, we believe that combining diverse features extracted from the knowledge resource in a balanced way can further improve the accuracy of semantic relatedness systems. To validate this hypothesis, we propose a novel SR method that naturally integrates diverse features weighted according to their importance for the task, and arrives at a single measure of relatedness between terms or concepts. In our studies we choose Wikipedia as the knowledge resource because of its broader coverage of concepts and richer lexical and structural knowledge than WordNet and Wiktionary; also because higher accuracy has been achieved when similar methods are tested with Wikipedia rather than WordNet. We extract six different types of lexical and structural knowledge and feed them as features to the random graph walk algorithm. The same method can be adapted to the usage of different resources rather than Wikipedia, by defining the kind of feature to extract according to the different resource. The random graph walk model is chosen for its robustness in dealing with multiple types of features (Iria, et al., 2007) and the representation of features in a natural and semantic manner, which facilitates the studies of feature effects. However, other models can be used, such as the cosine similarity.

To better understand the contribution of different features to the task of measuring semantic relatedness, we select a state-of-the-art dataset as training data and follow the method of Simulated Annealing (Nie, et al., 2005) to study the impact of different features and their importance. The method allows us to investigate the effects of altering feature weights on the accuracy of the system. The experiment results provide useful insight to the design of semantic relatedness measures. Firstly, different features contribute different weights to compute semantic relatedness. When combined under the random graph model, certain types of features reported in the literature prove to be more important than others, thus they receive higher weights in our approach. Secondly, combining diverse features in a balanced way leads to higher accuracy than if using single types of features. Next, we employ these findings in further sets of experiments to fully evaluate the method. To do so, we apply the learnt features together with their weights to a set of benchmarking datasets that have been used by a number of state-of-the-art works. We evaluate the systems accuracy using the same metric (co-relation with human judges) as reported in these works, and compare the results against their reported figures. We show that on several datasets our system achieves higher accuracy than some of the best results reported in the literature. In order to prove the true value of the method in enabling the semantic web, we also adapted this method to a sense disambiguation task, in which names of entities are to be disambiguated and associated with proper unique real-world object. Tested on one well-known state-of-the-art corpus for Named Entity Disambiguation, our system achieves higher accuracy than the best system reported in the literature.

The remaining of the chapter is organised as follows. Firstly we present a brief review of state of the art methods for computing semantic relatedness; next we describe in details the proposed method of using diverse weighted feature sets for computing SR and we show a set of experiments designed to study the selection of features and feature weights and to evaluate the accuracy of the proposed SR measure. Also we carry out experiments to apply the proposed method to a practical NLP task, to justify the usefulness of proposed novel measure in real applications.

BACKGROUND

There is abundant literature on computing semantic similarity and relatedness for both statistical and knowledge-based methods. The fundamental intuition behind statistical methods is that terms that share similar neighbours share similar semantics (Harris, 1970). For example, Matsuo et al. (2006), Chen et al. (2006) and Bollegala et al. (2007) query search engines using the pair of terms in question, then use returned page counts to compute collocation strength of the terms. Sahami and Heilmn (2006) use a similar approach, but make use of the snippets retrieved from search results to build an extended vector representation of input terms, and apply the cosine similarity function to compute a similarity score between the two vectors. Another web-based measure is the Google distance (Cilibrasi & Vitanyi, 2007): between two search terms it is calculated exploiting the total number of web pages searched by Google search engine, the number of Google hits for search terms separately and the number of web pages where terms co-occur (the normalised value is in the range $\{0, 1\}$; it is 0 if terms always co-occur, 1 if they never do).

Knowledge-based methods exploit information content and structural elements related to terms extracted from a knowledge resource; many of these methods are designed to compute "semantic similarity", which takes into account only hypernymy and hypynymy relations defined in a knowledge resource; others deal with more general "semantic relatedness", which encompasses all kinds of relations (hypernymy, hyponymy, antonymy, synonymy and functional) between terms and concepts (Strube & Ponzetto, 2006). One of such resources is WordNet, a lexical database of English, where nouns, verbs, adjectives and adverbs are grouped into sets of cognitive synonyms (synsets), each expressing a distinct concept (Miller, 1995). From WordNet it is possible to obtain both structural elements (taxonomy structure and relations between concepts) and information content, which can be used as features for semantic relatedness measures. Leacock and Chodorow (1998) measure similarity between two concepts by calculating the path length between the two synsets containing the terms, namely, counting the number of steps required to reach one synset from another by following hypernymy and hyponymy relations between them. The number is then normalized by the depth of the taxonomy. Resnik (1995b) proposes a measure that is built on the hypotesis that the similarity between two concepts is "the extent to which they share information in common". Specifically using WordNet, the similarity between two concepts is determined by the information content of their Least Common Subsumer (LCS), i.e. the lowest concept in the hierarchy that subsumes both concepts. Two similar metrics to Resnik's one are the ones by Lin (1998) and by Jiang and Conrath (1997). Lin (1998) defines a theoretical model for similarity which is applicable whenever the domain of interest has a probabilistic model (he shows how to apply the measure when dealing with ordinal values, with feature vectors, to calculate word similarity and also semantic similarity in taxonomy). The similarity between two concepts c_1 and c_2 is the ratio between the amount of information needed to state the commonality of c_1 and c_2 and the information needed to fully describe c_1 and c_2. Jiang and Conrath (1997) proposed a variation of Resnik measure, which also takes into account the link strength between a child c_i and its parent p. Wu & Palmer (1994) calculate the similarity between two concepts considering their depth, i.e. their distance from the root node. The similarity between concepts c_1 and c_2 takes into account their respective depth and the depth of their LCS. Banerjee & Pedersen (2003) proposed to use the gloss associated with a synset in WordNet. Similarity between two concepts is quantified by

the text overlap of the glosses of their containing synset. Hughes and Ramage (2007) apply a random graph walk model to compute semantic similarity of two terms by exploiting the relations between the terms extracted from WordNet.

Although WordNet is extensively used in this field and proved to be useful on open domain words, one of its major limitation is the lack of coverage for named entities and specialized concepts which are crucial to domain-specific problems (Bollegala, et al., 2007; Strube & Ponzetto, 2006). Moreover word senses evolve over time, which means that effort is needed to maintain the resource up-to-date (Bollegala, et al., 2007; Zesch, et al., 2008b).

Given these limitations, a natural choice is using collaborative knowledge resources (Zesch, et al., 2008b) which, due to the popularity of Web 2.0 technologies, are easily available, growing rapidly and well maintained. One of these is the Wiktionary[1], a multi-lingual free content dictionary covering over 270 languages and over 5 million entries inter-linked with semantic relations. The first attempt in using Wiktionary as a knowledge resource for semantic relatedness is by Zesch et al. (2008b), who adapted several WordNet based methods to Wiktionary by using equivalent features extracted from Wiktionary. An evaluation using seven different datasets shows better results with the usage of Wiktionary instead of WordNet over state-of-the-art WordNet-based SR. Weale et al. (2009) apply a page rank based algorithm to compute relatedness of words using Wiktionary, and tested their method in a synonym detection task. Müller and Gurevych (2009) use knowledge in Wiktionary to improve information retrieval systems. Essentially, their approach is based on aggregating the semantic relatedness between terms of each query and document term pair. For each word, texts of its corresponding Wiktionary entries are used to build representational concept vectors. When compared against a standard Lucene[2] search, their methods achieved better results on many datasets.

Due to the nature of collaborative authoring, Wiktionary overcomes the maintenance problem that arises in WordNet. However, being in the form of a word-based dictionary, it still suffers from very limited or no coverage of domain specific concepts or named entities. For this reason, more attention has been paid to Wikipedia in the research of semantic relatedness measures. Wikipedia is the world's most famous collaborative encyclopaedia. Contents in Wikipedia are mostly organized based on named entities (Kazama & Torisawa, 2007). Similar to Wiktionary, the first attempt of using Wikipedia in such tasks adapts WordNet-based measures to the Wikipedia knowledge resource. Strube and Ponzetto (2006) translated several WordNet-based approaches including that of Leacok and Chodorow (1998), Wu and Palmer (1994), Resnik (1995b), and Banerjee and Pedersen (2003) to make use of Wikipedia. For each approach, they identify the feature in Wikipedia that is equivalent to that used within WordNet, and demonstrate that the same approaches applied to Wikipedia achieve better results than using WordNet. Positive outcomes in this direction have also been reported by Zesch et al. (2008a). They implement a path-length based technique and a gloss-based technique; in the first one they use the category structure in Wikipedia as feature, while in the second one they use words contained within an article (a Wikipedia page) or only words from the first paragraph.

Turdakov and Velikhov (2008) apply semantic relatedness measures in the Word Sense Disambiguation (WSD) context. They analyze different types of links in Wikipedia and use those features with different weights. However, their method heavily relies on heuristics and they do not evaluate the system in the semantic relatedness task.

Gabrilovich and Markovitch (2007) represent each Wikipedia concept using a weighed vector of words that occur in the corresponding article, and then build an inverted index that maps each word into a list of concepts in which it appears. Thus to compute relatedness between two texts, a weighted vector of Wikipedia concepts is built for each text by aggregating the concept vectors of each word retrieved from the index. The vectors are then inputted to the cosine metric to derive a similarity score. Essentially, this is a statistic-based method other than knowledge oriented since the method treats contents in Wikipedia as large corpora and makes use of term distribution statistics. An extension of this direction is by Hassan and Mihalcea (2009) who introduce several modifications to improve Gabrilovich and Markovitch's approach. They replace the cosine similarity function with a different metric, taking into account the length of articles, and then placing more importance on category-type concepts. Essentially these methods treat content in a Wikipedia article as bag-of-words, and do not make use of the structural elements in Wikipedia. In addition, their approaches require pre-computing the inverted index of the entire Wikipedia knowledge resource. Given the size and growth of Wikipedia, producing and maintaining an up-to-date index of such kind can be computationally expensive.

Milne and Witten (2008) propose the Wikipedia Link-based Measure (WLM), which makes use of Wikipedia's hyperlink structure to define relatedness: semantic relatedness between terms is calculated only using the links found within their corresponding Wikipedia articles, rather than their textual content.

Han and Zhao (2010) propose the Structural Semantic Relatedness (SSR) measure. Their method calculates semantic relatedness by using diverse knowledge resources, including Wikipedia and WordNet as structured knowledge resources, and an unstructured corpus as a source of term co-occurrence statistics. Three state-of-the-art methods are chosen to calculate SR using each of the three resources. These are the WLM (Milne & Witten, 2008) for Wikipedia, (Lin, 1998) for WordNet and the Google Similarity distance (Cilibrasi & Vitanyi, 2007) for the unstructured corpus. For each pair of term, only one method is used to compute the semantic relatedness. The choice of method is determined by an arbitrary preference order. The semantic relatedness scores are used to plot a connected graph of input terms, which is then used to calculate the Structural Semantic Relatedness. Their work is not directly comparable with the one we are proposing in this work, because the effort is targeted at finding a way to combine diverse knowledge resources rather than improving accuracy of single semantic relatedness measures.

MOTIVATION BEHIND THIS WORK

We observe that one major limitation of existing work on semantic relatedness measures is that they typically make use of single or very limited choice of features, without considering the usefulness of multiple, diverse feature sets, or understanding the importance of different features in this task. For example, the majority of statistic-based methods use content words extracted from a corpus to build feature vectors, which are used to determine semantic relatedness. Particularly for knowledge-based methods, in which case the knowledge resources often contain diverse types of information content and structural elements, existing semantic relatedness measures simply make use of one or two types of features. And in cases where the methods are adapted from another knowledge resource (typically WordNet), the choice of features are restricted by the choice of measures. However, our analysis of related work shows that it is clear that different features can be equally useful to computing semantic relatedness when they are used separately. On the other hand, experiences from other information extraction tasks such as Named Entity Recognition (Grishman & Sundheim 1996) and relation extraction (Giuliano, et al., 2006) suggest that combining diverse and mutually exclusive features can lead to improved performance over systems that use very limited feature sets. These naturally lead to the question of whether we can combine diverse

features for computing semantic relatedness, and if so, what are the features to choose and how to balance them in a uniform model.

Due to this very motivation, this work is carried out to investigate the effects of using diverse feature sets and methods of feature weighting for the task of computing semantic relatedness. For this purpose, we propose a novel SR method that naturally integrates these features and arrives at a single measure of relatedness between terms or concepts. We opt for knowledge-based methods and choose Wikipedia as the structured knowledge resource in the study for two main reasons. Firstly, compared to other structured knowledge resources such as WordNet and Wiktionary, it has broader coverage of concepts and named entities, which is a major requirement for real-world applications. Secondly, it contains richer types of information content and structural elements, offering good test-beds for diverse features. We extract six different types of features and feed them to a random graph walk based algorithm to compute a semantic relatedness score. The random graph walk model is chosen for its robustness in dealing with multiple types of features (Iria, et al., 2007) and the representation of features in a natural and semantic manner, which facilitates the studies of feature effects. The following section presents the method in details.

A NOVEL SEMANTIC RELATEDNESS MEASURE

Given a pair of terms or concepts, our approach is designed to identify descriptions of these terms or concepts in the chosen knowledge resource, extract their relevant knowledge pieces that are to be used as features and aggregate these features to derive a measure of the strength of semantic relatedness between the terms or concepts. Therefore, the approach is naturally split into three steps: page retrieval, feature extraction and relatedness computation. Starting with an input set of terms, which are referred to as *surfaces*, the page retrieval step consists of searching within Wikipedia all pages that possibly describe the *surfaces*: all retrieved pages will be the *concepts* of interest. In the feature extraction step we build a feature space for each *concept*, i.e. information content and structural elements derived from Wikipedia. Finally, for the SR computation step, all *concepts*, features and relations are transformed into a graph representation, and applying a random graph walk we obtain a relatedness score between every pair of *concepts*. A detailed description of each step follows.

Page Retrieval

For each *surface* we query Wikipedia to retrieve all relevant pages. If the *surface* matches at least one entry in Wikipedia, a Wikipedia page is returned. This page can be either a single page or a disambiguation page (a special page in Wikipedia which lists different senses as links to other pages). A single page is returned when either the *surface* has only one sense defined in Wikipedia, or it has been defined the most often used common sense. In this case, we refer to this page as the *sense page* for the *concept*. If a disambiguation page is returned we follow every link and keep all *sense pages*, and expect our feature extraction and the semantic relatedness algorithm to naturally select the most related senses for the input pair of *surfaces*. To illustrate, suppose we have only two senses for the *surface* "queen" listed on the disambiguation page, which refer to "Queen, a British rock band formed in London in 1971" and "queen (chess), a chess piece"; likewise two senses for the *surface* "rook" are listed on disambiguation page as "rook, a chess piece" and "rook, a family of birds". We represent all four *concepts* using features extracted from their sense pages, and expect our algorithm to produce maximum relatedness score for the *concept* pair "queen (chess), a chess piece" and "rook, a chess piece" rather than other combinations, and we use this

maximum score as the final relatedness score for the input *surface* pair "queen" and "rook".

Feature Extraction Using Wikipedia

At the end of the Page Retrieval step we have for each *surface* one or more *concepts* from Wikipedia and for each *concept* we have its *sense page* (the whole Wikipedia page content); we use such *sense pages* to build the *concept* feature space. Features we extract from each page are essentially words, such as words from the title, describing nouns (words which describe the concept), words from the first section, frequent words, category words and words from outgoing links. Specifically, the initial features we selected for study are the followings:

1. Words from the titles of a page (*title_words*) – including words in the title of a *sense page* plus words from all redirecting links that group several *surfaces* of a single *concept* to this page.

2. Words from first section (*first_sec_words*), as opposed to top *n* most frequently used words in the entire page (*frequent_words_n*). We test each feature separately.

3. Words from categories (*cat_words*) assigned to a page – each page in Wikipedia is assigned several category labels. These labels are organized in a taxonomy-like structure. We retrieve the category labels by performing a depth limited search of 2, and split these labels to words. The depth of 2 is chosen because we observe that in many cases, the first level category assigned to a page is the title of the page itself. For example, the page of "Bronze Age" has one category "Bronze Age". For this reason, we always traverse the category hierarchy up to two levels to ensure useful categories are collected.

4. Words from outgoing links that are contained in a list structure on a page (*list_link_words*) – the intuition is that links found in list struc-

tures may be more important than other links on the same page, as suggested by Turdakov and Velikhov (2008). However, we take the "target" of a link rather than the "surface" of a link. E.g., in the page about "Queen (chess)", the first sentence "The Queen is the most powerful piece in the game of chess" contains a link "Chess_piece" with surface form "piece"; in such case, we take the target "Chess_piece" other than "piece".

5. Words from all other outgoing links excluding links extracted by feature 4. (*other_link_words*).

6. Words from the describing nouns (*desc_ noun_words*) - Kazama and Torisawa (2007) noted that, in the first sentence of a page, the head noun of the noun phrase just after *be* is most likely the hypernym of the concept described by the page. We extend their idea by keeping the entire noun phrase and also including the noun phrases connected by a correlative conjunction word; e.g., we keep the nouns marked in italic in the sentence "Leeds is a *city* and *metropolitan borough* in West Yorkshire, England", and refer to them as "describing nouns".

Once we extract all these features for each concept, next step concerns organizing the text features into a graph conforming to the random walk model.

Random Walk Graph Model

A random walk is a formalization of the intuitive idea of taking successive steps in a graph, each in a random direction (Lovász, 1993). The underneath hypothesis is that the "harder" it is to walk from a node to another, the less related the two nodes are. An advantage of the random-walk model is that it enables combining different features in a simple way, and deriving a single measure of relatedness between two entities (Iria, et al., 2007). Specifically, following Hughes and Ramage (2007) ap-

proach, we build an undirected weighted typed graph where all concepts identified in the page retrieval step and all their extracted features are both represented as nodes (of a different type).

The whole graph is a 5-tuple $G = (V, E, t, l, w)$, where:

- V is the set of nodes
- $E: V \times V$ is the set of edges that connect concepts and their features, representing an undirected path from concepts to their features, and vice versa
- $t: V \rightarrow T$ is the node type function, where $T = \{t_1, \ldots, t_{|T|}\}$ is a set of types
- $l: E \rightarrow L$ is the edge label function, where $L = \{l_1, \ldots, l_{|L|}\}$ is a set of labels that define relations between concepts and their features
- $w: L \rightarrow R$ is the label weighing function that assigns a weight to an edge in the set L.

Thus, given the features described in the previous section, we structure our problem domain with the types $T = \{concept, title\_words, cat\_words, first\_sec\_words/frequent\_words\_n, list\_link\_words, other\_link\_words, desc\_noun\_words\}$ and labels $L = \{has\_title\_words, has\_cat\_words, has\_first\_sec\_words/has\_frequent\_words\_n, has\_list\_link\_words, has\_other\_link\_words, has\_desc\_noun\_words\}$.

Figure 1 shows the graph representation model of concepts, features, and their relations. Circles indicate nodes (V); solid lines connecting nodes indicate edges (E), representing relations between concepts and features; italic texts indicate types of edges (L). The graph contains seven nodes. The two bigger circles indicate nodes of type concepts, which in this case report the concept id (*Wiki_1190* and *Wiki_5236*). The smaller circles are feature nodes: the white ones are of type *title_words* (*Forest* and *Coast*), the grey ones are of type *cat_words* (*Forestry, Lanforms* and *Coastal geography*). Concepts sharing same features will

Figure 1. Graph representation model of concepts, features, and their relations

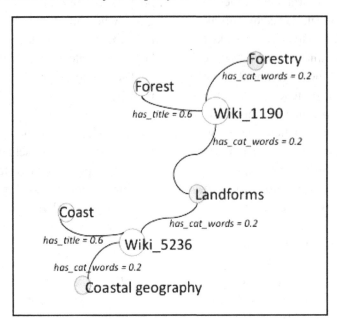

be connected via the edges that connect features and concepts. The two nodes of type *concept*, *Wiki_1190* and *Wiki_5236*, are connected via a node of type *cat_words*, which value is *Landforms*. Intuitively, the more features two concept nodes share, the more routes are available to connect them and therefore, to "walk" from one concept node to another. In the mean time, given a set of edges reaching out from one concept node, the more likely the connected routes (to other concepts via shared features) are chosen, the more related the two concepts are.

To model such "likeliness", we define weights for each edge type, which, informally, determine the relevance of each feature to establish the relatedness between any two concepts.

Let $L_{t_d} = \{l(x,y) : (x,y) \in E \cap t(x) = t_d\}$ be the set of possible labels for edges leaving nodes of type t_d. We require that the weights form a probability distribution over L_{t_d}, i.e.

$$\sum_{l \in L_{t_d}} w(l) = 1 \qquad [1]$$

Initially the weights can be uniformly distributed, i.e the weight for each edge type is 1/|L|, or can be assigned using diverse strategies. To tune the weight of different features, which we will refer to as a *weight model* (*wm*), we use a simulated annealing optimization method (Nie, et al., 2005). Details on this will be given in the next section and can be also found in (Zhang, et al., 2010).

We build an adjacency matrix of locally appropriate similarity between nodes as

$$W_{ij} = \begin{cases} \sum_{l_k \in L} \dfrac{w(l_k)}{|\,(i,\cdot) \in E : l(i,\cdot) = l_k\,|}, (i,j) \in E \\ 0, otherwise \end{cases}$$

$$[2]$$

Where W_{ij} is the ith-row and j^{th}-column entry of W, indexed by V. The above equation distributes uniformly the weight of edges of the same type (features) leaving a given node: given w(l_k) the weight assigned to an edge of a certain type l_k, for each node i, such weight is distributed among all edges of type l_k leaving node i.

Table 1. Adjacency matrix W for example in Figure 1

	Wiki_1190	**Wiki_5236**	**title_Forest**	**title_Coast**	**cat_Forestry**	**cat_ Landform**	**cat_Coastal Geography**
Wiki_1190	0	0	0.6	0	0.2	0.2	0
Wiki_5236	0	0	0	0.6	0	0.2	0.2
title_Forest	0.6	0	0	0	0	0	0
title_Coast	0	0.6	0	0	0	0	0
cat_Forestry	0.2	0	0	0	0	0	0
cat_Landform	0.2	0.2	0	0	0	0	0
cat_Coastal Geography	0	0.2	0	0	0	0	0

In the example reported in Figure 1 we only have two types of feature nodes: *title_words* and *cat_words*. The weight assigned to relative edges are w(*has_title_words*)=0.6 and w(*has_cat_words*)=0.4. In this case the weight for the edges *has_cat_words* is distributed as 0.2 for each edge, because both concepts have two nodes of type *cat_words*.

The adjacency matrix W for the example in Figure 1 is reported in Table 1.

Next we associate to each node of the graph the probability of a random walker traversing to an adjacent node *j*, expressed as $P^{(t)}(j|i)$ (probability to go from *i* to *j* in one step). These probabilities are expressed by the row stochastic matrix $D^{-1}W$, where *D* is the diagonal degree matrix given by

$$D_{ii} = \sum_{k} W_{ik} \qquad [3]$$

The value of the Diagonal matrix calculated from the example W matrix (Table 1) are [1, 0.6, 0.6, 0.2, 0.4, 0.2].

The random walk is then simulated by a matrix transformation using the formula

$$P^{(t)}(j|i) = [(D^{-1}W)^t]_{ij} \text{ (Iria, et al., 2007)} \qquad [4]$$

which means that relatedness between two nodes in the graph is given by the *t*-step transition probability $P^{(t)}(j|i)$. In this work we set *t* = 2 in order to prevent smoothing out the walk.

The resulting matrix after two steps for the example is shown in Table 2.

Table 2. 2-step transition probability matrix of adjacency matrix W (Table 1)

	Wiki_1190	**Wiki_5236**	**title_Forest**	**title_Coast**	**cat_Forestry**	**cat_ Landform**	**cat_Coastal Geography**
Wiki_1190	0.9	0.1	0	0	0	0	0
Wiki_5236	0.1	0.9	0	0.6	0	0	0
title_Forest	0	0	0.6	0	0.2	0.2	0
title_Coast	0	0	0	0.6	0	0.2	0.2
cat_Forestry	0	0	0.6	0	0.2	0.2	0
cat_Landform	0	0	0.3	0.3	0.1	0.2	0.1
cat_Coastal Geography	0	0	0	0.6	0	0.2	0.2

Table 3. Relatedness matrix for example in Figure 1

	Wiki_1190	Wiki_5236	title_Forest	title_Coast	cat_Forestry	cat_Landform	cat_Coastal Geography
Wiki_1190	1	0.11	0	0	0	0	0
Wiki_5236	0.11	1	0	0	0	0	0
title_Forest	0	0	0.67	0	0.22	0.22	0
title_Coast	0	0	0	0.67	0	0.22	0.22
cat_Forestry	0	0	0.67	0	0.22	0.22	0
cat_Landform	0	0	0.33	0.33	0.11	0.22	0.11
cat_Coastal Geography	0	0	0	0.67	0	0.22	0.22

In fact, the transition results in a sparse, non-symmetric matrix filled with probabilities of reaching node *i* from *j* after *t* steps. To transform probability to relatedness, we use the observation that the probability of walking from *i* to *j* then coming back to *i* is always the same as starting from *j*, reaching *i* and then coming back to *j*, given the undirected nature of the graph. Thus we define a transformation function as

$$\text{Rel}(i \mid j) = \text{Rel}(j \mid i) = \frac{P^{(t)}(i \mid j) + P^{(t)}(j \mid i)}{2}$$

[5]

and we normalize the score to range *{0, 1}* by using the maximum $\text{Rel}(i \mid j)$ as denominator to every value of $\text{Rel}(i \mid j)$ using

$$\text{Rel}(i \mid j) = \frac{\text{Rel}(i \mid j)}{Max_{\text{Rel}(i \mid j)}}$$

[6]

Table 3 reports the normalized relatedness scores for all concepts in the initial example graph (Figure 1). Because we are only interest in relatedness between nodes of type concept, in this case we have that relatedness between *Wiki_1190* and *Wiki_5236* is 0.11.

EXPERIMENTS

As aforementioned, the major hypothesis of this chapter is that combining diverse features extracted from a knowledge resource in a balanced way for a semantic relatedness method can outperform the same method that employs very limited sets of features. To justify this hypothesis, we have proposed using diverse features extracted from the Wikipedia knowledge base and naturally integrate them under the random walk model. This section first describes a set of experiments designed to analyse the balancing of different features (feature tuning), then shows experiments to compare results of our novel SR to the state-of-the art measures (evaluating SR) and at the end evaluates the usage of the novel SR measure within an application task (application results).

Feature Tuning

Under the random walk model, naturally, feature tuning can be achieved by using different combinations of features (Figure 1), and altering the distribution of weights for different types of features, using equation 1. Essentially, this is a parameter optimisation process, which takes a set of training data and optimises values of input parameters (choice of features and feature weights) to minimise the loss of accuracy of the automated system on the data. Typically, evaluating the ac-

Table 4. The best and the worst results obtained with initial feature sets and corresponding wm from feature tuning experiments (selected from 100 iterations of runs on Fin-200 dataset)

Feature	wm1	wm2	wm3	wm4	wm5	wm6
title_words	0.17	0.24	0.30	0.14	0.02	0.03
first_sec_words	0.15	0.1	0.14	0.31	0.28	0.24
cat_words	0.15	0.14	0.11	0.01	0.02	0.01
desc_noun_words	< 0.01	< 0.01	< 0.01	0.34	0.28	0.24
list_link_words	0.24	0.21	0.17	0.2	0.39	0.48
other_link_words	0.29	0.31	0.27	< 0.01	< 0.01	< 0.01
Correlation accuracy	0.39	0.387	0.381	0.17	0.167	0.165

curacy of semantic relatedness measures makes use of human judgments as gold standard. The datasets are usually organised as sets of pair of words, such as "apple" and "pear", and "Apple" and "Intel", for which annotators are required to assign a score within a scale of minimum and maximum values to indicate their subjective interpretation of the semantic relatedness between two words. System produced scores are then compared against human-rated values using a correlation coefficient function. For consistency with previous literature, we use the Spearman rank-order correlation coefficient (Spearman, 1987) for all our experiments.

For the purpose of feature tuning, we select the largest benchmarking dataset by Finkelstein et al. (2002). The dataset is split into two sets that are annotated by different annotators, one containing 200 pairs of words (Fin-200) and the other containing 153 pairs of words (Fin-153). We choose the larger part of this dataset (Fin-200) as the training data for feature tuning, and use the smaller set for evaluation in the following sections. We adopt the simulated annealing algorithm by Nie et al. (2005). The algorithm explores the search space of possible combinations of feature weights and iteratively reduces the difference in accuracy between human annotations and that of the automated system. The algorithm allows the proposed method to run on one dataset in an iterative manner. At each iteration, the algorithm

generates random feature weight for different types of features subject to equation 1, which we refer to as a *weight model* (wm). The weights are then used by the proposed method to compute semantic relatedness on the dataset and results are evaluated against the gold standard.

To begin with, we run our system on this dataset for 100 iterations using initial feature set as proposed in the feature extraction section, with uniform distribution of feature weights. We fix the number of iterations to 100 in all the following simulated annealing experiments. Due to the limitation of space, Table 4 only shows the highest and the lowest accuracies and the corresponding *wm* obtained in those iterations.

As shown in Table 4, *title_words, cat_words* and links (*list_link_words and other_link_words*) are more important features since the increase in their weights leads to improvements in system accuracy; on the other hand, the increase in the weight for feature *desc_noun_words* has the opposite effect, suggesting it a less useful feature. However, instead of dropping this feature entirely and losing potentially useful information, we refine the feature set by merging *desc_noun_words* into *cat_words* to become *cat_words_merged*. The intuition is that they bear similar semantics (e.g., hypernyms) and therefore, can be considered as similar types of features. Likewise, we merge *list_link_words* and *other_link_words* into *link_words_merged* as they are

Table 5. The best and the worst results obtained with refined feature sets and corresponding weight models from feature tuning experiments (selected from 100 iterations of runs on the Fin-200 dataset)

Feature	wm1	wm2	wm3	wm4	wm5	wm6
title_words	0.2	0.22	0.24	0.17	0.26	0.4
first_sec_words	0.05	0.05	0.06	< 0.01	<0.01	< 0.01
cat_words_merged	0.15	0.17	0.2	0.53	0.56	0.52
link_words_merged	0.6	0.56	0.5	0.29	0.17	0.07
Correlation accuracy	0.422	0.418	0.405	0.28	0.287	0.28

equally important features and are both outgoing links. We re-run simulated annealing for another 100 iterations on the same dataset using the revised feature set starting with uniform distribution of feature weights, and present results in Table 5.

As shown in Table 5, feature grouping further improves system accuracy. Also, the *wms* are generally consistent with the previous findings; that is, links on the page are more important features than others, and thus tend to receive higher weights; followed by *title_words* and *cat_words_merged*. However, this raised the question of whether it is beneficial to further group features and eventually arriving at a single type of feature. To test this, we carried out further sets of experiments by randomly grouping two types of features. However, the system could not outperform the best results obtained so far. For example, Table 6 shows results of grouping *title_words* and *cat_words_merged*, which leads to the top accuracy of 41.7. This suggests that it is useful to keep feature set diverse rather than over-grouping features.

Another observation based on Table 5 is that *first_sec_words* is a less useful feature as indicated by the low weight it receives under the best performing *wms*. This is possibly due to the varying sizes of first sections of Wikipedia pages that result in sparse feature spaces. For example, in some short articles, the first section consists of only one sentence. To improve this, we replaced it with the most frequent n words extracted from a page (*frequent_words_n*). Using this revised feature set, we re-run simulated annealing with different value of n. Results are shown in Table 7: this modification further improves the system performance, and the *wm* derived with different n tends to be consistent.

As a result of feature tuning and analysis, we obtain the best feature set and an optimum feature *weight model,* as summarized in Table 8.

In summary, results from feature tuning suggest that there is an optimum combination of features as well as the choice of feature weights for the task of computing semantic relatedness. On one hand, grouping features extracted from

Table 6. Best and worst results obtained with further grouped features and corresponding weight models from feature tuning experiments (selected from 100 iterations of runs on the Fin-200 dataset)

Feature	wm1	wm2	wm3	wm4	wm5	wm6
title+cat_words_merged	0.3	0.23	0.3	0.11	0.16	0.1
first_sec_words	0.07	0.15	0.19	< 0.01	< 0.01	< 0.01
link_words_merged	0.63	0.62	0.51	0.88	0.83	0.89
Correlation Accuracy	0.417	0.405	0.399	0.267	0.258	0.25

Table 7. Best results obtained by replacing the feature first_sec_words with n most frequent words, and varying the value n and weight models. Figures are obtained on the Fin-200 dataset after 100 iterations of runs

Feature	n=25	n=50	n=75	n=100
title_words	0.16	0.17	0.16	0.19
freq_words_n	0.28	0.30	0.39	0.32
cat_words_merged	0.11	0.12	0.1	0.11
link_words_merged	0.45	0.41	0.35	0.38
Correlation	0.382	0.44	0.455	0.41

Table 8. Final feature set and weight model

title_words	freq words_75	cat_words_merged	link_words_merged
0.16	0.39	0.1	0.35

Wikipedia by similar semantics achieve better results than treating them separately. On the other hand, over-grouping features towards the other extreme can damage the system accuracy. Different features contribute differently to semantic relatedness. The most indicative features for this specific task are the most frequent words on the page; followed by words from outgoing links on a page, words from titles and redirection links, and words from category labels. Additionally, most frequent words on a page are more useful features than words extracted from the first section. In addition, we carried out experiments using the exact phrases instead of treating them as words, which resulted in decreased accuracy. This can be explained by the observation that many information and structural elements extracted from Wikipedia can be too fine-grained, causing the feature space to be too sparse. For example, the page for "rabbit" has a category "Herbivorous animals"; and the page for "dog" has a category "Domesticated animals". The category labels are clearly too restrictive, and the most indicative information in this case is in the word "animals". Although using word-based

features can introduce noise, our experiments have shown that, in general, it leads to better accuracy.

Next, we apply these feature sets with the *wm* as shown in Table 8 to several major benchmarking datasets to thoroughly evaluate the proposed method for computing semantic relatedness.

Evaluating the Semantic Relatedness Measure

In addition to the Fin-200 dataset, we choose another three most often used benchmarking datasets to evaluate the proposed methods. These include the other part of Finkelstein's dataset (Fin-153) containing 153 pairs of words, the Rubenstein and Goodenough (1965) dataset consisting of 65 pairs of words (RG-65), the Miller and Charles (1991) dataset (MC-30) that contains a subset of 30 pairs from the RG-65 dataset. In order to justify that using the inferred diverse feature set and feature weights can produce better results than using single types of features, the baseline systems use the same proposed method, but using each type of the inferred feature separately (and thus not

Table 9. Comparison of the proposed method using diverse, weighted features against baselines. Bold text highlights the highest accuracy achieved

	Fin-200	*Fin-153*	*RG-65*	*MC-30*
RW-combined	**0.46**	**0.71**	**0.76**	**0.71**
RW-title_words	0.24	0.4	0.46	0.68
RW-freq_words	0.41	0.63	0.6	**0.71**
RW-cat_words	0.21	0.38	0.56	0.64
RW-link_words	0.37	0.59	0.57	0.46

weighted). Therefore, we have four baselines, namely, the random walk based method using only *title_words* as features (*RW-title_words*); only *freq_words_75* as features (*RW-freq_words*); only *cat_words_merged* as features (*RW-cat_words*); and only *link_words_merged* as features (*RW-link_words*). We use *RW-combined* to denote the proposed method with inferred feature set and weights. Table 9 compares the method against proposed baselines.

Next, we compare the proposed method against state-of-the-art systems on these datasets. Firstly, we select five widely accepted and frequently used WordNet based approaches, including Leacock and Chodorow (lch) (1998), Lin (lin) (1998), Wu and Palmer (wup) (1994), Jiang and Conrath (jc) (1997), and Resnik (res) (1995b). These

methods have been implemented in the Java WordNet::Similarity[3] package, which we use to produce results as shown in the upper section of Table 10. Additionally, we also compare the results against state-of-the-art methods that employ Wikipedia as the knowledge base. These are shown in the lower section of Table 10.

As it is shown in Table 9, using diverse weighted features significantly improves the accuracy of semantic relatedness measures under the same proposed method. This justifies our hypothesis that different types of features extracted from a knowledge base can all be useful to the task of computing semantic relatedness. Additionally, they complement each other if used in a properly balanced way. Comparing against the state-of-the-art methods using Table 10, we

Table 10. Comparison of the proposed system against state-of-the-art methods

	Fin-200	*Fin-153*	*RG-65*	*MC-30*
RW-Combined	0.46	**0.71**	0.76	0.71
WordNet method				
lch	0.24	0.32	**0.79**	0.75
lin	0.25	0.39	0.78	0.76
wup	0.24	0.37	0.78	0.77
jc	0.23	0.38	0.78	**0.81**
res	0.25	0.37	0.78	0.76
Wikipedia				
Zesch et al. (2008a) ESA[4]	0.31	0.62	n/a	n/a
Zesch et al. (2008a) Wiki	**0.5**	0.7	0.76	0.68
Strube & Ponzetto (2006)	n/a	0.55	0.69	0.67

notice that there is no single system or knowledge base that always outperforms others on all datasets. Specifically, all methods that use Wikipedia outperform WordNet-based methods on the Fin-153 and Fin-200 datasets. However, WordNet based methods achieve highest accuracy on the RG-65 and MC-30 datasets. This on one hand indicates that measuring semantic relatedness is not an easy task; on the other hand, suggests that different knowledge bases may contain complementary information. Compared to other Wikipedia based methods, the proposed method achieves highest accuracy on three out of the four datasets. As aforementioned, these systems only make use of one or two types of features extracted from Wikipedia. The improvement in accuracy by our system further confirms the hypothesis that using diverse weighted features extracted from a knowledge base can produce better results in computing semantic relatedness.

Application Results

In order to evaluate the usefulness of our method, we apply our SR method to a Named Entity disambiguation (NED) task. NED is the problem of mapping mentions of entities in a text with the object they are referencing. The set of possible entities for this task is supposed to predefined in an external repository, the *name inventory*, and the goal is establishing a unique mapping between a mention of name in a text, the surface form, and the real world object in the *name inventory*. The NED methodology used in this evaluation is designed to exploit SR scores (Gentile, et al., 2010). The hypothesis is that, given a set of mentions of names in a text, their meanings (the referred objects) are collectively defined by other entities. For example, "Apple" is likely to mean the American company if it occurs together with "Macintosh", "Microsoft" in the same document; but it is likely to mean "fruit" if it occurs with "pear", "passion fruit". Therefore, given:

- $S = \{s_1, ..., s_n\}$ the set of *surfaces* (mentions of entities in a text)
- $C = \{c_{1\_1}, c_{1\_2}, ..., c_{i\_k}, ..., c_{n\_k}\}$ the set of all their possible *concepts* from Wikipedia (where i is the index for surface s_i and k varies according to the number of possible concepts for s_i retrieved from Wikipedia)
- R the matrix of semantic relatedness, where each cell indicates the strength of relatedness between concept c_{i_t} and concept c_{j_z} (where $i \neq j$, which means that the concepts have been retrieved from different surfaces)

the NED algorithm is defined as a function f: $S \rightarrow C$, which given a set of *surfaces* S returns an unambiguous *concept* for each of them, using R. Three different functions f have been designed for such purpose, details can be found in Gentile et al. (2010). Briefly, the three functions are:

- The *highest method* ($f_{highest}$), where the choice is based on the highest value in the matrix R for each *concept*
- The *combination method* (f_{comb}), which combines for each *concept* the relatedness with all different *concepts* from different *surfaces*
- The *propagation method* (f_{prop}), which staring from highest relatedness values in R, recursively deletes *concepts* with lower scores until only one *concept* remains in R for each *surface*.

The corpus used for evaluating NED is the benchmarking dataset published by Cucerzan (2007). It is created based on 20 news stories, for each of which a list of named entities is extracted. Most names are ambiguous, since they point to multiple entries of entities defined in Wikipedia. The purpose of NED is to select the accurate Wikipedia entries for each name depending on the context collectively defined by other named entities in each news story. The number of entities

Table 11. Comparison of our NED system against state-of-the-art

f_{comb}	91.5%
f_{prop}	**68.7%**
$f_{highest}$	**82.2%**
Cucerzan (2007) baseline	51.7%
Cucerzan (2007) best	91.4%

in each story can vary from 10 to 50. For each news story, we take the extracted names as input to our SR method and compute pair-wise semantic relatedness between their underlying concepts. The result forms the semantic relatedness matrix R, which is then submitted to the three NED functions proposed before. The results of the NED experiment are shown in Table 11.

The best performing function is f_{comb}, which is the *combination method*. Its accuracy of 91.5% represents a result competitive to the state of the art. Indeed, the best figure reported by Cucerzan (2007) on the same dataset is of 91.4%. The same experiment, repeated on a different dataset, confirm the same trend (Gentile, et al., 2010), thus showing a profitable usage of SR for the purposes of Named Entity Disambiguation.

CONCLUSION AND FUTURE RESEARCH DIRECTIONS

In this chapter, we introduced a novel approach to measuring semantic relatedness between words or concepts using a random walk model. We investigate various features extracted from Wikipedia for a pair of words or concepts and their importance in measuring semantic relatedness. No single system reported in the literature always outperforms the others on all testing datasets. In general, by integrating various weighted features extracted from Wikipedia through a random walk model, we can obtain better results than WordNet-based approaches, and other Wikipedia-based approaches

that only make use of limited un-weighted features. Also, we empirically derived the best features and analyzed their importance for the semantic relatedness task. The conclusions from the analysis can be useful references to future research in computing semantic relatedness.

However, the effects of using a random walk model in combining diverse features are unclear. In the future, we will study and compare effects of other similarity functions with diverse feature sets in semantic relatedness task, and compare against other distributional models such as Latent Semantic Analysis (LSA) to investigate the possibility of improving performance using different approaches. Also, we will research the possibilities of integrating different lexical resources in a coherent methodology. In addition, we will look into adapting our methodology to computing semantic relatedness between longer text fragments, such as sentences and snippets, which is another major challenge in the studies of semantic relatedness.

REFERENCES

Banerjee, S., & Pedersen, T. (2003). Extended Gloss Overlaps as a Measure of Semantic Relatedness, *IJCAI-03, Proceedings of the Eighteenth International Joint Conference on Artificial Intelligence* (pp. 805-810). Boston: M. Kaufmann.

Bollegala, D., Matsuo, Y., & Ishizuka, M. (2007). *An Integrated Approach to Measuring Semantic Similarity between Words Using Information Available on the Web. HLT-NAACL* (pp. 340–347). The Association for Computational Linguistics.

Chen, H.-H., Lin, M.-S., & Wei, Y.-C. (2006). Novel association measures using web search with double checking. *ACL-44: Proceedings of the 21st International Conference on Computational Linguistics and the 44th annual meeting of the Association for Computational Linguistics* (pp. 1009-1016). Sydney, Australia: Association for Computational Linguistics.

Cilibrasi, R. L., & Vitanyi, P. M. B. (2007). The Google Similarity Distance. *IEEE Transactions on Knowledge and Data Engineering, 19*(3), 370–383. doi:10.1109/TKDE.2007.48

Cucerzan, S. (2007). Large-Scale Named Entity Disambiguation Based on Wikipedia Data, *Proceedings of the 2007 Joint Conference on Empirical Methods in Natural Language Processing and Computational Natural Language Learning (EMNLP-CoNLL)* (pp. 708-716). Prague, Czech Republic: Association for Computational Linguistics.

Finkelstein, L., Gabrilovich, E., Matias, Y., Rivlin, E., Solan, Z., & Wolfman, G. (2002). Placing search in context: the concept revisited. *ACM Transactions on Information Systems, 20*(1), 116–131. doi:10.1145/503104.503110

Gabrilovich, E., & Markovitch, S. (2007). Computing semantic relatedness using Wikipedia-based explicit semantic analysis. *IJCAI'07: Proceedings of the 20th international joint conference on Artificial intelligence* (pp. 1606-1611). Hyderabad, India: Morgan Kaufmann Publishers Inc.

Gentile, A. L., Zhang, Z., Xia, L., & Iria, J. (2010). Cultural knowledge for Named Entity Disambiguation: a graph-based Semantic Relatedness approach. *Serdica Journal of Computing, 4*(2), 217–242.

Giuliano, C., Lavelli, A., & Romano, L. (2006). Exploiting Shallow Linguistic Information for Relation Extraction From Biomedical Literature, *Proceedings of the 11th Conference of the European Chapter of the Association for Computational Linguistics (EACL 2006)*. Trento, Italy.

Grishman, R., & Sundheim, B. (1996). Message Understanding Conference- 6: A Brief History. *COLING* (pp. 466-471).

Han, X., & Zhao, J. (2010). *Structural Semantic Relatedness: A Knowledge-Based Method to Named Entity Disambiguation.* Paper presented at the the 48th Annual Meeting of the Association for Computational Linguistics, Uppsala, Sweden.

Harris, Z. (1970). *Distributional structure* (pp. 775–794). Papers in Structural and Transformational Linguistics.

Hassan, S., & Mihalcea, R. (2009). *Cross-lingual Semantic Relatedness Using Encyclopedic Knowledge, EMNLP* (pp. 1192–1201). Association for Computational Linguistics.

Hughes, T., & Ramage, D. (2007). Lexical semantic relatedness with random graph walks, *Proceedings of EMNLP* (Vol. 7).

Iria, J., Xia, L., & Zhang, Z. (2007). *WIT: Web People Search Disambiguation using Random Walks.* Paper presented at the Proceedings of the Fourth International Workshop on Semantic Evaluations (SemEval-2007).

Jiang, J., & Conrath, D. (1997). Semantic similarity based on corpus statistics and lexical taxonomy, *Proceedings of the International Conference on Research in Computational Linguistics* (pp. 19-33).

Kazama, J., & Torisawa, K. (2007). Exploiting Wikipedia as External Knowledge for Named Entity Recognition. *Joint Conference on Empirical Methods in Natural Language Processing and Computational Natural Language Learning* (pp. 698-707). Japan Advanced Institute of Science and Technologie.

Leacock, C., & Chodorow, M. (1998). *Combining local context and WordNet similarity for word sense identification, WordNet: An Electronic Lexical Database.* Cambridge, MA: MIT Press.

Lin, D. (1998). *An Information-Theoretic Definition of Similarity*. Paper presented at the Proceedings of the Fifteenth International Conference on Machine Learning.

Lovász, L. (1993). Random walks on graphs: A survey. *Combinatorics, Paul Erd\"os is Eighty, 2*, 1-46.

Matsuo, Y., Sakaki, T., Uchiyama, K. o., & Ishizuka, M. (2006). Graph-based word clustering using a web search engine. *EMNLP '06: Proceedings of the 2006 Conference on Empirical Methods in Natural Language Processing* (pp. 542-550). Sydney, Australia: Association for Computational Linguistics.

Miller, G., & Charles, W. (1991). Contextual correlates of semantic similarity. *Language and Cognitive Processes, 1*(6), 1–28. doi:10.1080/01690969108406936

Miller, G. A. (1995). WordNet: a lexical database for English. *Communications of the ACM, 38*(11), 39–41. doi:10.1145/219717.219748

Milne, D., & Witten, I. H. (2008). *An effective, low-cost measure of semantic relatedness obtained from Wikipedia links*. Paper presented at the Wikipedia and Artificial Intelligence: An Evolving Synergy Workshop at the Twenty-third AAAI conference on Artificial Intelligence (AAAI-08).

Müller, C., & Gurevych, I. (2009). Using Wikipedia and Wiktionary in domain-specific information retrieval, *CLEF'08: Proceedings of the 9th Cross-language evaluation forum conference on Evaluating systems for multilingual and multimodal information access* (pp. 219-226). Aarhus, Denmark: Springer-Verlag.

Nie, Z., Zhang, Y., Wen, J., & Ma, W. (2005). Object-level ranking: bringing order to Web objects. *WWW '05: Proceedings of the 14th international conference on World Wide Web* (pp. 567-574). Chiba, Japan: ACM.

Pearson, K. (1905). The Problem of the Random Walk. *Nature, 72*(1867).

Resnik, P. (1995a). Disambiguating noun groupings with respect to WordNet senses, *Proceedings of the 3th Workshop on Very Large Corpora* (pp. 54-68). ACL.

Resnik, P. (1995b). Using Information Content to Evaluate Semantic Similarity in a Taxonomy, *Proceedings of the 14th International Joint Conference on Artificial Intelligence* (pp. 448-453). Boston: Morgan Kaufmann.

Rubenstein, H., & Goodenough, J. B. (1965). Contextual correlates of synonymy. *Communications of the ACM, 8*(10), 627–633. doi:10.1145/365628.365657

Sahami, M., & Heilman, T. D. (2006). A web-based kernel function for measuring the similarity of short text snippets, *WWW '06: Proceedings of the 15th international conference on World Wide Web* (pp. 377-386). Edinburgh, Scotland: ACM.

Spearman, C. (1987). *The American Journal of Psychology; The Proof and Measurement of Association between Two Things. 100*(3/4), 441-471.

Strube, M., & Ponzetto, S. P. (2006). WikiRelate! Computing Semantic Relatedness Using Wikipedia, *Proceedings of The Twenty-First National Conference on Artificial Intelligence and the Eighteenth Innovative Applications of Artificial Intelligence Conference* (pp. 1419-1424). AAAI Press.

Turdakov, D., & Velikhov, P. (2008). Semantic Relatedness Metric for Wikipedia Concepts Based on Link Analysis and its Application to Word Sense Disambiguation, *SYRCoDIS* (Vol. 355). CEUR-WS.org.

Weale, T., Brew, C., & Fosler-Lussier, E. (2009). Using the Wiktionary Graph Structure for Synonym Detection, *Proceedings of the 2009 Workshop on The People's Web Meets NLP: Collaboratively Constructed Semantic Resources* (pp. 28-31). Suntec, Singapore: Association for Computational Linguistics.

Wu, Z., & Palmer, M. (1994). Verbs semantics and lexical selection, *Proceedings of the 32nd annual meeting on Association for Computational Linguistics* (pp. 133-138). Las Cruces, New Mexico: Association for Computational Linguistics.

Zesch, T., Müller, C., & Gurevych, I. (2008a). *Extracting Lexical Semantic Knowledge from Wikipedia and Wiktionary.* Paper presented at the Proceedings of the Sixth International Language Resources and Evaluation (LREC'08), Marrakech, Morocco.

Zesch, T., Müller, C., & Gurevych, I. (2008b). Using Wiktionary for Computing Semantic Relatedness, *Proceedings of the Twenty-Third AAAI Conference on Artificial Intelligence, AAAI 2008* (pp. 861-866). AAAI Press.

Zhang, Z., Gentile, A. L., Xia, L., Iria, J., & Chapman, S. (2010). A Random Graph Walk based Approach to Computing Semantic Relatedness Using Knowledge from Wikipedia, *Proceedings of the Seventh conference on International Language Resources and Evaluation (LREC'10)* (pp. 1394-1401). European Language Resources Association (ELRA).

ADDITIONAL READING

Budanitsky, A., & Hirst, G. (2006). Evaluating WordNet-based Measures of Lexical Semantic Relatedness. *Computational Linguistics, 32*(1), 13–47. doi:10.1162/coli.2006.32.1.13

Cha, S.-H. (2007). Comprehensive Survey on Distance/Similarity Measures between Probability Density Functions. *International journal of mathematical models and methods in applied sciences, 1*(4), 300-307.

Crestani, F. (2003). Combination of similarity measures for effective spoken document retrieval. *Journal of Information Science, 29*(2), 87–96. doi:10.1177/016555150302900201

Fernandez, M., Lopez, V., Sabou, M., Uren, V., Vallet, D., & Motta, E. (2008). *Semantic Search Meets the Web.* Paper presented at the IEEE International Conference on Semantic Computing.

Kaminski, G., Dridi, S., Graff, C., & Gentaz, E. (2009). Proceedings of the Royal Society B: Biological Sciences; Human ability to detect kinship in strangers' faces: effects of the degree of relatedness.

Kozima, H., & Furugori, T. (1993). Similarity between words computed by spreading activation on an English dictionary, *Proceedings of the sixth conference on European chapter of the Association for Computational Linguistics* (pp. 232-239). Utrecht, The Netherlands: Association for Computational Linguistics.

Lien, L., & Klein, P. (2009). Journal of Management. *Using Competition to Measure Relatedness, 35*(4), 1078–1107.

Mohler, M., & Mihalcea, R. (2009). Text-to-text semantic similarity for automatic short answer grading, *EACL '09: Proceedings of the 12th Conference of the European Chapter of the Association for Computational Linguistics* (pp. 567-575). Athens, Greece: Association for Computational Linguistics.

Pedersen, T. (2010). *Information Content Measures of Semantic Similarity Perform Better Without Sense-Tagged Text*. Paper presented at the Human Language Technologies: The 2010 Annual Conference of the North American Chapter of the Association for Computational Linguistics.

Pedersen, T., Pakhomov, S., Patwardhan, S., & Chute, C. (in press). Measures of semantic similarity and relatedness in the biomedical domain. *Journal of Biomedical Informatics*.

Pirró, G. (2009). A semantic similarity metric combining features and intrinsic information content. *Data & Knowledge Engineering, 68*(11), 1289–1308. doi:10.1016/j.datak.2009.06.008

Ponzetto, S. P., & Strube, M. (2007). Knowledge derived from wikipedia for computing semantic relatedness. *Journal of Artificial Intelligence Research, 30*(1), 181–212.

Ramage, D., Rafferty, A. N., & Manning, C. D. (2009). Random walks for text semantic similarity, *TextGraphs-4: Proceedings of the 2009 Workshop on Graph-based Methods for Natural Language Processing* (pp. 23-31). Suntec, Singapore: Association for Computational Linguistics.

Resnik, P. (1999). Semantic Similarity in a Taxonomy: An Information-Based Measure and its Application to Problems of Ambiguity in Natural Language. *Journal of Artificial Intelligence Research, 11*, 95–130.

Rodriguez, M., & Egenhofer, M. (2003). Knowledge and Data Engineering. *IEEE Transactions on; Determining semantic similarity among entity classes from different ontologies, 15*(2), 442-456.

Turney, P. (2006). Similarity of Semantic Relations. *Computational Linguistics, 32*(3), 379–416. doi:10.1162/coli.2006.32.3.379

Yeh, E., Ramage, D., Manning, C. D., Agirre, E., & Soroa, A. (2009). WikiWalk: random walks on Wikipedia for semantic relatedness, *TextGraphs-4: Proceedings of the 2009 Workshop on Graph-based Methods for Natural Language Processing* (pp. 41-49). Suntec, Singapore: Association for Computational Linguistics.

Zesch, T., & Gurevych, I. (2010). Wisdom of crowds versus wisdom of linguists - measuring the semantic relatedness of words. *Natural Language Engineering, 16*(1), 25–59. doi:10.1017/S1351324909990167

KEY TERMS AND DEFINITIONS

Graph: A representation of a set of interconnected objects. Connections are established between pairs of objects by means of links. The objects are called vertices or nodes, the links are called edges.

Knowledge Resource: A collection of data, which can be general purpose or about a specific domain, represented in machine-readable form.

Named Entity Disambiguation: Is the task of mapping the list of entities appearing in a text with the correct unique real-world objects respectively referred.

Natural Language Processing: A field of Information Science and Computational Linguistics which investigates on the properties of human language with the aim of automatically processing and understanding it.

Random Walk: A mathematical formalisation of a trajectory that consists of taking successive random steps. Could be applied on the line, on graphs, in the plane, in higher dimensions or on groups. The term has been introduced by Pearson (1905).

Semantic Relatedness: Calculated between two terms, quantifies how much they are associated to each other. Typically the calculation of this kind of measure exploits all kind of relations between concepts, such as hyponymy and hypernymy, together with antonymy, meronymy and other functional relations.

Semantic Similarity: Calculated between two terms, quantifies how much they are close to each other. Typically the calculation of this kind of measure only exploits is-a /kind-of relations (hyponymy and hypernymy) between concepts.

Wikipedia: A multi-lingual, free online encyclopedia that is collaboratively created and maintained by voluntary contributors. Knowledge in Wikipedia are organised based on articles, which are often descriptions of named entities. Information can be accessed by semi-structured and structured way.

WordNet: A lexical database of English, where nouns, verbs, adjectives and adverbs are grouped into sets of cognitive synonyms (synsets), each expressing a distinct concept.

ENDNOTES

[1] http://en.wiktionary.org, last retrieved on 3 Sept 2010

[2] http://lucene.apache.org, last retrieved on 3 Sept 2010

[3] http://www.informatics.sussex.ac.uk/users/drh21/, last retrieved on 3 Sept 2010

[4] This is the re-implementation of the ESA method (Gabrilovich & Markovitch, 2007), because the original authors did not report results on *Fin-153* or *Fin-200*

Chapter 6
Web Search Results Discovery by Multi–Granular Graphs

Gloria Bordogna
CNR-IDPA, Italy

Alessandro Campi
Politecnico di Milano, Italy

Giuseppe Psaila
Università di Bergamo, Italy

Stefania Ronchi
Politecnico di Milano, Italy

ABSTRACT

Graph-based visualization and exploration of results of a single Web search is becoming very popular with the wonderwheel of Google (http://www.googlewonderwheel.com/).

In this chapter, the authors propose a novel multi-granular framework for visualization and exploration of the results of a complex search process, performed by a user by submitting several queries to possibly distinct search engines. The primary aim of the approach is to supply users with summaries, with distinct levels of details, of the results for a search process. It applies dynamic clustering to the results in each ordered list retrieved by a search engine evaluating a user's query. The single retrieved items, the clusters so identified, and the single retrieved lists, are considered as dealing with topics at distinct levels of granularity, from the finest level to the coarsest one, respectively. Implicit topics are revealed by associating labels with the retrieved items, the clusters, and the retrieved lists. Then, some manipulation operators, defined in this chapter, are applied to each pair of retrieved lists, clusters, and single items, to reveal their implicit relationships. These relationships have a semantic nature, since they are labeled to approximately represent the shared documents and the shared sub-topics between each pair of combined elements. Finally, both the topics retrieved by the distinct searches and their relationships are represented through multi-granular graphs, that represent the retrieved topics at three distinct levels of granularity. The exploration of the results can be performed by expanding the graphs nodes to see their contents, and by expanding the edges to see their shared contents and their common sub-topics.

DOI: 10.4018/978-1-60960-881-1.ch006

INTRODUCTION

Graph-based visualization of Web search results has been recognized to be an effective way to provide a road and concise representation of the results; the user can quickly analyse graphs to understand if and how they are related to his/her information needs. This paradigm enables the simultaneous display of a large number of Web pages. It has been adopted for several different purposes:

- For providing an impressed view of the contents of a Web site, allowing users to deal with the results at a coarser grain, namely, the site level rather than the page level (McCrickard et al., 2007);
- For representing the inner structure of retrieved documents, mainly in the case of multimedia documents composed of distinct media sections (Worring, de Rooij and van Rijn, 2007);
- For representing the relationships between documents defined by both their in and out links and shared index terms (Angelaccio, Buttarazzi and Patrignanell, 2007; Thiel et al., 2007; Belew, 1989);
- For representing the inter structure of homogeneous sets of documents identified by flat and hierarchical clustering (de Graaf, Kok and Kosters, 2007);
- Last but not least, for visualizing and refining Web searches, as in the popular *wonderwheel* feature recently introduced by Google.

In this chapter, we propose a novel framework for the exploration of the results obtained by querying possibly distinct search engines during a complex search process; we also propose a multi-granular graph-based visualization of results.

Graphs are used to represent and visualize both the main retrieved topics and their approximate semantic relationships. Specifically, we define a multi-granular graph that consists of several graphs organized on distinct layers, which represent the topics dealt with in the retrieved documents and their relationships at distinct levels of details. This multi-granular representation is very effective to provide overviews at a glance of the retrieved topics at distinct levels.

Further, the representation of the retrieved contents is done by considering the user needs expressed in the query that retrieved the web page. So, since a web page can be retrieved by distinct queries, we derive multiple representations that focus its contents from distinct points of view.

This goal is also the same pursued by the application of hierarchical categorization and hierarchical clustering of the results of web searches. Nevertheless, our approach is different: we generate the topics and their approximate semantic relationships by employing clustering techniques in combination with the application of cluster manipulation operations. These operations aid the identification of ''hidden'' relevant topics, not necessarily top-ranked and highlighted in any of the retrieved result lists.

More precisely, our approach follows the following two steps.

- Firstly, the results in the lists, retrieved independently by possibly distinct search services (i.e. search engines) by evaluating possibly distinct queries, are clustered (each list is clustered independently of the others) The clustering of a results' list identifies a group of clusters which are considered the most general retrieved topics by a single query.
- Second, other hidden topics are revealed by combining both the ranked lists, i.e., the groups of clusters, the clusters, and the single retrieved items (that are represented by the web pages' titles and snippets) by means of manipulation operators defined in this chapter: these operations allow defining approximate semantic relationships

between the combined elements that high-light their shared sub-topics.

This way, topics can be analyzed at three levels of granularity: groups of clusters, clusters and documents. To discover their relationships, the manipulation operators are applied between pairs of groups. A first experimental validation of this approach, in which the user explicitly applies the manipulation operators, was performed by the aid of *Matrioshka*, a meta-search clustering environment (http://matrioshka.unibg.it) (Bordogna et al., 2011). This evaluation consisted in designing an experiment in which users submit the same query firstly directly to a search engine, and secondly indirectly by the aid of the *Matrioshka* meta-search system. The evaluation metrics were defined to quantify the user's gain in terms of precision and effort in retrieving relevant documents by means of *Matrioshka* with respect to using directly the search engine. The results obtained pointed out the need to introduce some automatic mechanism that helps users apply the manipulation operator and to visualize the discovered relationships between pairs of groups, clusters, and documents.

This is the motivation that brought us to define the multi-granular graph visualization of search results.

At each level of the multi-granular graphs, the nodes represent the topics in the elements of that level (groups, clusters, or documents), while the edges represent their relationships in terms of both shared documents and sub-topics. The generation of the multi-granular graph of a search process is obtained by applying the manipulation operators in a given order: we call this procedure an *Overview Script*.

First of all, the chapter discusses the background of the approach; then, it recaps the data model and defines the operators used for creating the graph; at this point, it introduces the concept of overview script that computes the edges of the graphs. Finally, it describes the graphs generated by the overview script.

BACKGROUND

Our proposal is related with three research fields: multi-document summarization, graph-based representations of search results, and graph mining.

Multi-document summarization is well known in both the artificial intelligence community and information retrieval community. Most of the proposed summarization techniques are query independent, and follow two alternative approaches: either they simply extract relevant passages from the set of documents by applying statistical analysis independently of the query that retrieved the documents, or they employ Natural Language Processing. A summary is then a phrase or a set of keywords that represents the topics of the set of documents.

Our approach can be regarded as a multi-document summarization task, since we also generate clusters by partitioning the results of a Web search in homogeneous sets, and represent the clusters' contents and their relationships by synthetic labels extracted from the documents in the clusters. These labels approximately synthesize the semantics of both the cluster topics and inter clusters' shared sub-topics.

Nevertheless, as the features of the documents used for clustering are extracted from the documents' dynamic snippets that contain the query terms, the generated clusters' labels are query dependent. This allows realizing an approximate synthesis of cluster contents that focalizes the context of the user's needs.

Further, not only the topics dealt with by each cluster are identified, but also the shared sub-topics between each pair of clusters. In the same manner, we also identify the topics of both each single retrieved document and single retrieved list.

To this aim, we combine the ranked lists, the clusters and the items in the ranked lists, through "intersection" operations, so as to identify other hidden topics, not necessarily relevant in any single cluster, nor top-rank in any single ranked list, but that are relevant to the global search process the user is engaged in, since they represent results and contents shared by multiple web searches.

Graph-based representations have been proposed in the Information Retrieval context for distinct purposes. In (Schenker, 2003; Markov et al., 2007) graph-based representations of documents are used as the basis for clustering and categorization. In (Leskovec et al., 2004) a graph-based representation of documents is used for generating graph-based summaries. Using deep linguistic analysis, they extract sub-structures from a document semantic graph in order to get a summary.

Conversely, Litvak and Last in their paper of (2008) generate summaries from graph-based representations with two distinct syntactic approaches, a supervised approach and an unsupervised approach; their techniques do not require almost any language-specific linguistic processing. In this context, graph's nodes stand for words/phrases and the edges represent syntactic relationships between them. The evaluation of this proposal reveals that most words that are highly interconnected with other words in the text of a document (except stop-words) should contribute to the summary.

Graph-based representations have also been proposed to represent the results of Web searches (Liu et al., 2009). The essential idea of these solutions is to model a network of multimedia documents as a graph, where the vertices represent information objects, e.g., concepts regarding the documents, as well as the documents themselves, or groups of them. The vertices of the graph are connected through weighted and directed edges, according to their logical relations, such as references (in and out links), or similarities (shared index terms).

Our proposal takes inspiration from these approaches: ranked lists, clusters, single web pages, as well as their inter-relationships, are represented by multi-granular graphs. These graphs constitute a graphical overview as a summary of the main retrieved topics.

Thus our approach can be regarded as a graph-based multi-document summarization task. However we assume a different meaning of the phrase "graph-based multi-document summarization" with respect to the one commonly adopted, like in (Erkan and Radev, 2004; Mihalcea, 2004; Wan, 2008), where either a graph-based representation of documents or a graph-based ranking algorithm is used to produce a textual multi-document summary.

The multi-granular graphs permit the visualization of multiple topics and their semantics relationships at the same level of detail, and the exploration of the relationships between topics of distinct levels, both in a top-down fashion, i.e., from the coarsest representation to the most detailed one, and in a bottom-up fashion.

Here comes the connection with graph mining that consists in exploring the nodes of a graph to discover their contents. Graph mining is used, for example, in indexing and retrieving images from image databases (Pan et al., 2007; Hsieh and Hsu, 2008).

In our framework, the relationships between topics and documents can be discovered: a user can get documents dealing with a topic represented by a node, or can get information about a ''hidden'' topic represented by an edge between pairs of nodes, simply by expanding nodes and edges.

MULTI-GRANULAR SUMMARIZATION OF WEB SEARCH RESULTS[1]

In this paragraph, we present the perspective of our proposal, and the operators for cluster manipulation that permit the discovery of retrieved topics and the approximate representation of their semantic relationships.

Basic Notions

In the following definitions, we introduce the necessary basic notions of the proposal to generate the information represented by the multi-granular graphs (Bordogna et al., 2008).

Consider a *query q* submitted to a search engine S; the query result is a ranked list of documents that contains *ranked items*.

Definition 1: Ranked Item

A *ranked item r* represents a document retrieved by a Web search. It is defined as a tuple:

$$r : (rid, uri, title, snippet, irank)$$

where: *rid* is a unique identifier of the ranked item in the overall database, *uri* is the *Uniform Resource Identifier* of the ranked Web document, *title* and *snippet* are the document title and snippet of the item (the snippet is an excerpt of the document, made by a set of sentences that contain the keywords of the query), and *irank* is a score (in the range [0, 1]) that expresses the estimated relevance of the retrieved document with respect to the query.

The same document is represented by distinct ranked items in distinct result lists. Therefore, we assume that a document is uniquely identified by its *uri* while it may have distinct *snippets* and *rank* when retrieved by different search engines. We compute the *irank* as a function of the position of the item in the query result list; this way, it is independent of the retrieval status value computed by the search engine that retrieved the document.

Definition 2: Cluster

A *cluster c* is a fuzzy set of ranked items, having a rank too. It is defined by a tuple:

$$C : (label, items, crank)$$

where *label* is an automatically generated set of terms that semantically synthesizes the cluster's contents. The generation is the result of application

of a function, named *SynthLabel* (Bordogna et al., 2008), that builds a representation of a cluster (more generally of any set of ranked items) by selecting meaningful terms from the titles and snippets of its ranked items.

A term is deemed meaningful on the basis of the evaluation of multiple criteria that are the following:

- The overall frequency of the term in the pool of titles and snippets of all ranked items in the cluster (or group of clusters);
- The percentage of the ranked items containing the term in the cluster (or group of clusters);
- The specificity of the term with respect to the other clusters, i.e., its discrimination power among the clusters (groups of clusters).

items is the fuzzy set of *ranked items* belonging to the cluster (a cluster can possibly contain only one single ranked item).

Finally, *crank* is a score (in the range [0, 1]) that represents a property of the cluster; the value is generated by the operator that generates the group. Some sample properties are the cluster's *relative cardinality* and *heterogeneity* (i.e., the dispersion of its ranked items in the term-vector space where they are represented). The complete data model, defined in (Bordogna et al., 2008), encompasses a large sets of properties. We omit them, because they are not relevant for the scope of the chapter.

Definition 3: Group

A *group g* is a non empty set of ranked clusters, defined by the tuple:

$$g : (id, label, clusters, keywords, session, v)$$

in which: *id* is a numeric unique identifier of the group, *label* is the label of the group automatically generated by the labeling function *SynthLabel* (Bordogna et al., 2008), *clusters* is a set of ranked clusters (where each cluster is ranked by the actual value of its *crank*), *keywords* is the set of weighted keywords that expresses a synthetic representation of the group contents, *session* is the identifier of the search process in which the group was generated and *v* is a Boolean value that defines the ''visibility'' of the group to the user: the group is visible (*v=true*) when it is generated by an explicit user operation (such as a query to a search engine); the group is not visible (*v=false*) when the group is automatically created by an operator executed by an overview script launched to generate the edges of a graph.

Notice that a ranked list can be regarded as a group containing just one single cluster, labeled with the query that retrieved it; consequently, a single ranked item in a list can be regarded as a group with one cluster containing only the ranked item as well.

Document Clustering

The first operation to performed is the clustering of the results of each query. To this end, in the prototypal implemented system *Matrioshka* (Bordogna et al., 2008a) the Lingo clustering algorithm is used (Osinski & Weiss, 2005). it is a dynamic clustering algorithm that applies Latent Semantic Analysis (Deerwester et al., 1990), a form of dimensionality reduction, so as to assign each item to more than one single cluster. It is based on the ''description come first approach'': it reverses the usual way of operating of other approaches where clusters are first generated and then, based on their contents, they are labeled. In contrast, Lingo, tries to avoid the generation of clusters which do not correspond with human understanding of their semantics, by first generating the candidate cluster labels, thus ensuring that what is created can be well perceivable by

a human. Then, it performs a Latent Semantic Analysis on the original term-document matrix by using Singular Value Decomposition: this way, it discovers possible existing latent structure of diverse concepts. Finally, it assigns documents with candidate labels based on their matching in the conceptual space, and retains only labeled clusters which have a minimum cardinality (Bordogna & Pasi, 2011).

We use *Lingo* to perform an efficient clustering on the basis of the titles and of the snippets of the retrieved documents. It is worth noticing that we do not need to access the text of the documents for extracting the features necessary to cluster them. We parse the result pages containing the first N results and extract all the information which constitutes the representation of a ranked item. *Matrioshka* performs lexicographic analysis, stop-words removal, conflation of terms having the same stem (recognized by applying the *Porter's* Algorithm), terms expansion by using *wordnet* (Fellbaum, 1998) to favor the clustering of documents, and finally filtering of the URI strings to uniquely identify the documents.

Finally, the *crank* of each cluster is computed as the average of the ranking values of its documents:

Operations Between Clusters

In order to generate the graphs, we need to define the intersection operation on clusters, and the intersection and coalescing operators on groups.

Broadly speaking, the intersection permits the identification of shared contents both between clusters and groups, while the coalescing operator permits merging all clusters in a group into a single cluster. In (Bordogna et al., 2008) the complete set of manipulation operators for groups of clusters is defined.

Hereafter, we introduce the two definitions of the intersection operation between clusters: the *ranked intersection*, named *RIntersect*, is a crisp operation, because it uniquely identifies the ranked items by their *uri*; the soft intersection, named

SIntersect, is a *soft* operation because it deals with the ranked items by representing them in a term vector space, like in the information retrieval vector space model (Salton, 1986).

Definition 4: Ranked Intersection

The operation *RIntersect*, denoted by $\cap^R$, takes two clusters of ranked items (R_1 and R_2) in input and generates a new cluster of ranked items R' that contains the common ranked items in both R_1 and R_2; two ranked items are considered to identify the same item if they have the same *uri*. The *irank* of r' in R' is defined as the minimum *irank* value of r_1 and r_2.

With such a strict definition of the intersection between clusters, the ranked items that represent duplicated web pages are filtered out from the result, since their *uris* are different.

In particular situations, this could be a limitation, since one would like to identify ranked items dealing with similar and duplicated topics. Let's consider, for example, the page of *Expedia* of the same hotel but retrieved in two different searches with two different dates of booking. They refer to the same hotel in the same Web site, but they have different *uri*s. With the *RIntersect* operator, these documents are not considered as the same document, even if their semantics is the same.

In order to overcome this limitation, the *Soft intersection* between clusters has been defined (Bordogna & Psaila, 2011). As a result, it yields a set R' generated considering the shared *contents* between the set of titles and snippets of the ranked items belonging to the input clusters. Thus, it identifies topics that approximately represent shared contents between clusters.

Definition 5: Soft Intersection

The operation *SIntersect*, denoted by $\cap^S$, performs the *content intersection* of two clusters of ranked items. It generates R', that contains all ranked

items r' such that there exists two ranked items $r_1 \in R_1$ and $r_2 \in R_2$ whose bags of words (identified by $b_1 = b_1[<t_1,w_1>,\ldots,<t_l,w_l>]$ and $b_2 = b_2[<t_1,w_1>,\ldots,<t_l,w_l>]$ respectively, where $w_i \in [0,1]$ is the weight of term t_i) extracted from their *titles* and *snippets*, satisfy the fuzzy relation:

$$similarity(b_1, b_2) = \frac{\sum_{<t_k,w_k>\in b_1 \wedge <t_j,w_j>\in b_2|t_k=t_j} \min(b_1[w_k], b_2[w_j])}{\sum_{<t_k,w_k>\in b_1 \wedge <t_j,w_j>\in b_2|t_k=t_j \vee \neg \exists (t_k=t_j)} \max(b_1[w_k], b_2[w_j])} > \varepsilon$$

where ε is a value in $[0,1]$ and *similarity* is defined as the fuzzy *Jaccard* coefficient between fuzzy sets (Miyamoto and Nakayama, 1986).

When such condition is satisfied, r' is defined as follows.

$$r' = r_1 \quad \text{if } inclusion(b_1, b_2) > inclusion(b_2, b_1)$$
$$r' = r_1 \quad \text{otherwise}$$

inclusion(x, y) is a fuzzy inclusion that computes a satisfaction degree in $[0,1]$ (Bordogna & Psaila, 2011).

This way, given a pair of similar ranked items r_1 and r_2, in the result, we retain the ranked item which has the most specific content, (as it can be guessed from titles and snippets). Most specific means that on the basis of the given representations of the two ranked items consisting of weighted index terms extracted from their titles and snippets, we are certain that all the terms that represent the selected ranked item are contained with a greater index term weight in the representation of the other ranked item.

Let us explain the rationale of this definition with a simple example. Given two documents, one dealing with Italian tourist places, and the second with Tourist places in the Mediterranean countries, they probably share most of the places listed in the first document, since Italy is a Mediterranean country, but the vice versa is unlikely to occur, since the second document contains also places of other countries such as Greece, Spain and so on. So, in the soft intersection we retain only the shared contents, i.e., the first document on Italian places.

The operation that unites two clusters of ranked items is the *Ranked Union*.

Definition 6: Ranked Union

The operation *Ranked Union*, denoted by $\cap^R$, takes two clusters of ranked items (R_1 and R_2) in input and generates a new cluster of ranked items R' that contains the ranked items of both R_1 and R_2, by removing the duplicated ranked items, i.e., those which have the same *uri*, $r_1.uri = r_2.uri$ In this case, r' *irank* is defined as the maximum *irank* value of $r_1.irank$ and $r_2.irank$.

Operators on Groups

In this paragraph, we resume the operators of the manipulation language that will be used in the generation of the graphs.

An *operator op* represents the application of an operator of the manipulation language (Bordogna et al., 2008) on (two) input groups, g_1, g_2, (some operators require just one input group) in order to obtain a resulting group g_{out}. It is defined as a tuple:

$$op : \Big(operator, g_1, rank, \big[g_2\big] \Big) = g_{out}$$

- First of all, *operator* is the name of the group operator. In the specific context of this paper, we constrain it to assume one of the following values
- $operator \in \{\cap^{GR}, \cap^{GS}, \oplus\}$
- in which: $\cap^{GR}$ represents the group ranked intersection operator, $\cap^{GS}$ represents the group soft intersection operator, and $\oplus$ represents the group coalescing operator.
- Second, *rank* is the name of the ranking method applied on the result of the opera-

tion, and can assume a value depending on the operator:

- $rank \in T_{operator}$
- in which $T_{operator}$ represents the set of admissible rank methods for the specific operator; for example, *cardinality*, *heterogeneity*, etc. (see (Bordogna et al., 2008)). In the context of this chapter, we will use only the *cardinality* ranking method that is defined as the number of items in the cluster.
- Second, g_1, g_2 and g_{out} are the identifiers of the two input groups and of the output group of the operation, respectively.

The group ranked intersection operators and the soft intersection operator are defined so as to exploit the *crisp* ranked intersection and the soft intersection between all the pairs of clusters originated from the two input groups.

Group Intersection Operators

Given two groups of clusters g_1 and g_2, both the group ranked intersection operator $\cap^{GR}$ and the group soft

Intersection operator $\cap^{GS}$, hereafter indicated simply by $\cap$, are defined as follows:

$$\cap : GxG \rightarrow G \qquad \cap (g_1, g_2) \rightarrow g',$$

where g' is the resulting group.

For each pair of clusters $c_1 \in g_1$, $c_2 \in g_2$, such that their intersection (either ranked $\cap^R$ or soft $\cap^S$, hereafter indicated simply by $\cap$) is not empty (i.e., $| c_1 .items \cap c_2 .items \neq 0|$), there is a cluster $c' \in g'$. c' is defined as follows:

$c'.items = c_1.items \cap c_2.items$,
$c'.label = SynthLabel(c'.items)$,
$c'.rank$ is computed as the average of the ranks of $c'.items$.

Group Coalescing Operator

The group coalescing operator $\oplus(g) = g'$, given an input group g generates a new group g' in such a way that g' contains only one cluster c' that is obtained by applying the ranked union operation $\cup^R$ to all clusters in g. This operator makes it possible to merge all clusters in a group into one global cluster.

The Multi-Granular Graph

In the proposed framework, the retrieved topics are represented by a multi-granular graph with three layers corresponding with three levels of granularity:

1. **Coarse level:** this corresponds with the top layer; in this level, a topic corresponds with the main shared contents in a *group* of clusters. A group is the overall set of documents, organized into clusters that has been retrieved by a single query or produced by the application of a group operator; this is the highest overview of retrieved results.
2. **Intermediate level:** this corresponds with the intermediate layer; a topic corresponds with the main shared contents of a *cluster* of documents; this is the intermediate overview.
3. **Fine level:** this corresponds with the terminal layer; a topic corresponds with the main contents of each single *document*; the description of these topics can be considered the most detailed summary of the Web results.

Each topic is summarized by a short phrase (a label or the document title) that expresses the most specific meaning of the topic, and by a set of weighted keywords which, on the other side, represents the exhaustive meaning of the topic.

We also provide a dual representation of the edges of a graph with distinct semantics:

- **Crisp relationship:** this relationship between pairs of topics instantiations (i.e. groups, clusters, documents) expresses the approximate semantics of shared common documents, where the shared common documents are identified by the ranked intersection $\cap^R$.
- **Soft relationship:** this relationships between pairs of topics instantiations (i.e. groups, clusters) expresses the approximate semantics of shared similar documents where the shared similar documents are identified by the *soft intersection* $\cap^S$.

In both cases, these edges are labeled with a set of keywords that approximately expresses the semantics of the shared documents. Also, a weight is associated with an edge, that is the relative cardinality of the shared set, i.e., the number of either common or similar documents with respect to their total amount.

The graph nodes are used to represent the topics of a level, while its edges represent the shared topics between pairs of nodes. Thus, we have three types of graphs, one on each layer, corresponding with the three levels (coarse, intermediate and fine) that are named *group graph, cluster graph* and *document graph*.

Overview Scripts

In this paragraph, a language for specifying an overview of a search process is defined. An *overview script* is a script of operators, the execution of which automatically creates the ingredients necessary for building the multi-granular graph of a search process. In the following, we rely on concepts and notations of well known BNF grammars.

Definition 7: Basic Overview

A *BASIC_OVERVIEW* is the non-terminal symbol for the specification of an operator on (two) input groups. It is defined as follows:

```
<BASIC_OVERVIEW>::=
  <CRISP_BASIC_OVERVIEW> | <SOFT_BASIC_OVERVIEW> |
<COALESCING_OVERVIEW>
<CRISP_BASIC_OVERVIEW>::=
  <INT_C_OP_NAME> "(" <C_GROUP_ID> "," <RANK> ","
<GROUP_ID> ")" "=" <GROUP_ID>
<SOFT_BASIC_OVERVIEW>::=
  <INT_S_OP_NAME> "(" <GROUP_ID> "," <RANK> ","
<GROUP_ID> ")" "=" <GROUP_ID>
<COALES_OVERVIEW>::=
  <COAL_OP_NAME> "(" <GROUP_ID> ")" "=" <GROUP_ID>
<C_GROUP_ID>::= <COALES_GROUP_ID> | <GROUP_ID>
```

- The symbols in the quotation marks (i.e. ") are terminal symbols of the grammar.
- $<INT\_C\_OP\_NAME> = \cap^{GR}$.
- $< INT\_S\_OP\_NAME > = \cap^{GS}$.
- $<RANK>$ = *cardinality* is the ranking method of the operator; it means that the *crank* of a generated cluster is the value of the cardinality of the cluster itself.
- $<COALES\_GROUP\_ID> = cg_n$ .id is the identifier of the *coalesced group*, generated by applying the *Group Coalescing* operator to the original group.
- $<COAL\_OP\_NAME> = \oplus$ is the name of the *Group Coalescing* operator, that generates a coalesced group cg_i from the input group g_i Notice that the cardinality of the resulting group is equal to the cardinality of the unique cluster contained in cg_i.
- $<GROUP\_ID> = g_n$ .id is the identifier of an input or output group. Notice that the output group is invisible.

Definition 8: Overview Script

The $<OVERVIEW>$ is the axiom symbol of the language, defined as follows:

```
<OVERVIEW>::=
  (<CRISP_BASIC_OVERVIEW> | <SOFT_BASIC_OVER-
VIEW>)+
```

An $<OVERVIEW>$ can thus specify a sequence of distinct operations on groups. In particular,

- the ranked (or soft) group intersection between two input groups;
- the ranked (or soft) group intersection between the coalescent groups of two input groups;
- the ranked (or soft) group intersection between an input group and the coalescent group of the other input group.

Definition of the Multi-Granular Graph

A multi-granular graph, hereafter indicated by *M_GRAPH*, is here defined as a set of graphs organized on three distinct layers which correspond with three levels of details of the representation of the Web search results: the *coarse* layer contains Group graphs, indicated by $GRAPH_g$, the *Intermediate* layer contains Cluster graphs, indicated by $GRAPH_c$, and the *fine* layer contains the Document graphs, indicated by $GRAPH_d$.

$$M\_GRAPH = \{GRAPH_{g1}, ..., GRAPH_{gn}, GRAPH_{cj}, ... GRAPH_{cm}, GRAPH_{di}, ... GRAPH_{dk}\}$$

In the case in which the user requests a multi-granular graph visualization, he/she can specify one or more groups g_1, g_2, ...,g_n, he/she wants to include in the coarse visualization layer. If he/she does not select any specific group, all groups generated till that time in the search process are considered.

An overview script for computing the necessary information for building the *M_GRAPH* must be defined and executed as follows.

Given a set of *n* groups $g_1, g_2, ..., g_n$, for each pair g_i and g_j of groups, with $i,j=1,...,n$. the script contains the following basic overviews.

$$\cap^{GR}(g_i, cardinality, g_j) = g_{ij}^R$$
$$\cap^{GS}(g_i, cardinality, g_j) = g_{ij}^S$$
$$\oplus(g_i) = \bar{g}_i$$
$$\oplus(g_j) = \bar{g}_j$$
$$\cap^{GR}(\bar{g}_i, cardinality, \bar{g}_j) = cg_{ij}^R$$
$$\cap^{GS}(\bar{g}_i, cardinality, \bar{g}_j) = cg_{ij}^S$$

The above script creates the output groups that are needed to compute the weights of the edges of the graphs in *M_GRAPH*.

Group Graph

The *nodes* of a coarse level graph represent the groups of clusters the user has selected, and in the case there is more than one single group, the edges between each pair of nodes represent the shared common documents and shared similar documents in the two associated groups.

Definition 9: Group Graph

The groups graph $GRAPH_g$ is defined as follows:

$$GRAPH_g := \langle N_g, E_{gc}, E_{gs} \rangle$$

in which: N_g is the set of nodes of the graph, that correspond with the groups the user has selected for the overview script; E_{gc} is the set of edges of the graph, that represent the shared common documents belonging to each pair of groups, while

E_{gs} is the set of edges of the graph, that represent the shared similar documents belonging to each pair of groups.

Formally, each node $n \in N_g$ is defined as the tuple:

$$n := (g_{id}, label, key, type)$$

where g_{id} is a group identifier, *label* is the group label (i..e, $g_{id}.label$), short description that expresses the specific semantics of the topic, *key* is the set of keywords of the group (i.e., $g_{id}.keywords$); *type* is the type of the node, in this case $^n group^n$, which identifies the granularity of the graph.

Formally, $ec_{ij} \in E_{gc}$ is defined as:

$$ec_{ij} := (label, rw, n_i, n_j)$$

in which *label* describes the *label* of the edge, that is the label of the group cg_{ij}^R generated by the overview script $(ie., cg_{ij}^R.label)$; n_i and n_j are the connected nodes associated with the groups g_i and g_j; the strength $_{rw}$ is a positive integer, that is the cardinality of the group cg_{ij}^R, i.e., the number of common shared documents between the two groups g_i and g_j. This way, $rw = 0$ if g_i and g_j do not have any common document, while $rw > 0$ in the case they share some common documents.

Likewise, $es_{ij} \in E_{gs}$ is defined as:

$$es_{ij} := (label, sw, n_i, n_j)$$

in which: *label* describes the *label* of the edge, that is the label of the group cg_{ij}^S generated by the overview script (i.e., $cg_{ij}^S.label$); n_i and n_j are the connected nodes associated with the groups

g_i and g_j; $_{sw}$ is the strength weight, that is the cardinality of the group cg_{ij}^S, i.e., the number of shared similar documents between the two groups g_i and g_j. In this way, we have $_{sw=0}$ if g_i and g_j do not have any similar documents (as defined by the soft intersection operator) while $_{sw>0}$ when they share some similar documents.

Notice that in the case of two groups, the more they are homogeneous in terms of contents, the more their relationships are strong (i.e., with high weight on the edge).

Cluster Graph

This is the clusters graph $GRAPH_c$ in which the nodes correspond to the clusters of one or more selected groups, and the edges correspond to the shared common documents and shared similar documents contained in the two clusters associated with the nodes they link.

Definition 10: Cluster Graph

The clusters graph is defined as:

$$GRAPH_c := \left\langle N_c, E_{cc}, E_{cs} \right\rangle$$

in which N_c is the set of nodes of the graph, that correspond with the clusters of the selected groups, while E_{cc} and E_{cs} are the sets of edges of the graph that represent the relationships between pairs of such clusters.

Like for the group graph, E_{cc} and E_{cs} are defined based on the evaluation of the ranked intersection and soft intersection between the clusters.

Each node $n \in N_c$ is defined as the tuple:

$$n := (c_{id}, label, key, g.id, type)$$

where c_{id} is the identifier of the cluster, $c_{id}.label$ is its label, *key* is the set of keywords of the cluster $c_{id}.q$, $_{g.id}$ is the identifier of the group the cluster belongs to, and *type* is the type of the node, that is, in this level, $_{\text{"cluster"}}$.

Each edge $ec_{hk} \in E_{cc}$ is defined as:

$$ec_{hk} := (label, rew, n_h, n_k)$$

in which *label* is the label of the edge, that is the label of the cluster rc_{hk} belonging to the group g_{ij}^R generated in the overview script by the ranked intersection of the two groups g_i and g_j to which the clusters belong; *rew* is the edge weight, that is the cardinality of the cluster rc_{hk}; n_h and n_k are the nodes (the clusters) connected by the edge.

Likewise $es_{hk} \in E_{cs}$ is defined as:

$$es_{hk} := (label, sew, n_h, n_k)$$

in which: *label* is the label of the edge, that is the label of the cluster sc_{hk} belonging to the group $g_{l,j}^S$ generated in the overview script by the soft intersection of the two groups g_i and g_j to which the clusters belong; *sew* is the edge weight, that is the cardinality of the cluster sc_{hk}; and n_h and n_k are the nodes (the clusters) connected by the edge.

Document Graph

This is the document level graph. It is defined as follows:

Definition 11: Document Graph

$$GRAPH_d := \langle N_d, E_{dc} \rangle$$

Figure 1. Groups involved in the overview procedure. These are the basis of the three levels graph

g_1: *Google!* -"Toronto"
cl.1: City of Toronto
cl.2: CBC Toronto News
cl.3: Travel Guide
cl.4: Toronto Zoo
cl.5: Tours
cl.6: Things to do in Toronto
cl.7: Toronto Ontario

g_2: *Yahoo!* -"Toronto"
cl.1: Toronto Raptors
cl.2: University of Toronto
cl.3: Architecture of Toronto
cl.4: Toronto Blue Jays
cl.5: Things to do in Toronto
cl.6: Wikipedia
cl.7: Events Restaurants
cl.8: Toronto Hotels
cl.9: Travel Guide
cl.10: Toronto Zoo
cl.10: Toronto Tourism

g_3: *Bing* -"Toronto"
cl.1: Events Restaurants
cl.2: Toronto Hotels
cl.3: City Guide
cl.4: Visit Toronto
cl.5: News Toronto GTA
cl.6: Fashion Group International
cl.7: Toronto Pearson International Airport

In which: N_d is the set of nodes of the graph; the nodes are the documents of the clusters belonging to the selected groups, while E_{dc} is the set of edges of the graph; the edges represent the relationships between pairs of documents. Note that these documents can belong to either the same cluster or different clusters.

Each node $n \in N_d$ is defined as the tuple:

$$n := (d_{id}, title, key, g.id, c.id, type),$$

Where d_{id} is the identifier of the document, i.e., of the ranked item, *title* is its title, *key* is the bag of keywords extracted from the document snippet and title, *g.id* and *c.id* are the identifiers of the group and cluster it belongs to, respectively, and *type* is the type of the node, that in this level is "document".

Each edge $ec_{xy} \in E_{dc}$ is defined as:

$$(ec := label, ew, n_x, ny)$$

in which *label* is defined by the list of the common words contained in both $n.key_x$ and $n.key_y$, and it summarizes the common contents of the two documents, n_x and n_y are the nodes (documents) connected by the edge, and *ew* is the edge weight,

defined by the number of common words in both $n.key_x$ and $n.key_y$, i.e., the length in terms of words of $ec_{xy}.label$.

EXAMPLE OF MULTI-GRANULAR GRAPH OF A WEB SEARCH PROCESS

Let's imagine we are interested in retrieving useful information about the city of *Toronto* and surroundings. We do not know a specific target for the search, but we are interested in deeply exploring search results. To this aim, we submit the generic query "Toronto" to the three search engines *Google*, *Yahoo* and *Bing*. The results are shown in Figure 1.

The execution of the overview script on the three resulting groups generates the multi-granular graph. The coarsest graph is the *group graph* depicted in Figure 2. It can be seen that the edges of the crisp group graph have more specific labels than the edges of the soft group graph, since they express the semantics of the shared documents and of the shared contents respectively.

Each edge of this graph can be explored by expanding it, to reveal the shared sub-topics of the connected groups. Let's suppose, for example,

Figure 2. Group Graph. Crisp and soft representations of the relationships between the three groups resulting from the query "Toronto" submitted to Google, Yahoo! and Bing

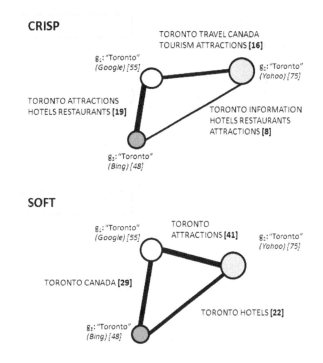

Figure 3. Cluster Graph. Fragment of the overall crisp relationships between the clusters of g_1 (grey nodes) and g_2 (white nodes)

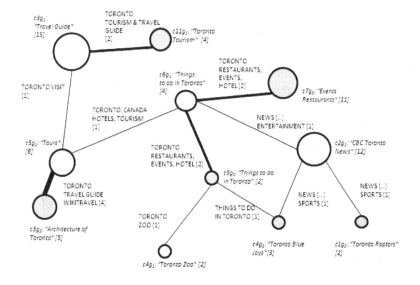

we are interested in *Attractions* in Toronto. We decide to investigate the relationships between groups g_1 ("Toronto - Google") and g_2 ("Toronto - Yahoo"), by expanding the corresponding edge. The results of this expansion is the cluster graphs presented in Figure 3 (crisp representation)

Figure 4. Cluster Graph. Fragment of the overall soft relationships between the clusters of g_1 and of g_2.

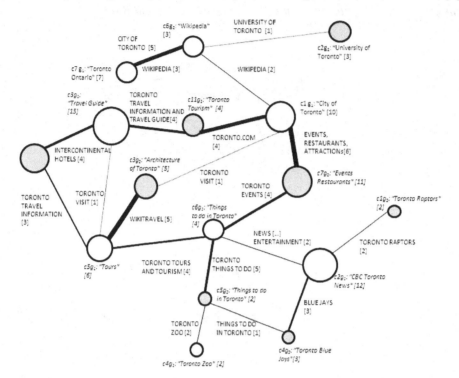

and in Figure 4 (soft representation) respectively. The two representations differ for some aspects: the first one has fewer nodes (clusters) than the second one and most of the nodes are weakly connected; the second one has more nodes (clusters) with strongest connections, and these connections have more general labels than those of the crisp representation.

Further, it can be seen that the strongest connections, such as the edge labeled "Toronto travel guide wiki" are between nodes of distinct colors (white and grey), which correspond with clusters belonging to distinct groups. The labels on these edges express the semantics of the shared contents of the results of "Google" and "Yahoo".

Finally we decide to conclude our exploration task consulting the documents belonging to the clusters "Travel Guide" and "Toronto Tourism", which are the closest to our need to discover Toronto and its beauties. Therefore, we expand the two clusters in order to obtain the related docu-

ment graph. The result of this operation is a soft representation of the semantic sharing identified between pairs of documents belonging to the two selected clusters, as shown in Figure 5.

CONCLUSION

In this chapter we proposed a multi-granular graph-based framework for visualization and exploration of the results of multiple Web searches; the goal is to tackle the pressing need for an effective way to explore the results of search processes. We propose a framework that allows the user to automatically generate an overview of all her/his searches of interest, and to explore it interactively by expanding nodes and edges in graphs. We believe that this framework is particularly useful in the context of Web meta-searches to make explicit the semantics of the shared common contents retrieved by distinct search engines as a result of

Figure 5. Document graph: soft relationships between the documents of the clusters ``Travel Guide''
and ``Toronto Tourism''.

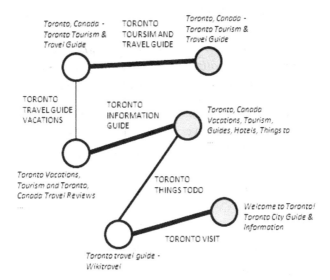

the same query. Its implementation and evaluation within the meta-search-clustering environment named *Matrioshka* (http://matrioshka.unibg.it) is ongoing. *Matrioshka* allows the user to perform different Web searches exploiting several search services (i.e. Google, Yahoo, Bing, Scholar), to cluster the results of each query and, further, to combine the obtained results through a set of manipulation operators. A first evaluation of the manipulation language, in which users directly select the operators and apply them to pairs of selected groups of clusters was performed and reported in (Bordogna et al., 2011). The results we obtained pointed out the need of a more practical and easy way to reveal the hidden relationships between pairs of groups of clusters, clusters, and documents. This evaluation motivated our further proposal of designing automatic overview scripts of manipulation operators, which can be executed by the users to detect the shared topics between search results organized into groups of clusters. The operators in the overview scripts include the ranked intersection, the soft intersection and the coalescing operator defined in this chapter. They are used to create the contents of the multi-granular graph. In fact, the multi-granular graph visualization modality has been added to provide the user with a tool for analyzing the results of an overview script.

Our proposal, starting from a set of selected results, is able to identify all the relationships between them at three different levels of granularity, groups, clusters and documents, and to represent their semantics in an approximate way through meaningful terms. This allows highlighting previously hidden contents not top-ranked in any of the retrieved lists.

Moreover, our solution is able to detect two types of relationships: *crisp* ones, that express the presence of common documents between clusters and groups of clusters, and *soft* ones, that express the presence of similar contents. The graphs representation allows users to explore the results of his/her searches, finding interesting hidden retrieved contents, thus getting suggestions for new searches.

REFERENCES

Angelaccio, M., Buttarazzi, B., & Patrignanell, M. (2007) Graph use to visualize web search results: Mywish 3.0. In *IV '07: Proceedings of the 11th International Conference Information Visualization* (pp. 245-250). IEEE Computer Society.

Belew, K. (1989) Adaptive information retrieval: Using a connectionist representation to retrieve and learn about documents. In *SIGIR '89: Proceedings of the 12th annual international ACM conference on Research and development in information retrieval* (pp 11-20). ACM Press.

Bordogna, G., Campi, A., Psaila, G., & Ronchi, S. (2008) A language for manipulating groups of clustered web documents results, In *ACM CIKM '08: Proceedings of the: the 17th ACM conference on Information and knowledge management* (pp 23-32). ACM Press.

Bordogna, G., Campi, A., Psaila, G., & Ronchi, S. (2008a). *An interaction framework for mobile web search.* In MoMM2008: Proceedings of the 6th International Conference on Advances in Mobile Computing and Multimedia, (pp. 183–191).

Bordogna, G., Campi, A., Psaila, G., & Ronchi, S. (2011). Disambiguated query suggestions and personalized content-similarity and novelty ranking of clustered results to optimize web searches. *Information Processing & Management.* .doi:10.1016/j.ipm.2011.03.008

Bordogna, G., & Pasi, G. (2011). *Soft Clustering for Information Retrieval Applications, WIREs Data Mining and Knowledge Discovery, electronic Journal Wiley & Sons* (pp. 1–9). Inc, January/February.

Bordogna, G., & Psaila, G. (2011) Soft Operators for exploring information granules of Web search results, In Proceedings of the *World Conference on Soft Computing*, May 23-25, San Francisco, 2011

de Graaf, E., Kok, J., & Kosters, W. (2007). Clustering improves the exploration of graph mining results. In *IFIP2007: Proceedings of the Articial Intelligence and Innovations 2007: from Theory to Applications, volume 247 of IFIP International Federation for Information Processing,* (pp 13-20). Springer Verlag.

Deerwester, S. C., Dumais, S. T., Landauer, T. K., Furnas, G. W., & Harshman, R. A. (1990). Indexing Latent Semantic Analysis. *Journal of the American Society for Information Science American Society for Information Science, 41*(6), 391–407. doi:10.1002/(SICI)1097-4571(199009)41:6<391::AID-ASI1>3.0.CO;2-9

Erkan, G., & Radev, D. R. (2004). Lexrank: Graph-based lexical centrality as salience in text summarization. *Journal of Artificial Intelligence Research, 22*, 457–479.

Hsieh, S., & Hsu, C. (2008). Graph-based representation for similarity retrieval of symbolic images. *Data & Knowledge Engineering, 65*(3), 401–418. doi:10.1016/j.datak.2007.12.004

Leskovec, J., Grobelnik, M., & Milic-frayling, N. (2004). Learning semantic graph mapping for document summarization. In Boulicaut J.B., Esposito F., Giannotti F., & Pedreschi D (Eds.): *ECML/PKDD-2004: Proceedings of the 15th European Conference on Machine Learning (ECML)8th European Conference on Principles and Practice of Knowledge Discovery in Databases,* Lecture Notes in Computer Science, 3202. Springer Verlag.

Litvak, M., & Last, M. (2008) Graph-based keyword extraction for single-document summarization. In *MMIES '08: Proceedings of the Workshop on Multi-source Multilingual Information Extraction and Summarization* (pp. 17-24). Association for Computational Linguistics.

Liu, Y., & Zhang, M. Ma., & Ru L. (2009) User browsing graph: structure, evolution and application, In *WSDM'09: Proceeedings of the Second ACM International Conference on Web Search and Data Mining,* ACM.

Markov, A., Last, M., & Kandel, A. (2007). Fast categorization of web documents represented by graphs. In *WEBKDD: Proceedings of Advances in Web Mining and Web Usage Analysis.* LNCS 4811, (pp 56-71).Springer Verlag.

Mccrickard, C. S., Mccrickard, D. S., & Kehoe, C. M. (2007). Visualizing search results using sqwid. In *WWW06: Proceedings of the sixth International World Wide Web Conference.* (pp. 65-77).

Mihalcea, R. (2004) Graph-based ranking algorithms for sentence extraction, applied to text summarization. In *ACL 2004: Proceedings of the Interactive poster and demonstration sessions,* (pp 20). Association for Computational Linguistics.

Miyamoto S., Nakayama, K., (1986) Similarity measures based on a fuzzy set model and applications to hierarechical clustering, *IEEE Trans. on Systems, Man and Cybernetics,* SMC-16, 3, (pp. 479-482).

Osinski, S., & Weiss, D. (2005). A concept-driven algorithm for clustering search results. *IEEE Intelligent Systems, 20,* 48–54. doi:10.1109/MIS.2005.38

Pan, J., Yang, H., Faloutos, C., & Duygulu, P. (2007). Crossmodal correlation mining using graph algorithms . In Zhu, X., Zhu, X., & Davidson, I. (Eds.), *Knowledge Discovery and Data Mining: Challenges and Realities with Real World Data* (pp. 274–294). Hershey, PA: IGI Global. doi:10.4018/978-1-59904-252-7.ch004

Salton, G. (1986). Recent trends in automatic information retrieval. In *SIGIR '86: Proceedings of the 9th Annual International ACM SIGIR Conference on Research and Development in Information Retrieval,* (pp.1-10). ACM press.

Schenker, A., Last, M., Bunke, H., & Kandel, A. (2003). Graph representations for web document clustering. In *IbPRIA03: Proceedings of the first Iberian Conference on Pattern Recognition and Image Analysis,* LNCS 2652. (pp. 935-942). Springer Verlag.

Thiel, K., Dill, F., Kotter, T., & Berthold, M. R. (2007). Towards visual exploration of topic shifts. Systems, *ISIC2007: Proceedings of the IEEE International Conference on Man and Cybernetics.* (pp.522-527).

Wan, X. (2008). An exploration of document impact on graph-based multi-document summarization. In *EMNLP '08: Proceedings of the Conference on Empirical Methods in Natural Language Processing,* (pp. 755-762). Association for Computational Linguistics.

Worring, M., de Rooij, O., & van Rijn, T. (2007). Browsing visual collections using graphs. In *MIR '07: Proceedings of the international workshop on Workshop on multimedia information retrieval* (pp.307-312). ACM press.

KEY TERMS AND DEFINITIONS

Cluster: Set of entities sharing some common properties and identified based on an unsupervised algorithm; also known as: group, container.

Clustering: An unsupervised machine learning technique capable to automatically partition a set of entities, described by a set of features, into disjoint groups, clusters. Also known as unsupervised learning mechanism, data mining technique.

Group Operator: A command of a cluster manipulation language that allows to combine clusters in several ways, for example by intersecting them to generate clusters containing common elements.

Labeling Function: A function that has the aim of identifying a phrase or a list of terms to represent the contents of a cluster or a group of clusters.

Multi-Granular Graph: A multi-granular graph consists of several graphs organized on distinct layers which represent a set of elements and their relationships (in the chapter the retrieved web pages) at distinct levels of details. A not terminal layer of a multi-granular graph has both nodes and edges which are represented as a graph of the lower level layer.

Search Service: A system, like a search engine over the internet or a database infrastructure, that assists a user in retrieving relevant information to his/her needs expressed by a query.

Term: A keyword or index term used to represent the content of a textual document that can be either manually assigned to the document or automatically extracted from its content by applying an indexing process, i.e., a full text indexing algorithm.

Chapter 7
Learning Full-Sentence Co-Related Verb Argument Preferences from Web Corpora

Hiram Calvo
Nara Inst. of Science & Technology, Japan

Kentaro Inui
Tohoku University, Japan

Yuji Matsumoto
Nara Inst. of Science & Technology, Japan

ABSTRACT

Learning verb argument preferences has been approached as a verb and argument problem, or at most as a tri-nary relationship between subject, verb and object. However, the simultaneous correlation of all arguments in a sentence has not been explored thoroughly for sentence plausibility mensuration because of the increased number of potential combinations and data sparseness. In this work the authors present a review of some common methods for learning argument preferences beginning with the simplest case of considering binary co-relations, then they compare with tri-nary co-relations, and finally they consider all arguments. For this latter, the authors use an ensemble model for machine learning using discriminative and generative models, using co-occurrence features, and semantic features in different arrangements. They seek to answer questions about the number of optimal topics required for PLSI and LDA models, as well as the number of co-occurrences that should be required for improving performance. They explore the implications of using different ways of projecting co-relations, i.e., into a word space, or directly into a co-occurrence features space. The authors conducted tests using a pseudo-disambiguation task learning from large corpora extracted from Internet.

DOI: 10.4018/978-1-60960-881-1.ch007

1. INTRODUCTION

A sentence can be regarded as a verb with multiple arguments. The plausibility of each argument depends not only on the verb, but also on other arguments. Measuring the plausibility of verb arguments is needed in several tasks such as Semantic Role Labelling, since grouping verb arguments and measuring their plausibility increases performance, as shown by Merlo and Van Der Plas (2009) and Deschacht and Moens (2009). Metaphora recognition requires this information too, since we are able to know common usages of arguments, and an uncommon usage would suggest its presence, or a coherence mistake (*v. gr. to drink the moon in a glass*). Malapropism detection can use the measure of the plausibility of an argument to determine misuses of words (Bolshakov, 2005) as in hysteric *center*, instead of *historic center*; density *has brought me to you*; *It looks like a* tattoo *subject*; and *Why you say that with* ironing? Anaphora resolution consists on finding referenced objects, thus, requiring among other things, to have information about the plausibility of arguments at hand, *i.e.*, what kind of fillers is more likely to satisfy the sentence's constraints, such as in: The boy plays with *it there*, *It* eats grass, I drank *it* in a glass.

This problem can be seen as collecting a large database of semantic frames with detailed categories and examples that fit these categories. For this purpose, recent works take advantage of existing manually crafted resources such as WordNet, Wikipedia, FrameNet, VerbNet or PropBank. For example, Reisinger and Paşca (2009) annotate existing WordNet concepts with attributes, and extend *is-a* relations, based on Latent Dirichlet Allocation on Web documents and Wikipedia; Yamada *et al.* (2009) explore extracting hyponym relations from Wikipedia using pattern-based discovery and distributional similarity clustering. The problem with the semantic frames approach for this task is that semantic frames are too general. For example Anna Korhonen (2000) considers the

verbs *to fly, to sail* and *to slide* as similar and finds a single subcategorization frame. On the other hand, n-gram based approaches are too particular, and even using a very big corpus (such as using the web as corpus) has two problems: some combinations are unavailable, or counts are biased by some syntactic constructions. For example, solving the PP attachment for *extinguish fire with water* using Google[1] yields *fire with water*: 319,000 hits; *extinguish with water*: 32,100 hits. Resulting in the structure *(extinguish (fire with water))* instead of *(extinguish (fire) with water)*. Thus, we need a way for smoothing these counts. This latter has been done by using Selectional Preferences since Resnik (1996) for verb to class preferences, and then generalized by Agirre and Martinez (2000) for verb class to noun class preferences. More recent work includes (McCarthy and Carroll, 2003), which disambiguate nouns, verbs and adjectives using automatically acquired selectional preferences as probability distributions over the WordNet noun hyponym hierarchy and evaluate with Senseval-2. However these aforementioned works have a common problem which is that they address separately each argument for a verb.

1.1. One Argument is Not Enough

Consider the following sentence:

There is hay at the farm. The cow eats it

We would like to connect it with hay, and not with farm. From selectional preferences we know that the object of eat should be something edible, so that we can say that hay is more edible than farm, solving this issue. From semantic frames, we have similar knowledge, but in a broader sense—there is an ingestor and an ingestible.

However, this information can be insufficient in some cases where the selectional preference depends on other arguments from the clause. For example:

Figure 1. A verb linking groups of related arguments

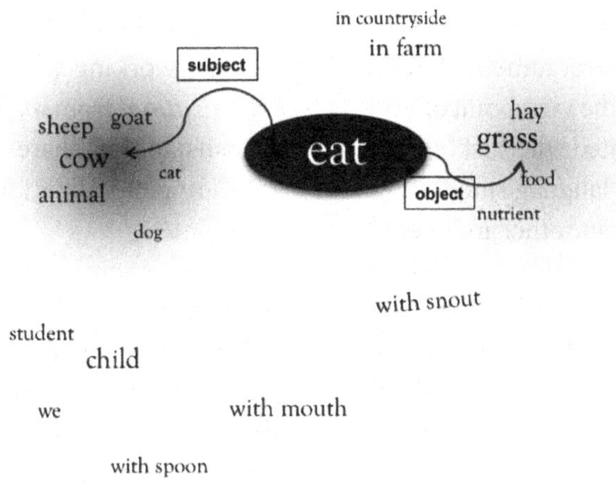

The cow eats hay but the man will eat it

In this case, it is not enough information to know that it should be edible, but also the resolution depends on who is eating. In this case it's unlikely that the man eats hay, so the sentence might refer to the fact that he will eat the cow. The same happens with other of arguments for verbs. For example, some of the FrameNet peripheral arguments for the ingestion frame are instrument, and place. However, there are some things that are ingested with some instrument —e.g. soup is eaten with a spoon, while rice is eaten with fork, or chopsticks, depending on who is eating; or at different places. Plausible argument extraction allows constructing a database dictionary of this kind of information, which can be regarded as common sense from the fact that it is possible to learn what kind of activities are performed by groups of entities automatically from large blocks of text. See Figure 1.

The goal of our work is to construct such a database. For this purpose we need to obtain information related to selectional preferences and semantic frames extraction.

In the next sections we will present related work, organized in several approaches (Section 2), then we will present a proposal based on the Word Space Model (Section 3), then a proposal based on language modelling (Section 4), and finally we present our major contributions (Section 5 and 6) which consist on interpolated PLSI for handling three co-related variables (Section 5), and then finally full co-occurrence handling via SVM learning from PLSI and co-occurrence features (Section 6). In each section we present several experiments in order to find how different parameters affect behaviour, as well as to compare different approaches.

2. APPROACHES FOR LEARNING VERB ARGUMENT PREFERENCES

The problem of automatic verb argument plausibility acquisition can be studied from several points of view. From the viewpoint of the kind of information extracted we can find related work for selectional preferences and semantic frames extraction. From the approach of selectional preferences, the task is focused on automatically obtaining classes of arguments for a given verb and a syntactic construction. From the approach of semantic frames, arguments are grouped by

139

the semantic role they have, regardless of the syntactic construction they have. This latter approach emphasizes the distinction between core (indispensable) and peripheral arguments. On the other hand, we can consider the viewpoint of how this information is represented: the task can be regarded as a case of statistic language modelling, where given a context—verb and other arguments, the missing argument should be inferred with high probability; or it can be regarded as a word space model task frequently seen in IR systems. In the next sections we present work related to this task from those different viewpoints.

2.1 Selectional Preferences

Selectional preferences acquisition can be regarded as one of the first attempts to automatically find argument plausibility. Early attempts dealt with simpler *<verb, argument>* pairs. Since the learning resource is sparse, all of these works use a generalization, or *smoothing* mechanism for extending coverage. Resnik (1996) uses WordNet for generalizing the object-argument. Agirre and Martinez (2001) use a class-to-class model, so that the both verb as well as the object-argument are generalized by belonging to a class using WordNet. McCarthy and Carrol (2006) acquire selectional preferences as probability distributions over the WordNet noun hyponym hierarchy. They use other argument relationships aside from object-argument. Padó and Lapata (2007) combine semantic and syntactic information by estimating his model using corpora with semantic role annotation (*i.e.* FrameNet, PropBank), and then applying class-based smoothing using WordNet.

2.2 Subcategorization Frames

The following works deal with the problem of semisupervised argument plausibility extraction from the subcategorization frames extraction approach. Salgeiro *et al.* acquire verb argument structures. They generalize nouns by using a

Named Entity Recognizer (IdentiFinder) and then they use the noisy channel framework for argument prediction. Examples of the kind of information they are working with are: *Organization* bought *organization* from *organization*, *Thing* bought the outstanding shares on date, and, sometimes without generalization, *The cafeteria bought extra plates*.

Another semi-supervised work is (Kawahara and Kurohashi, 2001). They generalize by using a manually created thesaurus. For finding case frames they use together with the verb, the closest argument, providing verb sense disambiguation for cases similar as the example that motivated us, presented in Section 1.

Next we discuss two different viewpoints for dealing with the verb argument information representation.

2.3 Word Space Model

Traditionally from Information Retrieval, words can be represented as documents and semantic context as features, so that it is possible to build a co-occurrence matrix, or word space, where each intersection of word and context shows the frequency count of each number. This approach has been recently used with syntactic relationships (Padó and Lapata, 2007). An important issue within this approach is the similarity measure chosen for comparing words (documents) given its features. Popular similarity measures range from simple measures such as Euclidean distance, cosine and Jaccard's coefficient (Lee, 1999), to measures such as Hindle's measure and Lin's measure.

In the next Sections we will present a simple proposal within the approach of the Word Space Model (Section 3); then we will present two algorithms within the language modelling approach (Section 0).

Table 1. Pseudo-Disambiguation Task Sample: choose the right option

verb	arg	option 1	option 2
add	subj: I	obj: gallery	obj: member
calculate	obj: flowrate	subj: worksheet	subj: income
read	obj: question	answer	stir
seem	it	just	unlikely
go	overboard	subj: we	subj: they
write	subj: he	obj: plan	obj: appreciation
see	obj: example	in: case	in: london
become	subj: they	obj: king	obj: park
eat	obj: insect	subj: it	subj: this
do	subj: When	obj: you	obj: dog
get	but	obj: them	obj: function
fix	subj: I	obj: driver	obj: goods
fix	obj: it	firmly	fresh
read	subj: he	obj: time	obj: conclusion
need	obj: help	before	climb
seem	likely	subj: it	subj: act

3. A WORD SPACE MODEL

We begin with a simple model for exploring the possibilities of the latter two approaches. In this section we propose a model based on the Word Space Model. Since we want to consider argument co-relation, we use the following information:

$P(v,r_1,n_1,r_2,n_2)$, where v is a verb, r_1 is the relationship between verb and n_1 (noun) as subject, object, preposition or adverb. r_2 and n_2 are analogous. If we assume that n has a different function when used with another relationship, then we can consider that r and n form a new symbol, called a. So that we can simplify our 5-tuple to $P(v,a_1,a_2)$. We want to know, given a verb and an argument a_1, which a_2 is the most plausible, we can write this as $P(a_2|v,a_1)$. For PLSI this can be estimated by

$P(a_2,v,a_1)=Sum(Z_i,P(z)\cdot P(a_2|z)\cdot P(v,a_1|z))$

For the word space model, we can build a matrix where a_2 are the rows (documents) and v,

a_1 are features. As this matrix is very sparse, we use a thesaurus for smoothing the argument values. For doing this, we loosely followed the approach proposed by (McCarthy *et al.*, 2004) for finding the predominant sense, but in this case we use the k nearest neighbours of each argument a_i to find the prevalence score of an unseen triple given its similarity to all triples present in the corpus, measuring this similarity between arguments. In other words, as in (McCarthy *et al.*, 2004, Tejada *et al.*, 2008a, 2008b) for WSD, each similar argument votes for the plausibility of each triple.

$$Prevalence(v,x_1,x_2) = \frac{\sum_{<v,a_1,a_2>\in T} sim(a_1,x_1)\cdot sim(a_2,x_2)\cdot P_{MLE}(v,a_1,a_2)}{\sum_{<v,a_1,a_2>\in T} sim\_exists(a_1,a_2,x_1,x_2)}$$

where T is the whole set of *<verb, argument_1, argument_2>* triples, P_{MLE} is the maximum likelihood of *<verb, argument_1, argument_2>* and

Table 2. Precision (P) and Recall (R) for each verb for 10 neighbours (WSM) and 10 topics (PLSI)

verb	triples	WSM-10		PLSI-10	
		P	**R**	**P**	**R**
eat	31	0.98	0.92	1.00	0.04
seem	77	0.88	0.09	0.64	0.38
learn	204	0.82	0.10	0.57	0.22
inspect	317	0.84	0.19	0.43	0.12
like	477	0.79	0.13	0.54	0.24
come	1,548	0.69	0.23	0.78	0.17
play	1,634	0.68	0.18	0.69	0.19
go	1,901	0.81	0.25	0.80	0.15
do	2,766	0.80	0.24	0.77	0.19
calculate	4,676	0.91	0.36	0.81	0.13
fix	4,772	0.90	0.41	0.80	0.13
see	4,857	0.76	0.23	0.84	0.20
write	6,574	0.89	0.31	0.82	0.15
read	8,962	0.91	0.36	0.82	0.11
add	15,636	0.94	0.36	0.81	0.10
have	127,989	0.95	0.48	0.89	0.03
average	11,401	0.85	0.30	0.75	0.16

$$sim\_exists\left(a_1, a_2, x_1, x_2\right) = \begin{cases} 1 & \text{if } sim(a_1, x_1) \cdot sim(a_2, x_2) > 0 \\ 0 & \text{otherwise} \end{cases}$$

For measuring the similarity between arguments, we built a thesaurus using the method described by Lin (1998a), using the Minipar browser (Lin, 1998b) over short-distance relationships, *i.e.*, we previously separated subordinate clauses. We obtained triples <v,a₁,a₂> from this corpus, which were counted, and these were used for both building the thesaurus as well as a source of verb and argument co-occurrences.

3.1. Evaluation

We compared these two models in a pseudo-disambiguation task following Weeds and Weir (2003). First we obtained triples $\rangle v, a_1, a_2 \langle$ from the corpus.

Then, we divided the corpus in training (80%) and testing (20%) parts. With the first part we trained the PLSI model and created the WSM. This WSM was also used for obtaining the similarity measure for every pair of arguments $a_2 a'_2$. Then we are able to calculate *Feasability(v,a₁,a₂)* For evaluation we created artificially 4-tuples: $\rangle v, a_1, a_2, a'_2 \langle$, formed by taking all the triples $\rangle v, a_1, a_2 \langle$ from the testing corpus, and generating an artificial tuple $\rangle v, a_1, a'_2 \langle$ choosing a random a'_2 with $r'_2 = r_2$, and making sure that this new random triple $\rangle v, a_1, a'_2 \langle$ was not present in the training corpus. The task consisted on selecting the correct tuple. Ties occur when both tuples are given the same score (and both are different from zero). See Table 1.

We compared two models based on the Statistical Language Model (See Section 3.2.1) and the Word Space Model approaches respectively. Using the patent corpus from the NII Test Collec-

Figure 2. Results for (topics)-PLSI and (neighbours)-WSM

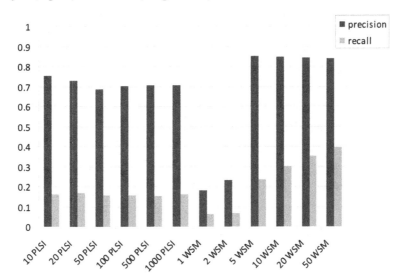

tion for Information Retrieval System, NTCIR-5 Patent (Fuji and Iwayama, 2005), we parsed 7300 million tokens, and then we extracted the chain of relationships on a directed way, that is, for the sentence: X add Y to Z by W, we extracted the triples: <add, subj-X, obj-Y>, <add, obj-Y, to-Z>, <add, to-Z, by-W>. We obtained 706M triples in the form $<v, a1, a2>$. We considered only chained asymmetric relationships to avoid false similarities between words co-occurring in the same sentence.

Following Weeds and Weir (2003), we chose 20 verbs, covering high-frequency verbs and low-frequency verbs and for each one we extracted all the triples $<v, a_1, a_2>$ present in the triples corpus. Then we performed experiments with the PLSI algorithm, and the WSM algorithm.

We experimented with different number of topics for the latent variable z in PLSI, and with different number of neighbours from the Lin thesaurus for expanding the WSM. Results are shown in Table 2 for individual words, 10 neighbours for WSM and 10 topics for PLSI. Figure 2 shows average results for different neighbours and topics.

3.2. Analysis

We have shown results for an algorithm within the WSM approach for unsupervised plausible argument extraction and compared with a traditional PLSI approach, obtaining particular evidence to support that it is possible to achieve good results with the method which votes for common triples using a distributional thesaurus. The results look consistent with previous works using distributional thesauri (Calvo *et al.,* 2005; Tejada *et al.*, 2008a; 2008b) (see Figure 2): adding information increases coverage with little sacrifice on precision.

We used no other resource after the dependency parser, such as named entity recognizers, or labelled data used for training a machine-learning algorithm, so that from that stage this algorithm is unsupervised.

For developing further this approach, it is possible to experiment with the upper limit of the increasing coverage, as each neighbour from the thesaurus is adding noise. We have experimented with building the thesaurus using the same corpus; however, significant differences could be found if using an encyclopaedia corpus for building the

Figure 3. Each document in PLSI is represented as a mixture of topics

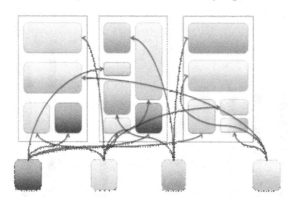

Table 3. Feasible arguments for (eat, subject: cow)

	Verb	Argument 1	Argument 2	Count	Sources
1	eat	subj: cow	obj: hay	0.89	2
2	eat	subj: cow	obj: kg/d	0.49	1
3	eat	subj: cow	obj: grass	0.42	12

dictionary, as broader and richer context could be found

As a future work it is also possible to explore the effect of using other similarity measures, as well as constructing a similarity table with simpler objects—a single noun instead of a composite object.

In the next section we explore other proposals within the Language Model.

3.2.1. Language modelling

We can regard the task of finding the plausibility of a certain argument for a set of sentences as estimating a word given a specific context. Particularly for this work we can consider context as the grammar relationships for a particular verb:

$$P(w,c) = P(c) \cdot P(c|w) \qquad (1)$$

which can be estimated in many ways, particularly, using a Hidden Markov Model, or using latent variables for smoothing, for PLSI (Hoffmann, 1999):,

$$P(w,c) = \sum_{z_i} P(z) \cdot P(w|z) \cdot P(c|z)$$

The conditional probability can be calculated from n-gram frequency counts.

4. THE DEPENDENCY LANGUAGE MODEL

Most of the previous work in SLM has been devoted to speech recognition tasks (Clarkson and Rosenfeld, 1997; Rosenfeld, 2000) using Maximum Entropy Models. Mostly because of space limitations, usually these models are limited to sequential 3-gram models. Several works have shown (Gao and Suzuki, 2003; Gao *et al.*, 2004) that relying only on sequential n-grams is not always the best strategy. Consider the example borrowed from (Gao and Suzuki, 2003): *[A baby]*

Table 4. Feasible arguments for (eat, subject: acid)

	Verb	Argument 1	Argument 2	Count	Sources
1	eat	subj:acid	obj:fiber	2	2
2	eat	subj:acid	obj:group	1	4
3	eat	subj:acid	obj:era	0.66	2
4	eat	subj:acid	away	0.25	40
5	eat	subj:acid	obj:digest	0.19	2
6	eat	subj:acid	of:film	0.18	2
7	eat	subj:acid	in:solvent	0.13	1
8	eat	subj:acid	obj:particle	0.11	4
9	**eat**	**subj:acid**	**obj:layer**	**0.10**	**3**

[in the next seat] cried [throughout the flight]. An n-gram model would try to predict *cried* from *next seat*, whereas a dependency language model (DLM) would try to predict *cried* from *baby*.

In this section we explore creating a DLM for obtaining feasible scenario fillers, which can be regarded as extracting selectional preferences (Resnik, 1996) but with a broader context for each filler. We show in Section 4.1.1 how this additional information helps choosing the best filler candidate; then in Sections 4.1.2 and 4.1.3 we present our implementations of two models for creating a DLM, one based on PLSI (Section 4.1.2) and one based on KNN (Section 4.1.3). In Section 4.2 we describe our experiments for comparing both algorithms in a pseudo-disambiguation task. We analyze our results in Section 4.3.

4.1. Models for Plausible Argument Estimation

4.1.1. Feasible Scenario Fillers

Let us consider that we want to find the most feasible thing eaten given the verb to eat. As eat has several senses, this filler could be food, or could be a material, depending on who is eating. See Table 3 and Table 4. In Table 3 the subject is cow. Count represents the total number of counts that voted for this combination divided by the number

of sources. These tables are actual output of our system (KNN DLM).

In Table 4, the subject is *acid*. It is possible to see the different adequate fillers depending on the subject doing the action.

If we consider the problem of estimating $P(a_2|v,a_1)$ instead of estimating only $P(a_2|v)$—where a_1 and a_2 are arguments, and v is a verb, the data sparseness problem increases. This has been solved mainly by using external resources such as WordNet (Resnik, 1996; McCarthy and Carroll, 2006; Agirre and Martinez, 2001); semantic-role annotated resources, *i.e.* FrameNet, PropBank (Padó and Lapata, 2007); a named entity recognizer, *e.g.* IdentiFinder (Salgeiro *et al.*, 2006); or other manually created thesaurus (Kawahara and Kurohashi, 2001).

A goal of this section is to find at which extent the information from the corpus itself can be used for estimating $P(a_2|v,a_1)$ without using additional resources. For this matter, several techniques are used for dealing with the data sparseness problem. We describe both of them in the next section.

4.1.2. PLSI – Probabilistic Latent Semantic Indexing

We can regard the task of finding the plausibility of a certain argument for a set of sentences as

Figure 4. Pseudo-algorithm for the K-nearest neighbours DLM algorithm

```
for each triple <v,a₁,a₂> with observed count c,
  for each argument a₁,a₂
    Find its k most similar words a₁ₛ₁...a₁ₛₖ,  a₂ₛ₁...a₂ₛₖ
      with similarities s₁ₛ₁, ..., s₁ₛₖ and s₂ₛ₁,...,s₂ₛₖ.
        Create a triple <v,a₁ₛᵢ,a₂ₛⱼ>
          Add c·s₁ₛi·s₂ₛⱼ to the count of votes of triple <v,a₁ₛᵢ,a₂ₛⱼ>
```

estimating a word given a specific context. Since we want to consider argument co-relation, we have

$$P\left(v, r_1, n_1, r_2, n_2\right)$$

where v is a verb, r_1 is the relationship between the verb and n_1 (noun) as subject, object, preposition or adverb. r_2 and n_2 are analogous. If we assume that n has a different function when used with another relationship, then we can consider that r and n form a new symbol, called a. So that we can simplify our 5−tuple $P\left(v, r_1, n_1, r_2, n_2\right)$ to $P\left(v, a_1, a_2\right)$.

We want to know, given a verb and an argument a_1, which a_2 is the most plausible argument, *i.e.* $P\left(a_2 \big| v, a_1\right)$. We can write the probability of finding a particular verb and two of its syntactic relationships as:

$$P\left(v, a_1, a_2\right) = P\left(v, a_1\right) \cdot P\left(a_2 \big| v, a_1\right),$$

which can be estimated in several ways. Particularly for this work, we use PLSI (Hoffmann, 1999) because we can exploit the concept of latent variables to deal with data sparseness.

The probabilistic Latent Semantic Indexing Model (PLSI) was introduced in Hofmann (1999), arose from Latent Semantic Indexing (Deerwester et al., 1990). The model attempts to associate an unobserved class variable $z \in Z = \{z_1, ..., z_k\}$, (in our case a generalization of correlation of the co-occurrence of v, a_1 and a_2), and two sets of

observables: arguments, and verbs + arguments. In terms of generative model it can be defined as follows: a v, a_1 pair is selected with probability $P(v, a_1)$, then a latent class z is selected with probability $P(z|v, a_1)$ and finally an argument a_2 is selected with probability $P(a_2|z)$. It is possible to use PLSI (Hoffmann, 1999) this said way, expressed also as (2).

$$P(v, a_1, a_2) = \overset{o}{\underset{z}{a}} P(Z_l) x P(a_2 \mid z_l) x P(v, a_1 \mid z_l) \tag{2}$$

z is a latent variable capturing the correlation between a_2 and the co-occurrence of (v, a_1) simultaneously. Using a single latent variable to correlate three variables may lead to a poor performance of PLSI, so that in next section we explore different ways of exploiting the smoothing by latent semantic variables.

4.1.3. K-Nearest Neighbours Model (Expansor)

This model uses the k nearest neighbours of each argument to find the plausibility of an unseen triple given its similarity to all triples present in the corpus, measuring this similarity between arguments. See Figure 4 for the pseudo-algorithm of this model.

As votes are accumulative, triples that have words with many similar words will get more votes.

Common similarity measures range from Euclidean distance, cosine and Jaccard's coefficient

(Lee, 1999), to measures such as Hindle's measure and Lin's measure (Lin, 1998a). Weeds and Weir (2003) show that the distributional measure with best performance is the Lin similarity, so we used this measure for smoothing the co-occurrence space, following the procedure as described in (Lin, 1998b).

4.2. Evaluation

For these experiments, we used the same setting presented in Section 3.1. We created artificially 4-tuples: $\langle v, a_1, a_2, a_2' \rangle$, formed by taking all the triples $\langle v, a_1, a_2 \rangle$ from the testing corpus, and generating an artificial triple $\langle v, a_1, a_2' \rangle$ choosing a random a_2' with r_2'=r_2 and making sure that this new random triple $\langle v, a_1, a_2' \rangle$ was not present in the training corpus. The task consisted on

As in Section 3.1 for evaluation we used the patent corpus from the NII Test Collection for Information Retrieval System, NTCIR-5 Patent (Fuji and Iwayama, 2005), we parsed 7300 million tokens with the MINIPAR parser (Lin, 1998b), and then we extracted the chain of relationships on a directed way, that is, for the sentence: *X add Y to Z by W*, we extracted the triples:

$$\langle add, sub - X, obj - Y \rangle,$$
$$\langle add, obj - Y, to - Z \rangle,$$

and

$$\langle add, to - Z, by - W \rangle$$

We obtained 177M triples in the form $\langle v, a_1, a_2 \rangle$

4.2.1. Comparing the Effect of Adding Context

For this experiment we created a joint mini-corpus consisting of 1,000 triples for each of the verbs from the patent corpus: (*add, calculate, come,*

do, eat, fix, go, have, inspect, learn, like, read, see, seem, write). We want to evaluate the impact of adding more information for verb argument prediction, so that we estimate the argument's plausibility given a verb $P(a_2|v)$ then we compare with using additional information from other arguments $P(a_2|v,a_1)$ for both models.

For completely new words sometimes it is not possible to do an estimate, henceforth, we measured precision and recall. Precision measures how many attachments were correctly predicted from the covered examples, and recall measures the correctly predicted attachment from the whole test set. We are interested on measuring the precision and coverage of these methods, so that we did not implemented any back off technique such as returning a default value for an undecided attachment.

4.3. Analysis

Operating separately on verbs (one mini-corpus per verb) yields better results for PLSI (precision above 0.8) while seems not affecting EXPANSOR KNN. For little context $P(a_2|v)$, PLSI works better than EXPANSOR KNN, for more context, $P(a_2|v,a_1)$, EXPANSOR KNN works better.

In general, PLSI prefers a small number of topics, even for a large corpus (around 20 topics for the largest corpus of experiments). EXPANSOR KNN seems to improve recall steadily when adding more neighbours, loosing a small amount of precision. Expanding with few neighbours (1~5) seems not to be very useful. Particularly it is possible to see in Figure 5 that when recall is very low, precision can go very high or very low. This is because when so few cases are solved, performance tends to be random. In general, results for recall seem low because for we did not use any back off method. If we compare the precision of the EXPANSOR KNN full model (based on more context) we can think of backing off to PLSI based on pairs $P(a_2|v)$. This would yield the best results, and it is left as future work.

Figure 5. Raw effect of adding more context: prediction based only on the verb versus prediction based on the verb plus one argument. EXPANSOR is the proposed KNN-based model

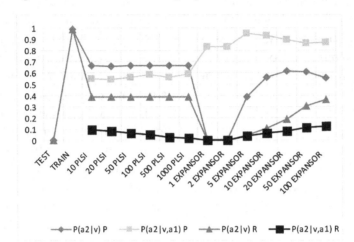

We evaluated two different Dependency Language Models with a pseudo-disambiguation test. The KNN based model outperforms the PLSI based model when more data is added, and thus creating data sparseness. Effective smoothing is achieved by voting using similarity measures from the Lin distributional thesaurus.

Since the PLSI model we have used up to these experiments is dealing with several arguments with a single latent variable, in the next section we will present an original improvement that consists on interpolating several PLSI models for handling multiple arguments.

5. INTERPOLATED PLSI

In this section we propose a new model called interpolated PLSI, which allows using multiple latent semantic variables, based on the algorithm described in Section 4.1.2.

5.1. iPLSI – Interpolated PLSI

The previous PLSI formula originally used crushes the association of information from a_2, and v, a_1 simultaneously into one single latent variable.

This caused two problems: first, data sparseness, and second, it fixed the correlation between two variables. Hence we propose a variation for this calculation by using interpolation based on each pair of arguments for a triple. Eq. Eq 3 shows an interpolated way of estimating the probability of a triple based on the co-occurrences of its different pairs. In

Additionally we test a model that considers additional information. See Eq. 4. Note that a_i (the latent variable topics) should not be confused with a_1 and a_2 (the arguments).

See Figure 5. for a graphical representation of this concept. Each latent variable is represented by a letter in a small circle. Big circles surround the components of the dependency triple to be estimated. A black dot shows the co-occurrence of two variables. All of them contribute for the estimation of the triple v, a_1, a_2.

5.2. Experiments

We compare these two models in a pseudo-disambiguation task as shown in Section 3.1. However, in order to have a wider range of co-occurrent words, for these evaluations we used the UkWaC corpus (Ferraresi et al. 2008.) This

Table 5. Results of the original PLSI and KNN algorithms for a test with the UKWaC corpus

Mode	Algorithm	Wordset size	Prec.	Recall	F-score
P(a2|v)	PLSI	1000	0.5333	0.2582	0.3479
	KNN	1000	0.7184	0.5237	0.6058
	PLSI	2500	0.5456	0.2391	0.3325
	KNN	2500	0.7499	0.5032	0.6023
P(a2|v,a2)	PLSI	1000	0.4315	0.1044	0.1681
	KNN	1000	0.8236	0.5492	0.6590
	PLSI	2500	0.3414	0.0611	0.1036
	KNN	2500	0.8561	0.6858	0.7615

corpus is a large balanced corpus of English from the UK Web with more than 2 billion tokens[2]. We created two wordsets for the verbs: *play, eat, add, calculate, fix, read, write, have, learn, inspect, like, do, come, go, see, seem, give, take, keep, make, put, send, say, get, walk, run, study, need,* and *become*. These verbs were chosen as a sample of highly frequent verbs, as well as not so frequent verbs. They are also verbs that can take a great variety of arguments, such as *take* (i.e., ambiguity is high). Each wordset contains 1000 or 2500 verb dependency triples per each verb. The first wordset is evaluated against 5,279 verb dependency triples, while the second wordset is evaluated against 12,677 verb dependency triples, corresponding roughly to 20% of the total number of triples in each wordset.

5.2.1. Results of Original Algorithm with New Corpus

In this section we present our results for this new corpus of the original PLSI and the KNN algorithms with the new corpus. Tests were carried out with one 7-topic variable for PLSI, and a 100 nearest neighbours expansion for KNN. We have shown in Section 4.2.1 that for estimating the probability of an argument a_2, $P(a_2|v,a_1)$ works better than $P(a_2|v)$. The following table confirms this for different wordset sizes. In most cases KNN performs better than original PLSI in precision

and recall (the best of the KNN variations is better than the best of the PLSI variations). Contrary to KNN, PLSI's performance increases as the wordset size is increased probably due to more confusion in using the same number of topics. This can be seen also in Figure 6 and Figure 7: recall improves slightly for bigger data sets and more topics.

5.2.2. Measuring the Learning Rate

This experiment consisted on gradually increasing the number of triples from 125 to 2000 dependency triples per verb to examine the effects of using smaller corpora. Results are shown in Figure 6. In this figure KNN outperforms PLSI when adding more data. KNN precision is higher as well in all experiments. The best results for PLSI were obtained with 10 topics, while for KNN the best results were obtained using 200 neighbours.

5.2.3. Results with No Pre-Filtering

Previous results used a pre-filtering threshold of 4, that is, triples with less than 4 occurrences were discarded. Here we present results with no pre-filtering. In Figure 7 results for KNN fall dramatically. PLSI is able to perform better with 20 topics. This suggests that PLSI is able to smooth better single occurrences of certain triples. KNN is better for working with frequently occurring triples. We

Figure 6. Average of Precision and Recall for the original PLSI and KNN showing learning rate (each series has different number of triples per verb, tpv). No frequency threshold was used. The numbers and the lower part show the number of topics for PLSI and the number of neighbours for KNN

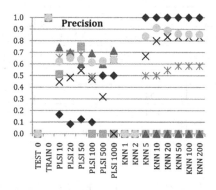
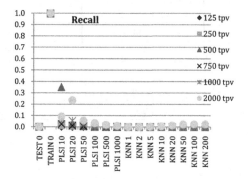

Figure 7. Precision and Recall for the original PLSI and KNN with learning rate (each series has different number of triples per verb, tpv). The frequency threshold for triples was set to 4. The numbers and the lower part show the number of topics for PLSI and the number of neighbours for KNN

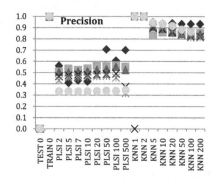
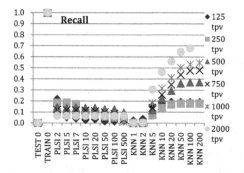

require a method that can handle occurrences of un-frequent words, since pre-filtering implies a loss of data that could be useful afterwards. For example, imagine that *tezgüino* is mentioned only once in the training test. We consider that it is important to be able to learn information for scarcely mentioned entities too. The next section presents results regarding to the improvement of using PLSI to handle non-filtered items.

$f(v)$, $f(a_1)$, and $f(a_2)$ are the observed probabilities of v, a_1 and a_2 respectively.

$$P_E(v, a_1, a_2) \mu f_m(v, a_1)f(a_2) + f_n(v, a_2)f(a_1) + f_o(a_1, a_2)f(a_2)$$

$$f_m(v, a_1) = \overset{o}{\underset{m}{a}} P(m_i) x P(v \mid m_i) x P(a_1 \mid m_i)$$

$$f_n(v, a_2) = \overset{o}{\underset{n}{a}} P(n_i) x P(v \mid n_i) x P(a_2 \mid n_i)$$

$$f_o(a_1, a_2) = \overset{o}{\underset{o}{a}} P(o_i) x P(a_1 \mid o_i) x P(a_2 \mid o_i)$$

(3)

Table 6. Comparison of different iPLSI modes, consisting on selecting different estimators. KNN is shown in the last row for reference

mode	Precision	Recall	mode	Precision	Recall
a,b,c	0.78	0.78	m,n,o	0.83	0.83
a	0.67	0.60	m	0.78	0.77
b	0.44	0.44	n	0.50	0.48
c	0.77	0.77	o	0.84	0.84
a,c	0.62	0.62	m,n	0.77	0.77
a,b	0.78	0.78	m,o	0.83	0.83
b,c	0.76	0.76	n,o	0.84	0.84
KNN	0.74	0.51	a,b,c,m,n,o	0.80	0.80

$$P_E(v, a_1, a_2) \gg f_m(v, a_1)f(a_2) + f_n(v, a_2)f(a_1) + f_o(a_1, a_2)f(a_2)$$
$$+ f_a(v, a_1, a_2) + f_b(v, a_1, a_2) + f_c(v, a_1, a_2)$$

$$f_a(v, a_1, a_2) = \overset{o}{\underset{a}{a}} P(a_i) x P(v, a_2 \mid a) x P(a_1 \mid a)$$
$$f_b(v, a_1, a_2) = \overset{o}{\underset{b}{a}} P(b_i) x P(a_1, a_2 \mid b_i) x P(v \mid b_i)$$
$$f_c(v, a_1, a_2) = \overset{o}{\underset{c}{a}} P(c_i) x P(v, a_1 \mid c_i) x P(a_2 \mid c_i)$$

$$(4)$$

5.3. iPLSI Results

As presented in Section 5.1, we test different models for combining the Latent Semantic Variables. The *mode* part shows the latent variables that were used for these tests. For example, for the *a,c* row, the estimation was carried using (5). Results are presented Table 6.

$$P_E(v, a_1, a_2) \gg f_a(v, a_1, a_2) + f_c(v, a_1, a_2) \qquad (5)$$

In Table 6, the best results were obtained for *o,* (using only the information from a_1, a_2) followed by *m,o*, which is combining the information from v, a_1 and a_1, a_2. The *m,n,o* and *n,o* modes include *n*, which has no impact in this test because it is always fixed, and helps little for deciding which triple is better. However, as we show in the following section, a test with pure n-grams (non

dependency triples, as in all previous tests) the three components (in this case *m, n,* and *o*), are contributing to the estimation.

5.4. N-grams Test

We conducted this test to attest that the three components are contributing to the interpolation, as well as avoiding the bias the parser might induce. The n-grams test was conducted by selecting trigrams of bigrams from the UKWaC corpus in a similar manner than the previous experiments, however in this case we did not use dependency relationships, but sliding windows of hexagrams distributed in trigrams in order to mimic the way function words (*v.gr.* prepositions or determiners) affect triplets in the dependency model. The n-grams were extracted for n-grams related to the same verbs described in Section 5.2. The task consisted, as with the dependency triples task, to choose one amongst two options of Pair 1. The correct case is the always first pair, although the system does not know about this. We used 80% of the trigrams as a base for prediction (training), and 20% for testing. Tests were conducted for 500 triples per verb to 5000 triples per verb, in the best performance models of the previous experiment (*m,n* and *m,n,o*).

From Table 6 we can see that *m,n,o* is always having the best performance.

Table 7. Results of iPLSI for hexagrams grouped as trigrams of bigrams. It shows that it is possible to select the correct trigram amongst two in 75% of the cases

Size, Mode	Prec.	Recall	Size, Mode	Prec.	Recall
500 m,n	0.75	0.70	2000 m,n,o	0.77	0.77
500 m,n,o	0.78	0.74	3000 m,n	0.70	0.70
1000 m,n	0.70	0.70	3000 m,n,o	0.75	0.75
1000 m,n,o	0.76	0.76	5000 m,n	0.72	0.72
2000 m,n	0.73	0.72	5000 m,n,o	0.76	0.76

5.5. Analysis

We have seen that the KNN algorithm outperforms single-variable PLSI, and we study the learning rate of both algorithms, showing that KNN increases recall when more data is added, without trading much recall; however, KNN requires strongly a pre-filtering phrase which eventually leads to an important loss of scarcely occurring words. These words are important to our purposes, because filtering them out would prevent us to generalizing rare words for measuring their plausibility. The iPLSI (interpolated PLSI) algorithm proposed here deals with that issue, yielding better results than single-variable PLSI. We have found that it is possible to select the most feasible hexagram out of two with a 75% of recall for raw n-grams grouped as trigrams of bigrams, and up to 83% recall for dependency trigrams. The conducted tests prove that it is possible to select the correct candidate for a triple, which can be regarded as part of a sentence. This allows calculating the most plausible argument in a sentence, using a broader context given by a verb and other argument.

iPLSI has outperformed the previous KNN model, but still there is room for improvement. Particularly, we are estimating co-occurrence of two arguments simultaneously. In order to determine if using more arguments is better for argument prediction we propose a model that allows this in the following section, and then compare with the previous approaches.

6. THE NEED FOR FULL CO-OCCURRENCE

We have shown previously that considering simultaneously three arguments yields better precision than only two, with certain loss of recall. Kawahara and Kurohashi (2006) perform verb disambiguation for learning preferences by differentiating the main verb with the closest argument. For example *play a joke* and *play a guitar* will have different argument preferences; however, in some cases this is not enough, as it can be seen in the following example, where the verb has different meanings depending of a far argument:

Play a scene for friends in the theatre

(to act), and

Play a scene for friends in the VCR

(to reproduce.)

Recent works have proposed a discriminative approach for learning selectional preferences, starting with Bergsma *et al.* (2008). Ritter *et al.* (2010) and Ó Séaghdha (2010) propose a LinkLDA (Latent Dirichlet Allocation) model with linked topic hidden variables drawn from the same distribution to model <subject, verb, object> combinations, such as <*man, eats, ramen*> and <*cow, eats, grass*>. However, these works consider at most tri-nary relations. Motivated by

Table 8. Co-occurrence table (verbs+nouns)

	with friend	in park
play	1	1
eat	1	
ball		1
yoyo	1	

the problem of considering as many arguments as possible for clustering verb preferences, we propose here a general model for learning all co-related preferences in a sentence, allowing us to measure the plausibility of its occurrence. In addition this model allows using both statistical resources as well as manual resources such as dictionaries or WordNet to improve the prediction. In this work we show an example of using PLSI, Mutual Information and WordNet for measuring this plausibility.

Furthermore, at this point there are several particular questions that we seek to answer. (1) For automatic learning, building the co-occurrence table out from real examples can be done in several different ways. Which one is better?; (2) Joining verb and nouns information in a single table is better for the model?; (3) Using an SVM trained only on PLSI information can perform better than the PLSI model itself?; (4) How this model performs when varying training information?; (5) Combining statistical information (PLSI and PMI) with manually crafted resources information such as WordNet improves results?; (6) Is it worth considering beyond tri-nary relationships?

6.1. Method

First we build the resource for counting co-occurrences. We do this by parsing the UKWaC corpus with MINIPAR (Lin, 1998) to obtain a lemmatized dependency representation. The UKWaC corpus (Ferraresi et al. 2008) is a large balanced corpus of English from the UK Web with more than 2 billion tokens. The sentence

Play a scene for friends in the theatre becomes: play obj:scene for:friend in:theatre. Then we pre-calculate the mutual information statistics between all pairs of words, *i.e.*, (play, obj:scene), (play, for:friend), (play, in:theatre), (obj:scene, for:friend), (obj:scene, in:theatre), (for:friend, in:theatre). We then proceed to calculate the topic representation of each word using PLSI.

As discussed previously in section 4.1.2 the probabilistic Latent Semantic Indexing Model (PLSI) (Hofmann, 1999) attempts to associate an unobserved class variable $z \in Z = \{z_1, ..., z_k\}$, and two sets of observable arguments. In terms of generative model it can be defined as follows: a document is selected with probability $P(d)$, then a latent class z is selected with probability $P(z|d)$ and finally a word w is selected with probability $P(w|z)$. This can be also alternatively represented as Eq. (6).

$$P(d, w) = \overset{o}{\underset{z}{a}} P(z_i) x P(d \mid z_i) x P(w \mid z_i) \qquad (6)$$

Given a set of sentences, there are several ways for considering what is a word and what is a document. We can consider grouping the documents by verb or by noun. That is, a document called *eat* will be for all the arguments co-occurring with the verb *eat*, or, a document called *ball* can be all the arguments and verbs co-occurring with this noun, such as *play, with:stripes, for:exercise*, etc. See g

Table 8. On the other hand, documents can be nouns only, and the co-occurrents would be verbs plus functions. See Table 9.

Table 9. Co-occurrence table (nouns only)

	play with	play at
yoyo	1	
ball	1	

Figure 8. Coverage, Precision and Recall of first experiment

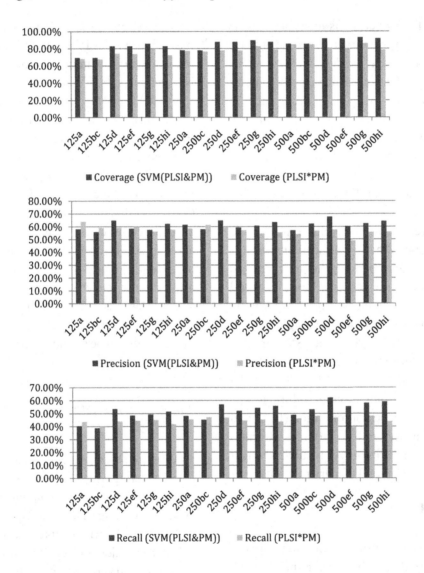

To summarize, the following different ways of building the sentence co-occurrence matrix for PLSI are listed below. fn means function:noun (*with:stripes*), v means verb (*play*), n noun (*ball*), vf means verb:function (*play:with*). In some cases Baroni and Lenci (2009) performed experiments with similar matrices. Their nomenclature is indicated in square brackets.

a. (fn|v,fn|v)

Table 10. Top concepts in WordNet.

dry_land_1	money_2
object_1	garment_1
being_1	feeling_1
human_1	change_of_state_1
animal_1	motion_2
flora_1	effect_4
artifact_1	phenomenon_1
instrument_2	activity_1
device_2	act_1
product_2	state_1
writing_4	abstraction_1
construction_4	attribute_1
worker_2	relation_1
creation_3	cognition_1
food_1	unit_6
beverage_1	relationship_3
location_1	time_1
symbol_2	fluid_2
substance_1	

bc. (fn,fn), (v,fn) [LCxLC, CxLC]
d. (v|n,fn)
ef. (v,fn), (n,fn) [CxLC,CxLC]
g. (n,vf|nf) [CxCL]
h,i. (n,vf) (n,nf)

Note that modes *a* and *bc* are the same, however *bc* considers building and training the PLSI model separately for nouns and verbs. The same happens for modes *d* and *ef* and *g* and *hi*. In the experiment section we detail results for each one of these different settings for building the sentence co-occurrence matrix for PLSI.

6.1.1. Assembling Features for SVM for Training and Testing

Once the PLSI and PMI resources are built, the training and test sentences are parsed with MINIPAR but only the first level shallow parse is used. We mapped features to positions in a vector. Every argument has a fixed offset, i.e., the subject will be always in the first position, the object in position 75, the arguments beginning with *in* at position 150, etc. In this way the co-relation can be captured by an SVM learner. We have chosen a second-degree polynomial kernel, so that it can capture combinations of features. Each one of the arguments is decomposed in several sub-features. These sub-features consist on the projection of each word in the PLSI topic space, the Pointwise Mutual Information (PMI) between target word and the feature word, and the projection of the feature word in the WordNet space.

The PMI was calculated as follows,

$$PMI(t_2, t_2) = \frac{\log P(t_1, t_2)}{P(t_1)P(t_2)}$$

Table 11. Simplified example representation for SVM training and testing (one long row)

verb	subj							obj (target)						
play	z_1	z_2	z_3	PMI	wn_1	wn_2	wn_3	z_1	z_2	z_3	PMI	wn_1	wn_2	wn_3
								0.3	0.2	0.5	1	0.8	0.3	0.2
	in							on						
	z_1	z_2	z_3	PMI	wn_1	wn_2	wn_3	z_1	z_2	z_3	PMI	wn_1	wn_2	wn_3
	0.4	0.3	0.8	0.4	0.2	0.4	0.3							
	with							for						
	z_1	z_2	z_3	PMI	wn_1	wn_2	wn_3	z_1	z_2	z_3	PMI	wn_1	wn_2	wn_3
								0.4	0.6	0.4	0.2	0.1	0.9	0.1

For an example on the data for learning, please refer to Table 11. This is the row corresponding to *play a scene for friends in theatre*. The word *scene* is projected in three topics z_1, z_2 and z_3 as 0.3, 0.2, 0.5 (note however that the experiments considered the projection unto 38 topics;) Then, we calculate the projection in a WordNet space for each word. This is done by calculating the *jcn* distance (Jiang and Conrath, 2007) with regard to 38 top concepts in WordNet shown in Table 10. The PMI value for the target word and every target word is also included: (*scene, scene*) 1, (*scene, in theatre*) 0.4, (*scene, for friends*) 0.2.

6.2. Experiments

Let us recall the questions we want to answer for these experiments from Section 6.

Following Weeds and Weir (2003) we perform experiments for a pseudo-disambiguation task. This task consisted on changing a target word (in this case, direct object) and then the system should identify the most plausible sentence considering the verb and all of its arguments. For example, for the sentences (i) *I eat* rice *with chopsticks at the cafeteria*; and (ii) *I eat* bag *with chopsticks at the cafeteria*, the system should be able to identify the first as the most plausible sentence. This experiment setting is similar to the previous experiments shown in Sections 3.1, 4.2, and 5.2, but in this case we are considering

full phrases instead of only quadruples. We obtained randomly 50 sentences from the WSJ corpus for the verbs: *play, eat, add, calculate, fix, read, write, have, learn, inspect, like, do, come, go, see, seem, give, take, keep, make, put, send, say, get, walk, run, study, need,* and *become*. These verbs were chosen as a sample of highly frequent verbs, as well as not so frequent verbs. They are also verbs that can take a great variety of arguments, such as *take* (i.e., ambiguity is high). For training we created wordsets for the same verbs. Each training wordset contains 125, 250 or 500 verb dependency triples per each verb. Varying size of training allows us to answer question number four. These wordsets were used for training the PLSI model, and also for creating the PMI database. Then, the same wordsets were used for training SVM. Each sentence was treated as a row, as described in Section 6.1.1, with each feature expanded in PLSI sub-features (topics). We generated two false examples randomly per each good example. For testing we generate a false for each existing test example.

At this point we have not included yet information about WordNet. This first experiment explores different ways of building the co-occurrence matrix, as described in Section 6.1 (questions number 1 and 2). We compare using PLSI and PM with and without SVM learning to answer question number 3. See results in Table 13.

Figure 9. Precision, Recall and F score (by training size and by method) for different training corpus' sizes (125, 250 and 500) and feature combinations (PMI, PLSI and WN)

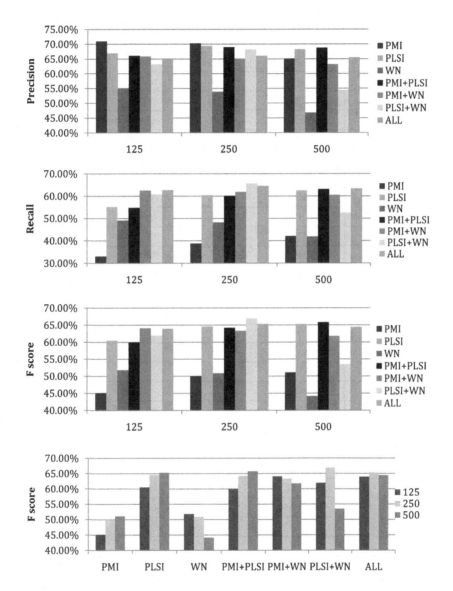

From Table 13 and Figure 8 we can see that in all cases considering all arguments improves performance (carried out by adding the SVM learning stage to the PLSI binary co-occurrences). In addition, whereas the *g* mode (n,vf|nf) for creating the co-occurrence matrix has greater coverage, by precision and recall mode *d* (v|n,fn) is always the best one. We observe also an increas-ing performance while increasing the amount of data in the training wordset.

Both the *g* and the *d* modes combine verbs and nouns, so that we can answer question two with a yes: it is better to join nouns and verbs in a single table.

Table 12. Results of pseudo-disambiguation task with different settings of PMI, PLSI and WordNet (WN)

PMI	PLSI	WN	Learning	Coverage	Precision	Recall	F
Wordset 125							
0	0	1	68.36%	89.44%	54.88%	49.09%	51.82%
0	1	0	89.59%	82.61%	66.96%	55.23%	60.53%
0	1	1	92.60%	**96.09%**	63.23%	60.76%	61.97%
1	0	0	93.63%	46.62%	**70.98%**	33.10%	45.15%
1	0	1	94.55%	94.88%	65.85%	**62.48%**	**64.12%**
1	1	0	97.14%	83.03%	66.09%	54.85%	59.95%
1	1	1	**98.01%**	**96.09%**	65.26%	62.71%	63.96%
Wordset 250							
0	0	1	67.85%	89.49%	53.87%	48.21%	50.88%
0	1	0	88.01%	87.02%	69.44%	60.43%	64.62%
0	1	1	90.82%	**96.28%**	68.22%	**65.69%**	**66.93%**
1	0	0	93.24%	55.18%	**70.34%**	38.81%	50.02%
1	0	1	93.78%	95.39%	64.86%	61.87%	63.33%
1	1	0	96.88%	87.12%	68.99%	60.11%	64.24%
1	1	1	**97.28%**	**96.28%**	66.10%	64.64%	65.36%
Wordset 500							
0	0	1	91.09%	89.49%	46.75%	41.84%	44.16%
0	1	0	86.75%	91.58%	68.32%	62.57%	65.32%
0	1	1	93.46%	96.79%	54.37%	52.63%	53.49%
1	0	0	92.95%	64.62%	65.11%	42.07%	51.11%
1	0	1	93.46%	95.72%	63.18%	60.48%	61.80%
1	1	0	96.65%	91.72%	**68.77%**	63.08%	**65.80%**
1	1	1	**96.68%**	**97.69%**	65.51%	**63.41%**	64.44%
Average							
0	0	1	91.09%	89.47%	51.83%	46.38%	48.96%
0	1	0	86.75%	87.07%	68.24%	59.41%	63.49%
0	1	1	93.46%	96.39%	61.94%	59.69%	60.80%
1	0	0	92.95%	55.47%	**68.81%**	37.99%	48.76%
1	0	1	93.46%	95.33%	64.63%	61.61%	63.08%
1	1	0	96.65%	87.29%	67.95%	59.35%	63.33%
1	1	1	**96.68%**	**96.69%**	65.62%	**63.59%**	**64.59%**

Table 13. Results of using different modes for building the co-occurrence matrix for PLSI, and using PLSI and PM with and without SVM learning

Train size	mode	SVM (PLSI&PM) Coverage	PLSI*PM Coverage	SVM (PLSI&PM) Precision	PLSI*PM Precision	SVM (PLSI&PM) Recall	PLSI*PM Recall
125	a	0.70	0.68	0.58	**0.64**	0.40	0.44
125	bc	0.69	0.68	0.56	0.59	0.39	0.40
125	d	0.83	0.74	0.65	0.59	0.54	0.44
125	ef	0.83	0.74	0.59	0.60	0.48	0.44
125	g	0.86	0.80	0.58	0.56	0.49	0.45
125	hi	0.83	0.72	0.62	0.58	0.51	0.42
250	a	0.78	0.78	0.62	0.59	0.48	0.45
250	bc	0.78	0.77	0.58	0.61	0.45	0.47
250	d	0.88	0.78	0.65	0.60	0.57	0.47
250	ef	0.88	0.78	0.59	0.57	0.52	0.45
250	g	0.90	0.83	0.61	0.55	0.54	0.45
250	hi	0.88	0.79	0.64	0.55	0.56	0.44
500	a	0.86	0.85	0.57	0.54	0.49	0.46
500	bc	0.85	0.85	0.62	0.57	0.53	0.48
500	d	0.92	0.81	**0.68**	0.58	**0.62**	0.47
500	ef	0.92	0.81	0.60	0.49	0.55	0.39
500	g	**0.93**	**0.86**	0.62	0.56	0.58	**0.48**
500	hi	0.92	0.79	0.64	0.56	0.59	0.44

6.2.1. Adding Manually Crafted Information

In this experiment we add manually crafted information into the model. As described in Section 6.1.1, we add information into the training and testing table about the distance to 38 common top concepts in WordNet. Table 12 shows the results obtained.

From Figure 9 it is possible to see that in most cases, combining the three sources of information improves the learning rate, although separately, PMI provides the highest learning rate. Coverage is always the best when combining the three resources. However, precision is better with PMI only for small amounts of training data, whereas PLSI gives better support when adding more data. Recall is greater for the cases involving the aid

of WordNet information. In average, except for precision, the best values are obtained when combining the three resources.

7. CONCLUSION AND FUTURE WORK

Despite the low amount of training data, we were able to obtain prediction rates above a trivial baseline of random selection between two options. With these experiments it was possible to determine the impact of using several resources, and also to measure the benefit of using an ensemble model for SVM with regard to a simple PLSI model. We found that considering all co-occurrences of arguments in a sentence increases recall by 10%. We also observed that, as expected, adding more data increases coverage; however, it increases recall in a greater extent using SVM over PLSI than in PLSI only. Using SVM increases coverage, precision and recall, even when trained with the same information available to PLSI. This suggests that generating negative examples randomly, and applying machine learning to this sample may improve performance of tasks using topic models.

We found also that the best mode to build the co-occurrence matrix for PLSI is mode d (v|n,fn), which corresponds in (Baroni and Lenci, 2009) work to the CxLC mode. We found also that building separately co-occurrence matrices for verbs and nouns does not improve the performance of the model; on the contrary, it worsens it. It is better to use a joint table of verbs and nouns because it is possible to share the information on the features between both groups of words. We proposed also that a single model to combine statistical information (PLSI and PMI) with manually crafted resources such as WordNet, and proved that performance increases in this way, however the increase was not as significative as we expected, as it is can be seen in Figure 9, where most of the contributing features are those from PLSI. However, as previously shown in Figure 8 and Table 13, SVM learning over PLSI has the advantage of being able to capture the co-relation of all arguments, as opposed than the pair-wise PLSI model.

Future work may consider exploring a three-variable mathematical model of PLSI instead of a pair wise interpolation, as well as other variants of iPLSI such as two-staged iPLSI, which would consist on relating two latent semantic variables with a latent variable in a second stage. Since the test we conducted creates random alternatives, our system might select more probable candidates than the actual one, such as given "cow eats hay in yard", selecting the randomly created "cow eats grass in yard" would count as negative results. Although the effect of this is expected to be low, it should be considered on further analyses.

As future work, we plan evaluating with larger wordsets, as well as evaluating the performance of our model in other tasks such as anaphora resolution or sentence coherence detection.

ACKNOWLEDGMENT

We thank the support of SNI, SIP-IPN, COFAA-IPN, and PIFI-IPN, CONACYT; and the Japanese Government; the first author is a JSPS fellow.

REFERENCES

Agirre, E., & Martinez, D. (2001). Learning class-to-class selectional preferences. *Workshop on Computational Natural Language Learning*, ACL.

Baroni, M., & Lenci, A. (2009). One distributional memory, many semantic spaces. *Proceedings of the EACL 2009 Geometrical Models for Natural Language Semantics (GEMS) Workshop*, East Stroudsburg PA: ACL, 1–8.

Bergsma, S., Lin, D., & Goebel, R. (2008). Discriminative Learning of Selectional Preference for Unlabeled Text. *Proceedings of the 2008 Conference on Empirical Methods in Natural Language Processing*, pp. 59–68

Bolshakov, I. A. (2005). An Experiment in Detection and Correction of Malapropisms through the Web . *LNCS, 3406*, 803–815.

Bolshakov, I. A., Galicia-Haro, S. N., & Gelbukh, A. (2005). *Detection and Correction of Malapropisms in Spanish by means of Internet Search*. TSD-2005 . *Springer LNAI, 3658*, 115–122.

Budanitsky, E., & Graeme, H. (2001). *Semantic distance in WorldNet: An experimental, application-oriented evaluation of five measures*, NAACL Workshop on WordNet and other lexical resources.

Calvo, H., Gelbukh, A., & Kilgarriff, A. (2005). *Automatic Thesaurus vs. WordNet: A Comparison of Backoff Techniques for Unsupervised PP Attachment.* LNCS 3406:177–188. New York: Springer.

Calvo, H., Inui, K., & Matsumoto, Y. (2009). Interpolated PLSI for Learning Plausible Verb Arguments, In *Proceedings of the 23rd Pacific Asia Conference on Language, Information and Computation*, pp.622–629.

Calvo, H., Inui, K., & Matsumoto, Y. (2009a). *Learning Co-Relations of Plausible Verb Arguments with a WSM and a Distributional Thesaurus.* Procs. of the 14th Iberoamerican Congress on Pattern Recognition, CIARP 2009, Springer, Verlag. To appear.

Calvo, H., Inui, K., & Matsumoto, Y. (2009b). *Dependency Language Modeling using KNN and PLSI.* Procs. of the 8th Mexican International Conference on Artificial Intelligence, MICAI 2009, Springer, Verlag, to appear.

Clarkson, P. R., & Rosenfeld, R. (1997). *Statistical Language Modeling Using the CMU-Cambridge Toolkit.* Procs. ESCA Eurospeech.

Deerwester, S., Dumais, S. T., Furnas, G. W., & Thomas, K. L, & Richard Harshman. (1990). Indexing by latent semantic analysis. *Journal of the American Society for Information Science American Society for Information Science*, 391–407. doi:10.1002/(SICI)1097-4571(199009)41:6<391::AID-ASI1>3.0.CO;2-9

Deschacht, K., & Moens, M. (2009). Semi-supervised Semantic Role Labeling using the Latent Words Language Model. Procs. 2009 Conf. on Empirical Methods in Natural Language Processing. *Proceedings of the 2009 conference on empirical methods in natural language processing (EMNLP 2009)*, pp. 21–29.

Ferraresi, A., Zanchetta, E., Baroni, M., & Bernardini, S. (2008). Introducing and evaluating ukWaC, a very large web-derived corpus of English. *Procs. of the WAC4 Workshop at LREC.* Marrakech, pp. 45–54.

Foley, W. A. (1997). *Anthropological linguistics: An introduction.* Boston: Blackwell Publishing.

Fuji, A., & Iwayama, M. (2005). *Patent Retrieval Task (PATENT).* Fifth NTCIR Workshop Meeting on Evaluation of Information Access Technologies: Information Retrieval, Question Answering and Cross-Lingual Information Access.

Gao J., J. Y. Nie, G. Wu, & G. Cao, (2004). *Dependence language model for information retrieval.* Procs. of the 27th annual international ACM SIGIR conference on Research and development in information retrieval, 170–177, 2004.

Gelbukh, A. & G. Sidorov, (1999). On Indirect Anaphora Resolution. PACLING-99, pp. 181-190.

Hoffmann, T. (1999). Probabilistic Latent Semantic Analysis. *Procs. Uncertainity in Artificial Intelligence'99, UAI,* 289–296.

Jiang, J., & Conrath, D. (1997). Semantic similarity based on corpus statistics and lexical taxonomy. In *Proc. of the International Conference on Research in Computational Linguistics.* ROCLING X.

Kawahara, D., & Kurohashi, S. (2001). Japanese Case Frame Construction by Coupling the Verb and its Closest Case Component. 1st Intl. Conf. on Human Language Technology Research, ACL.

Korhonen, A. (2000). Using Semantically Motivated Estimates to Help Subcategorization Acquisition. In *Proceedings of the Joint SIGDAT Conference on Empirical Methods in Natural Language Processing and Very Large Corpora.* Hong Kong. 216-223.

Lee, L., (1999). *Measures of Distributional Similarity.* Procs. 37th ACL.

Lin, D. (1998a). *Automatic Retrieval and Clustering of Similar Words*. Procs. 36th Annual Meeting of the ACL and 17th International Conference on Computational Linguistics.

Lin, D. (1998b). *Dependency-based Evaluation of MINIPAR*. Proc. Workshop on the Evaluation of Parsing Systems.

McCarthy, D. & J. Carroll. (2006). Disambiguating Nouns, Verbs, and Adjectives Using Automatically Acquired Selectional Preferences. *Computational Linguistics* 29-4, 639–654.

McCarthy, D., Koeling, R., Weeds, J., & Carroll, J. (2004). *Finding predominant senses in untagged text*. Procs 42nd meeting of the ACL, 280–287.

Merlo, P., & Van Der Plas, L. (2009). Abstraction and Generalisation in Semantic Role Labels: PropBank, VerbNet or both? *Procs. 47th Annual Meeting of the ACL and the 4th IJCNLP of the AFNLP*, pp. 288–296.

Padó, S. & M. Lapata, (2007). Dependency-Based Construction of Semantic Space Models. *Computational Linguistics* 33-2, 161–199.

Padó, U. M. Crocker, & F. Keller, (2006). *Modeling Semantic Role Plausibility in Human Sentence Processing*. Procs. EACL.

Parton, K., et al. (2009). *Who, What, When, Where, Why? Comparing Multiple Approaches to the Cross-Lingual 5W Task*. Procs. 47th Annual Meeting of the ACL and the 4th IJCNLP of the AFNLP, pp. 423–431.

Ponzetto, P. S., & Strube, M. (2006). *Exploiting Semantic Role Labeling, WordNet and Wikipedia for Coreference Resolution*. Procs. Human Language Technology Conference, NAACL, 192–199.

Reisinger, J & Marius Paşca. (2009). Latent Variable Models of Concept-Attribute Attachment. *Procs. 47th Annual Meeting of the ACL and the 4th IJCNLP of the AFNLP*, pp. 620–628.

Resnik, P. (1996). Selectional Constraints: An Information-Theoretic Model and its Computational Realization. *Cognition, 61,* 127–159. doi:10.1016/S0010-0277(96)00722-6

Ritter, A. Mausam & Oren Etzioni. (2010). A Latent Dirichlet Allocation method for Selectional Preferences, *Proceedings of the 48th Annual Meeting of the Association for Computational Linguistics,* 424–434.

Rosenfeld, R. (2000). Two decades of statistical language modeling: where do we go from here? *Proceedings of the IEEE, 88*(8), 1270–1278. doi:10.1109/5.880083

Salgueiro, P., Alexandre, T., Marcu, D., & Volpe Nunes, M. (2006). Unsupervised Learning of Verb Argument Structures. *Springer LNCS, 3878,* 2006.

Séaghdha, Ó. D. (2010). Latent variable models of selectional preference. *Proceedings of the 48th Annual Meeting of the Association of Computational Linguistics,* pp. 435–444.

Weeds, J. & D. Weir. (2003). A General Framework for Distributional Similarity, *Procs. conf on EMNLP,* 10, 81–88.

Yamada, I., Torisawa, K., Kazama, J., Kuroda, K., Murata, M., de Saeger, S., et al. (2009). Hypernym Discovery Based on Distributional Similarity and Hierarchical Structures. *Procs. 2009 Conf. on Empirical Methods in Natural Language Processing,* pp. 929–937.

ENDNOTES

[1] Google query as of April, 2010.
[2] A tool including queries to this corpus can be found at http://sketchengine.co.uk

Chapter 8
Evaluating and Enhancing Contextual Search with Semantic Similarity Data

Ana G. Maguitman
Universidad Nacional del Sur, Argentina

Carlos M. Lorenzetti
Universidad Nacional del Sur, Argentina

Rocío L. Cecchini
Universidad Nacional del Sur, Argentina

ABSTRACT

Performance evaluation plays a crucial role in the development and improvement of search systems in general and context-based systems in particular. In order to evaluate search systems, test collections are needed. These test collections typically involve a corpus of documents, a set of queries and a series of relevance assessments. In traditional approaches users or hired evaluators provide manual assessments of relevance. However this is difficult and expensive, and does not scale with the complexity and heterogeneity of available digital information. This chapter proposes a semantic evaluation framework that takes advantages of topic ontologies and semantic similarity data derived from these ontologies. The structure and content of the Open Directory Project topic ontology is used to derive semantic relations among a massive number of topics and to implement classical and ad hoc retrieval performance evaluation metrics. In addition, this chapter describes an incremental method for context-based retrieval, which is based on the notions of topic descriptors and topic discriminators. The incremental context-based retrieval method is used to illustrate the application of the proposed semantic evaluation framework. Finally, the chapter discusses the advantages of applying the proposed framework.

DOI: 10.4018/978-1-60960-881-1.ch008

INTRODUCTION

Contextual search is the process of seeking information related to a user's thematic context (Budzik et al., 2001; Maguitman et al., 2005a; Kraft et al., 2006; Ramirez & Brena, 2006). As is the case with conventional information retrieval (IR), evaluating the performance of contextual search requires experimenting with test collections. Relevance judgments of semantic relationships between topics and Web pages are crucial at the moment of building these test collections. However, human assessments of relevance are very hard to come by, especially when dealing with large and heterogeneous corpora. As a consequence, collecting relevance judgments is especially challenging and is one of the major bottlenecks in the development of thematic retrieval evaluation frameworks.

Automating the process of obtaining relevance judgments consistent with human-based assessments could greatly facilitate the implementation of robust evaluation tools for IR in general and contextual search in particular. Editor-driven topic ontologies such as ODP (Open Directory Project - http://www.dmoz.org) have enabled the design of automatic evaluation methodologies (Beitzel et al., 2005; Haveliwala et al., 2002; Menczer 2004). In these methodologies a document is assumed to be relevant to a specific topic if the document is classified under that topic. This gives rise to a large collection of relevance judgments for diverse topics. Since documents are classified into topics by human editors, these judgments can be taken as a gold standard and therefore are extremely valuable for evaluation purposes. In addition, the topic ontology hierarchical structure gives rise to semantic similarity measures between Web pages assigned to different but related topics (Haveliwala et al., 2002; Menczer 2004).

Inferring suitable semantic similarity measures based on the structure of topic ontologies is essential for the implementation of a fair evaluation framework based on ontologies such as the ODP. However, most existing approaches focus only on the hierarchical component of the ODP and fail to capture many semantic relationships induced by the ontology's non-hierarchical components (symbolic and related links). As a result, according to these approaches, the semantic similarity between Web pages in topics that belong to different top-level categories is zero even if the topics are clearly related.

In light of this limitation Maguitman et al. (2005b) proposed an information theoretic measure of semantic similarity that can be applied to objects stored in the nodes of arbitrary graphs, in particular topical ontologies that combine hierarchical and nonhierarchical components such as Yahoo!, ODP and their derivatives. Therefore, it can be usefully exploited to derive semantic relationships between massive numbers of topics as well as between those Web pages assigned to these topics, giving way to the design of more precise automatic evaluation methodologies than those that are based only on the hierarchical component of these ontologies. This makes it natural to implement a framework for assessing the performance of contextual search systems.

As part of the background discussion for this chapter, we will begin with an introduction to the challenge of building test collections and describe some methods that have been proposed to estimate semantic similarity for objects stored in taxonomies from taxonomies. We will then continue with the main focus of the chapter which includes a review of the graph-based measure of semantic similarity and a proposal to for evaluating contextual search using a framework that takes advantage of semantic similarity data. In order to illustrate the application of this new evaluation framework we will present and evaluate a semi-supervised-incremental algorithm for contextual-search based on the notions of topic descriptors and discriminators (Lorenzetti & Maguitman, 2009) and we will compare it with a simple algorithm that extracts terms directly from the user initial context and with a generalization of the Rocchio's method (Rocchio, 1971) known as the Divergence from Randomness mechanism with Bose-Einstein statistics (Bo1-DFR) (Amati, 2003). The chapter closes by showing the advantages of applying the proposed evaluation methodology and discusses a number of other applications where semantic similarity data derived from topic ontologies can be usefully exploited to evaluate and enhance the performance of information systems.

BACKGROUND

The Challenge of Building Test Collections

Building test collections is a crucial aspect of information retrieval experimentation in general and context-based search in particular. The predominant approach used for the evaluation of information retrieval systems, first introduced in the Cranfield experiments (Cleverdon, 1991), requires a collection of documents, a set of topics or queries, and a set of relevance judgments created by human assessors who mark the documents as relevant or irrelevant to a particular topic or query. However, reading large sets of document collections and judging them is expensive, especially when these documents cover diverse topics. In light of this difficulty a number of frameworks for automatic or semiautomatic evaluation have been proposed. A common approach that has been applied in automatic evaluations is based on the use of pseudo-relevance judgments automatically computed from the retrieved documents themselves. A simple framework based on these ideas is the one proposed in (Li & Shang, 2000). In this approach the vector space model is used to represent queries and results. Then, the relevance of each result is estimated based on the similarity between the query vector and the result vector. Another approach for automatic evaluation uses a list of terms that are believed to be relevant to a query (onTopic list) and a list of irrelevant terms (offTopic list) (Amitay et al., 2004). This evalua-

tion method scores every result d by considering the appearances of onTopic and offTopic terms in d. The authors show that their method is highly correlated with official TREC collections (Voorhees & Harman, 2005). Click-through data have also been exploited to assess the effectiveness of retrieval systems (Liu et al., 2007). However, studies suggest that there is a bias inherent in this data: users tend to click on highly ranked documents regardless of their quality (Boyan et al., 1996).

Topic Ontologies and Semantic Similarity

Editor-driven topic ontologies such as ODP (Open Directory Project) have enabled the design of automatic evaluation frameworks. These ontologies are means of classifying Web pages based on their content. In this classification, topics are typically organized in a hierarchical scheme in such a way that more specific topics are part of more general ones. In addition, it is possible to include cross-references to link different topics in a non-hierarchical scheme. The ODP ontology is the largest human-edited directory of the Web. It classifies millions of pages into a topical ontology combining a hierarchical and a non-hierarchical scheme. This topical directory can be used to measure semantic relationships among massive numbers of pairs of Web pages or topics.

Many measures have been developed to estimate semantic similarity in a network representation. Early proposals have used path distances between the nodes in the network (e.g. (Rada et al., 1989)). These frameworks are based on the premise that the stronger the semantic relationship of two objects, the closer they will be in the network representation. However, as it has been discussed by a number of sources, issues arise when attempting to apply distance-based schemes for measuring object similarities in certain classes of networks where links may not represent uniform distances (e.g., (Resnik, 1995)).

Figure 1. A portion of a topic taxonomy

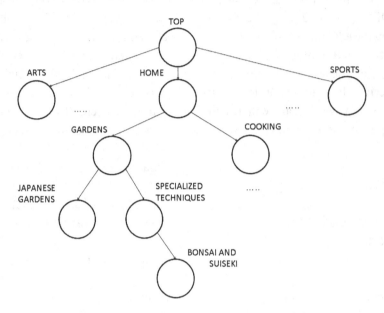

To illustrate the limitations of the distance-based schemes take the ODP sample shown in Figure 1. While the edge-based distance between the topics JAPANESE GARDENS and COOKING is the same as the one between the topics JAPANESE GARDENS and BONSAI AND SUISEKI, it is clear that the semantic relationship between the second pair is stronger than the semantic relationship between the first pair. The reason for this stronger semantic relationship lays in the fact that the lowest common ancestor of the topics JAPANESE GARDENS and BONSAI AND SUISEKI is the topic GARDENS, a more specific topic than HOME, which is the lowest common ancestor of the topics JAPANESE GARDENS and COOKING. To address the issue of specificity, some proposals estimate semantic similarity in a taxonomy based on the notion of information content (Resnik, 1995; Lin, 1998).

In information theory (Cover & Thomas, 1991), the information content of a class or topic τ is measured by the negative *log* likelihood, $-log$ $Pr(\tau)$, where $Pr(\tau)$ represents the prior probability that any object is classified under topic τ. In prac-

tice $Pr(\tau)$ can be computed for every topic τ in a taxonomy by counting the fraction of objects stored in node τ and its descendants out of all the objects in the taxonomy.

Based on this quantitative characterization of object commonality Resnik (1995) introduced an information theoretic definition of similarity that is applicable as long as the domain has a probabilistic model. This proposal can be used to derive a measure of semantic similarity between two topics τ_i and τ_j in an "is-a" taxonomy:

$$\sigma(\tau_i, \tau_j) = \max_{\tau_s \in S(\tau_i, \tau_j)} (-\log Pr(\tau_s)),$$

where $S(\tau_i, \tau_j)$ is the set of topics that subsume both τ_i and τ_j. Resnik's measure has been applied with some degree of success to diverse scenarios, including concept relatedness in WordNet (Pedersen et al, 2004) and protein similarity based on their Gene Ontology (GO) annotations (Lord et al., 2003). A limitation of Resnik's measure is that the similarities between all the children of a topic τ are identical, independently of their information content.

Lin (1998) has investigated an information theoretic definition of semantic similarity closely related to Resnik's measure. In Lin's proposal, not only the common meaning of the two topics but also their individual meaning is taken into account. Indeed, according to Lin's proposal, the semantic similarity between two topics τ_i and τ_j in a taxonomy is defined as a function of the meaning shared by the topics (represented by the most specific topic that subsumes τ_i and τ_j) and the meaning of each of the individual topics:

$$\sigma(\tau_i, \tau_j) = \max_{\tau_s \in S(\tau_i, \tau_j)} \frac{2 \log \Pr(\tau_s)}{\log \Pr(\tau_i) + \log \Pr(\tau_j)}.$$

Assuming the taxonomy is a tree, the semantic similarity between two topics τ_i and τ_j is then measured as the ratio between the meaning of their lowest common ancestor and their individual meanings. This can be expressed as follows:

$$\sigma_S^T(\tau_i, \tau_j) = \frac{2 \log \Pr(\tau_0(\tau_i, \tau_j))}{\log \Pr(\tau_i) + \log \Pr(\tau_j)},$$

where $\tau_0(\tau_i, \tau_j)$ is the lowest common ancestor topic for τ_i and τ_j in the tree.

Given a document d classified in a topic taxonomy, we use $\tau(d)$ to refer to the topic node containing d. Given two documents d_1 and d_2 in a topic taxonomy the semantic similarity between them is estimated as $\sigma_S^T(\tau(d_1), \tau(d_2))$. To simplify notation, we use $\sigma_S^T(d_1, d_2)$ as a shorthand for $\sigma_S^T(\tau(d_1), \tau(d_2))$. From here on, we will refer to measure σ_S^T as the tree-based semantic similarity. The tree-based semantic similarity measure for a simple tree taxonomy is illustrated in Figure 2. In this example, documents d_1 and d_2 are contained in τ_1 and τ_2 respectively, while topic τ_0 is their lowest common ancestor.

Figure 2. Lowest common ancestor in a topic taxonomy

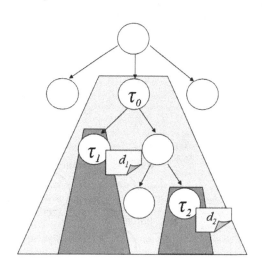

An important distinction between taxonomies and general topic ontologies such as ODP is that edges in a taxonomy are all "is-a" links, while in ODP edges can have diverse types such as "is-a", "symbolic" and "related". The existence of "symbolic" and "related" edges should be given due consideration as they have important implication in the semantic relationships between the topics linked by them. Consider for example the portion of the ODP shown in Figure 3. If only the taxonomy edges are considered, then the semantic similarity between the topics BONSAI AND SUISEKI and BONSAI would be zero, which does not reflect the strong semantic relationship existing between both topics. To address this limitation Maguitman et al. (2005b) defined a graph-based semantic similarity measure σ_S^G that generalizes Lin's tree-based similarity σ_S^T to exploit both the hierarchical and non-hierarchical components of an ontology. This measure is key for the definition of the evaluation framework for context-based search proposed in this chapter and will be discussed in detail in next section.

Figure 3. A portion of a topic ontology

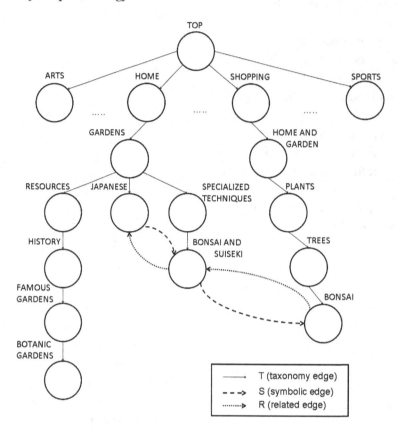

A NEW SEMANTIC FRAMEWORK FOR EVALUATING TOPICAL SEARCH METHODS

Graph-Based Semantic Similarity

In this section we outline work first reported in (Maguitman et al., 2005b), where we showed how to generalize the semantic similarity measure to deal with arbitrary graphs. We wish to define a graph-based semantic similarity measure σ_S^G that generalizes the tree-based similarity σ_S^T to exploit both the hierarchical and non-hierarchical components of an ontology. A topic ontology graph is a graph of nodes representing topics. Each node contains objects representing documents (pages). An ontology graph has a hierarchical (tree) compo-

nent made by "is-a" links, and a non-hierarchical component made by cross-links of different types.

For example, the ODP ontology is a directed graph $G = (V,E)$ where:

- V is a set of nodes, representing topics containing documents;
- E is a set of edges between nodes in V, partitioned into three subsets T, S and R, such that:
  - T corresponds to the hierarchical component of the ontology,
  - S corresponds to the non-hierarchical component made of "symbolic" cross-links,
  - R corresponds to the non-hierarchical component made of "related" cross-links.

Figure 4. A portion of a topic ontology populated with documents

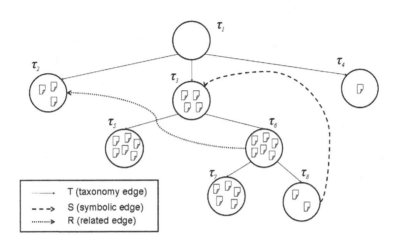

Figure 4 shows a simple example of an ontology graph G. This is defined by the sets $V = \{\tau_1, \tau_2, \tau_3, \tau_4, \tau_5, \tau_6, \tau_7, \tau_8\}$, $T = \{ (\tau_1, \tau_2), (\tau_1, \tau_3), (\tau_1, \tau_4), (\tau_3, \tau_5), (\tau_3, \tau_6), (\tau_6, \tau_7), (\tau_6, \tau_8) \}$, $S = \{ (\tau_8, \tau_7) \}$ and $R = \{ (\tau_6, \tau_2) \}$. In addition, each node τ contains a set of objects (documents). We use $|\tau|$ to refer to the number of objects stored in node τ (e.g., $|\tau_3| = 4$).

The extension of σ_S^T to an ontology graph raises three questions: (1) how to deal with edges of diverse type in an ontology, (2) how to find the most specific common ancestor of a pair of topics, and (3) how to extend the definition of subtree rooted at a topic for the ontology case. Different types of edges have different meanings and should be used accordingly. One way to distinguish the role of different edges is to assign them weights, and to vary these weights according to the edge's type. The weight $w_{ij} \in [0, 1]$ for an edge between topic τ_i and τ_j can be interpreted as an explicit measure of the degree of membership of τ_j in the family of topics rooted at τ_i. The weight setting we have adopted for the edges in the ODP graph is as follows: $w_{ij} = \alpha$ for $(i, j) \in T$, $w_{ij} = \beta$ for $(i, j) \in S$, and $w_{ij} = \gamma$ for $(i, j) \in R$. We set $\alpha = \beta = 1$ because symbolic links seem to be treated as first-class taxonomy ("is-a") links in the ODP Web interface.

Since duplication of URLs is disallowed, symbolic links are a way to represent multiple memberships. For example, in the ontology of Figure 3, a symbolic link is used to represent the fact that the pages in topic SHOPPING/HOME AND GARDEN/PLANTS/TREES/BONSAI also belong to topic HOME/GARDENS/SPECIAL-IZED TECHNIQUES/BONSAI AND SUISEKI. On the other hand, we set $\gamma = 0.5$ because related links are treated differently in the ODP Web interface, labeled as "see also" topics. Intuitively the semantic relationship is weaker.

As a starting point, let $w_{ij} > 0$ if and only if there is an edge of some type between topics τ_i and τ_j. However, to estimate topic membership, transitive relations between edges should also be considered. Let $\tau_i \downarrow$ be the family of topics τ_j such that there is a direct path in the graph G from τ_i to τ_j, where at most one edge from S or R participates in the path. We refer to $\tau_i \downarrow$ as the *cone* of topic τ_i. Because edges may be associated with different weights, different topics τ_j can have different degree of membership in $\tau_i \downarrow$.

We represent the graph structure by means of adjacency matrices and apply a number of operations to them. A matrix T is used to represent the hierarchical structure of the ontology. Matrix T codifies edges in T and is defined so that $T_{ij} = \alpha$ if $(i, j) \in T$ and $T_{ij} = 0$ otherwise. We use T with 1s on the diagonal (i.e., $T_{ii} = 1$ for all i). Additional adjacency matrices are used to represent the non-hierarchical components of an ontology. For the case of the ODP graph, a matrix S is defined so that $S_{ij} = \beta$ if $(i, j) \in S$ and $S_{ij} = 0$ otherwise. A matrix R is defined analogously, as $R_{ij} = \gamma$ if $(i, j) \in R$ and $R_{ij} = 0$ otherwise.

In the following we will define some basic fuzzy set theory operators that are necessary to compute the graph-based semantic similarity measure. A more elaborate introduction to fuzzy set theory is beyond the scope of this chapter and can be found in (Kandel, 1986).

Consider the operator $\vee$ on matrices, defined as $[A \vee B]_{ij} = \max(A_{ij}, B_{ij})$, and let

$G = T \vee S \vee R$. Matrix G is the adjacency matrix of graph G augmented with 1s on the diagonal.

We will use the MaxProduct fuzzy composition operator defined on matrices as follows:

$$\left[A \otimes B\right]_{ij} = \max_{k}(A_{ik} \cdot B_{kj}).$$

Let $T^{(1)} = T$ and $T^{(r+1)} \otimes T^{(1)} = T^{(r)}$. We define the closure of T, denoted T^+ as follows:

$$T^+ = \lim_{r \to \infty} T^r.$$

Finally, we compute the matrix W as $W = T^+ \otimes G \otimes T^+$. The element W_{ij} can be interpreted as a fuzzy membership value of topic τ_j in the cone $\tau_i\downarrow$, therefore, we refer to W as the fuzzy membership matrix of the graph G.

We illustrate the process of computing matrix W for the ontology presented in Figure 4. For this simple ontology, matrices T, S and R are defined as follows:

$$T = \begin{bmatrix} 1 & 1 & 1 & 1 & 0 & 0 & 0 & 0 \\ 0 & 1 & 0 & 0 & 0 & 0 & 0 & 0 \\ 0 & 0 & 1 & 0 & 1 & 1 & 0 & 0 \\ 0 & 0 & 0 & 1 & 0 & 0 & 0 & 0 \\ 0 & 0 & 0 & 0 & 1 & 0 & 0 & 0 \\ 0 & 0 & 0 & 0 & 0 & 1 & 1 & 1 \\ 0 & 0 & 0 & 0 & 0 & 0 & 1 & 0 \\ 0 & 0 & 0 & 0 & 0 & 0 & 0 & 1 \end{bmatrix}$$

$$S = \begin{bmatrix} 0 & 0 & 0 & 0 & 0 & 0 & 0 & 0 \\ 0 & 0 & 0 & 0 & 0 & 0 & 0 & 0 \\ 0 & 0 & 0 & 0 & 0 & 0 & 0 & 0 \\ 0 & 0 & 0 & 0 & 0 & 0 & 0 & 0 \\ 0 & 0 & 0 & 0 & 0 & 0 & 0 & 0 \\ 0 & 0 & 0 & 0 & 0 & 0 & 0 & 0 \\ 0 & 0 & 0 & 0 & 0 & 0 & 0 & 0 \\ 0 & 0 & 1 & 0 & 0 & 0 & 0 & 0 \end{bmatrix}$$

$$R = \begin{bmatrix} 0 & 0 & 0 & 0 & 0 & 0 & 0 & 0 \\ 0 & 0 & 0 & 0 & 0 & 0 & 0 & 0 \\ 0 & 0 & 0 & 0 & 0 & 0 & 0 & 0 \\ 0 & 0 & 0 & 0 & 0 & 0 & 0 & 0 \\ 0 & 0 & 0 & 0 & 0 & 0 & 0 & 0 \\ 0 & 0.5 & 0 & 0 & 0 & 0 & 0 & 0 \\ 0 & 0 & 0 & 0 & 0 & 0 & 0 & 0 \\ 0 & 0 & 0 & 0 & 0 & 0 & 0 & 0 \end{bmatrix}$$

The computation of matrices G, T^+ and W will result in the following:

$$G = \begin{bmatrix} 1 & 1 & 1 & 1 & 0 & 0 & 0 & 0 \\ 0 & 1 & 0 & 0 & 0 & 0 & 0 & 0 \\ 0 & 0 & 1 & 0 & 1 & 1 & 0 & 0 \\ 0 & 0 & 0 & 1 & 0 & 0 & 0 & 0 \\ 0 & 0 & 0 & 0 & 1 & 0 & 0 & 0 \\ 0 & 0.5 & 0 & 0 & 0 & 1 & 1 & 1 \\ 0 & 0 & 0 & 0 & 0 & 0 & 1 & 0 \\ 0 & 0 & 1 & 0 & 0 & 0 & 0 & 1 \end{bmatrix}$$

$$T^+ = \begin{bmatrix} 1 & 1 & 1 & 1 & 1 & 1 & 1 & 1 \\ 0 & 1 & 0 & 0 & 0 & 0 & 0 & 0 \\ 0 & 0 & 1 & 0 & 1 & 1 & 1 & 1 \\ 0 & 0 & 0 & 1 & 0 & 0 & 0 & 0 \\ 0 & 0 & 0 & 0 & 1 & 0 & 0 & 0 \\ 0 & 0 & 0 & 0 & 0 & 1 & 1 & 1 \\ 0 & 0 & 0 & 0 & 0 & 0 & 1 & 0 \\ 0 & 0 & 0 & 0 & 0 & 0 & 0 & 1 \end{bmatrix}$$

$$W = \begin{bmatrix} 1 & 1 & 1 & 1 & 1 & 1 & 1 & 1 \\ 0 & 1 & 0 & 0 & 0 & 0 & 0 & 0 \\ 0 & 0.5 & 1 & 0 & 1 & 1 & 1 & 1 \\ 0 & 0 & 0 & 1 & 0 & 0 & 0 & 0 \\ 0 & 0 & 0 & 0 & 1 & 0 & 0 & 0 \\ 0 & 0.5 & 1 & 0 & 1 & 1 & 1 & 1 \\ 0 & 0 & 0 & 0 & 0 & 0 & 1 & 0 \\ 0 & 0 & 1 & 0 & 1 & 1 & 1 & 1 \end{bmatrix}$$

The semantic similarity between two topics τ_1 and τ_2 in an ontology graph can now be estimated as follows:

$$\sigma_S^G(\tau_i, \tau_j) = \max_k \frac{2 \cdot \min(W_{ki}, W_{kj}) \cdot \log \Pr(\tau_0(\tau_i, \tau_j))}{\log \Pr(\tau_i \mid \tau_k) \cdot \Pr(\tau_k) + \log \Pr(\tau_j \mid \tau_k) \cdot \Pr(\tau_k)}.$$

The probability $\Pr(\tau_k)$ represents the probability that any document is classified under topic τ_k and is computed as:

$$\Pr(\tau_k) = \frac{\sum_{\tau_j \in V} W_{kj} \cdot |\tau_j|}{|U|},$$

where $|U|$ is the number of documents in the ontology.

The conditional probability $\Pr(\tau_i \mid \tau_k)$ represents the probability that any document will be classified under topic τ_i given that it is classified under τ_k, and is computed as follows

$$\Pr(\tau_i \mid \tau_k) = \frac{\sum_{\tau_j \in V} \min(W_{ij}, W_{kj}) \cdot |\tau_j|}{\sum_{\tau_j \in V} W_{kj} \cdot |\tau_j|}.$$

The proposed definition of σ_S^G is a generalization of σ_S^T. In other words, if σ_S^G is computed on the topics of a taxonomy (i.e., only "is-a" links are available) it will give us the same measures as σ_S^T.

In (Maguitman et al., 2005b) we reported a human-subject experiment to compare the proposed semantic similarity measure σ_S^G against Lin's measure σ_S^T. The goal of that experiment was to contrast the predictions of the two semantic similarity measures against human judgments of Web pages relatedness. To test which of the two methods was a better predictor of subjects' judgments of Web page similarity we considered the selections made by each of the human-subjects and computed the percentage of correct predictions made by the two methods. Measure σ_S^G was a better estimate of human-predictions in 84.65% of the cases while σ_S^T was a better predictor in 5.70% of the cases (the remaining 9.65% of the cases were undecided).

To provide stronger evidence supporting the effectiveness of σ_S^G as a predictor of human assessments of similarity, we conducted a new experiment, which is reported in (Magutiman et al., 2010). The goal of the second experiment was to determine if the rankings induced by σ_S^G were in accordance with rankings produced by humans. The result was an average Spearman rank correlation coefficient $\rho = 0.73$.

QUERY REFINEMENT AND TOPICAL SEARCH

Query refinement methods typically require explicit feedback, which is usually obtained from users who indicate the relevance of each of the retrieved documents. The best-known algorithm for relevance feedback has been proposed by Rocchio (1971). Given an initial query q a modified query q_m is computed as follows:

$$q_m = \alpha q + \beta \sum_{d_j \in D_R} d_j - \gamma \sum_{d_j \in D_N} d_j$$

where D_R and D_N are the sets of relevant and non-relevant documents respectively and α, β and γ are tuning parameters. A common strategy is to set α and β to a value greater than 0 and γ to 0, which yields a positive feedback strategy. When user relevance judgments are unavailable, the set D_R is initialized with the top k retrieved documents and D_N is set to $\varnothing$. This yields an unsupervised relevance feedback method.

Several successors of the Rocchio's method have been proposed with varying success. One of them is selective query expansion (Amati et al., 2004) which monitors the evolution of the retrieved material and is disabled if query expansion appears to have a negative impact on the retrieval performance. Other successors of the Rocchio's method use an external collection different from the target collection to identify good terms for query expansion. The refined query is then used to retrieve the final set of documents from the target collection (Kwok & Chan, 1998).

A successful generalization of the Rocchio's method is the Divergence from Randomness (DFR) mechanism with Bose-Einstein statistics (Bo1) (Amati, 2003). To apply this model, we first need to assign weights to terms based on their informativeness. The DFR weight $w(t)$ is estimated by the divergence between the term distribution in the top-ranked documents and a random distribution as follows:

$$w(t) = \mathrm{tf}_x \cdot \log_2 \frac{1 + P_n}{P_n} + \log_2(1 + P_n),$$

where tf_x is the frequency of the query term in the top-ranked documents and P_n is a number in the range [0,1] and is computed as the proportion of

documents in the whole collection that contains the term t. Finally, the query is expanded by merging the most informative terms with the original query terms.

The main problem of the Bo1 query refinement method is that its effectiveness is correlated with the quality of the top-ranked documents returned by the first-pass retrieval. If a search-context is available, it could be usefully exploited to guide the term selection process of query formulation.

Contextual search typically involves the automatic generation or refinement of queries based on the user thematic context. Several semi-supervised techniques that formulate queries from the user context have been proposed. For example, Watson (Budzik et al., 2001) uses contextual information from documents that users are manipulating to automatically generate Web queries from the documents, using a variety of term-extraction and weighting techniques to select suitable query terms. Watson then filters the matching results, clusters similar HTML pages, and presents the pages to the user as suggestions. Another such system is the Remembrance Agent (Rhodes & Starner, 1996), which operates inside the Emacs text editor and continuously monitors the user's work to find relevant text documents, notes, and emails previously indexed.

Other systems such as Letizia (Lieberman, 1995) and WebWatcher (Armstrong et al., 1995) use contextual information compiled from past browsing behavior to provide suggestions on related Web pages or links to explore next. SenseMaker (Baldonado & Winograd, 1997) is an interface that facilitates the navigation of information spaces by providing task specific support for consulting heterogeneous search services. The system helps users to examine their present context, move to new contexts or return to previous ones. SenseMaker presents the collection of suggested documents in bundles (their term for clusters), which can be progressively expanded, providing a user-guided form of incremental search.

The EXTENDER system (Maguitman et al., 2004; Maguitman et al., 2005a) applies an incremental technique to build up context descriptions. Its task is to generate brief descriptions of new topics relevant to a knowledge model under construction. Suitor (Maglio et al., 2000) is a collection of "attentive agents" that gather information from the users by monitoring users' behavior and context, including eye gaze, keyword input, mouse movements, visited URLs and software applications on focus. This information is used to retrieve context-relevant material from the Web and databases. Other methods support the query expansion and refinement process through a query or browsing interface requiring explicit user intervention (Scholer & Williams, 2002).

In this section we report an incremental context-based method that will be used to illustrate the application of the proposed evaluation framework. This method exploits the search context to go beyond the vocabulary of the initial document. It starts with a small number of terms randomly selected from the document under analysis and uses the full document as the initial search context. Using these terms, a set of queries are built and submitted to a search engine. After the first set of results has been obtained, the search context is used to refine/extend the set of terms used for the context description. Terms that appear *often* in search results similar to the search context tend to be good "descriptors" of the thematic context. On the other hand, terms that tend to occur *only* in results similar to the search context can serve as "discriminators".

In this approach *topic* descriptors and discriminators are considered higher-order notions and distinguished from the more basic notions of *document* descriptors and discriminators. Formally, given a collection of m documents and n terms we can build a $m \times n$ matrix H, such that $H_{ij}=k$, where k is the number of occurrences of term t_j in document d_i. We define discriminating power of a term in a document as a function δ: $\{d_0...,d_{m-1}\} \times \{t_0...,t_{n-1}\} \to [0,1]$:

$$\delta(d_i,t_j) = \frac{\text{sgn}(H_{ij})}{\sqrt{\sum_{k=0}^{m-1} \text{sgn}(H_{kj})}}$$

where $\text{sgn}(H_{ij})=0$ if $H_{ij} = 0$ and $\text{sgn}(H_{ij})=1$ if $H_{ij}>0$.

Analogously, we define descriptive power of a term in a document as a function λ: $\{d_0...,d_{m-1}\} \times \{t_0...,t_{n-1}\} \to [0,1]$:

$$\lambda(d_i,t_j) = \frac{H_{ij}}{\sqrt{\sum_{k=0}^{n-1} (H_{ik})^2}}$$

These simple notions of document descriptors and discriminators share some insight with standard IR proposals. However here we are interested in a topic-dependant definition of topic descriptors and discriminators. We formally define the descriptive power of a term in the topic of a document as a function Λ: $\{d_0...,d_{m-1}\} \times \{t_0...,t_{n-1}\} \to [0,1]$ calculated as follows:

$$\Lambda(d_i,t_j) = \begin{cases} 0 & \text{if } \sum_{k=0,\ k\neq i}^{m-1} sim(d_i,d_k) = 0 \\ \dfrac{\sum_{k=0,\ k\neq i}^{m-1} (sim(d_i,d_k) \cdot \lambda(d_k,t_j)^2)}{\sum_{k=0,\ k\neq i}^{m-1} sim(d_i,d_k)} & \text{otherwise} \end{cases}$$

where $sim(d_i,d_k)$ stands for some similarity measure between documents d_i and d_k. Thus the discriminating power of term t_j in the topic of document d_i is an average of the similarity of d_i to other documents discriminated by t_j. Indeed, the descriptive power of a term in a topic is defined using the simpler notions of document similarity and document descriptors: The topic descriptive power of a term t in the topic of a document d is a measure of the quality of t as a descriptor of documents similar to d.

Analogously, the discriminating power of a term t in the topic of a document d is quantified as the average of the similarity of d to other documents discriminated by t and is formally defined as a function $\Delta:\{d_0,...,d_{m-1}\} \times \{t_0,...,t_{n-1}\} \rightarrow [0,1]$ calculated as follows:

$$\Delta(d_i,t_j) = \sum_{\substack{k=0, \\ k \neq i}}^{m-1} (sim(d_k,d_i) \cdot \delta(d_k,t_j)^2)$$

Thus the discriminating power of term t_j in the topic of document d_i is an average of the similarity of d_i to other documents discriminated by t_j (the fact that this function gives us an average with a value between 0 and 1 is due to the the way function δ is computed).

To illustrate how topic descriptors and topic discriminators can be computed, consider the following matrix H representing a thematic context involving the *Java Virtual Machine* and four other documents associated with the term java (Lorenzetti & Maguitman, 2009):

$$H = \begin{array}{r} \\ \text{java} \\ \text{machine} \\ \text{virtual} \\ \text{language} \\ \text{programming} \\ \text{coffee} \\ \text{island} \\ \text{province} \\ \text{jvm} \\ \text{jdk} \end{array} \begin{array}{ccccc} d_0 & d_1 & d_2 & d_3 & d_4 \\ \left[\begin{array}{ccccc} 4 & 2 & 5 & 5 & 2 \\ 2 & 6 & 3 & 2 & 0 \\ 1 & 0 & 1 & 1 & 0 \\ 1 & 0 & 2 & 1 & 1 \\ 3 & 0 & 2 & 2 & 0 \\ 0 & 3 & 0 & 0 & 3 \\ 0 & 4 & 0 & 0 & 2 \\ 0 & 4 & 0 & 0 & 1 \\ 0 & 0 & 2 & 1 & 0 \\ 0 & 0 & 3 & 3 & 0 \end{array}\right] \end{array}$$

d_0 = user context
d_1 = expressotec.com
d_2 = netbeans.org
d_3 = sun.com
d_4 = wikitravel.org

The descriptive and discriminating powers of each term for the user context are as follows:

$$\lambda(d_0,t_j) \quad \delta(d_0,t_j)$$

	$\lambda(d_0,t_j)$	$\delta(d_0,t_j)$
java	0.718	0.447
machine	0.359	0.500
virtual	0.180	0.577
language	0.180	0.500
programming	0.539	0.577
coffee	0.000	0.000
island	0.000	0.000
province	0.000	0.000
jvm	0.000	0.000
jdk	0.000	0.000

Using $\lambda(d_0,t_j)$ as the vector representation of document d_0, we compute the cosine similarity between the user context (d_0) and the other documents, which results in the following:

$sim(d_0,d_1) = 0.399$ $sim(d_0,d_2) = 0.840$ $sim(d_0,d_3) = 0.857$ $sim(d_0,d_4) = 0.371$

Finally, the topic descriptive and topic discriminating powers of each term for the user context are as follows:

	$\Lambda(d_0,t_j)$	$\Delta(d_0,t_j)$
java	0.385	0.493
machine	0.158	0.524
virtual	0.014	0.566
language	0.040	0.517
programming	0.055	0.566
coffee	0.089	0.385
island	0.064	0.385
province	0.040	0.385
jvm	0.032	0.848
jdk	0.124	0.848

Guided by the notions of topic descriptors and discriminators, it is possible to incrementally learn novel context-specific terms and reinforce the weights of existing ones. These incremental methods identify topic descriptors and topic discriminators by analyzing the terms in retrieved documents. Consequently, they are not restricted to terms occurring in the originating search context, and if novel terms have high descriptive or discriminating power, they expand the vocabulary found in the initial document. In this incremental search process, the generation of second-round and subsequent queries can significantly benefit from a search context refined by the addition of good topic descriptors and discriminators.

In (Lorenzetti & Maguitman, 2009) we propose to apply these notions to incrementally refine queries based on the best descriptors and discriminators of the user's thematic context. A list of topic descriptors and topic discriminators is collected and updated at each iteration. Queries are formulated using a roulette selection mechanism where the probability of choosing a particular term t to form a query is proportional to the term combined weight as a descriptor and as a discriminator of the thematic context. Roulette selection is a technique typically used by Genetic Algorithms (Holland, 1975) to choose potentially useful solutions for recombination, where the fitness level is used to associate a probability of selection. This approach resulted in a non-deterministic exploration of term space that favored the fittest terms. More details about this search method can be found in (Lorenzetti & Maguitman 2009).

EVALUATION

Evaluation Setting

The goal of this section is to illustrate the application of the semantic evaluation framework by comparing the incremental context-based method described in the previous section against two other methods. The first is a baseline that submits queries directly from the thematic context and does not apply any refinement mechanism. The baseline randomly selects terms from the thematic context. The second method used for comparison is the Bo1-DFR method, which is a query refinement method that selects query terms based on the notion of term informativeness (introduced in the previous section).

To perform our tests we used 448 topics from ODP. The topics were selected from the third level of the ODP hierarchy. This selection guaranteed a good balance between specificity and generality. A number of constraints were imposed on this selection with the purpose of ensuring the quality of our test set. The minimum size for each selected topic was 100 URLs and the language was restricted to English. For each topic we collected all of its URLs as well as those in its subtopics. The total number of collected pages was more than 350.000. The Terrier framework (Ounis et al., 2007) was used to index these pages and to run our experiments.

In our tests we used the ODP description of each selected topic to create an initial context description. The incremental algorithm was run for each topic for at least 10 iterations, with 10 queries per iteration and retrieving 10 results per queries. The descriptor and discriminator lists at each iteration were limited to up to 100 terms each. In addition, we used the stopword list provided by Terrier, Porter stemming was performed on all terms and none of the query expansion methods offered by Terrier was applied.

In order to evaluate the proposed algorithm we used three metrics to assess query performance: Novelty-Driven Similarity, Precision and Semantic Precision. To implement the first two metrics as part of the proposed evaluation framework, the content and organization of ODP is taking into consideration. The third metric also considers the semantic relations existing among topics in ODP. These metrics are described below.

Novelty Driven Similarity

The Novelty-Driven Similarity is an ad hoc measure of similarity based on the classical cosine similarity measure (Baeza-Yates & Ribeiro-Neto, 1999). However, this new measure of similarity disregards the terms that form the query, overcoming the bias introduced by those terms and favoring the exploration of new material. Given a query q and documents d_i and d_j, the novelty-driven similarity measure sim^N is defined as:

$$sim^N(q, d_i, d_j) = sim^C(d_i / q, d_j / q),$$

where sim^C is the classical cosine similarity measure and the notation d_i / q stands for the representation of the document d_i with all the values corresponding to the terms from query q set to zero. The same applies to d_j / q.

Precision

The Precision evaluation metric is computed as the fraction of retrieved documents which are known to be relevant:

$$\text{Precision} = \frac{|D_A \cap D_R|}{|D_A|},$$

where D_A and D_R are the answer set and relevant set respectively. The relevant set for each analyzed ODP topic is set as the collections of its URLs as well as those URLs belonging to its subtopics.

Semantic Precision

Although Precision is a natural way of analyzing the accuracy of a retrieval method, it only looks at full relevance, disregarding documents that are partially relevant to the topic of interest. Other topics in the ontology could be semantically similar (and therefore partially relevant) to the topic of the given context. Therefore, we propose a measure of Semantic Precision defined as

$$\text{Precision}^S = \frac{\sum_{d \in D_A} \sigma_S^G(\tau(C), \tau(d))}{|D_A|},$$

where $\tau(C)$ is the ODP topic associated with the description used as the initial context, $\tau(d)$ is the topic of document d and $\sigma_S^G(\tau(C), \tau(d))$ is the graph-based semantic similarity between these two topics.

Results

Tables 1, 2 and 3 compare the performance of each of the tested method using Novelty-Driven Similarity, Precision and Semantic Precision. In the tables we can observe the means and confidence intervals of each of the methods.

Each of the three proposed measures provides a different stand on the data. According to the Novelty-Driven Similarity, the goal is to return novel material that is related to the topic at hand. In the case of Precision, those methods that focus on relevant material are favored over the others, while Semantic Precision has the capability of also taking partially relevant material into consideration. In all cases, the incremental context-based method yields the best results.

Table 1. Means and confidence intervals for the performance of the three algorithms based on Novelty-Driven Similarity

Novelty-Driven Similarity			
Method	Number of topics	Mean	95% C.I
Baseline	448	0.087	[0.0822;0.0924]
Bo1-DFR	448	0.075	[0.0710;0.0803]
Incremental	448	0.597	[0.5866;0.6073]

Table 2. Means and confidence intervals for the performance of the three algorithms based on Precision

Precision			
Method	Number of topics	Mean	95% C.I
Baseline	448	0.266	[0.2461;0.2863]
Bo1-DFR	448	0.307	[0.2859;0.3298]
Incremental	448	0.354	[0.3325;0.3764]

Table 3. Means and confidence intervals for the performance of the three algorithms based on Semantic Precision

Semantic Precision			
Method	Number of topics	Mean	95% C.I
Baseline	448	0.553	[0.5383;0.5679]
Bo1-DFR	448	0.590	[0.5750;0.6066]
Incremental	448	0.622	[0.6068;0.6372]

FUTURE RESEARCH DIRECTIONS

Context-based search is an active research area of continuing interest. Developing methods to evolve high-quality queries and collect context-relevant resources can have important implications on the way users interact with the Web. The evaluation of these methods can highly benefit from the use of semantic information stored in ontologies by applying a framework such as the one described in this work. The proposed framework can be adapted to evaluate different kinds of applications, were the identification of a theme or topic plays an important role. This includes: Task-Based Search (Leake et al., 2000), Resource Harvest for Topical Web Portals (Chakrabarti et al., 1999), Deep Web Search (Kautz et al., 1997) and Support for Knowledge Management (Leake et al., 2003).

However, the use of semantic similarity data does not need to be limited to the evaluation of topical retrieval system. Semantic similarity data can also be used to evaluate mechanisms for integrating and combining text and link analysis to derive measures of relevance that are in good agreement with semantic similarity. Phenomena such as the emergence of semantic network topologies can also be studied in the light of the proposed semantic similarity measure (Akavipat et al. 2006; Markines et al.2009). In the future, we expect to adapt the proposed framework to evaluate other information retrieval applications, such as classification and clustering algorithms.

CONCLUSION

This chapter presented a semantic framework for evaluating the performance and enhancing context-based search system. It reviews different methods for capturing semantic similarity data in topic ontologies and proposes to use a graph-based measure of semantic similarity to address the issue of partially relevant information. It then outlines the problem of query refinement and context-based search and sketches out the main elements of a system that performs incremental search based on a thematic context. This incremental system, together with a baseline and the Bo1-DFR methods are used to illustrate the application of the proposed evaluation framework.

Evaluation plays a crucial role in the development of search techniques, and heavily relies on telling apart relevant from irrelevant material, which is hard and expensive when performed manually. In light of the availability of semantic data, like the ODP ontology, we have proposed a semantic framework for identifying relevant and partially relevant resources for a topic of interest.

ACKNOWLEDGMENT

This research work is partially supported by Consejo Nacional de Investigaciones Científicas y Técnicas (CONICET – PIP 11220090100863) and Universidad Nacional del Sur (UNS – PGI 24/ZN13).

REFERENCES

Akavipat, R., Wu, L.-S., Menczer, F., & Maguit-man (2006). *Emerging semantic communities in peer Web search.* In P2PIR '06: Proceedings of the international workshop on Information retrieval in peer-to-peer networks, pages 1–8, New York: ACM Press.

Amati, G. (2003). *Probabilistic models for information retrieval based on divergence from randomness.* Unpublished doctoral dissertation, Department of Computing Science, University of Glasgow, UK.

Amati, G., Carpineto, C., & Romano, G. (2004). *Query difficulty, robustness and selective application of query expansion.* In Advances in Information Retrieval, 26th European Conference on IR research (pp. 127–137). Berlin / Heidelberg: Springer.

Amitay, E., Carmel, D., Lempel, R., & Soffer, A. (2004). *Scaling IR-system evaluation using term relevance sets.* In SIGIR '04: Proceedings of the 27th annual international ACM SIGIR conference on Research and development in information retrieval, pages 10–17, New York: ACM.

Armstrong, R., Freitag, D., Joachims, T., & Mitchell, T. (1995). A learning apprentice for the World Wide Web. In *AAAI spring symposium on information gathering* (pp. 6–12). WebWatcher.

Baeza-Yates, R., & Ribeiro-Neto, B. (1999). *Modern Information Retrieval.* Reading, MA: Addison-Wesley.

Baldonado, M. Q. W., & Winograd, T. (1997). *SenseMaker: an information-exploration interface supporting the contextual evolution of a user's interests.* In Proceedings of the SIGCHI conference on human factors in computing systems (pp. 11–18). New York: ACM Press.

Beitzel, S. M., Jensen, E. C., Chowdhury, A., & Grossman, D. (2003). *Using Titles and Category Names from Editor-Driven Taxonomies for Automatic Evaluation.* In CIKM '03: Proceedings of the 12th International Conference on Information and Knowledge Management (pp. 17–23), New York: ACM Press.

Boyan, J., Freitag, D., & Joachims, T. (1996). *A machine learning architecture for optimizing Web search engines.* In In AAAI Workshop on Internet-based Information Systems.

Budzik, J., Hammond, K. J., & Birnbaum, L. (2001). Information Access in Context. *Knowledge-Based Systems, 14*(1–2), 37–53. doi:10.1016/S0950-7051(00)00105-2

Chakrabarti, S., van den Berg, M. & Dom, B. (1999). *Focused crawling: a new approach to topic-specific Web resource discovery.* Computer Networks (Amsterdam, Netherlands: 1999), 31(11–16):1623–1640

Cleverdon, C. W. (1991). *The significance of the cranfield tests on index languages.* In SIGIR '91: Proceedings of the 14th annual international ACM SIGIR conference on Research and development in information retrieval, pages 3–12, New York: ACM Press.

Cover, T., & Thomas, J. (1991). *Elements of Information Theory.* New York: Wiley. doi:10.1002/0471200611

Haveliwala, T. H., Gionis, A., Klein, D., & Indyk, P. (2002). *Evaluating Strategies for Similarity Search on the Web.* In WWW '02: Proceedings of the 11th International Conference on World Wide Web, pages 432–442, New York: ACM Press.

Holland, J. H. (1975). *Adaptation in natural and artificial systems.* Ann Arbor: The University of Michigan Press.

Kandel, A. (1986). *Fuzzy Mathematical Techniques with Applications.* Reading, MA: Addison-Wesley.

Kautz, H., Selman, B., & Shah, M. (1997). The hidden Web. [AAAI Press.]. *AI Magazine, 18*(2), 27–36.

Kraft, R., Chang, C. C., Maghoul, F., & Kumar, R. (2006). *Searching with Context*. In WWW'06: Proceedings of the 15th International Conference Wide Web, pages 477–486, New York: ACM Press.

Kwok, K. L., & Chan, M. S. (1998). *Improving two-stage ad-hoc retrieval for short queries*. In SIGIR '98: Proceedings of the 21st Annual International ACM/SIGIR Conference on Research and Development in Information Retrieval (pp. 250–256). New York: ACM.

Leake, D., Maguitman, A. G., Reichherzer, T., Cañas, A., Carvalho, M., Arguedas, M., et al. (2003). *Aiding knowledge capture by searching for extensions of knowledge models*. In Proceedings of KCAP-2003. New York: ACM Press.

Leake, D. B., Bauer, T., Maguitman, A. G., & Wilson, D. C. (2000). *Capture, storage and reuse of lessons about information resources: Supporting task-based information search*. In Proceedings of the AAAI-00 Workshop on Intelligent Lessons Learned Systems. Austin, Texas (pp. 33–37). AAAI Press.

Li, L., & Shang, Y. (2000). A new method for automatic performance comparison of search engines. *World Wide Web (Bussum), 3*(4), 241–247. doi:10.1023/A:1018790907285

Lieberman, H. (1995). *Letizia: An agent that assists Web browsing*. In C. S. Mellish (Ed.), Proceedings of the fourteenth international joint conference on artificial intelligence. ijcai-95 (pp. 924–929). Montreal, Quebec, Canada: Morgan Kaufmann publishers.

Lin, D. (1998). *An Information-theoretic Definition of Similarity*. In Proceedings of the Fifteenth International Conference on Machine Learning (pp. 296–304). San Franciso, CA: Morgan Kaufmann Publishers Inc.

Liu, Y., Fu, Y., Zhang, M., Ma, S., & Ru, L. (2007). *Automatic search engine performance evaluation with click-through data analysis*. In WWW '07: Proceedings of the 16th international conference on World Wide Web (pp. 1133–1134). New York: ACM.

Lord, P. W., Stevens, R. D., Brass, A., & Goble, C. A. (2003). Investigating semantic similarity measures across the gene ontology: The relationship between sequence and annotation. *Bioinformatics (Oxford, England), 19*(10), 1275–1283. doi:10.1093/bioinformatics/btg153

Lorenzetti, C. M., & Maguitman, A. G. (2009). A Semi-Supervised Incremental Algorithm to Automatically Formulate Topical Queries. [Special Issue on Web Search.]. *Information Sciences, 179*(12), 1881–1892. doi:10.1016/j.ins.2009.01.029

Maglio, P. P., Barrett, R., Campbell, C. S., & Selker, T. (2000). *SUITOR: an attentive information system*. In Proceedings of the 5th international conference on intelligent user interfaces (pp. 169–176). New York: ACM Press.

Maguitman, A., Leake, D., & Reichherzer, T. (2005a). *Suggesting novel but related topics: towards context-based support for knowledge model extension*. In IUI '05: Proceedings of the 10th International Conference on Intelligent User Interfaces (pp. 207–214). New York ACM Press.

Maguitman, A., Leake, D., Reichherzer, T., & Menczer, F. (2004). *Dynamic extraction of topic descriptors and discriminators: Towards automatic context-based topic search*. In Proceedings of the thirteenth conference on information and knowledge management (CIKM) (pp. 463—472). Washington, DC: ACM Press.

Maguitman, A. G., Cecchini, R. L., Lorenzetti, C. M., & Menczer, F. (2010). *Using Topic Ontologies and Semantic Similarity Data to Evaluate Topical Search*. To appear in CLEI 2010. Asuncion, Paraguay.

Maguitman, A. G., Menczer, F., Roinestad, H., & Vespignani, A. (2005b). *Algorithmic Detection of Semantic Similarity.* In WWW '05: Proceedings of the 14th International Conference on World Wide Web (pp. 107–116). New York: ACM Press.

Markines, B., Cattuto, C., Menczer, F., Benz, D., Hotho, A., & Stumme, G. (2009) *Evaluating similarity measures for emergent semantics of social tagging.* In WWW '09: Proceedings of the 18th international conference on World Wide Web (pp. 641–650) New York: ACM Press.

Menczer, F. (2004). Correlated Topologies in Citation Networks and the Web. *The European Physical Journal B*, *38*(2), 211–221. doi:10.1140/epjb/e2004-00114-1

Ounis, I., Lioma, C., Macdonald, C., & Plachouras, V. (2008). *Research directions in Terrier.* Novatica/UPGRADE Special Issue on Web Information Access, Ricardo Baeza-Yates et al. (Eds), Invited Paper.

Pedersen, T., Patwardhan, S., & Michelizzo, J. (2004). *Wordnet: similarity – measuring the relatedness of concepts.* In Proceedings of the Nineteenth National Conference on Artificial Intelligence (AAAI-04), pages 1024–1025, 2004.

Rada, R., Mili, H., Bicknell, E., & Blettner, M. (1989). Development and application of a metric on semantic nets. *IEEE Transactions on Systems, Man, and Cybernetics*, *19*(1), 17–30. doi:10.1109/21.24528

Ramirez, E. H., & Brena, R. F. (2006). *Semantic Contexts in the Internet.* LA-WEB'06: Proceedings of the Fourth Latin American Web Congress, 74–81, Washington, DC, USA. IEEE Computer Society.

Resnik, P. (1995). *Using information content to evaluate semantic similarity in a taxonomy* (pp. 448–453). In IJCAI.

Rhodes, B., & Starner, T. (1996). *The remembrance agent: A continuously running automated information retrieval system.* In The proceedings of the first international conference on the practical application of intelligent agents and multi agent technology (PAAM '96) (pp. 487–495). London, UK.

Rocchio, J. J. (1971). Relevance feedback in information retrieval . In Salton, G. (Ed.), *The Smart retrieval system—Experiments in automatic document processing* (pp. 313–323). Englewood Cliffs, NJ: Prentice-Hall.

Scholer, F., & Williams, H. E. (2002). *Query Association for Effective Retrieval.* In Proceedings of the Eleventh International Conference on Information and Knowledge Management (pp. 324–331). New York: ACM Press.

Voorhees, E. M., & Harman, D. K. (2005). *Experiment and Evaluation in Information Retrieval.* Cambridge, MA: MIT Press.

ADDITIONAL READING

Billerbeck, B., Scholer, F., Williams, H. E., & Zobel, J. (2003). *Query expansion using associated queries.* In Proceedings of the Twelfth International Conference on Information and Knowledge Management (pp. 2–9) New York: ACM Press.

Bleuler, S., Laumanns, M., Thiele, L., & Zitzler, E. (2003). PISA—A platform and programming language independent interface for search algorithms. In C.M. Fonseca, P.J. Fleming, E. Zitzler, K. Deb, & L. Thiele (Eds.), *Evolutionary multicriterion optimization, 2632*, 494–508. Berlin: Springer-Verlag.

Buckley, C., Singhal, A., & Mitra, M. (1995). *New retrieval approaches using SMART*. In D.K. Harman (Ed.), Proceedings of the Fourth Text Retrieval Conference (Vol. Special Publication 500–236). Gaithersburg, MD: National Institute of Standards and Technology.

Caramia, M., Felici, G., & Pezzoli, A. (2004). Improving search results with data mining in a thematic search engine. *Computers & Operations Research, 31*(14), 2387–2404. doi:10.1016/S0305-0548(03)00194-1

Cecchini, R. L., Lorenzetti, C. M., Maguitman, A. G., & Brignole, N. B. (2008). Using genetic algorithms to evolve a population of topical queries. *Information Processing & Management, 44*(6), 1863–1878. doi:10.1016/j.ipm.2007.12.012

Cecchini, R. L., Lorenzetti, C. M., Maguitman, A. G., & Brignole, N. B. (2010). Multi-objective Evolutionary Algorithms for Context-based Search. *Journal of the American Society for Information Science and Technology, 61*(6), 1258–1274.

Chen, H., Shankaranarayanan, G., & She, L. (1998). A machine learning approach to inductive query by examples: An experiment using relevance feedback, ID3, genetic algorithms, and simulated annealing. *Journal of the American Society for Information Science American Society for Information Science, 49*(8), 693–705. doi:10.1002/(SICI)1097-4571(199806)49:8<693::AID-ASI4>3.0.CO;2-O

Drucker, H., Shahraray, B., & Gibbon, D. C. (2001). *Relevance feedback using support vector machines.* In Proceedings of the Eighteenth International Conference on Machine Learning (pp. 122–129). Williamstown, MA: Kaufmann.

Hawking, D., & Craswell, N. (2001). *Overview of the TREC-2001 Web track.* In E.M. Voorhees & D.K. Harman (Eds.), Proceedings of the Tenth Text Retrieval Conference TREC-2001 (Vol. Special Publication 500–250, pp. 61–67). Gaithersburg, MD: National Institute of Standards and Technology.

Hsinchun, C., Yi-Ming, C., Ramsey, M., & Yang, C. C. (1998). An intelligent personal spider (agent) for dynamic Internet/intranet searching. *Decision Support Systems, 23*(1), 41–58. doi:10.1016/S0167-9236(98)00035-9

In, H. T. '08: Proceedings of the nineteenth ACM conference on Hypertext and hypermedia (pp. 149–156) New York: ACM Press.

Jordan, C., & Watters, C. R. (2004). *Extending the Rocchio relevance feedback algorithm to provide contextual retrieval.* In Advances in Web Intelligence, Proceedings of the Second International Atlantic Web Intelligence Conference (Vol. 3034, pp. 135–144). Berlin/Heidelberg: Springer.

Kushchu, I. (2005). Web-based evolutionary and adaptive information retrieval. *IEEE Transactions on Evolutionary Computation, 9*(2), 117–125. doi:10.1109/TEVC.2004.842093

Leroy, G., Lally, A. M., & Chen, H. (2003). The use of dynamic contexts to improve casual internet searching. *ACM Transactions on Information Systems, 21*(3), 229–253. doi:10.1145/858476.858477

Maguitman, A. G., Menczer, F., Erdinc, F., Roinestad, H., & Vespignani, A (2006). Algorithmic

Markines, B., Roinestad, H. & Menczer, F. (2008.) *Efficient assembly of social semantic networks.*

Martin-Bautista, M. J., Vila, M.-A., & Larsen, H. L. (1999). A fuzzy genetic algorithm approach to an adaptive information retrieval agent. *Journal of the American Society for Information Science and Technology, 50*(9), 760–771. doi:10.1002/(SICI)1097-4571(1999)50:9<760::AID-ASI4>3.0.CO;2-O

Menczer, F., Pant, G., & Srinivasan, P. (2004). Topical Web crawlers: Evaluating adaptive algorithms. *ACM Transactions on Internet Technology, 4*(4), 378–419. doi:10.1145/1031114.1031117

Petry, F. E., Buckles, B. P., Prabhu, D., & Kraft, D. H. (1993). *Fuzzy information retrieval using genetic algorithms and relevance feedback*. In S. Bonzi (Ed.), Proceedings of the Fifty-sixth annual meeting of the American Society for Information Science (Vol. 30, pp. 122–125). Medford, NJ: Learned Information.

Proceedings of the 3rd international workshop on Link discovery (pp. 66–73,) New York: ACM Press.

Rijsbergen, C. J. v. (1979). *Information retrieval*. Newton, MA: Butterworth- Heinemann.

Somlo, G., & Howe, A. E. (2004). *QueryTracker: An agent for tracking persistent information needs*. In Proceedings of the Third International Joint Conference on Autonomous Agents and Multi-agent Systems (pp. 488–495). Los Alamitos, CA: IEEE Computer Society.

Stoilova, L., Holloway, T., Markines, B., Maguitman, A. G., & Menczer, F. (2005). *Givealink: mining a semantic network of bookmarks for Web search and recommendation*. In LinkKDD '05

Yang, J.-J., & Korfhage, R. (1993). *Query optimization in information retrieval using genetic algorithms*. In Proceedings of the Fifth International Conference on Genetic Algorithms (pp. 603–613). San Francisco: Morgan Kaufmann.

KEY TERMS AND DEFINITIONS

Context-Based Search: Process of searching resources (such as documents, images, music, etc.) related to a search context. The search context can be a document the user is editing, a Web page he or she is visiting, etc.

Corpus: A collection of documents in electronic form.

Information Theory: A branch of communications theory that involves the quantification of information. It was introduced by Claude E. Shannon in 1948.

Ontology: A formal description of concepts in a domain of discourse.

Retrieval Performance Evaluation Metric: A metric of some performance characteristic of a retrieval system. It typically involves counting the number of relevant resources and the number of resources retrieved by the system. Some standard performance evaluation metrics in information retrieval include Precision, Recall and F-score.

Semantic Similarity: A measure of the likeness of meaning between objects such as terms, documents or topics.

Topic Ontology: A formal specification of a set of topics, including associations of some kind among the topics. For example, a topic A could be a sub-topic of topic B or it could be related to topic C.

Chapter 9
Document Search Images in Text Collections for Restricted Domains on Websites

Pavel Makagonov
Mixtec Technological University, Mexico

Celia B. Reyes E.
Mixtec Technological University, Mexico

Grigori Sidorov
National Polytechnic Institute, Mexico

ABSTRACT

The main idea of the authors' research is to perform quantitative analysis of a text collection during the process of its preparation and transformation into a digital library for a website. They use as a case study the digital library of the website on Mixtec culture that we maintain. The authors propose using the concept of the text document search image (TDSI). For creating TDSIs they make analysis of word frequencies in the documents and distinguish between the Zipf's distribution that is typical for meaningful words and distributions approximated by an ellipse typical for auxiliary words. The authors also describe some analogies of these distributions in architecture and in urban planning. We describe a toolkit DDL that allows for TDSI creation and show its application for the mentioned website and for the corpus of dialogs with railway office information system.

DOI: 10.4018/978-1-60960-881-1.ch009

1. INTRODUCTION: RETRIEVAL PROBLEMS FOR DIGITAL LIBRARY OF NON-COMMERCIAL WEBSITE

The phenomenon of information overload in Internet means that the access to knowledge available on a website is a problem not only of search engines but also of the owners of the website. Usually, this website contains a large text collection for some restricted domain. The owners of such websites usually are not specialists in computational linguistics and they have neither tools nor time for a high-skilled job of applying natural language processing.

Various studies were carried out by researchers in the field of optimization of search engines. As the result of these efforts, some techniques of documents processing by search engines include working with metadata. It is assumed that metadata creation is done by the website managing team (usually, by the webmaster). Still, when a website contains a large text collection (roughly, more than 100 texts or more than 1,000,000 words) for a restricted topic, it takes a lot of time to create and publish its content for the semantic web. The problem is aggravated by the fact that there are two types of data for each piece of information: one for humans and the other one for computers. Note that the volume of data does not allow using manual processing fulfilled by professional linguists.

The main idea of our research is to perform quantitative analysis of a text collection during the process of its preparation and transformation into a digital library for a given website.

We carry out this analysis by applying heuristic algorithms that do not need large amount of manual data for learning and lead rapidly to useful results as far as both humans and search engines are concerned.

This analysis is useful at the initial stages of creation of a digital library for websites without using an expensive commercial toolkit and without involving a team of linguists. There are other research possibilities in the field of the semantic web; however, we propose the most simple and cheap approach, at least at the initial stage.

Our research was motivated by the necessity of creation of a digital library of the website devoted to the Mixtec culture, but in fact we consider that our solutions of this type of problems can be used in similar situations. At the last phase of the project for the development of a website about the Mixtec culture, a sub-site related to the digital (electronic) library was prepared[1].

The website (www.cumix.org.mx) is devoted to conserving and popularizing the culture of the Mixtec ethnic group. Mixtecs are a national minority of the Southern part of Mexico. The digital library contains all available text documents on history, culture, and modern life of this ethnic group. The website is non-commercial and has free access, as well as its digital library.

There are several problems related to obtaining texts for the website. The first one is free access (without payment and even without registration): authors would not to donate their literary works because in the majority of cases it is their source of living. Another reason is that authors prefer publishing in journals with a high impact factor rather than on the websites. Nevertheless, authors of the documents on non-commercial websites have an advantage of greater accessibility of their materials for the users and of increasing the effectiveness of searches for the materials they placed on their sites. In addition to the materials that have been especially prepared for the site and adapted to the potential users, there is a need to include materials from the collections of text documents that belong to the domain of the site. Usually, these documents are presented on the Internet by free access abstracts.

At the same time, conscientious authors of text materials offered for commercial access on the Internet are interested in better understanding of the content of their materials by the potential user who should be confident and well informed at the moment of making his/her purchase decision.

In many cases, the users feel that the abstract is insufficient for the full document representation. Partly it can be explained by the subjectivity of the authors' approach to writing an abstract.

In the case of literary works related to the Mixtec culture that are available on our website, a fee or registration process for accessing the information were not considered. Therefore, in cases when the author is not willing to authorize the publication of his/her complete work online, the only information available is the title and the name of the author due to the fact that in the real situation related to the literary works on the Mixtec culture, the texts usually do not include abstracts.

It is worth mentioning that the structural elements of a text, such as the introduction or the prologue of a book, the introduction or the conclusion of a paper, are not adequate abstracts and generally speaking cannot serve as substitutes for them.

In many cases, especially for scientific texts, abstracts do not include explanation of the process through which the results were obtained, that keeps them from being considered representative of the complete document.

In our previous work, it was shown that if we consider a collection of texts and their abstracts, there are no more than 40-45% of abstracts that can be identified as corresponding to their full texts (Makagonov, 2004).

The language of a website as a rule (and our website is not an exclusion) is adapted to the principal groups of the website potential visitors. Still, as the text documents are not prepared for being published on the Internet, the webmaster or the "owner" of the website has to consider the discrepancy between the cultural background of the author of the document and the main part of the users. It can be done through structuring of the digital library and through delivering additional information about the difficulties that can appear in the text. We did this for other useful websites linked with our website.

From all these, we can define the necessities of the administrator of a digital library (or the webmaster):

- Define themes that are not difficult for perception of a general public, as opposed to the general set of the texts located on the site.
- Group all texts into a specific set of clusters of a certain domain, probably taking into account the degree of difficulty for perception related with the author's style and genre.

To satisfy these needs, it is necessary to define the procedures for accomplishing at least two tasks:

- Create text document search images (TDSI), and
- Create a rapid prototype of the ontology for a text collection of a restricted domain, see, for example, (Makagonov, 2005; Gelbukh *et al*, 2010). Ontology is usually needed when a text collection exceeds a hundred of documents.

2. TEXT DOCUMENT SEARCH IMAGE

In the case of the website "Mixtec culture", we hope that the number of documents in the digital library will run up to thousand.

In both cases (when there is either a full text at the website or not) it is useful to create a text document search image (TDSI) that contains only words belonging to the domain of the text collection. TSDI helps to simplify retrieval of information both for Internet users and for search engines, because TSDI is smaller and easier for the semantic web to process than a full text document.

2.1 Necessity of a Text Document Search Image

TDSI can be used for referencing a webpage, a text file, as well as a physical resource such as a book in a digital library or in a bookstore where the document is available. It can be shown that the automation of the TDSI preparation increases the objectivity of its content. Obviously, it decreases the necessity of the human labor involved.

Creation of a digital library on the Internet can entail some limitations for making the documents available to public related to the following issues:

- There are authors who do not authorize online publications of their complete texts, or only authorize the publication of some fragments or a brief explanation of the content. However, all authors are keen to provide information about their work to public, because it is their promotion. For that reason the authors may authorize the manager of a digital library (the webmaster of the site) to give partial access to digitalized texts for her own purposes or for general public. For example, it is allowed to prepare an alphabetically ordered word list which is very easy to implement. In this case, the word list that represents the text can be used for creation of the TDSI. This TDSI is in many aspects equivalent to the original text and can be used for obtaining the statistics about the words in the text. In this case, the inconvenience is that we cannot get the statistics about words co-occurrences, i.e., about the words that appear together or at a short distance from the given word. For some tasks, information on word co-occurrences is important.

- There are situations when the authors or the editors who have the authorization to publish the text documents online, do not have the digitalized version[2] of the text document (say, it can be lost or it never existed in case of ancient documents, etc.). As a quick alternative, these documents can be scanned and then be available as images. Usually, it requires a lot of work to convert a text image (scanned) into a symbolic form. For publishing these texts in a form that allows them to be searched on the Internet, the manager of a digital library should convert these images into a text format (say, using an optical character recognition program). In order to create the TDSI for a text, it is not necessary to have access to all text properties, like figures, etc.; the only necessary thing is the text (sequence of characters) itself.

- Some of the texts have large images that occupy a lot of loading time, and in some cases, texts are too long for reading (or looking through). Users can save these long documents for later study. Usually, before saving the document, they should be sure that the document, no matter what size it has, is useful. In general, users do not read long texts while surfing in the Internet, they prefer to evaluate the text on a general level and then decide whether to save it or not. In case of very long texts, it is necessary to give the user a possibility of visualizing the group of key words that reflect the content of the original document. This opens a possibility to evaluate quickly if a text is useful.

Given the previously mentioned difficulties, we propose using TDSI that should have the size of an abstract – it contains not more than a thousand words, in general about 150-250 words –as it is usually recommended by organizing committees of scientific conferences. This size is acceptable for users who are used to working with abstracts.

Technically speaking, for the problem of selection of documents under the situation of a lack of time and resources, the following rules are applied: Our digital library serves first of all as a tool of dissemination of information of those authors who are supporters of "open information", who have already placed full-text information on other websites, who provide information in a digital form, and to those authors of hard-copy materials who have already provided a lot of information in a digital form before. The authors of hard-copy texts which have to be scanned come next.

2.2 Previous Work

In case of some digital libraries, the managers responsible for selection of texts for the library use text document search images (TDSI), for example, the IRBIS system (Brodovsky, 1999).

Before, we proposed an open access to full text document search images as "it does not violate the copyright because it is impossible to recover a full text of an article from such a document image" (Makagonov, 2004). This proposal was supported by other researchers, for example, (Alexandrov, 2005).

Generally speaking, the users of digital libraries work with documents in local networks, not on the Internet. Previously, it was shown that the TDSIs contain words of a domain orientated dictionary (DOD) (Makagonov, 2001). This dictionary can be organized in different ways. For example, in IRBIS system, it is made up of the words included in the documents in the digital library, which have a very high frequency or a frequency significantly higher than words of general use. Since the tools of the IRBIS system are oriented towards clustering of the TDSIs, the topics of the documents in these digital libraries may vary and for that reason it is necessary to group the texts by themes.

While IRBIS system was in practical use by librarians, we observed an ability of librarians to use TDSI for acquaintance with the content of a text document. So, it is also useful for website digital libraries.

Still, the text content retrieval with the help of TDSI is not so trivial and is based on creative abilities of the final user, especially when the user is familiar with the subject of the search. The users who have the knowledge about the domain are more successful.

The existing software package IRBIS cannot be used directly in our task for the following reasons:

- This tool is orientated towards Russian and English alphabets and does not accept specific letters in French, Spanish and other languages, like accents, tilde, etc.
- The objectives for the creation and usage of the DOD are also different; in our case, they are related to the search of texts in small libraries on the Internet as well as in digital libraries, so they entail different problems.
- The main problem with TDSIs in IRBIS is that it groups the texts by themes and sub-themes for proposing specific collections of documents. In our situation, the expected collection of documents in the library is not large, so we are not so interested in text classification. Our main problem is to attract the user to the library offering her the documents which she was looking for on the Internet.
- In our case, the theme of the texts in the library is more or less uniform, so we are more interested in obtaining certain characteristics of the texts which cannot be obtained through a set of key words. For example, these characteristics include the complexity of the document, the style, the type of a document or genre (scientific, poetry, essay, news, legend, etc.).

An add-on of the Google monitoring system Google Analytics® to the website on the Mixtec culture gave us the statistics of the keywords used in searches of the website visitors. These words used by the visitors are the words that brought them to the website on the Mixtec culture (Makagonov & Reyes, 2008). If these words are present in the document, they should be integrated into

TDSI because they correspond to the interests of the users.

In our case the structure of TDSI includes:

- Title of the document,
- Name of the author,
- Words from the DOD,
- Words used as keywords for searches by the users of the website on the Mixtec culture.

Some of these elements are stored separately in the digital library database. We are unaware about the free and easy-to-use software for the construction of DOD for digital libraries, so, further in this work we describe its development.

3. TOOLKIT FOR DIGITAL LIBRARY DEVELOPMENT

Many quantitative methods are commonly used in natural language processing for the semantic web, but it not easy to apply these methods in a given situation for a practical application. So usually the simplest available methods are applied taking into account that they give problem solutions with a sufficient degree of exactness.

For general analysis of a corpus of texts in a restricted domain, we have developed a toolkit– a group of algorithms and programs – called "System for Development of Digital Library" (system DDL). This toolkit includes algorithms specifically oriented for usage of the text document search image (TDSI). At the beginning of the processing, a Domain Orientated Dictionary (DOD) should be created that will be used at the subsequent steps of the algorithm. For this, we choose only content words whose relative frequencies in the corpus are very big in comparison with their frequencies in the common language. The DOD includes also the most frequent words from a special list generated by the search engine, namely, words using which the visitors have encountered the website

of the digital library (in our case, the website on the Mixtec culture).

3.1 Considerations and Methodology for Construction of Domain Orientated Dictionaries

Many linguists consider that in order to capture the meaning of a text, it is enough to take from the whole text just some most important words that represent the prevailing meaning of the dominant conceptual structures expressed in the text. Let us mention a few of them here:

- "If the most frequently used words are excluded from the dictionary[3], then we can guarantee that almost all remaining words will be "innovations", more precisely, the remaining words that have only one meaning (or at least not too many different meanings)" (Arapov, 1988).
- "A practical demonstration comes from the world of the poetic texts which are characterized by only one 'subject'" (Baevsky, 2001, p. 178), which is represented in the frequency dictionary.

At the beginning of word frequency lists for any language, if we order this list by frequency starting from the greater frequencies (ranking the words), we find mostly auxiliary words. They are markers of relations within a phrase and/or relations with the neighboring phrases. Outside the boundaries of such phrases, auxiliary words do not add any new or important content (meaning) to the text. In information retrieval these words are called "stop-words" and for many tasks in text analysis (especially for search engines development) they are ignored.

There is a great difference between meaningful (conceptual) words and stop-words (or auxiliary words) in their function in the text: the meaningful words are specific for every domain while auxiliary words have the same function in different domains. Auxiliary words serve as links between meaningful words. For example, auxiliary words are:

- Purely grammar words (prepositions, auxiliary verbs, articles, etc.),
- Anaphoric words which are words or phrases that refer to the previously mentioned item in the text (like personal pronouns), or
- Deictic words that specifies their referent in a given context (like demonstrative pronouns "this", "that", etc.).

None of these language phenomena bears information out of the context and that is why we can ignore them for our purposes.

3.1.1 Systemic Approach to Modeling a Domain Oriented Dictionary and a Dictionary of Stop-Words

Our approach is based on a very general idea (a systemic idea) that if language is a system, then language has elements and relations between these elements. The elements in a textual phrase are subjects, objects, predicates and circumstances expressed by the words that belong to a specific domain.

A collection of texts from the same domain is considered a system. These texts contain meaningful words that represent certain elements of this system. Auxiliary words usually are present in practically all systems. For this reason, they should not be too varied and will be practically the same for dictionaries of various domains. Among auxiliary words we can find conjunctions, prepositions, pronouns, articles, auxiliary verbs, pronominal and interrogative adjectives, adverbs of time, order, and amount; affirmative, negative, comparative, interrogative and relative adverbs, as well as adverbs of doubt. It is possible to find the main part of stop-words in a language grammar textbook.

Therefore, we can conclude that there are some very frequent words independent from the domain of a group of texts; these are auxiliary words. These auxiliary words or stop-words should be removed from the list of candidate words to be included in the collection DOD. Before removing auxiliary words, such list is called the ProtoDOD. Recall that the DOD is formed according to the criterion we adapted. A word belongs to the domain of a specific text collection if its relative frequency is higher – at least three times higher – than the frequency of the same word in the word frequency list of common language (Makagonov, 2001).

Our approach may be clarified by a deep analogy with the analysis of other social systems. Here we consider two of them: analysis of a city map and analysis of the facade of a building.

The first example is related to the analysis of distribution of the sizes of elements of a city and the intensity of links between these elements. We made our analysis for the city of Scalitsa (Scalica, Slovakia). The elements were defined step by step using the texture of the surface picture (see Figure 1a). We used the toolkit "Picture" (Makagonov, 2007). The same toolkit was applied for calculation of the area of every element, as well as for the centroids (the centers of gravity) of the area (R_N), of every (N) element.

We order the areas by their sizes. These elements are presented at a bi-logarithmical plot: logarithm of rank (N) is at the horizontal axis and logarithm of the size of the elements is at the vertical axis. As we can see in Figure 1b, the area-rank distribution of sizes of elements fits the straight line, which is a visualization of the well-known Zipf's law that corresponds to a linear function on a bi-logarithmic scale:

$$Y = B - A*X \qquad (1)$$

$$Y = \log(R_N), B = \log(R_0), X = \log(N), \qquad (2)$$

where A and B are positive constants.

Figure 1.The map of the city of Scalica as a system

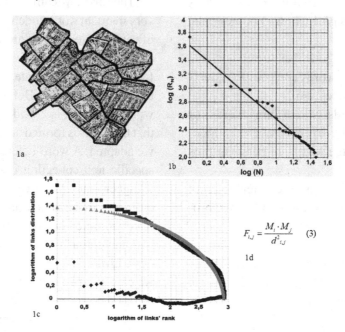

To represent the links between all elements, we chose an attractive (gravitational) model, which corresponds to formula (3) in Figure 1d of any two city's elements with indices *i* and *j* and with sizes M_i and M_j. Here $F_{i,j}$ is the Newtonian force of gravity of two masses of elements with indices *i* and *j*; $d_{i,j}$ is the distance between them.

We put these values of F in descending order and assign each a value for its rank. We then plot force against rank using a logarithmic scale on each axis (Figure 1c).

As it can be seen in Figure 1c, the distribution of links between elements can be approximated by an elliptical curve. The discrepancy of the distribution of links and the points of ellipse is more than 0.1 for only 12 initial points, and it is more than 0.07 only in 24 initial points out of 870 points of the curve.

The second example is related to facades of buildings. We obtained the Zipfian distribution of the details of the facade elements of buildings. An image of a building is shown in Figure 2a, its stepwise revealing of details is presented in Figure 2b, the area-rank distribution is given in

Figure 2c and the links between the elements of the building picture are given in Figure 2d.

There are much more examples, see, for instance, (Makagonov, 2007, 2008), of the fulfillment of Zipf's law as a criterion of integrity for various cities.

We use more or less the same approach for estimating the completeness of a list of words for a sub-language, for example, a sub-language of a writer, or a sub-language for text collections which belong to the same domain.

To show how to use the methods and tools developed, we have chosen two groups of texts that satisfy the previously mentioned requisites: a restricted domain and a relatively small size (for demonstration purposes). In this research, we use two text collections: the initial collection of the digital library of our website on the Mixtec culture and the collection of texts consisting in dialogs between the operators of the Information Desk of a railway office and their clients.

It is well known that for all text documents Zipf's law (Formula 4a) or its variant Zipf-Mandelbrot's law (Formula 4b) holds.

Figure 2.The facade of a building with the distribution of elements and the links between them

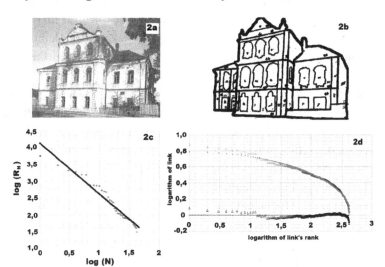

In its simplest form these laws can be described with the formulae:

$$F_i = A * i^{-k} \qquad (4a)$$

$$F_i = A * (i+b)^{-k}, \qquad (4b)$$

where F_i is the frequency of the word, and "i" is the rank of the word, i.e., the number of words in the word frequency list in a descending order. *A* and *b* are coefficients, and "*k*" is the power of the decrement of the frequency, which for many languages is practically equal to 1.

Piotrovsky (1975) showed that given a limit to the amount of elements in the language (words and letters), the distribution of these elements in a frequency list for a small sample size corresponds to Zipf-Mandelbrot's law, but when there is an increment of the amount of the distribution elements at the bi-logarithmic plot then the curve with a vertical asymptote at the right end will appear, and for the frequency list of the letters, the distribution at the bi-logarithmic plot got a form of a circumference. We check the case of the letters, and according to our results the same hypothesis holds. Now we will show that an upper right branch of the elliptical curve is a good approximation for

the list of frequencies of stop-words. The list of words of the DOD is never overflown, therefore it cannot be approximated by an ellipse, because in any domain it is necessary to involve new concepts and use new meaningful words. Many of these words are *hapax legomena,* i.e., the words that occur only once in a text collection.

Therefore, there are two poles in the vocabulary: on the one hand, the specific words for the given domain that cannot be found in other domains with similar frequency (clearly meaningful words), on the other hand, the words that are obligatorily in any real world text (clearly auxiliary words). The remaining words are situated between these two poles. There are two distributions of word frequencies (see Figure 3): the distribution of stop-words has the form of an ellipse $F_{SW}(N)$, while the distribution of domain specific words has the form according to the Zipf-Mandelbrot's law $F_{ZM}(N)$. The criterion to separate all words into these two groups is the minimum differences of frequency distributions and the corresponding laws: $F_{SW}(N)$ and $F_{ZM}(N)$.

3.1.2 Case of Text Collections on Websites

The distribution of the word frequencies in each text or in all the texts is calculated at the bi-logarithmic scale and it is shown in Figure 3. At the plot 3A the distribution of the frequencies of words from two samples is presented: a set of Spanish language newspapers (the grey curve), which serves as the list of word frequencies in the common language and a group of documents in the library of the website on the Mixtec culture. We can observe that the lines cross both axes approximately in the point 4.5, so we can say that this plot corresponds to Zipf's law as presented in formula (4a). The coefficients K of every curve almost coincide, because of that the right asymptotes of both curves are parallel. Still, there is an irregular form on both lines related with the values

where logs of word rank (i) at the horizontal axis have values from 0 to 1.5, which is not typical Zipf's or Zipf-Mandelbrot's distributions. This range corresponds to the first 32 words of the frequency list for both samples. Twenty seven of them are the same in both lists: *a, al, como, con, de, del, el, en, es, este, la, las, lo, los, más, no, o, para, por, que, se, su, sus, un, una, y* (*to, to¹, like, with, of, of, the, in, is, this, the, the, the, the, more, no, or, for, for, what, self, his, theirs, a, a, and*). The rest are twelve words, where six are taken from the newspapers: *ayer, ha, han, le, pero, sobre,* (*yestarday, has, have, him, but, over*) and another six are from the digital library *donde, entre, esta, son, méxico, mixteca (where, between, is, are, Mexico, Mixtec).* Among the six words from the library, there are two words "*Mixtec*" and "*Mexico*" that belong clearly to its domain. The other words are among the first 50

Figure 3. Frequency lists of words at the bi-logarithmic scale for the collection of digital library

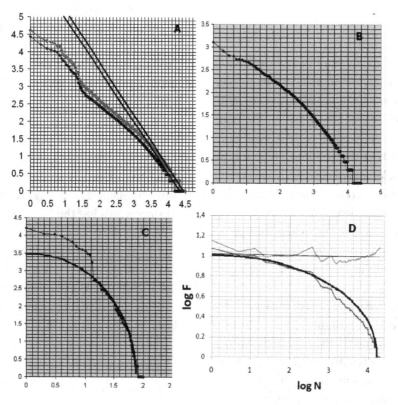

words in the list of the newspapers. The majority of the first 100 words in both distributions do not correspond to special topics; they are auxiliary words as we mentioned before.

A list of stop-words was constructed for the digital library (bottom left part in Figure 3C) using these words. Then we eliminated these stop-words from the distribution of words in the collection of documents on the website of the Mixtec culture. See the distribution of the rest of the words in the upper right part in Figure 3B. These words are called keywords or autonomous words.

As we can see in Figure 3D, the distribution of the letters in one of the texts of the text collection has the form of an ellipse. The difference (error) between this distribution and the curve of the ellipse is

$$error= ((\log N)/a)^2 + ((\log F)/b)^2 - 1 \qquad (5)$$

The curve that corresponds to the error shows that the comparison with the lineal trend has the closest fit equal to the value of "one" (a straight horizontal line at that level).

Now we can see that the curves that correspond to stop-words have the shape of the upper right branch of the elliptical curves – the case presented in Figure 3C, where only first thirteen words out of 300–400 ones do not fit precisely. We have

examples of a minor difference with the shape of an ellipse for both text collections. One of them is presented in Figure 4b.

3.1.3 Case of Text Collection of Dialogs

The short description of the text collection of dialogs (the length of talking, the lexicon size, etc.) is presented in (Bonafonte, 2000). The cluster analysis of the same corpus of the dialogs with the transportation Information Desk service was used in (Alexandrov, 2005) to reveal typical scenarios of dialogs. This data is useful for design of the automatic dialog systems. We used this approach in our early work related to the parameterization and cluster analysis (Makagonov, 1997), though it required hard work for manual parameterization of the set of dialogs.

In general, the purpose of the analysis of dialogs is the extraction of cognitive components. This is useful for philosophical analysis of literature, especially, for the case of the theater scripts, and for analysis of the spoken language. In our case, the purpose is to know what type of questions and problems the users of the information desk have. This would allow supply of the complementary information in a more effective manner, the arrangement of the information in an optimal manner, the preparation of the answers to the most

Figure 4. Distribution of words in the corpus of dialogs

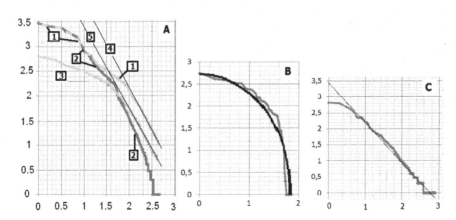

frequent questions beforehand, etc. In this case, the dialogs are frequently considered as discourses, given that there are at least two speakers and the text is related to a specific situation. Discourses are frequently called text collections of a restricted domain. Taking into account all these aspects, the proposed approach can be used for the analysis of discourses.

We used a corpus that contained 204 dialogs. They are very short texts, for this reason we chose 100 of the longest dialogs that cover 80% of the total corpus size.

Distribution of the words in the dialogs is shown in Figure 4A. The superior curve (number 1, F_{total}) is the distribution of the words of the whole collection. The curve located on the left (number 2) first coincides with the superior curve but then decreases rapidly; this curve corresponds to the distribution of the stop-words $F_{SW}(N)$. The lowest curve on the left side (number 3, $F_{protoDOD}$) is the distribution of words in the protoDOD, i.e., the distribution of the remaining part of the initial list after removing of the stop-words. In Figure 4A, for distributions of all words and for the protoDOD, we can see that the asymptotes F_{total} (curve number 4) and $F_{protoDOD}$ (curve number 5) are parallel. Therefore, the words of the complete list that are represented at the right side of the plot (and at the end of the list) are the words from the protoDOD only.

In case of the stop-words, we can use the positive as well as the negative deviation of the relative frequency in comparison with the frequency of the same word in the list of stop-words of the common language. This can be useful in preparation of a sub-dictionary of stop-words of different styles and for functional types of the lexicon of the dialog participants.

The distribution of the list of numerals is shown in Figure 4B. It also has a distribution at the bi-logarithmic scale that has a form of ellipse. This means that this group of words has the properties similar to auxiliary words.

The distribution of the list of all forms of the verbs in the text collection of dialogs is shown in Figure 4C. It corresponds to Zipf-Mandelbrot's law.

So, now we should decide which part of speech should be excluded from the DOD. It depends on the behavior of their frequency distributions at the right side of the bi-logarithmic plot: whether the right part of the curve has a vertical asymptote (in case of an ellipse) or it has an inclined asymptote.

Figure 5 shows:

- F1 and T1 is the right part of the distribution of the frequency of words in all dialogs and its lineal trend correspondingly;

- F2 and T2 is the right part of the distribution of the frequency of words of the protoDOD and its lineal trend.

- F3 and T3 is the right part of the distribution of the frequency of words of the protoDOD from which the verbs were removed (all their inflectional forms) and its lineal trend.

- F4 and T4 is the right part of the distribution of the frequency of the verbs in the dialogs and its lineal trend.

- D1-2 and T1-2 is the curves of the difference between F1-F2 and its lineal trend. D4-3 and T4-3 is the curve of the difference between F4-F3 and its lineal trend.

In Figure 5 we can see that the lines T_{1-2} and T_{4-3} are practically horizontal. The approximation of the difference D_{1-2} has a slope of only 5 degrees and the approximation of the D_{4-3} is a horizontal line. Therefore, the following distributions have the same form of Zipf's law:

- Verbs (without auxiliary verbs or verbs which are aimed to maintain the dialog, for example: look, tell me, call, etc.)

- The right part of the distribution of word frequencies from the whole dialog collection,

Figure 5. Logarithmic graphs of functions and corresponding linear trends

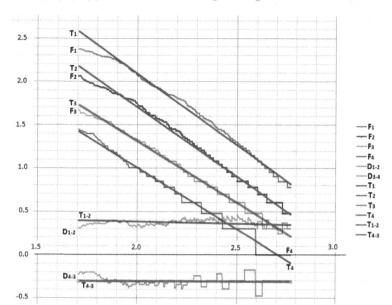

- The words from the protoDOD without the verbs.

On the basis of this data, we can formulate a (second) hypothesis, that this fact is the evidence that the groups of words that correspond to curves F2, F3, and F4 have the same structure as the right part of the distribution F1. Therefore, if they contain some sub-systems of words from the same text collection that have the same angle of the slope as their asymptotes then they can be united into one group because they are homogenous sub-groups of the whole system.

For defining the DOD for a website library, first we prepare a list of word frequencies in common language. In our case, we used more than 2 million words from the newspaper text collection. From this list, we keep the words which have the margin of error for frequency less than 35% of their values. Then we compare this list with the list of relative word frequencies from the text collection on the website (in our case, website on the Mixtec culture). The DOD_1 includes all words in the list from the website on the Mixtec culture

that have a frequency three times higher than they have in the list for the common language. We also define DOD_2, the final dictionary of our system, by adding to the DOD_1 the most frequent words provided by the search engine, i.e., the words that were used by the visitors of the website to find the site.

We prepared the DOD for the dialogs in the same manner excluding the last step.

3.1.4 Formulation of the Criterion

Finally, we can formulate the criterion related to the distribution of word frequencies. If any large fragment of the list of word frequencies has an elliptical distribution at the bi-logarithmic plot, then this fragment should be part of the list of stop-words. If it has the slope of the right asymptote of the distribution of the DOD, then it should belong to the DOD.

Like in other social systems, there are several types of elements (words) in the DOD of the text collections for restricted domains: 1) words that are elements of the system, 2) words that have the function of expressing the relations between the elements in the system and 3) words that belong to the super-system and some sub-systems. We found that there is strong analogy between the frequency distributions in linguistic systems and the distribution of parameters of the objects and their relations in urban planning.

3.2 TDSI and Additional Text Characteristics for Development of the Digital Library of the Website on the Mixtec Culture

Instead of the artificial measures that are typical for commercial websites for the launch and promotion of a new site, we propose another methodology for the webmaster to simplify the access to the information related to the text documents or to the text documents themselves: the TDSI. For preparation of the TDSI, we eliminate from the text the words that belong to the common language and leave the words that are specific for the domain of the document.

We created the toolkit that can be used by the webmasters of websites, which contain digital libraries of text documents for a restricted domain. Restricted domains offer some advantages as far as processing of the texts is concerned: usually, there is much less polysemy (when the same word or sign has various meanings or applications) and homonymy (words which have the same form but have different meanings).

It is also useful to propose some formal simple characteristics, which are similar to the widely accepted, though more complex, linguistic characteristics and to substitute them with their simpler analogs. These features should be sufficient to evaluate the level of interest in the text by its final user. This interest is determined by the correlation between the sub-language of the text and the language of the user. This is required for avoiding a negative attitude towards the text that can be produced by the sub-cultural differences between the language used by the author of the text (sender of the message) and that of the user

of the site (receiver of the message). In case of the texts on the websites, we can assume that they are already adequate for the language of the users.

For the automatic preparation of the TDSI and the calculation of certain characteristics of the texts, a non-commercial system (called DDL system) was developed and applied for the digital library of the website on Mixtec culture.

In addition, the DDL system contains tools that can be used for research related to the domain lexicon and for compilation of the following types of the dictionaries:

- Words common to all types (styles) of texts;
- Specific words reserved for functional styles of texts;
- Specific words reserved for inadequate styles of texts;
- Specific words reserved for specific styles of texts.

In the DDL system, we included a tool for calculation, using the least square method, the parameters of Zipf's law for each text without stop-words (or for a set of texts) and the differences between Zipf's law and the given sample, i.e., the difference in the distribution of words and the straight line at the bi-logarithmic scale corresponding to Zipf's law. Texts with very large differences should be removed from the group of documents for preparation of the DOD. Still, the final decision should be made by the webmaster. For the short texts, the relative difference is usually higher than for the long texts.

For each text, the average number of words per phrase (P_{aver}) and the average number of letters in the words (L_{aver}) is calculated (the latter is also related to the number of syllables that is approximately proportional to the number of letters).

The formula:

$$C = L_{aver} log (P_{aver})$$ (6)

is used to calculate the complexity C of the text.

Based on these characteristics, the webmaster can recommend some texts only for people with sufficient level of preparation or experience. The digital library of the website on the Mixtec culture describes documents using these characteristics of the complexity of the texts.

The structure of the TDSI includes: the title of the document, the author name, the words from the DOD_2 (which are obtained from the text document) and the pairs of words that appear together most frequently in the document. All auxiliary words (stop-words) are eliminated. Also, DDL contains a tool for construction of the Marcovian matrix of frequency for each pair of neighboring words in the text (disregarding stop-words), where the first word represents the left column of the matrix and the second word of the pair represents the first line of the matrix. We constructed the Marcovian matrix of frequencies for each pair of neighboring words for each text for the 234 most frequent words in the DOD_2. These pairs have different values. Some of them are the combinations of words from different phrases; generally these pairs occur only once in texts. These pairs are of no interest to our tasks and they are eliminated. The pairs that are found more than once in the texts are included into TDSI.

4. RETRIEVAL USING TDSI IN DIGITAL LIBRARIES

We carried out an experiment for evaluation of the effectiveness of the Internet search using TDSI by modeling a search method used by the majority of the experts on Mixtec culture. We elaborated a questionnaire about the search algorithm used by more than 30 experts in the Mixtec culture for discovering their search methodology. We used Delphi method (Dalkey, 1969) of revealing the priorities and statistical generalization of the results of sampling. From this questionnaire, we received the following parameters for the average search.

The average user generally uses three keywords in a search. In the first experiment, three key words were used, in the second and third experiments, four key words were used. The users consider viewing quickly not more than six pages (with ten links per page) without following each of the links. The user accesses not more than five links from each page of the results to revise them carefully. In average, thirty-eight minutes are dedicated to a search on a specific topic. The users achieve 79% success rate in their Internet searches.

The most common search algorithm is:

1. Search using "k" key words
2. Receive "N" pages of results
3. Make a quick revision of the first "M" pages and open "S" sites.
4. Finish if find what you wanted.
5. If not, repeat steps 1,2, and 3, "X" times with an adapted version of the keywords based on the analysis of the visited websites in the previous searches.

The algorithm was modified for preparation of the following experiment:

• Experts in the selected domain need to choose 11 key words for each document that form part of the TDSI;
• The described search algorithm is applied.

The percentage of success in the experiment (using the samples) is 53.3%. For the documents that were found on our website only, i.e., without counting the documents found on the Internet; the success rate was 50%. For the documents that were found on the Internet only, i.e., without counting the documents found on the website, the success rate was 56%. It is necessary to mention that using another search method, we can achieved better results because we did not consider as a success when in order to find a document on the website of the Mixtec culture it was necessary to review more than the first 60 sites. Namely, in cases when the document did not appear within the first 60 suggested documents, we stop the search process. In cases when the name of the document is known, the search for its name generates an absolute result.

In the case of digital library documents that were obtained from the popular websites, these sites have an advantage in the search process. For the documents that are represented only by their titles and the TDSI on the website on the Mixtec culture, the success with the TDSI use is considerable, but modest. Possibly, the use of broader samples will produce better results. In the near future, we plan to increase the number of documents in the collection of the digital library of the website on the Mixtec culture.

5. ANALYSIS OF DIALOGS USING DDL SYSTEM

DDL system is a rather flexible toolkit that can be used also for analysis of dialogs, for example, for studying the vocabulary that allows defining of the author styles and genres, or for some additional tasks like the following:

1. Receive and examine the word frequency list of the participants of the dialogs and compare them with other types of texts, the lists of frequencies of the meaningful and auxiliary words, the quantitative characteristics of the client or operator vocabulary;
2. Analyze through the Markovian Matrixes the peculiarities of the vocabulary of the operators and the clients;
3. Analyze which characteristics of complexity and emotionality are present in the vocabulary of the operators and the clients.

These possibilities were tested for the text collection of dialogs.

It is not necessary to examine the functional style of the dialogs in the text collection because it is already known. Nevertheless, the comparison

with other styles can be done. Also, it is possible to compare the styles of the clients and the operators of the information system.

Another possibility of the system is to support the creation of the typical topics which serve as a guide for the training of an operator, or classify the operators and the clients into the groups on the basis of some common behavior, or improve the information reference charts for the operators and the usage manuals for the clients.

During the analysis of stop-words in the phrases of the operators and the clients of the system we got the difference of 50% in the relative sum of the following words:

- For the operators: *a, en, luego, ahora, hasta, mismo, como, otro, ese, mejor, solo, las, le, un, usted, se, ver, son, tiene, vamos, va, he, digo, quiere (to, in, now, until, same, how, other, this, better, only, the, you, a, you, it, see, are, have, go, have, say, want).*
- For the clients: *vale, saber, hola, gracias, muchas, ah, aja, uh (worth, know, hello, thanks, very much, ahh, uh-huh, uh).*

The collection of dialogs as compared with other domains has the list of stop-words with more paralinguistic words. It is necessary to add emotional interjections such as: *ah, eh, eeh, eeeh, eehh, ajaja, huy, a-já, hum, hem, oh, (ahh, uhh, hmmm, well, oh, uh-huh, uh-uh)*etc.

Our system allows, with the abovementioned restrictions, to perform the lexicographic analysis leaving aside the problems related to the traditional sentence analysis (morphologic and syntax analysis) and to pass directly to semantic analysis.

For example, in the dialog number 204, among the phrases from the part of the operator, out of the 644 words the following 57 words belonging to the DOD are found: *Euromed, intercity, tarde, horas, llega, tren, trenes, Barcelona, vuelta, calcule, ejemplo, estrella, ida, momentito, pesetas, punto, sale, salidas, sants, sentido, talgo, viaje, aconsejo, antiguos, calculadora, capricho, casualidad, clase, combinar, departamentos, descuento, evidentemente, fecha, funciona, gana, hombre, idea, justo, lleva, media, minutos, parecidos, poquillo, puerta, puesto, renfe, revisar, Sevilla, suma, tiempo, turista, valga, volver, vuelve. (Euromed, intercity, late, hours, arrive, train, trains, Barcelona, return, estimate, example, star, departure, moment, pesetas, point, leaves, departures, sants, meaning, talgo, trip, suggest, old, calculator, whim, coincidence, class, combine, departments, discount, evidently, date, function, win, man, idea, just, take, half, minutes, similar, a little, door, stand, renfe, review, Sevilla, sum, time, tourist, worth, return, come back).*

So, we focus our efforts in detection of the meaning (conducting the semantic analysis) of this group of words. In case of the dialogs, we have the situation where the texts are "knowledge poor". For this reason, we did not filter the words of the protoDOD, but included all of them into the DOD. Additionally in this approach, there are some compensating measures that somehow substitute the morphological and syntax analysis.

Some of the results obtained from the analysis of the dialogs using the DDL toolkit are presented in Table 1.

The numerical values in Table 1 show that the clients are much more emotional and the operators are more cooperative in the dialog.

In the DDL system, the analysis of the preferred amount of letters of the dialog participants was included. We also used the calculation of the

Markovian matrices between the pairs of words and between the pairs of letters. This toolkit can be utilized for analysis of author style, for example, by detecting the stable word combinations from the given list.

It is useful to enrich the TDSI with pairs of words from the DOD. We also combine them with the pairs detected from word chains in the DOD in the way similar to the tool "Text Analyst" that is organized under the principles of neural networks (TextAnalyst, 2010).

We do not discuss here application of Zipf's law for evaluation of the level of harmony in text documents. In this case, the harmony is very close to the integrity of a text as related to its style.

6. RESTRICTIONS AND BENEFITS OF THE DDL SYSTEM

The DDL system that contains a set of programs is useful for the comparative analysis of a group of texts in a restricted domain. Also, it can be used in other fields of research with some restrictions:

1. The methods considered are neither suitable for the analysis of one (separate) short text, nor for large collections of long texts of non-restricted domain;

2. These methods are not suitable for the translation theory and for the development of specialized search engines.

Table 1. Numerical values of characteristics of the dialog participants

	Operator (logical dominance)	Client (emotional dominance)	Ratio "Client/Operator"
Duration of talk average (words quantity)	269	130	0.48
Length of group of average sentences in the DOD	52	24	0.46
Punctuation:			
Interrogation mark (?)	1547	13699	8.56
Exclamation mark (!)	96	861	8.97

Our approach is somewhat similar to automatic summarization because it is connected with the detection of information (content, knowledge) in the original text using computer tools. An example of the application of the summarization technology is search engines, such as Google. There are different types of summaries depending on the summarization method applied: extraction or abstraction. The extractive techniques copy the information considered most important by the search system and construct the abstract (for example, using the key clauses, sentences or paragraphs). The abstractive techniques involve representation of the document with further paraphrasing and reduction. In general, the abstraction can condense a text better than the extraction, but it requires the usage of much more advanced natural language processing methods, and also involves natural language generation technology, which makes it more difficult for its implementation. Our approach more resembles extractive summarization techniques.

Our system generates the TDSIs of the text based on a single source document in the restricted domain, while for preparation of the domain oriented dictionary (DOD) it uses multiple source documents of the domain.

Both development and usage of the DDL toolkit is in some aspects easier than metadata preparation. There are several reasons for this:

- Instead of the full grapheme analysis we combine the statistics of letters, punctuation marks, and calculate the Markovian matrices of frequencies for pairs of letters and pairs of words for every text.
- Instead of the complete morphological analysis of every sentence we apply only a text filtering through the lists of auxiliary words (stop-words) or through the DODs.
- Instead of the syntactic analysis of every sentence we carry on statistical analysis of punctuation marks of all text documents or of some essential parts of them.

- Instead of the semantic analysis of sentences we generate the TDSI (including pairs of words in the Markovian matrices) of the whole text and then we evaluate the text content using it.

Working with a restricted domain has an advantage from the point of view of the more simplicity of the text processing. For example, when we work with a corpus of a restricted domain, the problems with polysemy are reduced, "If we exclude from the dictionary a sufficient amount of the most common words, then almost all of the remaining words are univocal (have one sense in this text)" (Arapov, 1988).

7. POSSIBILITY TO APPLY ONTOLOGY PROTOTYPING

Learning ontology from text collections is useful for better understanding of the content of the collection and for development of applications based on ontology. Necessity of ontology or at least of its rapid prototype for a restricted domain is really important. It is obvious when we search a prospective theme or evaluate theme for possibility of financial support by the government or by the private investors, who are interested in certain research directions.

The creation of the rapid prototype of the ontology for a text collection is useful for structuring the collection itself, because this information is useful for guiding the users. We make use of our previous experience of this kind of work in the domain of parallel, concurrent, distributed, and simultaneous programming (Makagonov, 2005, 2006) and in the domain of certain topics related to newspapers. The minimum quantity of text documents, according to our experience, is at least 2,000 texts with at least 200 words on the average for the first case, or at least 600 texts with 500 words on the average for the second case.

The ontology constructing is reasonable if the collection size is not less than 300-400 thousand words, and the number of texts is much more than 100.

The size of our website digital library is not sufficient enough to show in a proper way the ontology construction. Out of 100 texts on the Mixtec culture we got only the two level hierarchy of clusters with the following concepts and subtopics: *government and cities, agricultural geography, handicraft, ancient arts and handicrafts, flora-fauna-nature, wealth and business, modern education, economics, Mesoamerican history, ancient religious rituals and tales, ancient philosophy*. It is easy to handle such a small set.

Our experience shows that if the text collection on a website is about or more than one million words, then it is worth creating ontology. At the same time for text collections of size less than 3,000 texts with less than 10 million words for a restricted domain, the ontology always contains rather various concepts. Usage of the TDSI enhances the possibility of search without using the advertising financial support for the site attendance.

We hope that the use of the DDL system would help to rapid prototyping of the ontology, though in our case we started with rather poor initial text collection and did not try this.

8. CONCLUSION

The digital library on the Mixtec culture was evaluated as a case study of a website with the digital library for online search of text documents. We showed that a specific text collection for a restricted domain of a reasonable size represents the suitable initial conditions for the successful analysis and solving problems related with the quantitative analysis of the text collections without any additional linguistic analysis, like morphological or syntactic analysis.

Restricted domain does not guarantee the absence but makes it less probable to encounter with the problems of homonymy and polysemy. It is useful to eliminate certain types of words in the text collection (auxiliary words, words from the general vocabulary) and leave only the vocabulary which is specific to the domain of the collection. Also, with certain degree of roughening, the linguistic analysis of sentences is substituted by the analysis of word frequency lists.

The flexible set of algorithms and software was developed for creating of a text document search image (TDSI), which is a set of words from the domain oriented dictionary (DOD). TDSI and DOD are specific for the collection. If the reader is not acquainted with the document, the TDSI can be used as the abstract and the DOD can be used for studying of the group of documents. If the reader already is acquainted with the document or the text collection, then he can learn new information by comparing it with other TDSIs and DODs.

TDSI construction is based on the idea that any text collection of a restricted domain is a system, which contains both elements and relations between these elements. The relations between the system elements are words that belong to "auxiliary" parts of speech, so called "stop-words". It is shown that for the typical complete systems the characteristics of distributions of their elements is according to Zipf-Mandelbrot's law, and the characteristics of distribution of auxiliary words is according a curve of an elliptical shape at the bi-logarithmic plot. The groups of words that satisfy the condition of being similar to the elliptical distribution are considered stop-word.

If we consider only TDSI, then the information about the author style is practically lost. So for evaluation of the degree of the text complexity from the point of view of personal style or understanding of differences between age and cultural groups, it is necessary to have text document image of other kind.

For construction of a search image of genre, author style, and for simplified evaluation of the complexity, we would propose to use the formulae like formula (6), based on the average length of words (counted in letters), the average length of a sentence (counted in words), and the ratio of punctuation marks. Sometimes, for evaluation of author style, the frequencies of auxiliary words of the text document are used. For detection of the authorship we will need to compile a corpus for its training and evaluation, i.e., prepare a collection of samples of the authors who wrote texts in our domain.

We analyzed typical methods of the users conducting an Internet search through the questionnaire. The questionnaire was applied to the users who are beginners in using the Internet, but who know something about our domain (the Mixtec culture). It was determined that more than 50% of the search attempts were successful in accessing the documents or their TDSIs in the digital library of the website.

REFERENCES

Alexandrov, M., Gelbukh, A., & Rosso, P. (2005). An Approach to Clustering Abstracts. *LNCS, 3513,* 275–285.

Alexandrov, M., Sanchis, E., & Rosso, P. (2005). *Cluster Analysis of Railway Directory Inquire Dialogs.* Proceedings of the 8th Intern. Conf. on Text, Speech and Dialog (TSD-2005) (pp. 385-390). Carlovy Vary, Czech Rep. *LNCS 3658.* Springer.

Arapov, M. V. (1988). *Cuantitative Linguistics.* Nauka.

Baevsky, V. S. (2001). Linguistic, semiotics, mathematics, and computational simulation of history of literature and poetry. *International Scientific Congress. Text, Intertext, Culture.* Azbukovnik (Ed.). Moscow.

Bonafonte, A., et al. (2000). Desarrollo de un sistema de dialogo oral en dominios restringidos. In *I Jornadas en Tecnología de Habla.* Sevilla. Spain.

Brodovsky, A. I., Makagonov, P., Ochagova, L. N., & Sboychakov, K. O. (1999). Information searching system for full texts database on the problem "Sustainable cities' development" based on IRBIS. *Computer techniques and technologies in libraries on the eve of Third Millennium* (pp. 57-63). Moscow.

Dalkey, N., C. (1969). An Experimental Study of Group Opinion: The Delphi Method. *Futures, 2*(3). Santa Monica.

Gelbukh, A., Sidorov, G., Lavin-Villa, E., & Chanona-Hernandez, L. (2010). Automatic Term Extraction using Log-likelihood based Comparison with General Reference Corpus. *Lecture Notes in Computer Science, 6177,* 248–255. doi:10.1007/978-3-642-13881-2_26

Makagonov, P. (1997). Evaluating the performance of city government: an analysis of letters by citizens to the Mayor by means of the Expert Assistant System. *Automatic Control and Computer Sciences*: *Vol. 31. N. 3* (pp. 11–19). New York: Allerton Press.

Makagonov, P., Alexandrov, M., & Gelbukh, A. (2004). Clustering Abstracts Instead of Full Texts. Text, *Speech, Dialog.* (pp. 129-135). *LNAI 3206, Springer.*

Makagonov, P., & Reyes, E. C. (2008). *Applying the Document Search Image from a Museum Site Digital Library to Simplify the Document Retrieval on the Internet. Fifteenth Jubilee international Conference.* Crimea, Russia: Libraries and Information Resources in the Modern World of Science, Culture, Education and Business.

Makagonov, P., & Ruiz, F. A. (2005). A Method of Rapid Prototyping of Evolving Ontologies. [Springer-Verlag.]. *Lecture Notes in Computer Science*, N3406.

Makagonov, P., Ruiz, F. A., & Gelbukh, A. (2006). Studying Evolution of a Branch of Knowledge by Constructing and Analyzing Its Ontology. *Lecture Notes in Computer Science Volume 3999, Natural Language Processing and Information Systems: 11th International Conference on Applications of Natural Language to Information Systems* (pp. 37–45). NLDB. Klagenfurt, Austria.

Makagonov, P., & Sánchez, P. Liliana, E. (2008) Simple applications of data mining and system approach to urban and regional problems analysis. *A Research Report in the Electronic Proceedings of International Workshop SoNet-08 Social Networks and Application Tools* (pp. 16-30).

Makagonov, P., & Sbochakov, K. (2004). Software for creating domain-oriented dictionaries and document clustering in full text database. In A. Gelbukh (Ed.), *Computational linguistics and intelligent text processing* (pp. 454-456*). Springer 2001. LNCS 2004.*

Makagonov, P., Sboychakov, K., & Sánchez, P. Liliana E. (2007). Método y herramienta computacional para medir y mejorar la armonía de proyectos arquitectónicos. *Vitrubio. Creatividad, ciencia: Volumen 1 Número 1.* (pp. 31-37). Facultad de arquitectura, diseño y urbanismo de la Universidad Autónoma de Tamaulipas, México.

Piotrovsky, M. (1975). *Text, computer, human being.* Nauka.

TextAnalyst Microsystems, Ltd. (2010). Retrieved from http://www.analyst.ru/

ENDNOTES

[1] This work was partly supported by CONA-CYT, National Council for Science and Technology, Mexico, Project No. 5777

[2] By digitalized version we mean the document represented as a sequence of letters, and not as scanned images. The images represent the first possible stage of digitalizing, but these images should be transformed into symbolic representation somehow. Usually either an OCR program (optical character recognition) or manual processing are applied.

[3] These words are called auxiliary words or "stop-words".

[4] Some Spanish words have different forms for singular/plural, masculine/feminine. We give just the plain English translation.

Chapter 10

Maximal Sequential Patterns:
A Tool for Quantitative Semantic in Text Analysis

René Arnulfo García-Hernández
Autonomous University of the State of Mexico, Mexico

J. Fco. Martínez-Trinidad
National Institute of Astrophysics, Mexico

J. Ariel Carrasco-Ochoa
National Institute of Astrophysics, Mexico

ABSTRACT

This chapter introduces maximal sequential patterns, how to extract them, and some applications of maximal sequential patterns for document processing and web content mining. The main objective of this chapter is showing that maximal sequential patterns preserve document semantic, and therefore they could be a good alternative to the word and n-gram models. First, this chapter introduces the problem of maximal sequential pattern mining when the data are sequential chains of words. After, it defines several basic concepts and the problem of maximal sequential pattern mining in text documents. Then, it presents two algorithms proposed by the authors of this chapter for efficiently finding maximal sequential patterns in text documents. Additionally, it describes the use of maximal sequential patterns as a quantitative semantic tool for solving different problems related to document processing and web content mining. Finally, it shows some future research directions and conclusions.

INTRODUCTION

In the last years, frequent pattern mining has been an intensively studied task into datamining (Han, Cheng, Xin, & Yan, 2007). Frequent patterns are itemsets, subsequences, or substructures that ap-

DOI: 10.4018/978-1-60960-881-1.ch010

pear in a data set with a frequency not less than a user-specified threshold. Frequent pattern mining constitutes an important step for mining associations, correlations, finding interesting relationships among data, data indexing, classification, clustering, text retrieval, among other data mining tasks. Besides, frequent patterns are useful for solving complex problems about data analysis.

Therefore, frequent pattern mining has become an important research area in datamining. Frequent pattern mining was first proposed in (Agrawal, Imielinski, & Swami, 1993) for market basket analysis, finding associations between the different items that customers place in their "shopping baskets". Since this first proposal there have been many research publications proposing efficient mining algorithms, most of them, for mining frequent patterns in transactional databases. However, mining frequent patterns in text document databases is a problem less studied in the literature. Sequential pattern mining in text document databases has the goal of finding all the subsequences that are contained at least β times in a collection of text documents or in a single text document, where β is a user-specified support threshold. This discovered set of frequent sequences contains the maximal frequent sequences (from now on we will use the term Maximal Sequential Patterns, MSP), which are not a subsequence of any other frequent sequence, in this way, the MSPs are a compact representation of the whole set of frequent sequences. Therefore, in the same way as occurs in transactional databases, the sequential pattern mining in text document databases plays an important role, because it allows identifying valid, novel, potentially useful and ultimately understandable patterns. Additionally, since maximal sequential patterns can be extracted from text documents independently of the language without losing their sequential nature they can be used to solve more complex problems as question answering, authorship attribution, automatic text summarization, document clustering, text retrieval, among others. All of them related to web content mining (Kosala & Blockeel, 2000; Srivastava, 2000; Zhang & Segall, 2009).

This chapter has five goals. First, it will introduce the problem of maximal sequential pattern mining when the data are sequential chains of words, which is a little studied problem in the literature. Second, it will define several basic/generic concepts and the problem of maximal

sequential pattern mining in text documents. Third, it presents two algorithms proposed by the authors of this chapter for efficiently finding MSPs in text documents. Fourth, it will describe the use of maximal sequential patterns as a quantitative semantic tool for solving different problems related to document processing and web content mining. Fifth, it will show future research directions and conclusions.

BACKGROUND

In the last decades, there has been a rapid growth of information stored in electronic devices. In (Leavit, 2002) the author reported that about the 20 percent of the electronic information in the companies is stored in structured databases, where objects or registers are easily accessible. This situation motivated the interest for analyzing information stored in this kind of databases. A research area that focuses on the analysis of information stored in structured databases is the *Knowledge Discovery* defined in (Fayad, Piatetsky-Shapiro, & Padhraic, 1996) as "the nontrivial process of identifying valid, novel, potentially useful, and ultimately understandable patterns in data". These patterns should be easily understandable by the user. The key step in the process of knowledge discovery in databases is *Datamining*, which following to (Fayad, Piatetsky-Shapiro, & Padhraic, 1996) is "a step in the Knowledge Discovery in Databases process that consists in applying data analysis and discovery algorithms that produce a particular enumeration of patterns (or models) over the data".

An important branch of data mining is the *Sequential Pattern Mining*, which finds high-frequency patterns. In (Agrawal & Srikant, 1995) the authors introduced it as follows. Given a database of transactions where each transaction is an ordered list of items, to find the maximal sequential patterns among all the patterns that have a certain user-specified minimum support, where the support is the number of transactions that contain the pattern. Frequent pattern mining has been a widely studied area in datamining research in the last years. There is abundant literature dedicated to frequent pattern mining research and tremendous progress about it. However, most of the algorithms for mining patterns solve problems related with transaction data in structured databases. A less studied problem is the one where the data are text or in general sequential chains of symbols.

In (Leavit, 2002) the author also reports that the 80 percent of electronic information stored by the companies is stored in unstructured databases, i.e., textual databases. In this context, the interest for discovering valid, novel, potentially useful, and user understandable patterns has motivated the emergence of *Knowledge Discovery from Text* (Feldman & Dagan, 1995; Kodratoff, 1999). In a similar way, the key step in this research area is *Text Mining*, "a step in the Knowledge Discovery from Text process that consists in applying text analysis and discovery algorithms that produce a particular enumeration of patterns (or models) over the text". Recently, mining frequent patterns over text or sequential chains of symbols has attracted many research interests.

Sequences or chains of symbols are an important type of data, which occur frequently in many scientific, medical, security, business and other applications. For example, DNA sequences encode the genetic makeup of humans and all species, and protein sequences describe the amino acid composition of proteins and encode the structure and function of proteins. Moreover, sequences capture how individual humans behave through various temporal activity records such as weblogs and customer purchase records (Dong & Pei, 2007). In this chapter, without loss of generality and for simplicity only sequences of textual data will be used, nevertheless the algorithms presented in this chapter can be applied over any other kind of sequences formed by chains of symbols.

In sequential pattern mining, a sequence of words is frequent if it appears at least in a certain number of documents. For example, the Figure 1a shows a document collection where each row is a document. Given a frequency threshold $\beta=2$, the sequences in the Figure 1b are the frequent sequences or sequential patterns extracted from the collection in Figure 1a. For example, the pattern *IS A BAD PRESIDENT* appears in the documents

Figure 1. a) Document collection containing five text documents. b) Sequential patterns extracted from the collection shown in a) using a frequency threshold $\beta=2$

a) Collection of five documents

1. *THE PRESIDENT OF THE UNITED STATES IS A BAD PRESIDENT*
2. *THE PRESIDENT GEORGE BUSH IS A BAD PRESIDENT*
3. *THE PRESIDENT GEORGE W. BUSH WAS A GOOD PRESIDENT*
4. *THE PRESIDENT BUSH WAS A BAD PRESIDENT*
5. *BUSH IS A BAD PRESIDENT*

b) Frequent word sequences from the last document collection

SIZE 1	SIZE 2	SIZE 3	SIZE 4	SIZE 5
1. *A*	9. *A BAD*	17. *A BAD PRESIDENT*	22. *IS A BAD PRESIDENT*	24. ***BUSH IS A BAD PRESIDENT***
2. *BAD*	10. *BAD PRESIDENT*	18. *BUSH IS A*	23. *BUSH IS A BAD*	
3. *BUSH*	11. *BUSH IS*	19. ***BUSH WAS A***		
4. *GEORGE*	12. *BUSH WAS*	20. *IS A BAD*		
5. *IS*	13. *IS A*	21. ***THE PRESIDENT GEORGE***		
6. *PRESIDENT*	14. *PRESIDENT GEORGE*			
7. *THE*	15. *THE PRESIDENT*			
8. *WAS*	16. *WAS A*			

1, 2, and 5, i.e, this sequence of words satisfies the frequency threshold.

From Figure 1b, we could conclude that discovering all sequential patterns is not useful for text analysis since only five small documents produce 24 sequential patterns. Consequently analyzing these sequential patterns could be as hard as analyzing the original documents. Fortunately, among the sequential patterns there some subfamilies that are very interesting; one of the most interesting and useful family is the one containing sequential patterns that are not contained in any other sequential pattern, i.e., the maximal sequential patterns (MSPs).

In our example, the maximal sequential patterns, using a threshold of frequency $\beta=2$, are those that appear highlighted in boldface in Figure 1b.

An interesting property of the maximal sequential patterns is that any subsequence contained in a maximal sequential pattern is also a sequential pattern and it has at least the same frequency that the maximal pattern. In other words, a maximal sequential pattern is a compact representation of the entire set of sequential sub-patterns formed from it.

Another interesting problem is to discover sequential patterns into a single document. This problem has some characteristics that make it particularly different from the problem above discussed, because for finding a maximal sequential pattern in a collection of documents, the collection by itself determines through the size of the content of each document where the sub-patterns that form the maximal sequential pattern can appear. On the other hand, to find a maximal sequential pattern in a single document is more difficult because of the limit of each sub-pattern that form the maximal sequential pattern is not known a priori, i.e., the initial and end positions that delimit the sub-patterns are not known a priori. Moreover, these relative positions will depend on the frequency threshold and they should allow determining the longest sequence that defines a maximal sequential pattern. For this reason, we will assume mutually excluded maximal sequential patterns. Therefore, the end position of a maximal sequential pattern must appear before the initial position of the following place where the same maximal sequential pattern appears. For example, consider the document <A,A,A,A,A,A,A,A,A,A> if the frequency threshold is $\beta=2$ the maximal sequential pattern <A,A,A,A,A> appears two times in the document. The Figure 2a shows (with bold shadowed numbers) the initial and end positions

Figure 2. a) Positions for the maximal sequential pattern <A,A,A,A,A>, using $\beta=2$. b) Positions for the maximal sequential pattern <A,A,A>, using $\beta=3$

a) $\beta=2$

Document	A	A	A	A	A	A	A	A	A	A
Position	**1**	2	3	4	**5**	**6**	7	8	9	**10**

b) $\beta=3$

Document	A	A	A	A	A	A	A	A	A	A
Position	**1**	2	**3**	**4**	5	**6**	**7**	8	**9**	10

Document	A	A	A	A	A	A	A	A	A	A
Position	**1**	2	**3**	**4**	5	**6**	7	**8**	9	**10**

Document	A	A	A	A	A	A	A	A	A	A
Position	**1**	2	**3**	4	**5**	6	**7**	**8**	9	**10**

Document	A	A	A	A	A	A	A	A	A	A
Position	1	**2**	3	**4**	**5**	6	**7**	**8**	9	**10**

where the maximal sequential pattern appears in the document. In our example, if the frequency threshold is $\beta=3$ then the maximal sequential pattern is <A,A,A>. The Figure 2b shows (with bold shadowed numbers) all the different initial and end positions that must be analyzed for computing the maximal sequential pattern <A,A,A>. This example allows stressing the difference of the problem for finding sequential patterns into a single document versus finding sequential patterns in a collection of documents.

ALGORITHMS FOR FINDING SEQUENTIAL PATTERNS ON TEXT

In this section, we will review some of the most successful algorithms for finding maximal sequential patterns.

GSP Algorithm

The first algorithm proposed for finding maximal sequential patterns is *GSP* (Srikant & Agrawal, 1996). *GSP* is based on the AprioriAll algorithm (Agrawal & Srikant, 1994), which is an algorithm for finding al frequent itemsets. The *GSP* algorithm starts finding the set of sequential patterns of size 1 with a frequency support greater than a threshold specified by the user. This implies to traverse the whole database for computing the frequency of each sequence. Using the sequential patterns of size 1 *GSP* generates the set of all the sequential patterns of size 2. In order to reduce the number of traverses of the whole database, the algorithm uses the anti-monotony property, which assures that if a sequence is not frequent then all of its super-sequences are also not frequent. Thus, for computing the sequential patterns of size 3, the algorithm generates candidate sequential patterns built from the sequential patterns of size 2. In general, for generating the candidate sequential patterns of size $k+1$, *GSP* checks, among the sequential patterns of size k, if the k-1 elements in

the suffix of a sequential pattern A match with the k-1 elements in the prefix of a sequential pattern B. Then the algorithm generates the candidate of size $k+1$ that results of concatenating the sequential pattern A and the last element in the pattern B. Once the algorithm has computed all the candidate sequential patterns of size $k+1$, it traverses the database for checking which candidate patterns satisfy the frequency threshold. These sequential patterns will be used for generating candidates of size $k+2$. Those sequential patterns that do not generate sequential patterns of size $k+1$ are maximal sequential patterns. If in an iteration of this process, the algorithm does not generate candidates, it ends.

GSP has two important characteristics; the first one is that it only needs little memory for generating a candidate sequential pattern. This characteristic makes the algorithm able to work with large databases. The second characteristic is that in the iteration $k+1$ all the sequential patterns of size k are generated. It allows the algorithm, in each iteration, reducing the search space. Nevertheless, this last characteristic becomes in its main drawback since in the first iterations more candidate sequential patterns are generated. However, the majority of these candidate sequences do not appear in the database but the algorithm, for computing the frequency of each candidate, has to traverse the database. If the size of the alphabet or the number of chains in the database is large this drawback is more evident. In (Antunes & Oliveira, 2003; Antunes, 2005) it was shown that the performance of *GSP* is affected when the number of chains in the database and the size of the maximal sequential patterns grow.

MineMFS Algorithm

Ahonen proposed the *MineMFS* algorithm (Ahonen, 1999; Ahonen, 1999a, Ahonen & Doucet, 2005). This algorithm is the first one addressing the problem of finding maximal sequential patterns in text document collections.

The algorithm *MineMFS* finds the sequential patterns of size 1 and 2 in the same way as *GSP*. After, for each sequential pattern of size k, the algorithm does a depth-first search growing the sequential patterns of size k by concatenating at every possible position, the sequential patterns of size 1; and traversing the database for checking if the new candidates of size $k+1$ satisfy the threshold frequency. This growth process follows until the algorithm does not generate candidates, i.e., the algorithm has found a maximal sequential pattern. Once the candidate patterns of size $k+1$ are computed, the algorithm prunes or deletes those candidate patterns contained in a maximal sequential pattern previously found, and the growth process is applied again until no more candidates are found.

PrefixSpan Algorithm

The *PrefixSpan* algorithm (Pei, et al, 2001) proposed a new approach for finding sequential patterns avoiding the generation of candidates. The algorithm follows a divide and conquer strategy for recursively building patterns through projected databases denoted as (α-DB). A projected database is a set of sub-patterns, in the original database, that are suffixes of patterns containing the prefix α. The *PrefixSpan* algorithm starts computing the patterns of size 1 that fulfill the frequency threshold in the database. Later, for each pattern of size 1, *PrefixSpan* computes its projected database and finds the patterns (only those having as prefix the pattern of size 1) that fulfill the frequency threshold in the projected database. The pattern of size 1 grows concatenating it with each element of the pattern found in the projected database generating patterns of size 2; this process is recursively repeated growing the pattern until the projected database is empty.

The strategy followed by *PrefixSpan* divides the problem of finding sequential patterns in dependence of the number of patterns found, reducing the search space in each growth step.

The most time consuming step of this algorithm is to compute the projected databases. However, according to the results shown in (Pei, et al., 2001; Pei, et al., 2004) *PrefixSpan* outperforms the performance of *GSP*. It is important to highlight that this algorithm computes all the sequential patterns. Thus for computing the maximal sequential patterns another process for selecting them is needed.

GenPrefixSpan Algorithm

Antunes proposed the *GenPrefixSpan* algorithm (Antunes& Oliveira, 2003) as an extension of *PrefixSpan*. The algorithm works in the same way as *PrefixSpan* but the projected databases include all the patterns having α as prefix, instead of only including the first apparition as *PrefixSpan* does. This algorithm has the same problem that *PrefixSpan*, in terms of time, for computing the projected databases and since it computes all the sequential patterns, another process for selecting the maximal sequential patterns is needed.

cSPADE Algorithm

Zaki proposed the *cSPADE* algorithm (Zaki, 2000). For computing the frequency of the patterns of size 1 the algorithm does not traverse the whole database, instead, *cSPADE* stores in lists, called *IdLists*, the positions where these patterns appear in the database. Later given two patterns of size 1, p_1 and p_2, *cSPADE* uses the lists denoted as *IdList*(p_1) and *IdList*(p_2) to determine where the pattern p occurs. The computation of *IdList*(p) is a kind of join denoted $join(p_1, p_2)$. There are several different merge and join operations used depending on the form of p_1 and p_2 for merging and on the form of p_1, p_2 and p for joining. Once all patterns of size k are found, *cSPADE* uses two patterns of size k having the same k-1 prefix to generate a pattern of size $k+1$, this operation is known as merge.

The *cSPADE* is one of the fastest algorithms for finding all the sequential patterns (Pei, et al., 2004).

Since their conception, the above-described algorithms find maximal sequential patterns in transactional datasets. The unique algorithm specially designed for solving the problem in unstructured datasets or text documents is *MineMFS*. Moreover, none of these algorithms can solve the problem of finding maximal sequential patterns into a single text document. As we highlighted previously, this problem has some characteristics that makes it different. In the next section, we introduce two algorithms, the first one finds maximal sequential patterns in a text document collection, in the same way as *MineMFS* does but our algorithm is much faster than *MineMFS*. The second algorithm solves the problem of finding maximal sequential patterns in a single text document.

MAXIMAL SEQUENTIAL PATTERN MINING IN TEXT DOCUMENTS

In this section, two algorithms one for mining all maximal sequential patterns in a document collection (*DIMASP-C*) and the second for all mining maximal sequential patterns in a single document (*DIMASP-D*), are introduced. Both of them build a data structure containing all the different pairs of contiguous words in the document or in the collection and the sequential relations among them. Then the algorithms, following a pattern-growth strategy, find the maximal sequential patterns into this structure.

Finding all the MSP in a Document Collection

The problem of finding patterns in text document collections, in the same way as in transactional databases, assumes that each document of the collection is a transaction in the database. In this way, a sequence of items in a document will be a

pattern in the collection if it appears in a certain number of transactions or documents.

A sequential pattern S, denoted by $<s_1,s_2,\ldots,s_k>$, is an ordered list of k elements called items, which appear in at least β documents in the collection. The frequency of a sequential pattern is also denoted by S_f or $<s_1 s_2 \ldots s_n>_f$. A sequential pattern S is β-frequent in the collection if $S_f \geq \beta$. The number of elements in a pattern S is the length of the pattern denoted by $|S|$. A k-pattern denotes a pattern of length k. Let $P=<p_1 p_2 \ldots p_n>$ and $S=<s_1 s_2 \ldots s_m>$ be sequential patterns, P is a sub-pattern of S, denoted $P \subseteq S$, if there exists an integer $i \geq 1$, such that $p_1=s_i$, $p_2=s_{i+1}, p_3=s_{i+2},\ldots,p_n=s_{i+(n-1)}$. A sequential pattern S is maximal if S is not a subsequence of any other sequential pattern in the collection. Therefore, given a document collection, the problem consists in finding all the maximal sequential patterns in the document collection.

DIMASP-C Algorithm

The basic idea of *DIMASP-C* consists in finding all the sequential patterns in a data structure. The data structure stores all the different pairs of contiguous words that appear in the documents, without losing their sequential order. Given a threshold β specified by the user, *DIMASP-C* reviews if a pair is β-frequent. In this case, *DIMASP-C* grows the sequence in order to determine all the possible maximal sequential patterns containing such pair as a prefix. A possible maximal sequential pattern (*PMSP*) will be a maximal sequential pattern (MSP) if it is not a subsequence of any previous MSP. This implies that the algorithm deletes all the stored MSP, which are subsequence of the new *PMSP*. The proposed algorithm is composed of three steps described as follows:

In the first step, for each different word in the collection, *DIMASP-C* assigns an integer number as identifier. In addition, for each identifier, the frequency is stored, i.e., the number of documents where it appears. The algorithm uses these identifiers instead of the words, in order to reduce the storage requirements and to speed up comparisons. Figure 4a shows an example for a collection containing four documents.

In the second step (Figure 3), *DIMASP-C* builds a data structure, from the collection, storing all the pairs of contiguous words $<w_i,w_{i+1}>$ that appear in a document and some additional information for preserving their sequential order. The data structure is an array containing in each cell four elements. The first one is a pair of words $C=<w_i,w_{i+1}>$. The second one is the frequency of the pair (C_f). The third element is a Boolean mark and finally a list Δ containing nodes δ. Each node δ stores a document identifier ($\delta.Id$), an index ($\delta.Index$) of the cell where the pair appears

in the array, a link ($\delta.NextDoc$) to maintain the linked *List*Δ and a link ($\delta.NextNode$) to preserve the sequential order of the pairs with respect to the document, where they appear. Therefore, the number of different documents in the *List*Δ is C_f. This step works as follows: for each pair of words $<w_i,w_{i+1}>$ in the document D_J, if the pair $<w_i,w_{i+1}>$ does not appear in the array, it is added, and its position is stored in *index*. In the position *index* of the array, the algorithm adds a node δ at the beginning of *List*Δ. The added node δ has J as $\delta.Id$, *index* as $\delta.index$, $\delta.NextDoc$ is linked to the first node of *List*Δ and $\delta.NextNode$ is linked to the next node δ corresponding to $<w_{i+1},w_{i+2}>$ of the document D_J. If the document identifier ($\delta.Id$) is

Figure 3. Algorithms of steps 2 and 3 of DIMASP-C

Step 2: Algorithm to construct the data structure from the DDB	Step 3: Algorithm to find all MSP
Input: A document database (*DDB*) **Output:** The Array **For** all the documents $D_J \in DDB$**do** Array $\leftarrow$ Add a document (D_J) to the array end-for	**Input:** Structure from step 2 and β threshold **Output:** MSP set For all the documents $D_J \in DDB$**do** MSP set $\leftarrow$ Find all MSP w.r.t. the document (D_J)
Step 2.1: Algorithm to add a document	**Step 3.1: Algorithm to find all MSP with respect to the document D_J**
Input: A document D_J**Output:** The Array **For** all the pairs $<w_i,w_{i+1}> \in D_J$**do** $\delta_i \leftarrow$ Create a new **Pair** δ $\delta_i.Id \leftarrow J$ //Assign the document identifier to the node δ $index \leftarrow$ Array[$<w_i,w_{i+1}>$] //Get the index of the cell $\delta_i.index \leftarrow index$ //Assign the index to the node δ $\alpha \leftarrow$ Get the first node of *List*Δ **If** $\delta_i.Id \neq \alpha.Id$**then** //the document identifier is new in *List*Δ Increment Cf //increment the frequency $\delta_i.NextDoc \leftarrow \alpha$ //link the node α at the beginning of *List*Δ *List*$\Delta \leftarrow$ Add δ_i as the first node //link it at the beginning $\delta_{i-1}.NextNode \leftarrow \delta_i$ //do not lose the sequential order *end-if* *end-for*	**Input:** A D_J from the data structure and a β threshold **Output:** The MSP set w.r.t. to D_J **For** all the nodes $\delta_i \in D_J i=1,\dots n$, i.e., $<w_i,w_{i+1}> \in D_J$**do** If $Array[\delta_i.index].frequency \geq \beta$**then** $PMSP \leftarrow Array[\delta_i.index].<w_i,w_{i+1}>$ //the initial pair $\Delta' \leftarrow$ Copy the rest of the list of Δ beginning from $\delta_i.NextDoc$ $\Delta'_f \leftarrow$ Number of different documents in Δ' $\delta'_i \leftarrow \delta_i$ **While** $\Delta'_f \geq \beta$ do the growth the *PMSP* $\Delta'' \leftarrow Array[\delta'_{i+1}.index].list$ $\Delta' \leftarrow \Delta' \& \Delta''$ i.e.$\{ \alpha \in \Delta' | (\alpha.index = \delta'_{i+1}) \wedge (\delta'_{i+1}.NextNode = \alpha)\}$ $\Delta'_f \leftarrow$ Number of different documents in Δ' If $\Delta'_f \geq \beta$**then** to grow the *PMSP* $Array[\delta'_{i+1}.index].mark \leftarrow$ "used" $PMSP \leftarrow PMSP + Array[\delta'_{i+1}.index].<w_{i+1}>$ $\delta'_i \leftarrow \delta'_{i+1}$ i.e. $\delta'_i.NextNode$ end-while
Step 3.1.1: Algorithm to add a PMSP to the MSP set	If $|PMSP| \geq 3$**then** add the *PMSP* to the MSP set MSP set $\leftarrow$ add a k-*PMSP* to the MSP set //step 3.1.1

Input: A k-*PMSP*, MSP set   **Output:** MSP set
If (k-*PMSP* $\in k$-MSP set) **or**
(k-*PMSP* is subsequence of some longer k-MSP) **then**
    // do not add anything
return MSP set
else //add as a MSP
k-MSP set $\leftarrow$ add k-*PMSP*
    {**delete** $S \in$ MSP set | $S \subseteq k$-*PMSP* }
return MSP set
	end-for
	For all the cells $C \in Array$**do** the addition of the 2-MSP
	If $C_f \geq \beta$ and $C.mark =$ "not used" then add it as 2-MSP
	    2-MSP set $\leftarrow$ add $C.<w_i,w_{i+1}>$

Figure 4. Data structure built by DIMASP-C for a document collection. a) Document database and its identifier representation; b) Data structure built for the document collection in a)

a) Collection of four documents

D_J	Document database
1	From George Washington to George W. Bush are 43 Presidents
2	Washington is the capital of the United States
3	George Washington was the first President of the United States
4	The President of the United States is George W. Bush
	Identifier representation
1	<1,2,3,4,2,5,6,7,8,9>
2	<3,10,11,12,13,11,14,15>
3	<2,3,16,11,17,18,13,11,14,15>
4	<11,18,13,11,14,15,10,2,5,6>

b) Data structure for the above document collection

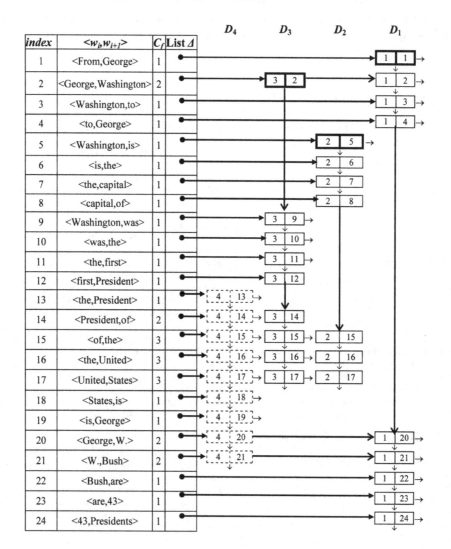

new in *List*Δ, then the frequency of the cell (C_f) is increased. The Figure 4b shows the data structure built from the document collection in Figure 4a.

In the last step (see Figure 3), given a frequency threshold β, *DIMASP-C* uses the constructed structure for mining all the maximal sequential patterns in the collection. For each pair of words stored in the structure, *DIMASP-C* verifies if this pair is β-frequent, in such case *DIMASP-C*, using the structure, grows the pattern while its frequency (the number of documents where the pattern can grow) remains greater or equal than β. When a pattern cannot grow, it is a possible maximal sequential pattern (*PMSP*), and the algorithm updates the maximal sequential pattern set. Since *DIMASP-C* starts finding 3-MSP or longer, then at the end, all the β-frequent pairs that were not used for any *PMSP* and all the β-frequent words that were not used for any β-frequent pair are added as maximal sequential patterns.

In order to reduce the number of comparisons when the algorithm adds a new *PMSP* to the MSP set (see Figure 3). The algorithm stores a MSP according to its length, it means, there is a k-MSP set for each k. In this way, before adding a k-PMSP as a k-MSP, the k-*PMSP* must not appear in the k-MSP set and it must not be subsequence of any longer k-MSP. Additionally, when the algorithm adds a *PMSP* it also deletes all its subsequences.

For avoiding repeating all the work for discovering all the MSP when new documents arrive to the database, *DIMASP-C* only processes the new documents. First, in the step 1, the algorithm assigns an integer number as identifier to the new words. Then *DIMASP-C* only uses the step 2.1 (see Figure 3) to add the information of the new documents to the data structure. Finally, the step 3.1 (see Figure 3) is applied on the new documents using the old MSP set, to discover the new MSP set. For example, Figure 4b shows with dotted lines the new part of the data structure when the document 4, of Figure 4a, is added as a new document. This strategy works only if the

algorithm uses the same value of β, however for a different value of β the algorithm only have to apply the discovery step (step 3, Figure 3) without rebuilding the data structure. This is an attractive characteristic that other algorithms do not have, since those algorithms must to compute since the beginning all the MSPs.

In order to show the performance of *DIMASP-C*, we present some experiments using the well-known reuters-21578 document collection (Lewis, 1997). After pruning 400 stop-words, this collection has 21,578 documents with around 38,565 different words from 1.36 million words used in the whole collection. The average length of the documents was 63 words. In all the experiments we used the first 5000, 10000, 15000 and 20000 documents.

The Figure 5a shows the time of *DIMASP-C* (with all its steps), *cSPADE*, *GenPrefixSpan*, *DELISP* and *GSP* algorithms using a frequency threshold value β=15 for computing all the MSP in the reuters-21578 document collection. The Figure 5b shows the same comparison but eliminating the worst algorithm (GSP), in this figure it is possible to see that *DELISP* is not as good as it seems to be in the Figure5a. In this experiment, *GenPrefixSpan* had memory problems; therefore, it only could run with the first 5000 and 10000 documents. The Figure 5c compares only *DIMASP-C* against the fastest algorithm *cSPADE* using a frequency threshold value β=15. The Figure 5d shows a linear scalability of *DIMASP-C* using a frequency threshold value β=5, 15, and 30. An additional experiment with the lowest frequency threshold value β=2 was performed, in this experiment *DIMASP-C* found a MSP of length 398 because there is a duplicated document in the collection, the Figure 5e shows these results.

In order to evaluate the incremental scalability of *DIMASP-C*, in the Figure 5f we report the time of the algorithm for adding 1000 documents, after processing 4000, 9000, 14000 and 19000 documents. In this figure, we also report the results of *cSPADE*, which needs to compute all the MSPs

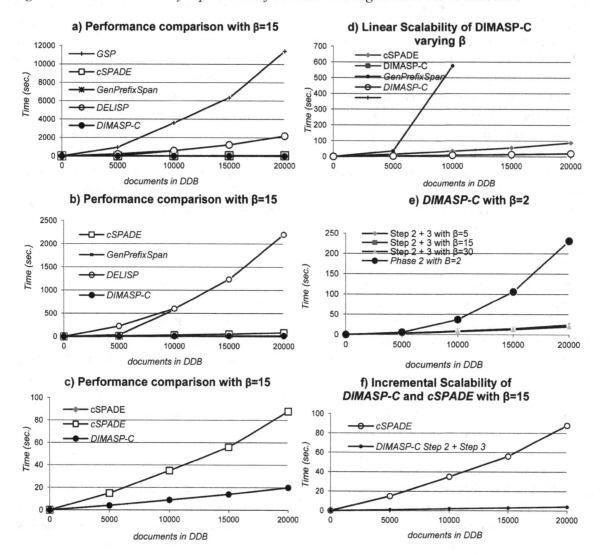

Figure 5. Time and scalability experiments of DIMASP-C using Reuters-21578 collection

since the beginning when we add the last 1000 documents.

For all the experiments with *DIMASP-C* we used a computer with an Intel Centrino Duo processor running at 1.6 GHz with 1GB RAM. All the algorithms are programmed in C++.

Space and Time Complexity Analysis

If *n* is the number of words in the document collection, then the structure built in step 2 (Figure 3) uses *n* nodes δ. If *m* is the number of all the different pairs of words in the document collection, then the array built in step 2 has a size of *m*. Therefore, the algorithm in step 2 needs a time of $\theta(n)$ and a space of $\theta(n+m)$. For example, the reuters-21578 document collection has for the first 20000 documents n=1,124,897 words with m=661,598 different pairs of words. In this case, *DIMASP-C* uses 17.16 MB for the all the nodes δ and 10 MB for the array, therefore the program uses 27.16 MB for the structure of the first 20000 documents.

The step 3 (Figure 3) has the worst time when all the documents in the collection are equal and the lowest frequency threshold is used (β=2). In this case, the q documents of length p will produce qp sequential patterns if $q \geq \beta$ with lengths of $p, p-1, p-2, ..., 1$ therefore the average length is

$$\left(p + 1 \right) \left(\frac{p}{2} \right) = \left(\frac{p^2 + p}{2} \right).$$

Consequently, the worst time is

$$O \left(pq \left(\frac{p^2 + p}{2} \right) \right) = O \left(\left(\frac{qp^3 + qp^2}{2} \right) \right) = O \left(qp^3 \right),$$

but in this case, according to the step 3.1.1.1 (Figure 3) *DIMASP-C* only needs a space for keeping only one maximal sequential pattern of length p.

Finding all the MSP in a Single Document

At first glance, we could solve the problem of finding patterns in a single document, by dividing the document into sections or paragraphs. Then we could apply algorithms for finding all the MSP in a document collection. However, we would need to define where to cut the document and the result would depend on this division. In addition, following this approach, a sequence of items will be a pattern in the document if it appears in many sections or paragraphs without taking into account the number of times the sequence appears inside each section or paragraph. This situation makes this problem different; therefore, we will consider that a sequence of items in a document

will be a pattern if it appears enough times inside the document.

Let $X \subseteq S$ and $Y \subseteq S$ then X and Y are mutually excluded sequential patterns if X and Y do not share items i.e., if ($x_n = s_i$ and $y_1 = s_j$) or ($y_n = s_i$ and $x_1 = s_j$) then $i < j$. A sequential pattern S is frequent in a document T, if it is contained at least β times in T in a mutually excluded way. A sequential pattern S is maximal if S is not a subsequence of any other sequential pattern in the document. Therefore, given a text document, the problem consists in finding all the maximal sequential patterns in the document.

DIMASP-D Algorithm

Similar to *DIMASP-C*, the idea of *DIMASP-D* consists in finding all the sequential patterns in a data structure, but in this case, the algorithm builds the structure from a single document. This structure stores all the different pairs of contiguous words that appear in the document, without losing their sequential order. Given a frequency threshold β specified by the user, *DIMASP-D* reviews if a pair is β-frequent. In this case, *DIMASP-D* grows the pattern in order to determine all the possible maximal sequential patterns containing such pair as a prefix. The proposed algorithm has three steps described as follows:

In the first step, the algorithm assigns an identifier for each different word in the document.

The second step (see Figure 6) consists in building the data structure. *DIMASP-D* will construct a data structure similar to the structure used for a document collection. But in this case, since only one document is stored in the structure, the document index is not needed, instead of it, the position of the pair inside the document is stored, as it is shown in Figure 7, this position is used to avoid overlapping among the instances of a maximal sequential pattern that appear into the document.

In the last step (see Figure 6), *DIMASP-D* finds all the maximal sequential patterns in a similar way as *DIMASP-C*, but now the algorithm verifies

Figure 6. Algorithms of steps 2 and 3 of DIMASP-D

Step 2: Algorithm to construct the data structure from a single document	Step 3: Algorithm to find all MSP

Input: A document T
Output: The data structure
For all the pairs $[t_i, t_{i+1}] \in T$ **do**
if $[t_i, t_{i+1}]$ it is not in *Array*, add it
PositionNode.Pos ← *index* ← *Array*$[t_i, t_{i+1}]$
Array[index].Positions ← **New***PositionNode*
Array[index].Freq ← *Array[index].Freq*+ 1
Array[LastIndex].Positions.NextIndex ← *index*
Array[LastIndex].Positions.NextPos ← *PositionNode*
LastIndex ← *index*;
End-for
	Input: Data structure from phase 2
	Output: MSP list
	Actual ← 1 //First element of *NextPos* in *List*
	while*Actual* ≠ 0 **do**
	if*Array[Actual].Frequency* ≥ β**then**
	temporal ← Copy (*Array[Actual].Positions*)
	PMS ← *Array[Actual].Id*1 + *Array[Actual].Id*2
	aux ← *Array[Actual].NextIndex*
	while aux ≠ 0 **do** //expand the 2-sequence
	temporal ← **Match**((*temporal.Pos* + 1) *AND*
	(*Array[aux].Positions.Pos*)
	If | *temporal* | ≥ β **then**
	if*aux* = *Array***then** there is a cycle,
	PMSP ← **Cycle**(β, *temporal*, *Array*, *Actual*, *aux*)
	If the *PMSP* cannot grow **then** exit from the while
	else*PMSP* ← *PMSP* + *Array[aux].Id*2
	aux ← *Array[Actual].NextIndex*
	end-while
	delete all the MSP ⊆*PMSP*
	if (*PMSP*⊄ MSP) **then** MSP ← Add(*PMSP*)
	Actual ← *Array[Actual].NextIndex*
	end-while

Figure 7. a) Data structure built by DIMASP-D for the text: "esadeladesad" b) Node for positions list

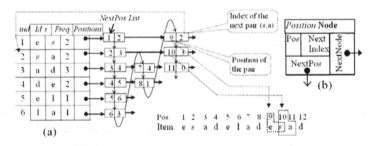

the frequency of a MSP inside the document, counting how many times a pattern appears without overlapping.

In order to show the performance of *DIMASP-D*, we chose from the collection Alex (Lease-Morgan, 2002) the document "Autobiography" by Thomas Jefferson with around 243,115 chars corresponding to: 31,517 words (approx. 100 pages); and the document "LETTERS" by Thomas Jefferson with around 1,812,428 chars and 241,735 words (approx. 800 pages). In both documents, we did not remove the stop words; we only deleted the numbers and punctuation symbols. In order to show the behavior of *DIMASP-D* regarding the number of words in the document, we computed the MSP using *DIMASP-D* with the minimum threshold value, β=2.

The Figure 8 shows the time of *DIMASP-D* processing different quantities of words for Autobiography and LETTERS. In the Figure 8a, the horizontal axis represents the amount of words (in thousands) processed by *DIMASP-D*, while the vertical axis represents the time in seconds; we started with 5,000 words incrementing 5,000

Figure 8. Processing time of DIMASP-D with β=2 and with different values of β, as well as the amount of MSP generated for different values of β; for the documents "Autobiography" and "LETTERS"

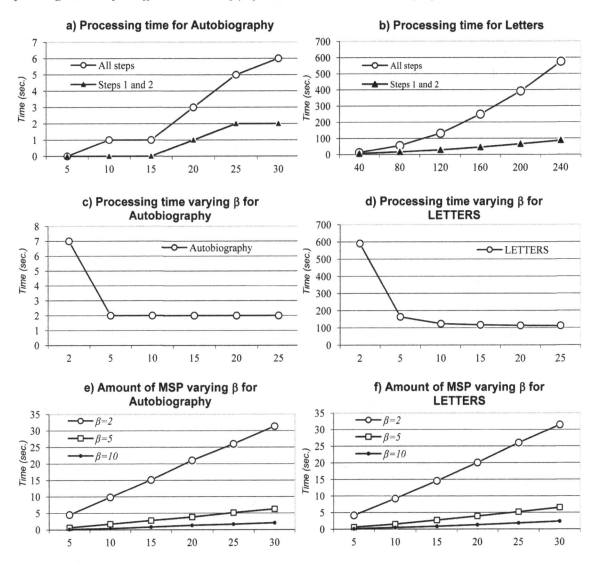

words each time. In the Figure 8b, the horizontal axis also represents the amount of words (in thousands); in this experiment, we used an increment of 40,000 words. In this figure, we can see, for both documents, how the processing time grows when the number of processed words is increased. In both graphs we show separately the time for steps 1 and 2 of *DIMASP-D*.

For the same documents, in the Figure 8c and 8d, we show the performance in time (seconds)

of our algorithm using the whole documents for different values of the frequency threshold β. This figure allows seeing the performance of our algorithm for different values of β.

Furthermore, we have included in the Figures 8e and 8f an analysis of the number of MSP obtained from "Autobiography" and "LETTERS" for different values of β. In this figure, the horizontal axis represents the amount of words (in thousands) processed by *DIMASP-D* and the vertical axis represents the number of MSP in hundreds.

Additionally to these experiments, we ran *DIMASP-D* with $\beta=2$ using "An Inquiry into the nature ..." by Adam Smith, the biggest document from the Alex collection. This document contains 2,266,784 chars corresponding to 306,156 words (approx. 1000 pages), *DIMASP-D* computed all the MSPs in 1,223 seconds (approx. 20 min). For all the experiments with *DIMASP-D* we used a computer with an Intel Centrino Duo processor running at 1.6 GHz with 1GB RAM. *DIMASP-D* was also programmed in C++.

MSPS AS A QUANTITATIVE SEMANTIC TOOL FOR TEXT ANALYSIS

The research about automatic text analysis depends on a computable representation of natural language texts. In general, text representation models specify the kind of mathematical entity (e.g. sets, graphs, feature distributions among others) used to represent texts and their constituents. One of the most prominent representation models in this area is the bag-of-words approach (G. Salton 1989) which represents texts in a vector space where the dimension of the vectors is defined by the lexical features whose values depend on local (i.e. text-specific) and global (i.e. corpus-specific) weighting parameters. Since its beginning, this model proved to be successful in representing texts in the area of information retrieval (G. Salton 1989). Nevertheless, the main problem of this model is that it does not take into account the structure of the content. That is, the model computes a vector space for the input corpus as a whole, without taking into account the order of the elements in the texts.

Maximal sequential patterns by its nature capture, in a quantitative way through the frequency threshold, the relations among the items (words, or chains of symbols) in the texts. It provides rich information, useful for revealing the most frequent

ideas in a text. The maximal sequential patterns define not only regularities in the text; they also provide semantic information since a sequence of words have more semantic information than only one word or a set of words as in the bag-of-words approach.

In the next sections, we will show the use of maximal sequential patterns as a semantic tool for solving different problems related to document processing and Web content mining. This last defined as the extraction and integration of useful data, information and knowledge from Web page contents (Cooley et al., 1997; Kosala & Blockeel, 2000; Liu, 2005). Therefore, document processing and Web content mining are highly related to text mining, information retrieval and natural language processing (Liu & Chang, 2004). Recently, a number of researchers make use of patterns (common sentences used to express certain facts or relations), which can be automatically extracted from text and used for clustering documents, finding concepts, relations among concepts, authorship attribution of documents, and text summarization, among others. Another research direction in this area is question answering from the Web. Although question answering was first studied in information retrieval literature, it becomes very important on the Web as the Web offers the largest source of information and the objective of many Web search queries is to obtain answers to some simple questions. To extend question answering to the Web by query transformation, query expansion, and taking into account the semantic information, is also a very useful task.

Document Clustering

Document clustering has the objective of discovering groups of similar documents, which are dissimilar to documents belonging to other groups. Since MSPs allow preserving document semantic, it makes sense to use them for representing documents for clustering.

In (Hernández-Reyes, et al., 2006), each document of a collection is represented by means of its

MSPs (extracted using *DIMASP-D*). In this work, the authors show the advantages of using MSPs for representing documents, over other models like bag-of-words model (representing documents by their words) and the *n*-gram model (representing documents by sequences of words of fixed size *n*). For representing documents as vectors of terms (words, *n*-grams or MSPs), there are different ways for term weighting. For example: Boolean, Frequency (*TF*), Inverse frequency (*IDF*), and Frequency-Inverse frequency (*TF-IDF*). The Boolean term weighting only considers the presence or absence of each different term in a document. The *TF* term weighting uses the frequency of each term in a document as its weight. The *IDF* term weighting computes the weight of a term using its frequency in the whole collection. The *TF-IDF* term weighting computes the weight of a term using its frequency in the document jointly with its frequency in the whole collection. In (Hernández-Reyes, et al., 2006), supposing that

bigger MSPs preserve more information about document semantic, the authors proposed a new term weighting based on the length of the MSPs.

In order to show the advantages of using MSPs as document representation for clustering, the authors built four sub-collections, from the Reuters-21578 collection. For each sub-collection, the number of documents and classes, as well as the number of words, 2-grams, and MSPs using $\beta=2$, with and without stop words (*SW*), are shown in Figure 9a.

From the Figure 9a, we can see that using MSPs for representing documents allows reducing data dimensionality between 60% and 69% regarding the word model; and between 78% and 81% regarding the 2-gram model. This reduction is very important because after term weighting each document is represented as a numerical vector whose length is the number of terms. However, each term of the MSP representation contains

Figure 9. a) Number of terms obtained for each representation model and sub-collection. b) Quality results, according to the general F-measure, for each sub-collection

a) Description for each representation model and sub-collection

	Collection-1	*Collection-2*	*Collection-3*	*Collection-4*
Documents	*100*	*120*	*120*	*253*
Classes	*2*	*3*	*3*	*5*
Words with SW	*2456*	*3195*	*3952*	*5768*
2-grams with SW	*7697*	*9128*	*9541*	*17534*
MFS's with SW	*1023*	*1635*	*1864*	*2746*
Words without SW	*1546*	*2354*	*2541*	*4294*
2-grams without SW	*3357*	*7652*	*7768*	*12927*
MFS's without SW	*484*	*726*	*821*	*1693*

b) Quality results for each sub-collection.

Representation	*weights*	*Collection-1*	*Collection-2*	*Collection-3*	*Collection-4*
Words	*Boolean*	*0,88865*	*1,00000*	*0,90756*	*0,91238*
Words	*TF-IDF*	*0,88865*	*1,00000*	*0,90756*	*0,91238*
2-grams	*Boolean*	*0,88865*	*1,00000*	*0,90712*	*0,91221*
2-grams	*TF-IDF*	*0,87635*	*1,00000*	*0,90765*	*0,91071*
MFS's	*Boolean*	*0,88865*	*1,00000*	*0,90076*	*0,91238*
MFS's	*TF-IDF*	*0,87825*	*1,00000*	*0,90076*	*0,91031*
MFS's	*Length*	*0,87825*	*0,98735*	*0,90076*	*0,91045*

more semantic information than each term of the word representation.

The authors clustered each one of these sub-collections applying the *k*-means algorithm using the cosine as similarity measure and setting *k* as the number of classes in the respective sub-collection. Figure 9b shows the quality results, according to the general *F*-measure, for each sub-collection of the Reuters-21578 collection.

From these results, it can be noticed that MSPs allow obtaining similar cluster quality, according the *F*-measure, but with a shorter representation. The short representations through the MSPs, shown in the Figure 9a, support the hypothesis that MSPs are able to capture the document semantic contained in the sequential order of the words.

Authorship Attribution

Since MSPs preserve document semantic and style, using them would be useful for solving the problem of authorship attribution. Authorship attribution is the task of identifying the author of a given text. For example in (Coyotl-Morales et al., 2006), the problem of authorship attribution is faced as a supervised classification problem. Thus given a sample of documents for some authors, the authorship of a new document must be determined. The problem consists in using the sample information for determining the class (author) of new documents.

Following this idea, in (Coyotl-Morales et al., 2006) each document in the training sample is represented by its MSPs using different frequency threshold values. Initially the threshold value is set to 2, and it is incremented until the current threshold value does not allow obtaining MSPs with two or more words. The MSPs extracted in this way are used as Boolean attributes for the vector space model of the training sample. Using this training sample, a supervised classifier can be use to determine the authorship of new documents.

In order to show the effectiveness of using MSPs as document representation for authorship attribution, in (Coyotl-Morales et al., 2006) the authors used a corpus containing poems obtained from the Web, which contains 353 poems written by 5 authors. The results, using the Naïve Bayes supervised classifier, compared against other representation models applying 10-fold cross validation, are shown in Figure 10.

From these results, we can see that, since the MSPs allow preserving document semantic and style, they got better accuracy, precision, and recall than the word and *n*-gram models.

Question Answering

Question answering has as objective to answer user specific questions expressed in natural language. A question answering system, unlike traditional information retrieval systems, provides the user a

Figure 10. Accuracy, average Precision and average Recall, for each representation model

Kind of features	Accuracy	Avg. Precision	Avg. Recall
Functional words	*41.0%*	*0.42*	*0.39*
Content words	*73.0%*	*0.78*	*0.73*
All kind of words	*73.0%*	*0.78*	*0.74*
Unigrams and bigrams	*78.8%*	*0.84*	*0.79*
Unigrams, 2-grams and 3-grams	*76.8%*	*0.84*	*0.77*
Maximal Sequential Patterns	*83.0%*	*0.87*	*0.82*

specific answer for the question, instead of a set of documents that probably contain the answer.

In (Denicia-Carral et al., 2006) the authors use definition text patterns to create a definition question answering system. A definition text pattern is a text pattern commonly used by authors to introduce new concepts in a text. Definition text patterns are useful to find the answer of a specific question, since the answer would probably appear in a text following one of these definition patterns. MSPs are useful to find definition text patterns, since they are patterns that frequently appear in a text or in a text collection.

The proposed system uses a set of pairs concept-description to find definition text patterns. First, the system substitutes each instance of each concept in a text collection by a special term *<CONCEPT>*, and each description by a special term *<DESCRIPTION>*. Then *DIMASP-C* finds all the MSP in the collection, and only the MSPs having the next structure are preserved.

<left-frontier-string><DESCRIPTION><center-string><CONCEPT><right-frontier-string>
<left-frontier-string><CONCEPT><center-string><DESCRIPTION><right-frontier-string>

To answer a specific question, the question answering system searches for fragments of text following any of the definition text patterns, but containing the specific concept of the question. If at least one definition text pattern is found, the *<DESCRIPTION>* corresponding to the most frequent definition text pattern is returned as the answer. Some examples of definition text patterns found in a collection of documents in Spanish are:

El <DESCRIPTION>, <CONCEPT>, ha
del<DESCRIPTION>, <CONCEPT>.
El ex <DESCRIPTION>, <CONCEPT>,
por el <DESCRIPTION>, <CONCEPT>.
El <DESCRIPTION>, <CONCEPT>, se
del<DESCRIPTION> (<CONCEPT>).

que la <DESCRIPTION> (<CONCEPT>)
de la <DESCRIPTION> (<CONCEPT>) en
del<DESCRIPTION> (<CONCEPT>) y
en el <DESCRIPTION> (<CONCEPT>)
de la <DESCRIPTION> (<CONCEPT>) en

In this way, for the question *¿Qué es la ONU?*, the requested concept is *"ONU"*, therefore if a document contains the text:

El delegado de la Organización de las Naciones Unidas (ONU) en México dijo......

The last pattern of the list would be found in the following form:

de la <DESPRIPTION: Organización de las Naciones Unidas> (<CONCEPT:ONU>) en

Then the answer for the question could be: *"Organización de las Naciones Unidas"*.

The authors report some experiments using the Spanish CLEF05 data set, which includes a collection of 454,045 documents, and a set of 50 definition questions. In this collection, the system reaches an overall accuracy of 84%, while in the CLEF 2005 edition the best result was 80%. These good results shows that MSPs, which retain part of the document semantic, are useful for finding good text patterns that allow improving question answering systems.

Mining Hyponyms from the Web

A hyponym is a word that has all semantic features of another more general word (its hypernym), but the hyponym adds some extra semantic features, which make it different from its hypernym. For example, the hypernym *"day"* has the hyponyms *"Monday"*, *"Tuesday"*, etc.

The relations between hyponym and hypernym are useful for a broad range of applications in Web content mining and automatic text processing. For example, in information retrieval, it is very useful to know the relation between hyponym and hypernym for recovering documents if the words of the query do not appear in the source documents. In this case, we can use the hypernym to extend the search.

Since the hypernym represents the class of another word (hyponym), then it could be useful for document clustering task because the hypernym could represent in some way a cluster of documents. This idea could be especially useful in text summarization task, since the hypernym could help to express in a shorter text a more general meaning.

In (Ortega-Mendoza et al., 2007), the authors use *DIMASP-C* for extracting text patterns involving hyponym-hypernym pairs. These patterns have one the following forms:

<left-frontier-string>HYPONYM<center-
    string>HYPERNYM
HYPERNYM<center-string>HYPONYM<right-
    frontier-string>

Given a collection of documents where all pairs hyponym-hypernym have been detected and marked, *DIMASP-C* is used for finding all MSPs of the marked collection, and only those where a pair hyponym-hypernym appears are preserved. The objective is to find text configurations commonly used for establishing a hyponym-hypernym relation, for example:

a HYPONYM is a HYPERNYM that

Once these patterns have been extracted, they can be used for detecting similar configurations that appear in non-marked documents extracted from the Web. The objective is to detect new hyponym-hypernym pairs. Notice that if a specific hypernym is fixed, the set of hyponym-hypernym pairs found by the system constitutes a list of hyponyms of the specific hypernym.

For testing this approach for hyponym mining, a set of 25 seed instances were used with Google in order to retrieve 500 text segments per seed. This way, a corpus of 12,500 segments expressing the hyponym relation, was constructed. From this corpus, 43 hyponym-hypernym configurations were extracted. The next are some examples of the discovered patterns:

the HYPONYM is a HYPERNYM that
the HYPONYM is the single HYPERNYM
the HYPONYM is one of the HYPERNYM more
the HYPONYM are a HYPERNYM
the use of HYPONYM as HYPERNYM

For mining hyponyms, each one of the 43 patterns was instantiated using the next hypernyms: "bank", "disease", "feline", "profession" and "stone". Using the instantiated patterns as Web queries, 851 candidate hyponyms were extracted: 193 related to "*bank*", 307 to "*disease*", 9 to "*feline*", 226 to "*profession*", and 116 to "*stone*". The found hyponym-hypernym configurations reflect the fact that MSPs preserve document semantic, since they preserve the relation of a hypernym with its hyponyms.

Automatic Text Summarization

Automatic text summarization consists in reducing the size of a document, but preserving the essential information contained in the original document. Since MSPs are statements that frequently appear in a document, they have relation to the semantic content of a document. Therefore, it makes sense to use them for text summarization.

In (Romyna, et al., 2009) and (Garcia, et al., 2008 & 2008-1) a summary is extracted by using *k*-means for grouping the sentences of a document and selecting a representative sentence from each group. For representing the sentences of a document, the authors used words, *n*-grams and MSPs. The method first extracts MSPs of a document by separating the document in sentences and applying *DIMASP-C*, considering each sentence as a separate document. For each document repre-

Figure 11. a) F-measure results for different representation models; b) Recall, Precision and F-measure results for different sentence selection options

a) F-measure results for different representation models

Model	Boolean	TF	IDF	TFIDF	Average
Words	0.44374	0.44037	0.43949	0.43996	0.44089
2-gram	0.43814	0.43824	0.43927	0.43953	0.43879
3-gram	0.44054	0.43519	0.44640	0.44127	0.44086
4-gram	0.43511	0.43510	0.44027	0.43142	0.43547
5-gram	0.43617	0.43892	0.44340	0.43604	0.43864
MSPs	0.44520	0.43979	0.43953	0.44056	0.44127

b) Recall, Precision and F-measure results for different sentence selection options

Terms	Weighting	Recall	Precision	F-measure
MSPs	Frequency	0.44085	0.45564	0.44796
MSPs	Boolean	0.44128	0.45609	0.44840
n-grams	Frequency	0.44609	0.45953	0.45259
n-grams	Boolean	0.38364	0.40277	0.39284
words	Frequency	0.43711	0.45099	0.44383
Words	Boolean	0.43711	0.45099	0.44383

sentation model, the authors evaluated Boolean, *TF*, *IDF*, and *TF-IDF* weighting schemas. In order to test which model is better for text summarization, the document collection DUC-2002 (used in the Document Understanding Conference 2002) containing 567 news in English with two human-created summaries, was used. After several experiments, the authors determined that MSPs got the best results for text summarization using the document collection DUC-2002. The *F*-measure results for different representation models appear in Figure 11a.

Another common strategy for text summarization consists in weighting the sentences of a document and extracting the best ones according to these weights. In (Ledeneva, et al., 2008), for weighting a sentence, the authors used the sum of the weights of its terms (in particular, they used Boolean and frequency term weighting). This work evaluated three different kinds of terms: MSPs, *n*-grams appearing in the MSPs, and words appearing in the MSPs. Once the method computes the weight of each sentence in a document, the method chooses the *k* sentences with highest weights as summary of the document. The Figure

11b shows the results of this text summarization method over the DUC-2002 document collection.

The results in Figure 11a show that, since the MSPs preserve semantic information and constitute a good document representation schema for clustering, they are useful for text summarization by clustering. Additionally, MSPs obtain good results for text summarization when they are used for ranking sentences.

FUTURE RESEARCH DIRECTIONS

Given the wide scope of applications, researches pointing to better scalable algorithms for searching maximal sequential patterns, as well as, to develop new applications of this kind of patterns, are very important. Moreover, researches pointing to find new ways for taking advantage of the MSPs, for applications where they have been already applied, are also important.

The bottleneck of maximal frequent pattern mining in text is not only on whether we can compute the complete set of maximal sequential patterns efficiently but also on whether we can derive a compact but also high quality set of maximal sequential patterns useful in applications. Therefore, much research is still needed to substantially reduce the size of derived patterns and enhance the quality of patterns for specific applications.

Another little explored research direction is the use of MSPs for information retrieval systems, in this direction, a preliminary study where the MSPs are used in combination with the bag-of-word model, in order to improve information retrieval systems appears in (Doucet & Ahonen-Myka, 2004). An interesting research in information retrieval is to recover documents similar to a given sample document. In this direction, the user provides a sample document, as a query, and the answer must be a set o documents whose topic is related to the sample document. For applying this idea to recover documents from the web, some MSPs can be used by a traditional information retrieval system, in order to obtain a first set of documents. After, a more detailed analysis, for re-ordering these documents, could be done using the MSP of the sample. In this way, the user is provided with a list of documents ordered according to the semantic similarity to the query document.

Although this chapter focuses on maximal sequential patterns where all words appear contiguously in a document, this is not the only approach. Sometimes two phrases could be not exactly the same, because one of them includes some extra words. In order to face this situation, research related to allowing a gap between the words of a MSP is another important research direction, where some ideas have been proposed (Antunes et al., 2003)

Finally, we need mechanisms for deep understanding and interpretation of maximal sequential patterns. The main research work on pattern analysis has been focused on words appearing in a pattern and their frequency. However the semantic of a maximal sequential pattern includes deeper information: what is the meaning of a pattern? What are the synonym patterns? What are the typical documents or sentences where these patterns reside?, etc. A deep understanding of frequent patterns is essential to improve the interpretability and the usability of frequent patterns. A first study in this direction over partially structured and structured data is presented in (Mei et al, 2006).

CONCLUSION

In this chapter, we introduced the maximal sequential pattern mining problem when the data are sequential chains of words or text, a problem little studied in the literature. In addition to the traditional problem treated by different researchers, we also introduced the problem for finding maximal sequential patterns into a single document. We presented an overview of the most successful algorithms for finding maximal sequential patterns; the majority of these algorithms (except *MineMFS*) were proposed for structured databases. Therefore, we introduced *DIMASP-C* and *DIMASP-D*; the former an algorithm specially proposed for discovering maximal sequential patterns from a text document collection, which is faster than the other existent algorithms. The second algorithm is an algorithm for discovering maximal sequential patterns in a single text document. This algorithm has a good performance in time and in the same way that *DIMASP-C* is an incremental algorithm; it means that our algorithms do not need to computed, from the beginning, the MSPs every time new documents are added to a database.

Maximal sequential patterns by its nature capture, in a quantitative way through the frequency threshold, the relations among items (words, or chains of symbols) in texts. The maximal sequential patterns define not only regularities in text; they also provide semantic information since a sequence of words has more semantic information than only a word or a set of words. Following this idea, we presented the use of maximal sequential patterns (computed by our algorithms) as a quantitative semantic tool for solving different problems related to document processing and Web content mining. In these problems, we showed that the semantic of the documents, preserved by the MSPs, helped to improve the quality of the results.

At the end of this chapter, we described some future research directions that constitute a challenge and mark that a depth research is still needed on several critical issues in this area so that it may have long lasting and deep impact in text analysis, information retrieval, natural language processing and text mining applications.

REFERENCES

Agrawal, R., Imielinski, T., & Swami, A. (1993). Mining association rules between sets of items in large databases . In Buneman, P., & Jajodia, S. (Eds.), *ACM-SIGMOD international conference on management of data* (pp. 207–217). New York: ACM Press.

Agrawal, R., & Srikant, R. (1994). Fast algorithms for mining association rules. In J. B. Bocca, M. Jarke, & C. Zaniolo (Eds.), *Int. Conf. Very Large Databases* (pp.487-499). San Francisco: Morgan Kaufmann.

Agrawal, R., & Srikant, R. (1995). Mining sequential patterns. In P. S. Yu & A. S. P. Chen (Eds.), *Eleventh International Conference on Data Engineering* (pp.3-14). IEEE Computer Society Press.

Ahonen, H. (1999). Finding all maximal frequent sequences in text. In I. Bratko & S. Dzeroski (Eds.).*International Conference on Machine Learning* (pp. 11–17).San Francisco: Morgan Kaufmann.

Ahonen, H. (1999a). Knowledge discovery in documents by extracting frequent word sequences. *Library Trends*, *48*(1), 160–181.

Ahonen, H., & Doucet, A. (2005). Data mining meets collocations discovery . In Arppe, A. (Eds.), *Inquiries into Words, Constraints, and Contexts* (pp. 194–203). Juho Tupakka.

Antunes, C. (2005). *Pattern mining over nominal event sequences using constraint relaxations*. Unpublished doctoral dissertation, Instituto Superior Técnico, Lisboa.

Antunes, C., & Oliveira, A. (2003). Generalization of pattern-growth methods for sequential pattern mining with gap constraints . In Perner, P., & Rosenfeld, A. (Eds.), *Machine Learning and Data Mining in Pattern Recognition, 2734* (pp. 239–251). Springer Verlag. doi:10.1007/3-540-45065-3_21

Cooley, R., Mobasher, B., & Srivastava, J. (1997). Web Mining: Information and Pattern Discovery on the World Wide Web. ictai, pp.0558. 9th International Conference on Tools with Artificial Intelligence (ICTAI '97).

Coyotl-Morales, R. M., Villaseñor-Pineda, L., Montes-y-Gómez, M., & Rosso, P. (2006). *Authorship Attribution Using Word Sequences*. 11thIberoamerican Congress on Pattern Recognition (CIARP'2006), LNCS vol. 4225. Springer Verlag.

Denicia-Carral, C., Montes-y-Gómez, M., Villaseñor-Pineda, L., & García Hernández, R. A. (2006). *A Text Mining Approach for Definition Question Answering*. 5th International Conference on NLP (Fintal 2006), LNAI, Vol. 4139, Springer-Verlag, pp. 76–86.

Dong, G., & Pei, J. (2007). *Sequence Data Mining*. Heidelberg: Springer.

Doucet, A., & Ahonen-Myka, H. (2004). *Non-Contiguous Word Sequences for Information Retrieval*. Proceedings of the Workshop on Multiword Expressions: Integrating Processing, Association for Computational Linguistics, Barcelona, Spain, pp. 88-95.

Fayad, U., Piatetsky-Shapiro, G., & Padhraic, S. (1996). From data mining to knowledge discovery in databases. *AI Magazine, 17*, 37–54.

Feldman, R., & Dagan, I. (1995). Knowledge discovery in textual databases (KDT). In U.M. Fayyad and R. Uthurusamy (Eds.), *International Conference on Knowledge Discovery* (pp. 112-117). AAAI Press.

García-Hernández, R. A., Ledeneva, Y., Gelbukh, A., & Gutierrez, C. (2008). An Assessment of Word Sequence Models for Text Summarization. Special issue: Advances in Intelligent and Information Technologies. *Research in Computing Science, 38*, 253–262.

García-Hernández, R. A., Montiel, R., Ledeneva, Y., Rendón, E., Gelbukh, A., & Cruz, R. (2008). *Text Summarization by Sentence Extraction Using Unsupervised Learning.* 7th Mexican International Conference on Artificial Intelligence (MICAI08), Lecture Notes in Artificial Intelligence, Springer-Verlag, Vol. 5317 pp. 133-143.

Han, J., Cheng, H., Xin, D., & Yan, X. (2007). Frequent pattern mining: current status and future directions. *Data Mining and Knowledge Discovery, 15*, 55–86. doi:10.1007/s10618-006-0059-1

Hernández-Reyes, E., García-Hernández, R. A., Carrasco-Ochoa, J. A., & Martínez-Trinidad, J. Fco.(2006). Document Clustering based on Maximal Frequent Sequences. 5th International Conference on NLP (Fintal 2006), Tapio Salakoski et al. (Eds.). LNCS Vol. 4139, Springer-Verlag, Turku, Finland, August 2006, pp. 257-267.

Kodratoff, Y. (1999). Knowledge discovery in texts: A definition and applications. In Z. W. Ras and A. Skowron (Eds.). *International Symposium on Foundations of Intelligent Systems.* Vol. 1609. (pp. 16–29). Springer-Verlag.

Kosala, R., & Blockeel, H. (2000). Web mining research: a survey. *SIGKDD Explorations Newletters, 2*, 1–15. doi:10.1145/360402.360406

Lease-Morgan, E. (2002). *Alex Catalogue of Electronic Texts.* Retrieved from http://infomotions.com/alex

Leavitt, N. (2002). Data mining for the corporate masses. *Computer, 35*(5), 22–24. doi:10.1109/MC.2002.999772

Ledeneva, Y. (2008). *Effect of Preprocessing on Extractive Summarization with Maximal Frequent Sequences.* LNAI 5317, pp. 123-132, Springer-Verlag. Lewis, D.D. (1997). *Reuter-21578 Text Categorization Test Collection Distribution 10.* Retrieved from http://kdd.ics.uci.edu/databases/reuters21578/reuters21578.html.

Liu, B. (2005). *Web Content Mining.* Tutorial at the 14th International World Wide Web Conference, May 10-14, Chiba, Japan.

Liu, B., & Chang, K. (2004). Special issue on Web content mining. *SIGKDD Explorations, 6*(2), 1–4. doi:10.1145/1046456.1046457

Mei, Q., Xin, D., Cheng, H., Han, J., & Zhai, C. (2006, August). *Generating semantic annotations for frequent patterns with context analysis.* Paper presented at the 2006 ACM SIGKDD international conference on knowledge discovery in databases (KDD'06), Philadelphia, USA.

Montiel Soto, R., García-Hernández, R. A., Ledeneva, Y., & Cruz Reyes, R. (2009). Comparación de Tres Modelos de Texto para la Generación Automática de Resúmenes. [Sociedad Española para el Procesamiento del Lenguaje Natural.]. *Revista de Procesamiento del Lenguaje Natural, 43*, 303–311.

Ortega-Mendoza, R. M., Villaseñor-Pineda, L., & Montes-y-Gómez, M. (2007). *Using Lexical Patterns For Extracting Hyponyms from the Web.* 6th Mexican International Conference on Artificial Intelligence (MICAI 2007), LNAI 4827, Springer-Verlag.

Pei, J., Han, J., Asl, M. B., Pinto, H., Chen, Q., Dayal, U., & Hsu, M. C. (2001). *Prefixspan mining sequential patterns efficiently by prefix projected pattern growth.* Paper presented at 17th International Conference on Data Engineering, Heidelberg, Germany.

Pei, J., Han, J., Mortazavi-Asl, B., Wang, J., Pinto, H., & Chen, Q. (2004). Mining sequential patterns by pattern-growth: the prefixspan approach. *Transactions on Knowledge and Data Engineering, 16*(11), 1424–1440. doi:10.1109/TKDE.2004.77

Salton, G. (1989). *Automatic text processing: The transformation, analysis, and retrieval of information by computer.* Reading, MA: Addison-Wesley.

Srikant, R., & Agrawal, R. (1996). Mining sequential patterns: Generalizations and performance improvements. In P. M. G. Apers, M. Bouzeghoub, & G. Gardarin (Eds). *Intl. Conf. Extending Database Technology, 1057*, 3–17. Springer-Verlag.

Srivastava, J., Cooley, R., Deshpande, M., & Tan, P. N. (2000). Web usage mining: discovery and applications of usage patterns from web data. *SIGKDD Explorations Newletters, 1*(2), 12–23. doi:10.1145/846183.846188

Zaki, M. J. (2000, November). *Sequence mining in categorical domains: incorporating constraints.* Paper presented at 9th international conference on Information and knowledge management, McLean, Virginia, USA.

Zhang, Q., & Segall, R. S. (2009). Web mining: a survey of current research, techniques, and software. [IJITDM]. *International Journal of Information Technology & Decision Making, 7*(4), 683–720. doi:10.1142/S0219622008003150

Chapter 11
Topic Discovery in Web Collections via Graph Local Clustering

Sara Elena Garza Villarreal
Universidad Autónoma de Nuevo León, Mexico

Ramón Brena
Tec de Monterrey, Mexico

ABSTRACT

This chapter presents an approach for discovering and describing thematically related document groups (topics) by means of graph clustering; this approach responds to the need of organizing information in massive Web collections. Because a Web collection is hyperlinked, we can view it as a directed graph, whose vertices represent its pages and whose arcs represent links among these pages. This being the case, the authors assume that topics will be graph clusters, where a graph cluster is a group of vertices with numerous arcs to the inside of the group and few arcs to the outside of it. In that sense, our topic mining task is mainly focused on clustering the document graph; to cope with scalability issues and enable the discovery of overlapping clusters, we particularly use a local approach, which maximizes a density-based fitness value over the neighborhoods of different starting points. Moreover, with the intent of enriching the discovered clusters, we include the calculation of semantic descriptors.

Our approach was tested over the Wikipedia collection and we observed—by different means—that the resulting clusters in fact correspond to cohesive topical document groups, which leads us to conclude that topic mining can be treated as a graph clustering problem.

An extensive review of existing literature on clustering and topic mining is given throughout the chapter as well.

DOI: 10.4018/978-1-60960-881-1.ch011

1. INTRODUCTION

Recently, the Web has turned into a dynamic, heterogeneous, massive—and almost chaotic—information spot. Naturally, the organization of such information becomes almost imperative for having a usable cyberspace. To carry out this apparently complicated endeavor, several alternatives have been proposed, e.g. manual directories and ontologies. However, because the Web is latently self-organized (Flake, 2002), options in the fashion of soft computing may also be used to uncover its hidden semantics.

Within the area of information organization, a challenging task concerns *automatic topic discovery*, which broadly consists of extracting the themes that are present in a document collection. Not only is there room left for exploring this discipline (particularly on the Web), but also the potential for generating valuable applications—e.g. visualization and semantic information retrieval—is released with its accomplishment. Now, for soft topic discovery, we can take advantage of a Web collection's *structure* (i.e. hyperlinks), as this information source is language independent and less ambiguous than text. In that sense, we propose to find topics with the aid of hyperlink-based document clustering. Because the size of Web collections is large, we specifically consider the use of *Graph Local Clustering* ("GLC"), a methodology that explores a corpus by neighborhoods (Virtanen, 2003). Knowing that the Wikipedia corpus is interesting, complex, and popular, we have taken it as our case study.

Our main contributions, which shall be covered after introducing relevant background (Section 2), consist of a topic discovery conceptual model, a GLC-based clustering algorithm, a set of suitable properties for the topic domain (these three points are discussed on Section 3), a set of topics extracted from Wikipedia, and evidence of the method's effectiveness (Section 4). Related work and conclusions are given on Sections 5 and 6.

2. BACKGROUND AND STATE OF ART

Hyperlink-based topic extraction with Wikipedia as a case study suggests a review in three dimensions: (1) Web structure mining for group detection, (2) topic mining, and (3) semantic information extraction in Wikipedia (which we can refer to also as "Wikipedia mining").

2.1 Basic Concepts and Notation

In order to have a better understanding of the fore coming sections, we will define some basic concepts and introduce the necessary mathematical notation. Regarding the essential vocabulary, a list of the most common terms, along with a succinct description and their respective synonyms is to be provided. As for synonyms, although they will usually express the same concept, it is important to clarify that they might occasionally exhibit slightly different meanings; whenever this is the case, it will be opportunely noted. Now, concerning notation, the most part will be used to denote graph theory concepts.

Taking into account that our field of study is multi-disciplinary, it is necessary to list our essential vocabulary:

- **Element**. Atomic entity.
  - Synonyms: *node, vertex, member, document, article, actor, page, webpage, object.*
- **Link**. Relationship between entities.
  - Synonyms: *arc/edge, hyperlink, tie.*
- **In-link**. An arc incident *upon* a vertex v_i ($v_j \rightarrow v_i$).
- **Out-link**. An arc incident *from* a vertex v_i ($v_i \rightarrow v_j$).
- **Corpus**. Document collection (universe).
  - Synonyms: *collection, document graph.*
- **Group**. Entity conglomeration.
  - Synonyms: *cluster, community, subgroup, sub-graph, document set.*

- **Grouping**. Set of groups.
  - Synonyms: *clustering, partition (exclusive), cover (overlapping)*.
- **Group detection**. Act of gathering elements into groups.
  - Synonyms: *clustering, group discovery*.
- **Topic**. Subject matter.
  - Synonyms: *theme, thematic*.

Some of the previous descriptions are still abstract, but suffice to get an initial idea of the implied concept.

The second part of the current section consists of introducing graph-theoretic notation. While certain definitions (graph, vertex degree, adjacency matrix) are assumed to be known, others shall be provided during the rest of the section.

Let us start by defining a cut. A *cut* is a graph partition that creates two disjoint and non-empty sets of vertices, namely S and $\overline{S}$, $(\overline{S} = V - S)$. The *edge-cut* is the set of edges that "cross" the partition by having one endpoint in and the other one in $\overline{S}$; the cardinality of this set is called the *cut size* and is denoted by $c\ (S, \overline{S})$.

Now, let us assume that we have a cluster C (equivalent, in practical terms, to a cut) on an unweighted, undirected graph, and that C has two kinds of edges: internal and external, the former being edges that have both endpoints on cluster members (these do not belong to the edge-cut) and the latter being edges that have one endpoint on a cluster member and the other on a cluster non-member (and thus belong to the edge-cut set). The number of external edges of C is considered to be the *external degree* ($\deg_{ext}[C]$), and analogously, the number of internal edges is the *internal degree* ($\deg_{int}(C)$). More formally:

$$\deg_{int}(C) = |\{(u,v): (u,v) \in E \wedge u,v \in C\}|, \quad (1)$$

$$\deg_{ext}(C) = |\{(u,v): (u,v) \in E \wedge (u \in C \wedge v \notin C)\}|. \quad (2)$$

Also, note that this edge classification can be extended to vertices, resulting that, for a particular vertex of C we have: $\deg(v) = \deg_{int}(C) + \deg_{ext}(C)$.

Another important concept is the *neighborhood* of a vertex; for a vertex v, it consists of the set of vertices that share an edge with v (denoted by $\Gamma[v]$).

Having covered this aspect, let us describe the state of the art regarding group detection via Web structure mining.

2.2 Web Structure Mining for Group Detection

Let us describe at this moment the organization of the current discussion. The central point concerns reviewing the different *methods* for group detection; to understand the most general notions of these, it is necessary to go through *prior work*, mostly represented by complex networks (e.g. citation and social nets). Afterwards, to have a clearer picture of the environment our discussed methods work on, it is convenient to enumerate the specific *tasks* they carry out for discovering distinct *group types*. Furthermore, this implies analyzing the assorted *metrics* and *information matrices* they use and then describe the methods properly, by classifying them; now, considering that the Web environment exhibits several special features, we might also mention how methods *overcome complexity* issues. Our final point of discussion covers the *evaluation* schemes that have been employed to validate results.

Prior studies and related areas. Web structure mining is rooted in the analysis of complex networks—systems whose topological features make them stand as the middle point between regular and random graphs. According to Newman's classification (2003), these networks can be divided into four main categories: social, informational, technological, and biological. From these, we are mainly interested in the first two, as they provide the main foundations for link analysis. From Social Network Analysis (SNA), which formally studies interactions among social entities (persons, organizations, parties, etc.), two important "inherited" concepts are *cohesive sub-groups* and *centrality*; while the former stand for subsets with relatively strong, direct, intense, frequent, or positive ties (Wasserman, 1994), the latter measures the relative importance of an actor, either at a local (network sub-group) or global scale (the whole network). From citation analysis (a.k.a. "bibliometrics"), which is devoted to studying aspects related to article, journal, and book citations, a pair of fundamental concepts is given by co-citation (Small, 1973) and bibliographic coupling (Kessler, 1963). While co-citation states that two documents are similar if they are simultaneously cited by the same sources, bibliographic coupling considers a pair of documents to be similar if they both cite the same documents.

The Web as a graph. Because documents and hyperlinks can be respectively visualized as the nodes and edges of a graph, there have been several initiatives to explore and treat the Web as a complex network. These works have exhibited network properties and structure of the Web, new random models to fit its behavior, and link mining algorithms.

Groups. Three main types of groups can be distinguished in Web structure mining: distinctive-feature groups, common trait groups, and cohesive groups. While the first constitute a proper subset of distinguished members (e.g. hubs and authorities), the second hold together similar elements (e.g. a cluster gathered by co-citation affinity), and the third represent densely-linked structures (e.g. communities).

Sub-tasks. Each of the aforementioned group types is related to different detection sub-tasks. In that sense, *resource discovery* finds distinctive feature groups, *pattern-based clustering* (data clustering) detects common trait groups, and *community identification* (network clustering) obtains cohesive groups.

Resource discovery. It consists of finding popular pages (authorities) and hubs (lists of authorities) given a "broad" query; for example, for "Harvard University", an authority could be its homepage http://www.harvard.edu and a hub could be a page that lists sites of universities. This task is also known as "topic distillation".

Regarding community detection and pattern-based clustering, they have a common root: clustering. This discipline is the most important

Table 1. Clustering types

Criterion	Types
Structure	**Flat:** Clusters are all at the same level **Hierarchical:** Clusters are nested into more general ones-
Group membership	**Exclusive:** Partitional. Every element belongs to exactly one cluster. **Overlapping:** Non-exclusive. Elements can belong to one or more clusters. **Fuzzy:** Every element belongs to all clusters with a membership value ranging from 0 (does not belong) to 1 (completely belongs).
Coverage	**Total:** All elements are assigned to a cluster. **Partial:** Not every element ends up in a cluster.
Conformation approach	**Agglomerative:** Bottom-up. Starts with one cluster per element. **Divisive:** Top-down. Starts with all elements in a single cluster.
Randomness	**Deterministic:** No randomness introduced. The same result is always achieved given a data set. **Stochastic:** Randomness introduced. Implies running the clustering process several times to get the best results.
Information management	**Network-based:** Graph-theoretic methods are used for clustering. **Pattern-based:** Similarity between pairs of information patterns is used.

unsupervised learning task, and concerns the conformation of distinct groups (clusters) over an object collection. Unlike with classification and other supervised methods, the number and composition of the clusters is initially unknown. A general description of its most important types has been summarized in Table 1. From Table 1, we can see that the *information management* criterion splits clustering into the two subdivisions of our interest: pattern-based (usually known as *data clustering*) and network-based (commonly known as *graph clustering*).

Pattern-based clustering. Widely reviewed by Jain et al. (1999), this clustering type groups patterns according to their *similarity*, where a pattern is usually understood as a *feature vector* and similarity—or dissimilarity—implies a certain kind of affinity (e.g. Euclidean-space proximity or conceptual alikeness). Classical clustering approaches include k-means, hierarchical clustering, fuzzy c-means, and Gaussian mixtures. Other relevant techniques for our domain are sub-space clustering, density-based clustering, ant-based clustering, spherical k-means, kernel k-means, ant-based clustering.

Pattern-based clustering is applicable to linked environments if we are able to *transform link-related data* into a collection of features; for example, from an adjacency matrix, each row can be taken as a feature vector, where each feature is given by the presence or absence of a link. Similarly, common connections between nodes could be translated into patterns of co-citation and bibliographic coupling that can be clustered by any traditional algorithm.

Community identification. This task involves finding sets of webpages that have more links to elements *inside* the set than *outside* of it (Flake, 2000)—this is actually equivalent to dense subgraph extraction in graph mining (Cook, 2006). These sets are called *communities*, and such congregations usually indicate persons sharing common interests or webpages talking about the same theme. The previous definition is the one commonly accepted, although literature offers

other formal and alternative conceptions for a community—for example, consider the definitions by Radicchi et al. (2004), Kumar et al. (2000), and Liu (2007). For further reading on community identification in general (not only for the Web), see the survey by Puig (2007).

As a final remark about data and network clustering, it seems relevant to mention that there are clustering techniques that stand in between of these two. For example, similarity-based graphs have given rise to algorithms such as METIS (Karypis, 1999a), Chameleon (Karypis, 1999b), and the Jarvis-Patrick (1973) method.

Metrics, matrices, and other computations. Because pattern-based clustering requires affinity metrics and matrices, and community identification relies on group quality measurements and SNA-related calculations, let us briefly list some of these:

- **Metrics**
  - *Pairwise similarity*. Affinity between pairs of elements. Usually used for data clustering. Examples: co-citation, bibliographic coupling, structural similarity, and set-related metrics, such as the Jaccard index and the Dice coefficient.
  - *Group quality*. Cohesion of elements gathered in a collection. Usually used for network clustering. Examples: conductance, local density, relative density, and modularity. Relative density, in particular, is very relevant for the present research; it consists of the ratio of internal links of a cluster (Equation 3).
- **Matrices**. Adjacency, weighted adjacency, co-citation, and Laplacian are several of the most used.

Other computations. Other relevant computations include edge betweenness and the relative strength ratio (Equations 4 to 6) of a cohesive sub-group, which is utilized in Social Network Analysis.

$$\rho(C) = \frac{\deg_{\mathrm{int}}(C)}{\deg_{\mathrm{int}}(C) + \deg_{ext}(C)} \qquad (3)$$

$$rsr(C) = \frac{rs_i(C)}{rs_e(C)} \qquad (4)$$

$$rs_i(C) = \frac{\deg_{\mathrm{int}}(C)}{|C| - 1} \qquad (5)$$

$$rs_\in(C) = \frac{\deg_{ext}(C)}{|V| - |C|} \qquad (6)$$

Methods for group detection. Regarding detection methods found in literature—which are aligned to the tasks and group types we have previously mentioned—, these can be classified according to their *modus operandi*. In that sense, we have similarity-based, cut-based, spectral, and based on structure search.

- **Similarity-based.** Methods based on pattern similarity basically solve the data clustering task, as they group webpages according to pairwise affinity. A pioneering effort in this line is given by Pirolli et al. (1996), since their method mixes text, hyperlinks, and even weblogs to carry out categorization and prediction tasks. It is interesting to note that, indeed, this kind of methods tend to employ hybrid information sources.

- **Cut-based.** Also known as *modularity-based*, these methods use community detection algorithms that work with graph cuts. This class of methods can be further divided into two sub-classes: link-count and flow approaches. While the former are highly based on vertex and cluster degrees, the latter address the problem of finding groups as a *max-flow/min-cut theorem* issue. Respective representatives of such orientations are Virtanen/Schaeffer (2005), who proposes a local type of graph clustering for coping with large scale graphs, and Flake et al. (2002), whose contribution is seminal for community detection based solely on structure.

- **Spectral.** Relying on spectral graph theory, these methods can be considered as part of the pattern-similarity techniques, but deserve to be placed apart for their great prominence in the Web meaningful group detection domain. Probably the most important work regarding this type of methods is the HITS (Hypertext Induced Topic Search) algorithm (Chakrabarti, 1998; Chakrabarti 1999; Kleinberg 1999), which discovers hubs and authorities by means of principal eigenvectors.

- **Methods based on structure search.** These look for certain patterns in graphs, and basically involve detecting various special kinds of sub-graphs and components with particular features. A representative work here is the one of Kumar et al., which presents the "trawling" process for identifying emerging communities (Kumar, 2000); the basic assumption is that communities are characterized by dense directed bipartite graphs.

A complementary classification of link-based methods can be made by taking into account the view of the search space; this results in *global* and *local* approaches—the first exploring all the search space and the second only local neighborhoods. Even when this type of classification seems logical, actually the limits of one approach versus the other are not quite neat. This is because certain methods claim to be global, but operate using local views of the Web. In that sense, only the works by Schaeffer and Kumar are clearly stated as local and global, respectively.

Overcoming complexity. Because the Web regards a massive collection, detection methods have to address complexity. A common option consists of achieving efficiency, either on algorithms, data structures, or both. Another important technique is given by problem decomposition, which has been carried out by considering only relevant subsets of the Web (obtained by means of queries and the use of local search) or parallelizing. Approximate answers and pruning of irrelevant material have also been utilized to solve complexity-related issues.

Evaluation. For assessing results, there are three principal validation schemes: internal, external, and relative. As for internal validation, it is based on the groups' intrinsic properties; in contrast, external validation requires a pre-established result model, i.e. a set of reference classes. With regard to relative evaluation, the basic idea is to compare different approaches by using certain criteria.

- **Internal evaluation.** This kind of scheme can actually be divided into benchmarking and intra cluster compactness vs. inter-cluster separation. The first consists of surpassing an accepted threshold, and the second one concerns measuring the proximity (where proximity stands for either similarity or dissimilarity) between pairs of elements from the same cluster and then contrasting them against the proximity found between pairs of elements of different clusters. This information is usually displayed in *visual similarity matrices*, where each cell stands for the proximity between two clusters.

- **External evaluation.** This type of evaluation is generally carried out with accuracy-based metrics, such as precision (correctness), recall (completeness), and F-score (balance between precision and recall); a typical graphs for portraying results are the precision-recall curve and the F-score curve.

A complementary validation type regards indirect evaluation, which consists of assessing a method's effectiveness by observing how well it leverages a certain *primary task* (e.g. browsing). This is especially useful for comparing methods more "neutrally".

Finally, it is worth mentioning that evaluating non-partitional clusterings is challenging to some extent, as validation techniques specifically designed for overlapping structures (covers and fuzzy groups) are scarce.

2.3 Topic Mining

When dealing with collection topics and their automatic identification, we are confronted with a wide variety of representations, approaches, tasks, and information. The former reveals a couple of aspects: on one hand, the *topic discovery* concept is not precise and, as a matter of fact, acts more like an umbrella that covers a considerable number of other concepts and methods. Let us briefly review some of the most substantial.

Topic representations. Topics, so far, can be conceived as word-oriented, document-oriented, or object-oriented. Word-oriented notions share a *descriptive* view of topics that consists of *word collections*; these include models and labels. Document-based conceptions, on their own, present an *enumerative* view of topics as *document lists*; such lists can be composed of URL's, titles, or representative keywords of each document. Object-oriented notions can be seen as a combination of word and document approaches.

Topic mining tasks and pure approaches. Another key classification criterion is the kind of topic mining approach. We can distinguish two main types: pure and hybrid. The first only use one type of basic task and utilize one type of representation. The second, on the other hand, principally mix basic tasks, information sources, and/or representations. According to literature, we may consider the following as basic tasks:

- **Labeling**. Consists of *naming* the topic. Other more technical names for this task concern *cluster annotation* and *cluster labeling*. A representative method for this task is suggested by Stein and Eissen (2004); this method annotates groups in a hierarchical fashion according to ontologies and term frequencies.

- **Distillation**. Consists of detecting the *authoritative* documents of the topic. Equivalent to the previously discussed *resource discovery* task, and is also known as *broad topic search* (or just "topic search"). Distillation is best appreciated on the works by Kleinberg (1999) and Chakrabarti et al. (1998; 1999)—the same group, actually. Regarding the first, topics are depicted as URL lists. With respect to the second, the approach can be seen as an upgrade of the HITS algorithm (now referred to as the *Clever system*), since it addresses some of its issues, such as straying and multi-topic pages.

- **Modeling**. Refers to *characterizing* the topic in probabilistic terms and is also referred to as topic analysis. A characteristic approach that consists of producing generative models for scientific topics is supplied by Griffiths and Steyvers (2004); such method views topics as probability distributions over words, and considers each document as a mixture of these themes.

- **Enumeration**. Refers to *listing* the elements of the topic. Technically conceptualized as *dense sub-graph extraction* (graph mining task), *blockmodeling* (SNA task), and *group detection* (link mining task). Pure enumeration approaches can be initially exemplified with Flake's maximum-

flow Web communities (2000), which are topically related (this was previously discussed).

Hybrid approaches. Regarding hybrid approaches, we can still subdivide works into several categories by assigning *paradigms*. On a first instance, flows composed of different tasks. For example, Schwartz et al. (2001) and Sista et al. (2002)—the same group—, who tackle the problem of *Unsupervised Topic Discovery* (UTD); the method (modeling-labeling) basically consists of characterizing topics via probabilistic tools, and then extracting human-readable names from an annotated corpus using classification. In that sense, the "unsupervised" term is awarded to the task because no training corpus is used to generate the topic models.

Other paradigm for hybrid works *information incorporation*, in which evidence combination is assumed to yield better results. An instance of this is given by the work of Jo et al. (2007), which integrates co-citation and term information to obtain more accurate topic models.

Two additional tasks that are worth to be mentioned, but are not the focus of our analysis are topic *segmentation* and Topic Detection and Tracking (TDT). The first one is dedicated to fragment texts (documents) in such a way that every "chunk" of information stands for a different topic. The second (TDT) is a *sui generis super-task* is totally committed to event-based organization of broadcast news (Allan, 2002).

Another interesting aspect with regard to topic mining approaches concerns the distinction between *important* and *unimportant* topics. For example, Griffiths and Steyvers talk about *hot vs. cold* topics, Ertöz and et al. (2003) about *dominant vs. non-dominant* themes, and Wartena and Brussee (2008) imply this distinction as *prominent vs. ordinary* topics.

2.4 Wikipedia Mining

Efforts concerning Wikipedia use for extracting semantics can be seen as having a three-fold division. First, we have *hard vs. soft approaches*, being the use of ontologies the main difference between these kinds of methods (we may consider this categorization as *Semantic Web paradigm*). Second, we can distinguish works that consider Wikipedia only as a rich information *source* from those that use Wikipedia both as a *source* for semantics and a *destination* over which the extracted knowledge can be applied (let us define this as the *type of use* given to the corpus). Finally, works can be differentiated according to the *type of information* used (content, structure, or both). Two efforts worth mentioning are DBPedia, which extracts semantics from Wikipedia infoboxes (Auer, 2007) and Yago, an ontology created from Wikipedia (Suchanek, 2008).

3. METHOD

To discuss our topic discovery method, it is essential to describe our conceptual model as a first instance, since this model depicts our general solution strategy. Once having explained such conceptual framework, it is possible to go deeper into the concrete discovery method, which is based on the graph local clustering (GLC) methodology. Our final stop shall be the calculation of topic properties.

3.1 Conceptual Model

To be able to explain our technique for topic discovery and the aspects it involves, let us start by conceptualizing a topic as a *document group whose semantics imply a common theme among its elements*. Regarding the first part of the definition, "a document group", we have seen that this topic conception is not uncommon to find in literature; actually, such definition allows us to treat topic discovery as a clustering problem—which is not an uncommon approach either. However, because we are not content with merely producing a *rough* grouping (obviating semantics), it becomes necessary to introduce the second part of our definition, "whose semantics imply a common theme among its elements". To make the semantics of the discovered clusters more explicit, from a series of possible actions that may be taken, we consider two in particular:

• Presenting it as a usable piece of information

Figure 1. Topic discovery layered conceptual model

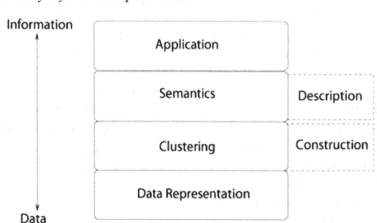

- ◦ Naming the theme that gathers the documents together
- ◦ Extracting the essence of the topic
- Validating that it is indeed a topic

With this definition, it is possible to use clustering as our main engine for a "rough" group discovery and then wrap a semantic (topical) context around this procedure. A natural model that serves for this purpose is given by a layered architecture—specifically, a four-layered model (see Figure 1). On this architecture, data is abstracted to facilitate clustering at the lowest level, while clustering takes place at the second one, and the discovered groups are given meaning at the third layer; finally, at the uppermost layer (which lies out of our scope), the discovered topics are used for a variety of applications.

Therefore, our general solution for topic discovery consists of clustering first, without taking into account the context, and, afterwards, calculating properties (i.e., cluster features) to make the semantics of the context more explicit. The former process shall be carried out with a local graph clustering approach and the latter with ranking and selection operations.

3.1.1 Elements from the Formal Conceptual Framework

Before describing the details for the topic discovery process, let us formalize the main *elements* of our conceptual framework. In that sense, our universe of discourse is given by the *corpus* (document collection). This entity is represented by a *directed graph* (Equation 7).

$$G=(V, E) \tag{7}$$

The vertex set V of this graph stands for the collection's documents the arc set E depicts hyperlinks connecting these.

In contrast to the corpus, which is our coarsest element, a document constitutes an atomic piece of information. From it, we can distinguish two important components: text and hyperlinks. In that sense, a document can be considered as the duple shown in Equation 8.

$$d_j = (L_j, W_j) \tag{8}$$

From the former equation, note that:

- L_j represents the set of neighbors of the document and corresponds to a set
  - ◦ $L_j = \{l: l \in V \land ([d_j, l] \in E \lor [l, d_j] \in E)\}$
- W_j corresponds to a duple $W_j = (A_j, B_j)$, where:
  - ◦ A_j is the anchor text of the document (a set of words)
  - ◦ B_j is the rest of the text (also a set)

Now, a topic—our entity of major interest—can be formally defined as in Equation 9.

$$T_i=(C_i, P_i) \tag{9}$$

From this definition, let us note that:

- C_i is the document cluster of the topic, which is actually a subset of the corpus graph vertex set
  - ◦ $C_i \subset V$
- $P_i = (K_i, R_i)$ represents a duple of topic properties, where:
  - ◦ K_i is the topic tag and is denoted by a set of keywords
    - $K_i \subset \left\{ w_i : w_i \in \bigcup_0^{|C_i|} W_j \right\}$
  - ◦ R_i is a subset of the most representative documents, according to some ranking metric
    - $R_i \subset C_i$

Some examples (from a movie context) of this formalization consist of the following:

Document:

nicole=({oscar, renee, russell, tom}, [{"Nicole", "Kidman"}, {"Nicole", "Kidman"}])

Topic:

LOTR=({frodo, Gandalf, lotr1, lotr2, lotr3, peter}, [{"lord", "rings", "movies"}, {lotr1, lotr2, lotr3}])

As just stated, the first example represents a document (let us just assume that the text of the documents and their title is the same, for space reasons), and the second one represents a topic.

Operations compose another important part of our conceptual framework; however, these shall be explained along with our approach.

3.2 Graph Local Clustering for Topic Discovery

Our basic assumption is that *topics have the structure of a social community*, where—by definition—there are more connections to the inside than to the outside of the group. For example, let us consider an article about basketball: it seems more natural to think of this document as having links towards and from articles like "Michael Jordan" and "NBA", i.e. documents belonging to the same subject matter, than to "mathematics" or "chaos theory", i.e. documents belonging to different topics. In fact, the notion of a document being similar in content to the ones linking it has been empirically proven by Menczer (2001).

Being this the case, we can discover topics by searching for structures whose number of internal links surpasses the number of external ones—i.e., by looking for nuclei or "peaks" of high relative density. This kind of task is precisely executed by *graph clustering techniques* (a.k.a. community detection methods). Nevertheless, because topics are overlapping by nature and Web collections are usually massive, a non-exclusive approach that achieves a certain degree of scalability is desirable. As a consequence, we propose to adapt the Graph Local Clustering (GLC) methodology

(Virtanen, 2003; Schaeffer, 2005) for our purposes, as it complies with these three needs: finds communities, is prepared for detecting covers, and can process large graphs.

GLC employs *local search* to detect cohesive sub-graphs by iteratively including and excluding elements in the *vicinity* of a starting point (an initial document set called "seed"), such that a *density-based fitness value* is increased (therefore note that it can be seen as a constructive "bottom-up" method).

For instance, let us suppose that our starting point is a node A (then our seed S consists of $\{A\}$ and the resulting cluster C_i initially is equal to this same set), and this node has a neighborhood $L_A = \{B, C, D\}$; if the addition of node B shows to improve the current fitness value (e.g., relative density), then this element becomes part of the current document cluster, i.e. $C_i = \{A, B\}$. In that case, the new neighborhood to explore for the next round becomes $\{L_A \cup L_B\} - C_i$ (note that those nodes already included in the cluster should be left out of the neighborhood to avoid cycles); now, let us assume that, after several rounds $C_i = \{A, B, C, H, J, T\}$. If it is determined that deletion of improves the fitness value, then the new current cluster is $C_i - \{H\}$. Eventually, this cluster construction method complies with a termination criterion and we have discovered *one* cohesive group; the repetition of this procedure at the end yields a set of clusters—that is, a *clustering* of the graph. By carrying out this method, the three demands previously stated are fulfilled on the following ways:

- By attempting to maximize a fitness function based on density, the mechanism actually tries to discover a community "around" the starting point, thus concerning a community detection method.
- By searching on local neighborhoods, the mechanism avoids working with the entire graph at once (a practically impossible

Figure 2. Clustering functions

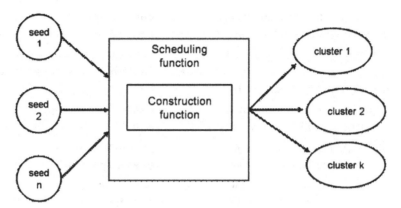

endeavor with a massive collection), thus achieving scalability.

• By creating clusters on an individual basis, the mechanism can be left unaware of which elements already belong to previously discovered groups, hence being left free to further include such elements in other clusters where they show to improve cohesion. Thus, overlapping structures (covers) are produced.

It is important to mention that, while GLC as a methodology provides general guidelines for locally discovering communities, specific details such as the search strategy, fitness function, and criteria for addition, deletion, termination, and seed processing are driven by the context and its needs. Consequently, the particular version designed for topic discovery in web collections is part of our contributions, as it varies from the original algorithm proposed by Virtanen/Schaeffer for studying network properties with the Chilean web; for example, our GLC version is the first one that considers overlapping clusters (previous attempts are partitional).

3.2.1 Topic Discovery Algorithms

As previously mentioned, our method focuses on "peaks", and a rough algorithm that we could use to detect them is the following:

1. Choose a starting position that has not been explored.
2. Find a cohesion peak given this initial position (note that cohesion, fitness, density, and relative density are being used as equivalent terms).
3. Discard those positions that are part of the peak's mountain.
4. Repeat until there are no positions left to explore.

Regarding step 2, we can consider it as covering a "depth" component of our topic discovery problem, as it is completely committed towards identifying a (single) peak of high relative density; steps 1, 3, and 4, instead, seem to handle a breadth component, since they assure that the whole document collection is scanned for group detection. By making this distinction between components, it is possible to define a pair of functions to carry out the discovery endeavor: (1) an embedded *construction function* that receives an initial position (seed) and returns the topical cluster (peak, nucleus) this position leads to and (2) a *scheduling function* that receives a set of possible starting positions and returns the corresponding set of clusters, which is generated by "iterating" the construction function. This relationship is illustrated in Figure 2.

Construction function (). Equation 10 formally presents this function; here, S_i is an input seed set (generally consisting of only one element) and φ is a set of tunable parameters. In order to describe these, let us first explain some basic aspects of the construction process. As already stated, it follows a GLC approach, which implies the selection of a search strategy and a fitness function for grouping. To define these two, we can consider an Ockham's razor principle, hence parting from a simple base and adding sophistication as needed; being this the case, a first-choice hill-climbing algorithm with relative density as fitness metric seems an adequate option. For such a mechanism, we defined the next features (parameters):

- **Element removal**. Inclusion of element elimination.
- **Candidate ordering**. Order in which nodes are revised for possible addition.
- **Neighborhood type**. Whether to choose all the neighbors of a node for the candidate set (complete neighborhood) or only the ones linked by the node (partial neighborhood).
- **Seed expansion**. Number of elements the seed should include.

Quantum. Time limit inclusion / amount of time units.

$$F(S_i, \varphi) = C_i \tag{10}$$

Figure 3 depicts the construction process with more detail; in fact, note that element removal and quantum use are explicitly portrayed here. On the next section, we will see how these and

Figure 3. Construction process algorithm

Description: Receives as input a seed S (initial set of documents) and returns a document cluster C_i. In each iteration, a new element is added to the cluster by choosing the candidate that yields the first density improvement; each time an element becomes part of the cluster, its neighbors become candidates for inclusion to the cluster at the next iteration. When relative density can no longer be increased or a specified time limit is reached, the algorithm stops. Finally, element removal is carried out as post-processing.

```
function CONSTRUCT-GLC-TOPIC(S)
  C_i ← S
  N ← CREATE-NEIGHBORHOOD(C_i)
  repeat
    ρ_curr ← ρ(C_i)
    while candidate not found ∧ neighbors left to explore do
      n_j ← next neighbor from N
      if ρ(C_i ∪ n_j) > ρ_curr then
        add n_j to C_i
        UPDATE-NEIGHBORHOOD(N, n_j)
      end if
    end while
  until (ρ_new = ρ_curr) ∨ time limit is reached

  C_i ← REMOVAL(C_i)
  return C_i
end function
```

the rest of the parameters were tuned and finally included (or excluded in some cases).

Scheduling function (χ). Equation 11 shows the formal definition of this function and how it can be depicted in terms of the construction function; is a list of seed sets, ψ concerns a parameter that indicates seed ordering and selection, and **CL** is the produced clustering.

$$\chi(S, \psi) = \mathbf{CL}, \chi(S, \psi) = F_{Si\epsilon S}(Si\,\varphi), \forall\, Si \qquad (11)$$

Regarding the seed list, it initially consists of all the documents from the corpus and is managed *dynamically*, as seeds that belong to documents already clustered (or initially clustered but then removed from the final cluster) are deleted from it.

3.3 Cluster Properties

As stated previously, to uncover the semantics of our rough clusters and present them as a usable piece of information for applications, we propose the extraction of two properties: a *topic tag* (K_i) and a set of the topic's *most representative documents* (R_i). For the case of tags, we use the classical tf-idf term weighting scheme. For the representative document subset, we employ centrality (a ranking metric for social networks). Formally, the calculation functions of these properties could be represented as in Equations 12 and 13, respectively.

$$\pi_k\left(\bigcup_0^{|C_i|} W_j\right) = K_i \qquad (12)$$

$$\pi_r(C_i) = R_i \qquad (13)$$

Let us describe each property with more detail and explain its obtainment as well (See Figure 4)

3.3.1 Topic Tags

The aim of the tag property is to *name* a topical cluster---in other words, to concretely state the theme that gathers the document set together. Furthermore, tags (usually managed as keyword

Figure 4. Tag generating function

Description: Receives the vocabulary from a C_i document cluster (denoted by W_i) and a number k of desired keywords as input for composing a topic tag (a set of terms K_i), which is returned as result. To determine the keywords, word ranking according to tf-dif weights is performed first. Before adding a keyword to the final tag, the stem of such keyword is verified against a set of stems (conveniently called *Stems*); if the stem is already in this set, the word is discarded. Keywords continue to be added one by one until the tag meets the desired length (set size).

```
function GENERATE-TAG(Wᵢ,k)    /*Get tag of length k*/
    W* ← ranking of Wᵢ according to tf-idf

    for j← 1, k do
        wⱼ ← next word from W*
        stemⱼ ← STEM(wⱼ)
        if stemⱼ ∉ Stems then
            add wⱼ ∈ W* to Kᵢ
            add stemⱼ to Stems
        end if
    end for

    return Kᵢ
end function
```

Figure 5. Representative subset generating function

Description: Receives a document set (cluster) C_i and a number k of desired outstanding members to produce a document subset R_i. Document ranking according to degree centrality is performed, and the top k documents are selected as members of R_i.

```
function REP-DOCS(C_i, k)      /*Get k most central documents*/
  R*← ranking of C_i according to degree centrality

  for j← 1, k do
    add r_j ∈ R* to R_i
  end for

  return R_i
end function
```

collections), make a topic *searchable* and are becoming universally accepted as descriptors for WWW resources (Treese, 2006; Smith, 2008).

Regarding the method for (automatic) keyword extraction, a direct option is to use the tf-idf (text frequency-inverse document frequency) term weighting scheme (Salton, 1988), which assigns importance scores to words according to their frequency in the document and the entire collection. This approach is solid and has previously been utilized for automatic tagging (Brooks, 2006; Chirita 2007).

In order to adapt tf-idf to our context, each document cluster is treated as a pseudo-document; therefore, frequency measurements are carried out as if the terms found in the cluster all belonged to a single piece of information. Furthermore, stemming has to be considered in order to prevent redundancy.

3.3.2 Set of Representative Documents

The goal of the representative document subset descriptor is to *capture* the essence of a topical cluster; in that sense, we could consider it as the "heart" of the topic. In that sense, it structures (presents in an organized manner) the topic and synthesizes it.

Because obtaining the most outstanding documents for a given cluster can be treated as a ranking problem, we can use SNA centrality/prestige measurements---certainly not uncommon measurements for Web data, as they are calculated in Google's famous PageRank (Brin, 1998). Now, for prestige calculation, there are several alternative measures, e.g. degree, eigenvector, and betweenness. From these, we find *degree centrality* as convenient and useful for several motives: it concerns a light-weight metric, it is acquainted with our link-count working approach, and it is best suited for measuring *local relevance* (Scott, 2000; Feldman, 2007).

To measure node prestige in a cluster, we can see the cluster as a network by itself, thus eliminating external links from consideration when carrying out calculations. As a consequence, we only take as neighbors of a node those vertices that are inside the cluster, even though this given node has more neighbors on the actual document graph. For example, if a node "A" has ten neighbors in the document graph, but only seven belong to the cluster where "A" is in, then its neighborhood size is seven. This calculation is done (independently) for every cluster "A" is in. The formula for *cluster degree centrality* is shown in equations 14 and 15. On the other hand, Figure 5 presents how to generate the tag.

Table 2. Examples of cluster properties (tag and document subset)

Tag (K)	Most representative documents (R)
software, windows, system, computer, server	Computer software Windows NT Random access memory
hiv, aids, infection, antiretroviral, virus	Antiretroviral drug AIDS pandemic AIDS in the United States
jedi, wars, star, palpatine, skywalker	Star Wars: Clone Wars Star Wars Jedi Knight: Jedi Academy Star Wars Jedi Knight: Dark Forces II
algebra, vector, space, frac, group	Field (mathematics) Topological space Determinant Matrix (mathematics) Polynomial

$$C_D(v) = \frac{\Gamma(v, C_i)}{|C_i|} \qquad (14)$$

$$\Gamma(v, C_i) = \{n: n \in C_i \wedge ((v, n) \in E \vee (n, v) \in E)\} \qquad (15)$$

Finally, let us present several examples of topic properties; these are shown in Table 2.

4. EXPERIMENTS AND RESULTS

The primary intention of validation in our case consists of supporting a fundamental hypothesis: *the discovered groups are topics*. As a consequence, the aim of the evaluation procedure is to *provide evidence of the clusters' topical coherence* (also referred to as "topicness" or "topicality"). However, before getting into validation details (e.g., setup, results, and findings), it is necessary to first describe the clustering performed on the Wikipedia corpus and condense the most important results (i.e., report the inputs, parameters, and outputs).

4.1 Clustering Wikipedia

To test our method, topic extraction via GLC and property calculation were carried out over the popular corpus of Wikipedia.

Parameter refinement. Before properly discussing experiments and results, it is important to describe how clustering parameters were tuned. Such process was carried out by generating two Wikipedia sub-collections and running exploratory experiments on them, where each experiment counted with a different parameter setup. With respect to the sub-collections, these were automatically gathered by only keeping those nodes whose degree fell into a particular range (hence pruning out the rest); these corpora consisted of several thousands of articles and hundreds of thousands of links. Moreover, the inclusion and value of parameters was evaluated according to quality (resulting relative density, coverage, and redundancy) and feasibility (time and memory). The final choices concern the following:

- Element removal inclusion
- Partial neighborhood exploration
- Candidate sorting according to the number of prospective internal links
- Random seed selection

- Time limit inclusion

The seed expansion feature was finally not included, as the tradeoff was larger than the actual benefits.

Dataset. The specific dataset, pre-processed with a script called *Wikiprep*, consisted of 800, 000 articles and 20 million links. After clustering, more than 55,000 topics with community structure (i.e. $\rho \leq 0.5$) were found.

4.2 Topic Validation

To assess the quality of the discovered clusters, we employed both internal and external evaluation techniques over a sample of clusters. Internal validation was applied to gather a preliminary assessment of cluster quality and group cohesion, while external validation was carried out with the clear intent of having a more thorough evaluation of our results. Let us detail each of these.

4.2.1 Internal Evaluation

To do internal evaluation, we relied on (a) intra-cluster vs. inter-cluster proximity (a.k.a. *compaction* and *separation*) and (b) a benchmark for structural cohesion. Regarding the former, it concerns a straightforward evaluation metric, as the elements of a cluster should be, by definition, more similar to each other than to elements of different clusters (i.e., intra-cluster proximity should be greater than inter-cluster proximity). With respect to the latter, surpassing an external quality threshold indicates that a cluster is well-formed.

To display intra vs. inter-cluster proximity results, we used visual similarity matrices, where a high compaction and a low separation are both indicated by an outstanding main diagonal on the matrices. Overall proximity between a pair of clusters—denoted by a cell of the matrix—was based on the average proximity between all pairs of documents from these clusters. For the case of compaction, the document pairs were from the

same cluster; for separation, each pair consisted of documents from different clusters. Formally:

$$compactness(C_i) = \frac{\sum proximity(d_a, d_b)}{|C_i|(|C_i|-1)}, d_a, d_b \in C_i$$

$$separation(C_i, C_j) = \frac{\sum proximity(d_a, d_b)}{|C_i|(|C_j|)},$$
$$d_a \in C_i, d_b \in C_j, i \neq j$$

$$proximity(d_a, d_b) =$$
$$cosim(d_a, d_b) \lor sr(d_a, d_b) \lor J(d_a, d_b)$$

Proximity metrics. Three different metrics were utilized: cosine similarity, semantic relatedness, and the Jaccard index.

- **Cosine similarity (cosim).** Cosine similarity measures the "cosine of the angle" between a pair of documents by calculating the normalized dot product between two document vectors—traditionally, term weight vectors previously obtained from text frequencies; values range from 0 (no similarity) to 1 (identical). Because there is no text involved in the clustering process, this metric is actually orthogonal to our method, hence constituting a form of semantic validation (structural cohesion is being backed-up with textual similarity).
- **Semantic relatedness (sr).** Created specifically for the Wikipedia domain and in spirit similar to co-citation—in fact based on the Normalized Google Distance (Cilibrasi, 2007), this measurement obtains the distance between a pair of articles by means of their in-links. A distance of 0 indicates a high similarity, and an infinite distance indicates no similarity at all.

- **Jaccard index (J).** This well-known index reports the similarity between two sets (also ranges from 0 to 1, where 1 implies that the sets are identical). For our case, each set is composed by a document's outlinks—therefore note that the index particularly resembles bibliographic coupling here. Along with semantic relatedness, the Jaccard metric represents an alternative way to measure structural properties (similarity, more than anything), as opposed to relative density, which measures cohesion.

Sampling. Because pairwise comparisons are very expensive for a considerable number of clusters, sampling was required; however, instead of only gathering a random sample, a systematic one was obtained by sorting clusters according to their relative density and selecting one at every k steps (as to complete a sample of n elements). By

choosing elements in this form, we tried to assure that groups with various densities and sizes would be part of the sample. Another action taken to save costs was to use only a representative amount of documents for each cluster; therefore, each of the evaluated groups was depicted by a subset of the 30 most outstanding documents (according to the previously used centrality metric).

Benchmark setup. To complement the results obtained from the similarity matrices, we compared our clusters against a benchmark as well. For this case, the chosen metric was SNA's relative strength ratio, which should be greater than 1.0 if a cluster is cohesive. Because calculating this ratio is not expensive, it was possible to evaluate all of our groups.

Results and Discussion

From the former calculations (depicted in Figure 6), intra-cluster similarity was on average

Figure 6. Resulting similarity matrices (from top to bottom and left to right): cosine, Jaccard, and semantic relatedness. Note that for semantic relatedness low values are favorable, as it consists of a distance (dissimilarity metric)

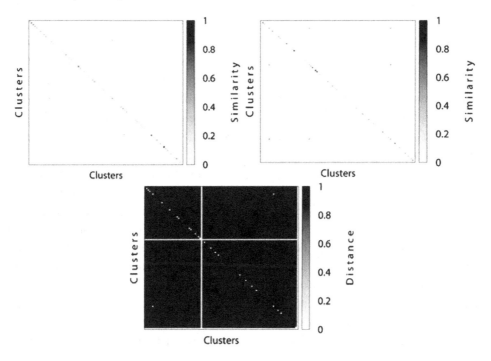

46 times higher than inter-cluster similarity for cosine similarity and 190 times higher for the Jaccard index; for semantic relatedness, the ratio of unrelated articles (infinite values) was twice as higher among elements of different clusters.

For results regarding the relative strength ratio, let us note that less than 1% of the clusters lied below the threshold. On the other hand, it is also interesting to observe that there was a positive correlation (0.21) between the strength ratio and relative density, although this is partly expected, as both measurements have similar foundations.

As discussion for these results, it seems fair to state that our internal validation outcomes reveal a well formed clustering. Regarding this aspect, the three chosen metrics for compaction and separation support this claim on an individual and collective basis; the former is accomplished by the consistent depiction of a cluster compliance *pattern* and the latter is achieved by the *coverage* of different perspectives (e.g. similarity and dissimilarity, text and links, semantic and clustering levels etc.). The group quality (benchmark) measurement, on its own, represents an alternative form of proving cohesion.

Nevertheless, it also seems fair to discuss the limitations of this kind of evaluation. Perhaps one of the most important concerns *scalability* (both for the validation approach itself and visualization tools); in that sense, the larger the sample the more expensive the evaluation procedure became. Therefore, with this validation approach we can obtain only a *partial perspective* of quality. Similarly, the strength ratio solely provides an initial quality insight.

4.2.2 External Evaluation

Since external evaluation requires pre-defined references or models for comparison, we chose to employ (a) Wikipedia's category network and (b) human criteria. The aim with the category network was to measure the existing correspondence between our grouping and an established

classification, hence assuming that if a particular discovered group matches a Wikipedia category, it can effectively be considered as a topic. Similarly, we assume that if a human being is able to identify a document group as a topic, the group is indeed held together by a common thematic.

4.2.2.1 Alignment with Wikipedia's Category Network

Because almost every Wikipedia article is contained into one or more categories, and these are arranged into a loose hierarchical structure—by "loose", we mean that the hierarchy is not strictly enforced—, it is possible to extract a category network from the corpus. This "wisdom of crowds" resource is reliable (is constantly revised by Wikipedia editors), has been previously employed in other works (Schönhofen, 2006), and can be used for overlapping schemes; as a result, it seems an adequate choice for gathering a set of reference classes.

As previously mentioned, the idea with this set of reference classes was to create an alignment, where a given cluster is the best for a given category and vice versa, to subsequently obtain standard accuracy measurements. To achieve this alignment, we had to enforce a hierarchy out of the network (create a category tree, properly) and make sure that every cluster would be matched with the most appropriate category, in terms of size. Additionally, uncategorized elements had to be taken into account to avoid affecting our final scores. Details of the process can be consulted in (Garza, 2010).

Results. Table 3 shows the most significant results from the alignment. In general, the average F-score is neither excellent nor poor; nevertheless, it is important to highlight that more than 20% of the clusters accomplished a perfect or nearly perfect score (most of these had also a relative density near 1.0). Probably the most relevant one concerns the correlation found between relative density and F-score, which was of 0.34 (moderate); such correlation proves our intuitive assumption

Figure 7. Experiment design for user tests

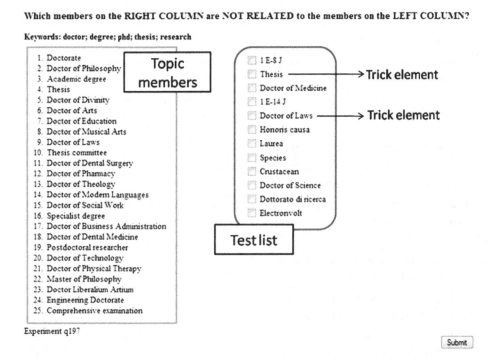

Experiment q197

Table 3. Alignment results

Aligned clusters	2,053
Relative density (avg.)	0.62
F-score (avg.)	0.53
Cluster size (avg.)	177

of structure (relative density) indicating topicality. F-score and precision curves can be appreciated in Figure 7, along with user tests.

4.2.2.2 Tests with Users

A user-based task that allows expressing evaluation results in terms of accuracy (recall, precision) and has been used recently on the topic mining domain consists of *outlier detection*—see, for example, the *topic intrusion* task designed by Boyd et al. (2009). In that sense, by correctly detecting elements that do not correspond to a given document group, the users are actually acknowledging that the presented cluster makes sense to them; if,

on the other hand, they cannot spot such spurious elements, this probably means that a topic is not being identified out of the group.

Design and setup. On each individual test (one per cluster), users were basically presented two lists: a list of topic members (positive examples) and a test list, where part of the elements were also topic members, but another fraction consisted of outliers, i.e., non-related items (see Figure 7). Consequently, the task consisted of detecting all of the latter. For the test set, 200 clusters were randomly selected; to avoid unknown themes, pure English person names and geographical clusters were discarded. For each cluster, its 30 most rep-

Table 4. User test results

	Precision	Recall	F-score
Min.	0.2	0.2	0.2
Max.	1.0	1.0	1.0
Avg.	0.92	0.93	*0.92*
Answered—366 Valid—327 (89%)			

resentative documents were taken, five of these being placed (by chance) on the test list and the rest on the topic members list. Similarly, several elements were drawn from different clusters to conform the outliers on the test list (the clusters and outlier elements being chosen at random as well). Moreover, to prevent careless answers (e.g., a user selecting all items on the test list), a pair of items belonging to the topic members list was copied into the test list; tests having both of these elements marked as outliers (an event that could happen with a probability of less than 0.7%) were discarded. This test set was uploaded to Amazon's Mechanical Turk (http://www.mturk.com), a reliable on-line platform that hosts tasks to be performed by anonymous workers (users) for a certain fee. Another copy of the test set was printed and handed to directly contacted users—mainly students from our university.

Results. A total of 366 tests were answered—327 of which were valid (89%). The achieved F-score was of 0.92 on average, and this greatly supports the central hypothesis. More results are reported in Table 4 and Figure 8.

5. RELATED WORK

To have a better understanding of how the presented work is different from other approaches, let us start by classifying it according to the taxonomies stated at the background section; such classification can be appreciated in Table 5.

Now, let us briefly describe approaches that fit into one or more areas covered by our method

as well, with the intent of highlighting similarities and differences.

Topic + Web structure mining. Modha and Spangler (2003) present hypertext clustering based on three pillars: a hybrid similarity metric, a novel variant of k-means, and the inclusion of proper-

Figure 8. External evaluation results. FC=F-score curve for category alignment tests (scores sorted in descending order), PRC=Precision vs. recall standard 11-level curve for category alignment tests, FU=F-score curve for user tests, and PRU=Precision vs. recall curve for user tests

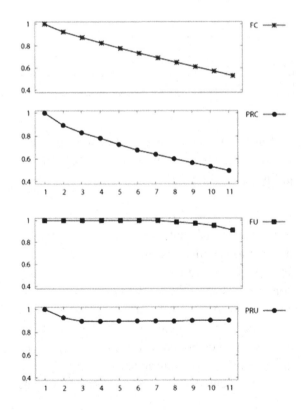

Table 5. Classification for the approach

Web Structure Mining	
Approach type	Cut-based, link count approach
Discovered group type	Cohesive groups
Complexity management	Problem decomposition (local search, mainly)
Sub-task	Network (graph) clustering
Topic mining	
Representation	Object-oriented (document list + label)
Approach type	Hybrid
Sub-task	Flow: Enumeration → labeling, distillation
Wikipedia mining	
Semantic Web paradigm	Soft
Information source	Structure
Use	Source and destination

ties (information ``nuggets'') into the clustering process. The topic mining task is composed by enumeration, labeling, and distillation. Resembling some aspects of this work, He et al. (2001) do topic enumeration and distillation by clustering webpages with a spectral method that employs a hybrid similarity metric; the central aim is to enhance information organization by presenting a list of the authoritative webpages given a user information request.

Although these works discover groups of topically-related documents and either refine those groups or calculate properties as well, they carry out a different kind of task: data clustering. In that sense, their working paradigm is different from the one we use. Furthermore, their information source is mixed, as text and structure are simultaneously used for measuring similarity.

Topic + Wikipedia mining. Topic modeling by grouping keywords with a novel distance metric based on the Jensen-Shannon divergence (which originally calculates the similarity between a pair of probability distributions) is the main contribution of the work by Wartena and Brussee (2008); such approach is tested over a subset of the Dutch Wikipedia and a handful of its categories and shows to yield correct results. On the other hand,

Schönhofen (2006) does topic labeling with the aid of the on-line encyclopedia's base of categories; in that sense, the aim is to assign labels from a fixed set to a group of documents. For this case, the fixed label set is represented by categories from Wikipedia, as this corpus is considered a taxonomy of wide coverage.

This other pair of initiatives can be clearly differentiated from our approach in the type of topic mining task they perform, as the former executes modeling, and the latter carries out labeling. Moreover, in the case of Schönhofen, his work uses Wikipedia more as a source of information than a target corpus.

Graph Local Clustering. The already mentioned work of Virtanen/Schaeffer (2003), which validates graph generative models to gain insight on the cluster formation process of the Web, introduces the GLC method. The general motivation for such approach is placed upon pointing out that global approaches do not scale well for large graphs. Consequently, a graph local clustering approach that combines simulated annealing with a fitness function composed of local and relative density is presented and applied over the largest connected component of the Chilean Web to produce a flat partition of pages. A more recent approach (but almost identical in spirit to the original GLC) is presented by Lancichinetti et al. (2009); such approach consists of a local clustering algorithm that detects hierarchical covers.

Both of these works are closely related to ours in the sense that they introduce a methodology from which our method is actually a variant. However, the key difference is precisely given by the topic domain, i.e. the semantics of the method. Similarly, these approaches are focused solely on grouping, while we also consider description (topic properties).

6. CONCLUSION

We have presented a mechanism for automatic topic discovery, which is based on a layered conceptual model where clustering and semantics management are the main components. The particular approach is centered on graph clustering, as the aim is to find communities, based on the assumption that these tend to represent topics on information networks. To deal with massive structures (common on the Web domain) and detect overlapping communities, we specifically use a graph local clustering approach, which consists of a simple base (hill-climbing and relative density) and a set of domain-oriented tunable parameters. The overall mechanism is divided into two functions: a construction function that discovers a single topic given an initial seed and a scheduling function that iterates the former with a dynamic list of seeds to produce a clustering over the whole document collection. Another important part of the approach is the calculation of topic properties; in our case, we extract a topic tag and a set of representative documents by means of ranking and selection procedures. Our approach has been tested with various validation techniques and results indicate that our discovered groups are topics indeed.

6.1 Concluding Remarks

Throughout the present work, we found out that a high relative density in node groups indicates that these nodes (documents) tend to share a common thematic in Wikipedia-like encyclopedic knowledge corpora. Furthermore, this was shown on an experimental basis—mainly by comparing these groups (clusters) against a set of reference classes (categories) that belong to the case study corpus (Wikipedia) and with the aid of human judgment. Also, topics can be detected (constructed) with an approach solely based on structure by searching for highly interlinked (dense) sub-graphs on the corpus; to identify such sub-graphs, we only require to have the links among documents. Additionally, our specific approach is able to consider the whole document collection by focusing on specific regions or (local) neighborhoods at a given time. As a result, the corpus is not viewed all at once, but by parts. That way, all the search space is gradually covered when attempting to place the different documents into one or more topical clusters and scalability is achieved.

Other interesting remarks are given by the mechanism's behavior. On one hand, we were able to notice that the construction algorithm is not challenged by complicated but by complex structures. In that sense, if the explored structures were clearly communities, topics could be easily detected, despite the size of such communities; on the contrary, intricate structures were hard (mostly in terms of time) for the algorithm. Another important feature of our approach is that it finds a specific kind of topics, namely *communitarian topics*; such groups are both highly cohesive and treat a certain thematic. Related to the former is the fact that our method actually discovers meta-topics, if we consider that Wikipedia articles by themselves already constitute a topic. Finally, given that our GLC-based algorithm is committed towards discovering nuclei of high relative density regardless of the starting point (therefore being able to discard this point at the end if it shows not to be part of the nucleus after all), it can be considered as a corpus-centered mechanism—unlike other approaches that are committed instead of finding a group tightly related to their seed.

6.2 Future Work

Future work can be headed towards different directions, as to know:

- **Management of temporal aspects**. Because repositories tend to change over time (documents are constantly modified, added, and deleted), it would be convenient for the method to care about these issues.
- **Hierarchical grouping**. Just as topics are overlapping by nature, they are also hierarchical by nature. As a consequence, it becomes practically necessary to consider how to produce this kind of scheme.
- **Refinements and variants**. There is a significant number of variants that could be tried out; for instance, weighted graphs and other types of networks (perhaps social ones).
- **Incorporation of alternative information sources**. As we just said, our method discovers cohesive groups; however, we strongly believe that the inclusion of other information sources, such as text, can result in the extraction of topics that are not necessarily cohesive.

ACKNOWLEDGMENT

We would like to thank the National Council of Science and Technology (CONACYT), as well as the Context Intelligence Research Chair from the Tec de Monterrey, Campus Monterrey, Elisa Schaeffer, and Eduardo Ramírez for their support and contributions towards the present research project.

REFERENCES

Allan, J. (2002). *Introduction to topic detection and tracking*. Boston: Kluwer Academic Publishers.

Auer, S., & Lehmann, J. (2007). *What have Innsbruck and Leipzig in common? Extracting semantics from Wiki content*. Lecture Notes in Computer Science 4519, 503. Boyd-Graber, J, Chang, J, Gerrish, S, Wang, C, & Blei, D. (2009). *Reading Tea Leaves: How Humans Interpret Topic Models*. [NIPS]. *Advances in Neural Information Processing Systems*, 31.

Brin, S., & Page, L. (1998). The anatomy of a large-scale hypertextual. *Web search engine* . *Computer Networks and ISDN Systems*, *30*, 1–7, 107–117. doi:10.1016/S0169-7552(98)00110-X

Brooks, C., & Montanez, N. (2006). Improved annotation of the blogosphere via autotagging and hierarchical clustering. In *Proceedings of the 15th international conference on World Wide Web*, ACM, pp. 632.

Chakrabarti, S., Dom, B., Gibson, D., Kleinberg, J., Kumar, R., & Raghavan, P. (1999). Mining the link structure of the World Wide Web. *IEEE Computer*, *32*(8), 60–67.

Chakrabarti, S., Dom, B., Gibson, D., Kumar, S., Raghavan, P., Rajagopalan, S., & Tomkins, A. (1998). Experiments in topic distillation In *ACM SIGIR Workshop on Hypertext Information Retrieval on the Web*, Melbourne, Australia.

Chirita, P., Costache, S., Nejdl, W., & Handschuh, S. (2007). P-tag: large scale automatic generation of personalized annotation tags for the web In *Proceedings of the 16th international conference on World Wide Web*, 854. New York: ACM.

Cilibrasi, R., & Vitanyi, P. (2007). The Google Similarity Distance. *IEEE Transactions on Knowledge and Data Engineering*, *19*, 370–383. doi:10.1109/TKDE.2007.48

Cook, D., & Holder, L. (2006). *Mining graph data*. New York: Wiley-Interscience. doi:10.1002/0470073047

Ertöz, L., Steinbach, M., & Kumar, V. (2003). Finding topics in collections of documents: A shared nearest neighbor approach. *Clustering and Information Retrieval, 1*, 83–104.

Feldman, R., & Sanger, J. (2007). *The text mining handbook*. New York: Cambridge University Press.

Flake, G., Lawrence, S., & Giles, C. (2000). Efficient identification of Web communities. In *Proceedings of the sixth ACM SIGKDD international conference on Knowledge discovery and data mining*, pp. 150–160. New York: ACM.

Flake, G., Lawrence, S., Giles, C., & Coetzee, F. (2002). Self-organization and identification of Web communities. *Computer, 35*(3), 66–70. doi:10.1109/2.989932

Flake, G., Pennock, D., & Fain, D. (2003). The self-organized Web: The yin to the Semantic Webs yang. *IEEE Intelligent Systems, 18*(4), 75–77.

Garza, S. (2010). *A process for extracting groups of thematically related documents in encyclopedic knowledge web collections by means of a pure hyperlink-based clustering approach*. PhD Thesis, May 2010, Tecnologico de Monterrey, Mexico.

Griffiths, T. L., Steyvers, M., & Tenenbaum, J. B. (2007). Topics in semantic representation. *Psychological Review, 114*, 211–244. doi:10.1037/0033-295X.114.2.211

He, X., Ding, C., Zha, H., & Simon, H. (2001). Automatic topic identification using webpage clustering. In *Proceedings IEEE International Conference on Data Mining, San Jose, CA*, pp. 195–202.

Jain, A., Murty, M., & Flynn, P. (1999). Data clustering: a review. *ACM Computing Surveys, 31*(3), 264–323. doi:10.1145/331499.331504

Jarvis, R., & Patrick, E. (1973). Clustering using a similarity measure based on shared near neighbors. *IEEE Transactions on Computers, 22*(11), 1025–1034. doi:10.1109/T-C.1973.223640

Jo, Y., Lagoze, C., & Giles, C. (2007). Detecting research topics via the correlation between graphs and texts. In *Proceedings of the 13th ACM SIGKDD international conference on Knowledge discovery and data mining*, ACM, pp. 379.

Karypis, G., Han, E., & Kumar, V. (1999). Chameleon: A hierarchical clustering algorithm using dynamic modeling. *IEEE computer 32*(8), 68–75.

Karypis, G., & Kumar, V. (1999). A fast and high quality multilevel scheme for partitioning irregular graphs. *SIAM Journal on Scientific Computing, 20*(1), 359. doi:10.1137/S1064827595287997

Kleinberg, J. (1999). Authoritative sources in a hyperlinked environment. *Journal of the ACM, 46*(5), 604–632. doi:10.1145/324133.324140

Kumar, R., Raghavan, P., Rajagopalan, S., Sivakumar, D., Tompkins, A., & Upfal, E. (2000). The Web as a graph. In *Proceedings of the nineteenth ACM SIGMOD-SIGACT-SIGART symposium on Principles of database systems*, pp. 1–10. New York: ACM

Kumar, R., Raghavan, P., Rajagopalan, S., & Tomkins, A. (1999). Trawling the web for emerging cyber-communities. *Computer Networks, 31*(11), 1481–1493. doi:10.1016/S1389-1286(99)00040-7

Lancichinetti, A., Fortunato, S., & Kertesz, J. (2009). Detecting the overlapping and hierarchical community structure in complex networks. *New Journal of Physics, 11*, 033015. doi:10.1088/1367-2630/11/3/033015

Liu, B. (2007). *Web data mining: exploring hyperlinks, contents, and usage data*. New York: Springer.

Menczer, F. (2001). *Links tell us about lexical and semantic Web content*. Arxiv preprint cs/0108004.

Modha, D., & Spangler, W. (2003). *Clustering hypertext with applications to Web searching*. US Patent App 10/660,242.

Newman, M. (2003). The structure and function of complex networks. *SIAM Review, 45,* 167–256. doi:10.1137/S0036144450342480

Pirolli, P., Pitkow, J., & Rao, R. (1996). Silk from a sow's ear: extracting usable structures from the Web. In *Proceedings of the SIGCHI Conference on Human factors in computing systems: common ground*, pp.118–125. New York: ACM.

Puig-Centelles, A., Ripolles, O., & Chover, M. (2007). Identifying communities in social networks: a survey. In *Proceedings of the IADIS International Conference Web Based Communities*, pp. 350–354.

Radicchi, F., Castellano, C., Cecconi, F., Loreto, V., & Parisi, D. (2004). Defining and identifying communities in networks. *Proceedings of the National Academy of Sciences of the United States of America, 101*(9), 2658–2663. doi:10.1073/pnas.0400054101

Schaeffer, S. (2005). Stochastic local clustering for massive graphs. *Advances in Knowledge Discovery and Data Mining, 3518,* 354–360. doi:10.1007/11430919_42

Schönhofen, P. (2006). Identifying document topics using the Wikipedia category network. In *Proceedings of the 2006 IEEE/WIC/ACM International Conference on Web Intelligence*, IEEE Computer Society Washington, DC, USA, pp. 456–462.

Schwartz, R., Sista, S., & Leek, T. (2001). Unsupervised topic discovery. In *Proceedings of workshop on language modeling and information retrieval*, pp. 72–77.

Scott, J. (2000). *Social Network Analysis: a handbook* (2nd ed.). Thousand Oaks, CA: SAGE Publications.

Sista, S., Schwartz, R., Leek, T. R., & Makhoul, J. (2002). An algorithm for unsupervised topic discovery from broadcast news stories. In *Proceedings of the second international conference on Human Language Technology Research, pp. 110-114*. San Francisco: Morgan Kaufmann Publishers Inc.

Smith, G. (2008). *Tagging: People-powered Metadata for the Social Web*. Berkeley, CA: New Rider Press.

Stein, B., & Zu-Eissen, S. (2004). Topic identification: Framework and application. In *Proceedings International Conference on Knowledge Management, 399*, pp. 522–531.

Suchanek, F., Kasneci, G., & Weikum, G. (2008). Yago: A large ontology from Wikipedia and Wordnet Web. *Semantics: Science . Services and Agents on the World Wide Web, 6*(3), 203–217. doi:10.1016/j.websem.2008.06.001

Treese, W. (2006). Web 20: is it really different? *netWorker, 10*(2), 15–17. doi:10.1145/1138096.1138106

Virtanen, S. (2003). Clustering the Chilean Web. In *Proceedings of the 2003 First Latin American Web Congress*, pp. 229–231.

Wartena, C., & Brussee, R. (2008). *Topic detection by clustering keywords*. In DEXA 2008: 19th International Conference On Database & Expert Systems Applications Proceedings.

Wasserman, S., & Faust, K. (1994). *Social Network Analysis: Methods and Applications*. New York: Cambridge University Press.

Compilation of References

Agirre, E., & Martinez, D. (2001). Learning class-to-class selectional preferences. *Workshop on Computational Natural Language Learning*, ACL.

Agrawal, R., Imielinski, T., & Swami, A. (1993). Mining association rules between sets of items in large databases. In Buneman, P., & Jajodia, S. (Eds.), *ACM-SIGMOD international conference on management of data* (pp. 207–217). New York: ACM Press.

Agrawal, R., & Srikant, R. (1994). Fast algorithms for mining association rules. In J. B. Bocca, M. Jarke, & C. Zaniolo (Eds.), *Int. Conf. Very Large Databases* (pp.487-499). San Francisco: Morgan Kaufmann.

Agrawal, R., & Srikant, R. (1995). Mining sequential patterns. In P. S. Yu & A. S. P. Chen (Eds.), *Eleventh International Conference on Data Engineering* (pp.3-14). IEEE Computer Society Press.

Ahonen, H. (1999a). Knowledge discovery in documents by extracting frequent word sequences. *Library Trends*, *48*(1), 160–181.

Ahonen, H., & Doucet, A. (2005). Data mining meets collocations discovery. In Arppe, A. (Eds.), *Inquiries into Words, Constraints, and Contexts* (pp. 194–203). Juho Tupakka.

Ahonen, H. (1999). Finding all maximal frequent sequences in text. In I. Bratko & S. Dzeroski (Eds.).*International Conference on Machine Learning* (pp. 11–17).San Francisco: Morgan Kaufmann.

Akavipat, R., Wu, L.-S., Menczer, F., & Maguitman (2006). *Emerging semantic communities in peer Web search.* In P2PIR '06: Proceedings of the international workshop on Information retrieval in peer-to-peer networks, pages 1–8, New York: ACM Press.

Alexandrov, M., Gelbukh, A., & Rosso, P. (2005). An Approach to Clustering Abstracts. *LNCS, 3513,* 275–285.

Alexandrov, M., Sanchis, E., & Rosso, P. (2005). *Cluster Analysis of Railway Directory Inquire Dialogs.* Proceedings of the 8th Intern. Conf. on Text, Speech and Dialog (TSD-2005) (pp. 385-390). Carlovy Vary, Czech Rep. *LNCS 3658.* Springer.

Allan, J. (2002). *Introduction to topic detection and tracking.* Boston: Kluwer Academic Publishers.

Amati, G. (2003). *Probabilistic models for information retrieval based on divergence from randomness.* Unpublished doctoral dissertation, Department of Computing Science, University of Glasgow, UK.

Amati, G., Carpineto, C., & Romano, G. (2004). *Query difficulty, robustness and selective application of query expansion.* In Advances in Information Retrieval, 26th European Conference on IR research (pp. 127–137). Berlin / Heidelberg: Springer.

Amitay, E., Carmel, D., Lempel, R., & Soffer, A. (2004). *Scaling IR-system evaluation using term relevance sets.* In SIGIR '04: Proceedings of the 27th annual international ACM SIGIR conference on Research and development in information retrieval, pages 10–17, New York: ACM.

Angelaccio, M., Buttarazzi, B., & Patrignanell, M. (2007) Graph use to visualize web search results: Mywish 3.0. In *IV '07: Proceedings of the 11th International Conference Information Visualization* (pp. 245-250). IEEE Computer Society.

Antunes, C., & Oliveira, A. (2003). Generalization of pattern-growth methods for sequential pattern mining with gap constraints. In Perner, P., & Rosenfeld, A. (Eds.), *Machine Learning and Data Mining in Pattern Recognition, 2734* (pp. 239–251). Springer Verlag. doi:10.1007/3-540-45065-3_21

Antunes, C. (2005). *Pattern mining over nominal event sequences using constraint relaxations.* Unpublished doctoral dissertation, Instituto Superior Técnico, Lisboa.

Arapov, M. V. (1988). *Cuantitative Linguistics.* Nauka.

Armstrong, R., Freitag, D., Joachims, T., & Mitchell, T. (1995). A learning apprentice for the World Wide Web. In *AAAI spring symposium on information gathering* (pp. 6–12). WebWatcher.

Auer, S., & Lehmann, J. (2007). *What have Innsbruck and Leipzig in common? Extracting semantics from Wiki content.* Lecture Notes in Computer Science 4519, 503. Boyd- Graber, J, Chang, J, Gerrish, S, Wang, C, & Blei, D. (2009). *Reading Tea Leaves: How Humans Interpret Topic Models.* [NIPS]. *Advances in Neural Information Processing Systems, 31.*

Baevsky, V. S. (2001). Linguistic, semiotics, mathematics, and computational simulation of history of literature and poetry. *International Scientific Congress. Text, Intertext, Culture.* Azbukovnik (Ed.). Moscow.

Baeza-Yates, R., & Ribeiro-Neto, B. (1999). *Modern Information Retrieval.* Reading, MA: Addison-Wesley.

Baeza-Yates, R. A., & Raghavan, P. (2010). Next Generation Web Search. In Ceri, S., & Brambilla, M. (Eds.), *Search Computing* (pp. 11–23). Berlin, Heidelberg: Springer. doi:10.1007/978-3-642-12310-8_2

Bai, J., Nie, J. Y., & Cao, G. (2005). Integrating Compound Terms in Bayesian Text Classification. In A. Skowron et al. (Ed.), *IEEE / WIC / ACM International Conference on Web Intelligence (WI 2005).* 19-22, September 2005, Compiegne, France.

Baldonado, M. Q. W., & Winograd, T. (1997). *SenseMaker: an information-exploration interface supporting the contextual evolution of a user's interests.* In Proceedings of the SIGCHI conference on human factors in computing systems (pp. 11–18). New York: ACM Press.

Banerjee, S., & Pedersen, T. (2003). Extended Gloss Overlaps as a Measure of Semantic Relatedness, *IJCAI-03, Proceedings of the Eighteenth International Joint Conference on Artificial Intelligence* (pp. 805-810). Boston: M. Kaufmann.

Baroni, M., & Lenci, A. (2009). One distributional memory, many semantic spaces. *Proceedings of the EACL 2009 Geometrical Models for Natural Language Semantics (GEMS) Workshop,* East Stroudsburg PA: ACL, 1–8.

Beitzel, S. M., Jensen, E. C., Chowdhury, A., & Grossman, D. (2003). *Using Titles and Category Names from Editor-Driven Taxonomies for Automatic Evaluation.* In CIKM '03: Proceedings of the 12th International Conference on Information and Knowledge Management (pp. 17–23), New York: ACM Press.

Belew, K. (1989) Adaptive information retrieval: Using a connectionist representation to retrieve and learn about documents. In *SIGIR '89: Proceedings of the 12th annual international ACM conference on Research and development in information retrieval* (pp 11-20). ACM Press.

Berger, A., & Lafferty, J. (1999). Information Retrieval as Statistical Translation. *In Proceedings of the 22nd ACM SIGIR Conference on Research and Development in Information Retrieval.* 222-229. Berkeley, CA, USA.

Bergsma, S., Lin, D., & Goebel, R. (2008). Discriminative Learning of Selectional Preference for Unlabeled Text. *Proceedings of the 2008 Conference on Empirical Methods in Natural Language Processing,* pp. 59–68

Berry, M. W., & Castellanos, M. (2008). *Survey of Text Mining II clustering, classification and retrieval.* London: Springer.

Berry, M. W., Dumais, S. T., & O'Brien, G. W. (1995). Using linear algebra for intelligent information retrieval. *SIAM Review, 37*(4), 573–595. doi:10.1137/1037127

Blei, D., Ng, A., & Jordan, M. I. (2003). Latent Dirichlet allocation. *Journal of Machine Learning Research, 3,* 993–1022.

Blei, D., Gri, T., Jordan, M., & Tenenbaum, J. (2004). Hierarchical topic models and the nested chinese restaurant process. *Advances in Neural Information Processing Systems, 16.*

Blei, D., Ng, A., & Jordan, M. (2003). Latent dirichlet allocation. *Journal of Machine Learning Research, 3,* 993–1022.

Blei, D. & Lafferty, J., (2009). Visualizing topics with multi-word expressions. Retrieved from http//arxiv.org/abs/0907.1013.

Blei, D., & Lafferty, J. (2007). A correlated topic model of science. *I*(1), 17-35.

Bollegala, D., Matsuo, Y., & Ishizuka, M. (2007). *An Integrated Approach to Measuring Semantic Similarity between Words Using Information Available on the Web. HLT-NAACL* (pp. 340–347). The Association for Computational Linguistics.

Bolshakov, I. A. (2005). An Experiment in Detection and Correction of Malapropisms through the Web. *LNCS, 3406,* 803–815.

Bolshakov, I. A., Galicia-Haro, S. N., & Gelbukh, A. (2005). *Detection and Correction of Malapropisms in Spanish by means of Internet Search.* TSD-2005. *Springer LNAI, 3658,* 115–122.

Bonafonte, A., et al. (2000). Desarrollo de un sistema de dialogo oral en dominios restringidos. In *I Jornadas en Tecnología de Habla.* Sevilla. Spain.

Bordogna, G., Campi, A., Psaila, G., & Ronchi, S. (2011). Disambiguated query suggestions and personalized content-similarity and novelty ranking of clustered results to optimize web searches. *Information Processing & Management..*doi:10.1016/j.ipm.2011.03.008

Bordogna, G., & Pasi, G. (2011). *Soft Clustering for Information Retrieval Applications, WIREs Data Mining and Knowledge Discovery, electronic Journal Wiley & Sons* (pp. 1–9). Inc, January/February.

Bordogna, G., & Psaila, G. (2011) Soft Operators for exploring information granules of Web search results, In Proceedings of the *World Conference on Soft Computing,* May 23-25, San Francisco, 2011

Bordogna, G., Campi, A., Psaila, G., & Ronchi, S. (2008) A language for manipulating groups of clustered web documents results, In *ACM CIKM '08: Proceedings of the: the 17th ACM conference on Information and knowledge management* (pp 23-32). ACM Press.

Bordogna, G., Campi, A., Psaila, G., & Ronchi, S. (2008a). *An interaction framework for mobile web search.* In MoMM2008: Proceedings of the 6th International Conference on Advances in Mobile Computing and Multimedia, (pp. 183–191).

Boyan, J., Freitag, D., & Joachims, T. (1996). *A machine learning architecture for optimizing Web search engines.* In In AAAI Workshop on Internet-based Information Systems.

Boyd-Graber, J., Chang, J. J., Gerrish, S., Wang, C., & Blei, D. (2009). Reading tea leaves How humans interpret topic models. In Bengio, Y., Schuurmans, D., Lafferty, J., Williams, C. K. I., & Culotta, A. (Eds.), *Advances in Neural Information Processing Systems* (pp. 288–296).

Brin, S., & Page, L. (1998). The anatomy of a large-scale hypertextual. *Web search engine. Computer Networks and ISDN Systems, 30,* 1–7, 107–117. doi:10.1016/S0169-7552(98)00110-X

Broder, A. (2002). A taxonomy of web search. *SIGIR Forum, 36*(2), 3–10. doi:10.1145/792550.792552

Brodovsky, A. I., Makagonov, P., Ochagova, L. N., & Sboychakov, K. O. (1999). Information searching system for full texts database on the problem "Sustainable cities' development" based on IRBIS. *Computer techniques and technologies in libraries on the eve of Third Millennium* (pp. 57-63). Moscow.

Brooks, C., & Montanez, N. (2006). Improved annotation of the blogosphere via autotagging and hierarchical clustering. In *Proceedings of the 15th international conference on World Wide Web,* ACM, pp. 632.

Budanitsky, E., & Graeme, H. (2001). *Semantic distance in WorldNet: An experimental, application-oriented evaluation of five measures,* NAACL Workshop on WordNet and other lexical resources.

Budzik, J., Hammond, K. J., & Birnbaum, L. (2001). Information Access in Context. *Knowledge-Based Systems, 14*(1–2), 37–53. doi:10.1016/S0950-7051(00)00105-2

Byrne, E., & Hunter, A. (2005). Evaluating violations of expectations to find exceptional information. *Data & Knowledge Engineering, 54*(2), 97–120. doi:10.1016/j.datak.2004.09.003

Calvo, H., Gelbukh, A., & Kilgarriff, A. (2005). *Automatic Thesaurus vs. WordNet: A Comparison of Backoff Techniques for Unsupervised PP Attachment.* LNCS 3406:177–188. New York: Springer.

Calvo, H., Inui, K., & Matsumoto, Y. (2009). Interpolated PLSI for Learning Plausible Verb Arguments, In *Proceedings of the 23rd Pacific Asia Conference on Language, Information and Computation*, pp.622–629.

Calvo, H., Inui, K., & Matsumoto, Y. (2009a). *Learning Co-Relations of Plausible Verb Arguments with a WSM and a Distributional Thesaurus.* Procs. of the 14th Iberoamerican Congress on Pattern Recognition, CIARP 2009, Springer, Verlag. To appear.

Calvo, H., Inui, K., & Matsumoto, Y. (2009b). *Dependency Language Modeling using KNN and PLSI.* Procs. of the 8th Mexican International Conference on Artificial Intelligence, MICAI 2009, Springer, Verlag, to appear.

Chakrabarti, S., Sarawagi, S., & Sudarshan, S. (2010). Enhancing Search with Structure. *A Quarterly Bulletin of the Computer Society of the IEEE Technical Committee on Data Engineering*, *33*(1), 1–13.

Chakrabarti, S., Dom, B., Gibson, D., Kleinberg, J., Kumar, R., & Raghavan, P. (1999). Mining the link structure of the World Wide Web. *IEEE Computer*, *32*(8), 60–67.

Chakrabarti, S., Dom, B., Gibson, D., Kumar, S., Raghavan, P., Rajagopalan, S., & Tomkins, A. (1998). Experiments in topic distillation In *ACM SIGIR Workshop on Hypertext Information Retrieval on the Web*, Melbourne, Australia.

Chakrabarti, S., van den Berg, M. & Dom, B. (1999). *Focused crawling: a new approach to topic-specific Web resource discovery.* Computer Networks (Amsterdam, Netherlands: 1999), 31(11–16):1623–1640

Chang, J., & Blei, D. M. (2010). Hierarchical relational models for document networks. *The Annals of Applied Statistics*, *4*(1), 124–150. doi:10.1214/09-AOAS309

Chang, J., Boyd-Graber, J., Gerrish, S., Wang, C., & Blei, D. (2009). Reading tea leaves: How humans interpret topic models. In *Neural information processing systems*. NIPS.

Chang, J., Boyd-Graber, J., & Blei, D. (2009). Connections between the lines: augmenting social networks with text. In *Proceedings of the 15th ACM SIGKDD international conference on Knowledge discovery and data mining* (p. 169–178). ACM.

Chen, S. F., & Goodman, J. T. (1999). An Empirical Study of Smoothing Techniques for Language Modeling. *Computer Speech & Language*, *13*(4), 359–393. doi:10.1006/csla.1999.0128

Chen, H.-H., Lin, M.-S., & Wei, Y.-C. (2006). Novel association measures using web search with double checking. *ACL-44: Proceedings of the 21st International Conference on Computational Linguistics and the 44th annual meeting of the Association for Computational Linguistics* (pp. 1009-1016). Sydney, Australia: Association for Computational Linguistics.

Chirita, P., Costache, S., Nejdl, W., & Handschuh, S. (2007). P-tag: large scale automatic generation of personalized annotation tags for the web In *Proceedings of the 16th international conference on World Wide Web*, 854. New York: ACM.

Chu, H. (2003). *Information representation and retrieval in the digital age.* Information Today Inc.

Cilibrasi, R. L., & Vitanyi, P. M. B. (2007). The Google Similarity Distance. *IEEE Transactions on Knowledge and Data Engineering*, *19*(3), 370–383. doi:10.1109/TKDE.2007.48

Cilibrasi, R., & Vitanyi, P. (2007). The Google Similarity Distance. *IEEE Transactions on Knowledge and Data Engineering*, *19*, 370–383. doi:10.1109/TKDE.2007.48

Clarkson, P. R., & Rosenfeld, R. (1997). *Statistical Language Modeling Using the CMU-Cambridge Toolkit.* Procs. ESCA Eurospeech.

Cleverdon, C. W. (1991). *The significance of the cranfield tests on index languages.* In SIGIR '91: Proceedings of the 14th annual international ACM SIGIR conference on Research and development in information retrieval, pages 3–12, New York: ACM Press.

Cook, D., & Holder, L. (2006). *Mining graph data.* New York: Wiley-Interscience. doi:10.1002/0470073047

Cooley, R., Mobasher, B., & Srivastava, J. (1997). Web Mining: Information and Pattern Discovery on the World Wide Web. ictai, pp.0558. 9th International Conference on Tools with Artificial Intelligence (ICTAI '97).

Cover, T. M., & Thomas, J. (1991). *Elements of information theory*. Wiley. doi:10.1002/0471200611

Cover, T., & Thomas, J. (1991). *Elements of Information Theory*. New York: Wiley. doi:10.1002/0471200611

Coyotl-Morales, R. M., Villaseñor-Pineda, L., Montes-y-Gómez, M., & Rosso, P. (2006). *Authorship Attribution Using Word Sequences*. 11thIberoamerican Congress on Pattern Recognition (CIARP'2006), LNCS vol. 4225. Springer Verlag.

Cucerzan, S. (2007). Large-Scale Named Entity Disambiguation Based on Wikipedia Data, *Proceedings of the 2007 Joint Conference on Empirical Methods in Natural Language Processing and Computational Natural Language Learning (EMNLP-CoNLL)* (pp. 708-716). Prague, Czech Republic: Association for Computational Linguistics.

Cuevas, A., & Guzman-Arenas, A. (2008). A language and algorithm for automatic merging of ontologies. In Rittgen, P. (Ed.), *Handbook of Ontologies for Business Interaction* (pp. 381–404). Hershey, PA: IGI Global.

Cybenko, G., & Berk, V. H. (2007). Process Query Systems. *IEEE Computer*, 62-70.

Dalkey, N., C. (1969). An Experimental Study of Group Opinion: The Delphi Method. *Futures, 2*(3). Santa Monica.

de Graaf, E., Kok, J., & Kosters, W. (2007). Clustering improves the exploration of graph mining results. In *IFIP2007: Proceedings of the Articial Intelligence and Innovations 2007: from Theory to Applications, volume 247 of IFIP International Federation for Information Processing*, (pp 13-20). Springer Verlag.

Deerwester, S. C., Dumais, S. T., Landauer, T. K., Furnas, G. W., & Harshman, R. A. (1990). Indexing Latent Semantic Analysis. *Journal of the American Society for Information Science American Society for Information Science, 41*(6), 391–407. doi:10.1002/(SICI)1097-4571(199009)41:6<391::AID-ASI1>3.0.CO;2-9

Deerwester, S., Dumais, S. T., Furnas, G. W., & Thomas, K. L, & Richard Harshman. (1990). Indexing by latent semantic analysis. *Journal of the American Society for Information Science American Society for Information Science*, 391–407. doi:10.1002/(SICI)1097-4571(199009)41:6<391::AID-ASI1>3.0.CO;2-9

Dempster, A. (1968). A generalization of Bayesian inference. *Journal of the Royal Statistical Society. Series B. Methodological*, (30): 205–247.

Denicia-Carral, C., Montes-y-Gómez, M., Villaseñor-Pineda, L., & García Hernández, R. A. (2006). *A Text Mining Approach for Definition Question Answering*. 5th International Conference on NLP (Fintal 2006), LNAI, Vol. 4139, Springer-Verlag, pp. 76–86.

Denoeud, L., & Guénoche, A. (2006). Comparison of distance indices between partitions. *Studies in Classification, Data Analysis, and Knowledge Organization*, 21-28.

Deschacht, K., & Moens, M. (2009). Semi-supervised Semantic Role Labeling using the Latent Words Language Model. Procs. 2009 Conf. on Empirical Methods in Natural Language Processing. *Proceedings of the 2009 conference on empirical methods in natural language processing (EMNLP 2009)*, pp. 21–29.

Dhillon, I. S., Mallela, S., & Modha, D. S. (2003). Information-theoretic co-clustering. In *Kdd '03: Proceedings of the ninth acm sigkdd international conference on knowledge discovery and data mining* (pp. 89–98). New York: ACM.

Dong, G., & Pei, J. (2007). *Sequence Data Mining*. Heidelberg: Springer.

Doucet, A., & Ahonen-Myka, H. (2004). *Non-Contiguous Word Sequences for Information Retrieval*. Proceedings of the Workshop on Multiword Expressions: Integrating Processing, Association for Computational Linguistics, Barcelona, Spain, pp. 88-95.

Duan, Q., Miao, D., & Chen, M. (2007). Web Document Classification Based on Rough Set. In A. An, et al. (Ed.), *Lecture Notes in Computer Science 4482, Rough Sets, Fuzzy Sets, Data Mining and Granular Computing, 11th International Conference, RSFDGrC 2007*. 240-247, May 2007, Toronto, Canada.

Dubois, D., & Prade, H. (1988). *Possibility Theory*. New York: Plenum.

Duda, R. O., Hart, P. E., & Stork, D. G. (2000). *Pattern Classification* (2nd ed.). New York: Wiley-Interscience.

Dumais, S. T., Furnas, G. W., Landauer, T. K., Deerwester, S., & Harshman, R. (1988). Using latent semantic analysis to improve access to textual information. In *Chi '88: Proceedings of the sigchi conference on human factors in computing systems* (pp. 281–285). New York: ACM.

Erkan, G., & Radev, D. R. (2004). Lexrank: Graph-based lexical centrality as salience in text summarization. *Journal of Artificial Intelligence Research*, *22*, 457–479.

Ertöz, L., Steinbach, M., & Kumar, V. (2003). Finding topics in collections of documents: A shared nearest neighbor approach. *Clustering and Information Retrieval*, *1*, 83–104.

Fayad, U., Piatetsky-Shapiro, G., & Padhraic, S. (1996). From data mining to knowledge discovery in databases. *AI Magazine*, *17*, 37–54.

Feldman, R., & Sanger, J. (2007). *The text mining handbook*. New York: Cambridge University Press.

Feldman, R., & Dagan, I. (1995). Knowledge discovery in textual databases (KDT). In U.M. Fayyad and R. Uthurusamy (Eds.), *International Conference on Knowledge Discovery* (pp. 112-117). AAAI Press.

Ferraresi, A., Zanchetta, E., Baroni, M., & Bernardini, S. (2008). Introducing and evaluating ukWaC, a very large web-derived corpus of English. *Procs. of the WAC4 Workshop at LREC*. Marrakech, pp. 45–54.

Finkelstein, L., Gabrilovich, E., Matias, Y., Rivlin, E., Solan, Z., & Wolfman, G. (2002). Placing search in context: the concept revisited. *ACM Transactions on Information Systems*, *20*(1), 116–131. doi:10.1145/503104.503110

Flake, G., Lawrence, S., Giles, C., & Coetzee, F. (2002). Self-organization and identification of Web communities. *Computer*, *35*(3), 66–70. doi:10.1109/2.989932

Flake, G., Pennock, D., & Fain, D. (2003). The self-organized Web: The yin to the Semantic Webs yang. *IEEE Intelligent Systems*, *18*(4), 75–77.

Flake, G., Lawrence, S., & Giles, C. (2000). Efficient identification of Web communities. In *Proceedings of the sixth ACM SIGKDD international conference on Knowledge discovery and data mining*, pp. 150–160. New York: ACM.

Foley, W. A. (1997). *Anthropological linguistics: An introduction*. Boston: Blackwell Publishing.

Fowlkes, E. B., & Mallows, C. L. (1983). A method for comparing two hierarchical clusterings. *Journal of the American Statistical Association*, *78*(383), 553–569. doi:10.2307/2288117

Fuji, A., & Iwayama, M. (2005). *Patent Retrieval Task (PATENT)*. Fifth NTCIR Workshop Meeting on Evaluation of Information Access Technologies: Information Retrieval, Question Answering and Cross-Lingual Information Access.

Furnas, G. W., Landauer, T. K., Gomez, L. M., & Dumais, S. T. (1987). The vocabulary problem in human-system communication. *Communications of the ACM*, *30*(11), 964–971. doi:10.1145/32206.32212

Furnas, G. W., Landauer, T. K., Gomez, L. M., & Dumais, S. T. (1984). Statistical semantics: analysis of the potential performance of keyword information systems. 187–242.

Gabrilovich, E., & Markovitch, S. (2007). Computing semantic relatedness using Wikipedia-based explicit semantic analysis. *IJCAI'07: Proceedings of the 20th international joint conference on Artificial intelligence* (pp. 1606-1611). Hyderabad, India: Morgan Kaufmann Publishers Inc.

Gao J., J. Y. Nie, G. Wu, & G. Cao, (2004). *Dependence language model for information retrieval*. Procs. of the 27th annual international ACM SIGIR conference on Research and development in information retrieval, 170–177, 2004.

García-Hernández, R. A., Ledeneva, Y., Gelbukh, A., & Gutierrez, C. (2008). An Assessment of Word Sequence Models for Text Summarization. Special issue: Advances in Intelligent and Information Technologies. *Research in Computing Science*, *38*, 253–262.

García-Hernández, R. A., Montiel, R., Ledeneva, Y., Rendón, E., Gelbukh, A., & Cruz, R. (2008). *Text Summarization by Sentence Extraction Using Unsupervised Learning.* 7th Mexican International Conference on Artificial Intelligence (MICAI08), Lecture Notes in Artificial Intelligence, Springer-Verlag, Vol. 5317 pp. 133-143.

Garza, S. (2010). *A process for extracting groups of thematically related documents in encyclopedic knowledge web collections by means of a pure hyperlink-based clustering approach.* PhD Thesis, May 2010, Tecnologico de Monterrey, Mexico.

Gelbukh, A., Sidorov, G., Lavin-Villa, E., & Chanona-Hernandez, L. (2010). Automatic Term Extraction using Log-likelihood based Comparison with General Reference Corpus. *Lecture Notes in Computer Science, 6177,* 248–255. doi:10.1007/978-3-642-13881-2_26

Gelbukh, A. & G. Sidorov, (1999). On Indirect Anaphora Resolution. PACLING-99, pp. 181-190.

Gentile, A. L., Zhang, Z., Xia, L., & Iria, J. (2010). Cultural knowledge for Named Entity Disambiguation: a graph-based Semantic Relatedness approach. *Serdica Journal of Computing, 4*(2), 217–242.

Girolami, M., & Kabán, A. (2003). *On an equivalence between plsi and lda* (pp. 433–434). SIGIR.

Giuliano, C., Lavelli, A., & Romano, L. (2006). Exploiting Shallow Linguistic Information for Relation Extraction From Biomedical Literature, *Proceedings of the 11th Conference of the European Chapter of the Association for Computational Linguistics (EACL 2006).* Trento, Italy.

Griffiths, T. L., & Steyvers, M. (2004). Probabilistic Topic Models, Finding scientific topics. [Palo Alto, CA: Stanford University.]. *Proceedings of the National Academy of Sciences of the United States of America, 101,* 5228–5235. doi:10.1073/pnas.0307752101

Griffiths, T. L., & Steyvers, M. (2004, April). Finding scientific topics. *Proceedings of the National Academy of Sciences of the United States of America, 101*(Suppl 1), 5228–5235. doi:10.1073/pnas.0307752101

Griffiths, T. L., Steyvers, M., & Tenenbaum, J. B. (2007). Topics in semantic representation. *Psychological Review, 114,* 211–244. doi:10.1037/0033-295X.114.2.211

Grishman, R., & Sundheim, B. (1996). Message Understanding Conference- 6: A Brief History. *COLING* (pp. 466-471).

Guadarrama, S., & Garrido, M. (2008). Concept-Analizer A tool for analyzing fuzzy concepts. In Magdalena, L., Ojeda-Aciego, M., & Verdegay, J. L. (Eds.), *Proceedings of the Information Processing and Management of Uncertainty in Knowledge-Based Systems, IPMU08.* (pp. 1084-1089). Torremolinos, Malaga, Spain.

Guzman-Arenas, A., Cuevas, A., & Jimenez, A. (2011). The centroid or consensus of a set of objects with qualitative attributes. *Expert Systems with Applications, 38,* 4908–4919. doi:10.1016/j.eswa.2010.09.169

Guzman-Arenas, A., & Jimenez, A. (2010). Obtaining the consensus and inconsistency among a set of assertions on a qualitative attribute. *Journal Expert Systems with Applications (*37), 158-164.

Guzman-Arenas, A., & Levachkine, S. (2004a). Hierarchies Measuring Qualitative Variables. *Lecture Notes in Computer Science LNCS* (2945), 262-274.

Guzman-Arenas, A., & Levachkine, S. (2004b). Graduated errors in approximate queries using hierarchies and ordered sets. *Lecture Notes in Artificial Intelligence* LNAI (2972), 139-148.

Halevy, A., Norvig, P., & Pereira, F. (2009). The unreasonable effectiveness of data. *IEEE Intelligent Systems, 24*(2), 8–12. doi:10.1109/MIS.2009.36

Han, J., Cheng, H., Xin, D., & Yan, X. (2007). Frequent pattern mining: current status and future directions. *Data Mining and Knowledge Discovery, 15,* 55–86. doi:10.1007/s10618-006-0059-1

Han, X., & Zhao, J. (2010). *Structural Semantic Relatedness: A Knowledge-Based Method to Named Entity Disambiguation.* Paper presented at the the 48th Annual Meeting of the Association for Computational Linguistics, Uppsala, Sweden.

Harris, Z. (1970). *Distributional structure* (pp. 775–794). Papers in Structural and Transformational Linguistics.

Hassan, S., & Mihalcea, R. (2009). *Cross-lingual Semantic Relatedness Using Encyclopedic Knowledge, EMNLP* (pp. 1192–1201). Association for Computational Linguistics.

Haveliwala, T. H., Gionis, A., Klein, D., & Indyk, P. (2002). *Evaluating Strategies for Similarity Search on the Web.* In WWW'02: Proceedings of the 11th International Conference on World Wide Web, pages 432–442, New York: ACM Press.

He, X., Ding, C., Zha, H., & Simon, H. (2001). Automatic topic identification using webpage clustering. In *Proceedings IEEE International Conference on Data Mining, San Jose, CA*, pp. 195–202.

Hernández-Reyes, E., García-Hernández, R. A., Carrasco-Ochoa, J. A., & Martínez-Trinidad, J. Fco.(2006). Document Clustering based on Maximal Frequent Sequences. 5th International Conference on NLP (Fintal 2006), Tapio Salakoski et al. (Eds.). LNCS Vol. 4139, Springer-Verlag, Turku, Finland, August 2006, pp. 257-267.

Hofmann, T. (1999). Probabilistic Latent Semantic Analysis. [Stockholm.]. *Proceedings of Uncertainty in Artificial Intelligence, UAI, 99,* 289–296.

Hofmann, T. (2001). Unsupervised learning by probabilistic latent semantic analysis. *Machine Learning, 42*(1-2), 177–196. doi:10.1023/A:1007617005950

Hofmann, T. (1999). Probabilistic latent semantic indexing. In *Sigir '99: Proceedings of the 22nd annual international acm sigir conference on research and development in information retrieval* (pp. 50–57). New York: ACM.

Holland, J. H. (1975). *Adaptation in natural and artificial systems.* Ann Arbor: The University of Michigan Press.

Hotho, A., Staab, S., & Stumme, G. (2003). Ontologies improve text document clustering. In *Third IEEE International Conference on Data Mining (ICDM'03)* (pp. 541-545). Published by the IEEE Computer Society.

Hsieh, S., & Hsu, C. (2008). Graph-based representation for similarity retrieval of symbolic images. *Data & Knowledge Engineering, 65*(3), 401–418. doi:10.1016/j.datak.2007.12.004

Hughes, T., & Ramage, D. (2007). Lexical semantic relatedness with random graph walks, *Proceedings of EMNLP* (Vol. 7).

Hunter, A., & Konieczny, S. (2008). Measuring inconsistency through minimal inconsistent sets. *Proceedings of the* 11th *International Conference on Knowledge Representation.* (pp. 358-366). Stratham, NH: AAI Press.

International Data Corporation. (2010). *The Digital Universe Decade, Are You Ready?* http//www.emc.com/collateral/demos/microsites/idc-digital-universe/iview.htm.

Iria, J., Xia, L., & Zhang, Z. (2007). *WIT: Web People Search Disambiguation using Random Walks.* Paper presented at the Proceedings of the Fourth International Workshop on Semantic Evaluations (SemEval-2007).

Jain, A., Murty, M., & Flynn, P. (1999). Data clustering: a review. *ACM Computing Surveys, 31*(3), 264–323. doi:10.1145/331499.331504

Jansen, B. J., Booth, D. L., & Spink, A. (2009). Patterns of query reformulation during web searching. *Journal of the American Society for Information Science and Technology, 60*(7), 1358–1371. doi:10.1002/asi.21071

Jarvis, R., & Patrick, E. (1973). Clustering using a similarity measure based on shared near neighbors. *IEEE Transactions on Computers, 22*(11), 1025–1034. doi:10.1109/T-C.1973.223640

Jelinek, F. (1990). Self-Organized Language Modeling for Speech Recognition, In B. A. Wei & K. F. Lee (Ed.), *Readings in Speech Recognition* (pp. 450-505). Los Altos, CA: Morgan Kaufmann publishing.

Jiang, J., & Conrath, D. (1997). Semantic similarity based on corpus statistics and lexical taxonomy. In *Proc. of the International Conference on Research in Computational Linguistics.* ROCLING X.

Jimenez, A. (in press). *Characterization and measurement of logical properties of qualitative values organized in hierarchies.* Mexico City, Mexico. *CIC-IPN.*

Jo, Y., Lagoze, C., & Giles, C. (2007). Detecting research topics via the correlation between graphs and texts. In *Proceedings of the 13th ACM SIGKDD international conference on Knowledge discovery and data mining,* ACM, pp. 379.

Joachims, T. (2002). *Learning to classify text using support vector machines Methods, theory, and algorithms.* London: Springer.

Johnson, S. C. (1967). Hierarchical Clustering Schemes. *Psychometrika, 32*(3), 241–254. doi:10.1007/BF02289588

Kandel, A. (1986). *Fuzzy Mathematical Techniques with Applications*. Reading, MA: Addison-Wesley.

Karypis, G., & Kumar, V. (1999). A fast and high quality multilevel scheme for partitioning irregular graphs. *SIAM Journal on Scientific Computing, 20*(1), 359. doi:10.1137/S1064827595287997

Karypis, G., Han, E., & Kumar, V. (1999). Chameleon: A hierarchical clustering algorithm using dynamic modeling. *IEEE computer 32* (8), 68–75.

Kautz, H., Selman, B., & Shah, M. (1997). The hidden Web. [AAAI Press.]. *AI Magazine, 18*(2), 27–36.

Kawahara, D., & Kurohashi, S. (2001). Japanese Case Frame Construction by Coupling the Verb and its Closest Case Component. 1st Intl. Conf. on Human Language Technology Research, ACL.

Kazama, J., & Torisawa, K. (2007). Exploiting Wikipedia as External Knowledge for Named Entity Recognition. *Joint Conference on Empirical Methods in Natural Language Processing and Computational Natural Language Learning* (pp. 698-707). Japan Advanced Institute of Science and Technologie.

Kim, S. B., Han, S., Rim, H. C., & Myaeng, S. H. (2006). Some effective techniques for naive bayes text classification. *IEEE Transactions on Knowledge and Data Engineering, 18*(11), 1457–1466. doi:10.1109/TKDE.2006.180

Kleinberg, J. (1999). Authoritative sources in a hyperlinked environment. *Journal of the ACM, 46*(5), 604–632. doi:10.1145/324133.324140

Kodratoff, Y. (1999). Knowledge discovery in texts: A definition and applications. In Z.W. Rasand A. Skowron (Eds.). *International Symposium on Foundations of Intelligent Systems*. Vol. 1609. (pp. 16–29). Springer-Verlag.

Korhonen, A. (2000). Using Semantically Motivated Estimates to Help Subcategorization Acquisition. In *Proceedings of the Joint SIGDAT Conference on Empirical Methods in Natural Language Processing and Very Large Corpora*. Hong Kong. 216-223.

Kosala, R., & Blockeel, H. (2000). Web mining research: a survey. *SIGKDD Explorations Newletters, 2*, 1–15. doi:10.1145/360402.360406

Kraft, R., Chang, C. C., Maghoul, F., & Kumar, R. (2006). *Searching with Context*. In WWW'06: Proceedings of the 15th International Conference Wide Web, pages 477–486, New York: ACM Press.

Kumar, R., Raghavan, P., Rajagopalan, S., & Tomkins, A. (1999). Trawling the web for emerging cyber-communities. *Computer Networks, 31*(11), 1481–1493. doi:10.1016/S1389-1286(99)00040-7

Kumar, R., Raghavan, P., Rajagopalan, S., Sivakumar, D., Tompkins, A., & Upfal, E. (2000). The Web as a graph. In *Proceedings of the nineteenth ACM SIGMOD-SIGACT-SIGART symposium on Principles of database systems*, pp. 1–10. New York: ACM

Kwok, K. L., & Chan, M. S. (1998). *Improving two-stage ad-hoc retrieval for short queries*. In SIGIR '98: Proceedings of the 21st Annual International ACM/SIGIR Conference on Research and Development in Information Retrieval (pp. 250–256). New York: ACM.

Lancichinetti, A., Fortunato, S., & Kertesz, J. (2009). Detecting the overlapping and hierarchical community structure in complex networks. *New Journal of Physics, 11*, 033015. doi:10.1088/1367-2630/11/3/033015

Landauer, T. K., Foltz, P. W., & Laham, D. (1998). An Introduction to Latent Semantic Analysis. *Discourse Processes, 25*, 259–284. doi:10.1080/01638539809545028

Leacock, C., & Chodorow, M. (1998). *Combining local context and WordNet similarity for word sense identification, WordNet: An Electronic Lexical Database*. Cambridge, MA: MIT Press.

Leake, D. B., Bauer, T., Maguitman, A. G., & Wilson, D. C. (2000). *Capture, storage and reuse of lessons about information resources: Supporting task-based information search*. In Proceedings of the AAAI-00 Workshop on Intelligent Lessons Learned Systems. Austin, Texas (pp. 33–37). AAAI Press.

Leake, D., Maguitman, A. G., Reichherzer, T., Cañas, A., Carvalho, M., Arguedas, M., et al. (2003). *Aiding knowledge capture by searching for extensions of knowledge models*. In Proceedings of KCAP-2003. New York: ACM Press.

Lease-Morgan, E. (2002). *Alex Catalogue of Electronic Texts*. Retrieved from http://infomotions.com/alex

Leavitt, N. (2002). Data mining for the corporate masses. *Computer, 35*(5), 22–24. doi:10.1109/MC.2002.999772

Ledeneva, Y. (2008). *Effect of Preprocessing on Extractive Summarization with Maximal Frequent Sequences.* LNAI 5317, pp. 123-132, Springer-Verlag. Lewis, D.D. (1997). *Reuter-21578 Text Categorization Test Collection Distribution 10.* Retrieved from http://kdd.ics.uci.edu/databases /reuters21578/reuters21578.html.

Lee, L., (1999). *Measures of Distributional Similarity.* Procs. 37th ACL.

Leskovec, J., Grobelnik, M., & Milic-frayling, N. (2004). Learning semantic graph mapping for document summarization. In Boulicaut J.B., Esposito F., Giannotti F., & Pedreschi D (Eds.): *ECML/PKDD-2004: Proceedings of the 15th European Conference on Machine Learning (ECML)8th European Conference on Principles and Practice of Knowledge Discovery in Databases,* Lecture Notes in Computer Science, 3202. Springer Verlag.

Levachkine, S., & Guzman-Arenas, A. (2007). Hierarchy as a new data type for qualitative variables. *Journal Expert Systems with Application, 32*(3), 139–148.

Levachkine, S., Guzman-Arenas, A., & de Gyves, V. P. (2005). The semantics of confusion in hierarchies: from theory to practice. ICCS 05 (Ed). *13th International Conference on Conceptual Structures: common semantics for sharing knowledge.* (pp. 94-107). Kassel, Germany.

Li, L., & Shang, Y. (2000). A new method for automatic performance comparison of search engines. *World Wide Web (Bussum), 3*(4), 241–247. doi:10.1023/A:1018790907285

Li, R. M., Kaptein, R., Hiemstra, D., & Kamps, J. (2008, April). Exploring topic-based language models for effective web information retrieval. In E. Hoenkamp, M. de Cock, & V. Hoste (Eds.), *Proceedings of the dutch-belgian information retrieval workshop (dir 2008), maastricht, the netherlands* (pp. 65–71). Enschede: Neslia Paniculata. http://eprints.eemcs.utwente.nl/12277/.

Li, W. B., Sun, L., Feng, Y. Y., & Zhang, D. K. (2008). Smoothing LDA Model for Text Categorization. In H. Li et al. (Ed.), *Lecture Notes in Computer Science, Volume 4993/2008, 4th Asia Information Retrieval Symposium, AIRS 2008,* 83-94, January, 2008, Harbin, China.

Li, W., & McCallum, A. (2006). Pachinko allocation: Dag-structured mixture models of topic correlations. In *Icml '06: Proceedings of the 23rd international conference on machine learning* (pp. 577–584). New York: ACM.

Lieberman, H. (1995). *Letizia: An agent that assists Web browsing.* In C. S. Mellish (Ed.), Proceedings of the fourteenth international joint conference on artificial intelligence. ijcai-95 (pp. 924–929). Montreal, Quebec, Canada: Morgan Kaufmann publishers.

Lin, J. (1991). Divergence Measures Based on the Shannon Entropy. *IEEE Transactions on Information Theory, 37*(I), 145–151. doi:10.1109/18.61115

Lin, D. (1998). *An Information-theoretic Definition of Similarity.* In Proceedings of the Fifteenth International Conference on Machine Learning (pp. 296–304). San Franciso, CA: Morgan Kaufmann Publishers Inc.

Lin, D. (1998a). *Automatic Retrieval and Clustering of Similar Words.* Procs. 36th Annual Meeting of the ACL and 17th International Conference on Computational Linguistics.

Lin, D. (1998b). *Dependency-based Evaluation of MINIPAR.* Proc. Workshop on the Evaluation of Parsing Systems.

Litvak, M., & Last, M. (2008) Graph-based keyword extraction for single-document summarization. In *MMIES '08: Proceedings of the Workshop on Multi-source Multilingual Information Extraction and Summarization* (pp. 17-24). Association for Computational Linguistics.

Liu, B., & Chang, K. (2004). Special issue on Web content mining. *SIGKDD Explorations, 6*(2), 1–4. doi:10.1145/1046456.1046457

Liu, B. (2007). *Web data mining: exploring hyperlinks, contents, and usage data.* New York: Springer.

Liu, B. (2005). *Web Content Mining.* Tutorial at the 14th International World Wide Web Conference, May 10-14, Chiba, Japan.

Liu, D. X., Xu, W. R., & Hu, J. N. (2009). A feature-enhanced smoothing method for LDA model applied to text classification. In: International Conference on Natural Language Processing and Knowledge Engineering (NLP-KE). 1- 7, September 2009, Dalian, China.

Liu, Y., & Zhang, M. Ma,, & Ru L. (2009) User browsing graph: structure, evolution and application, In *WSDM '09: Proceeedings of the Second ACM International Conference on Web Search and Data Mining,* ACM.

Liu, Y., Fu, Y., Zhang, M., Ma, S., & Ru, L. (2007). *Automatic search engine performance evaluation with click-through data analysis.* In WWW '07: Proceedings of the 16th international conference on World Wide Web (pp. 1133–1134). New York: ACM.

Lord, P. W., Stevens, R. D., Brass, A., & Goble, C. A. (2003). Investigating semantic similarity measures across the gene ontology: The relationship between sequence and annotation. *Bioinformatics (Oxford, England), 19*(10), 1275–1283. doi:10.1093/bioinformatics/btg153

Lorenzetti, C. M., & Maguitman, A. G. (2009). A Semi-Supervised Incremental Algorithm to Automatically Formulate Topical Queries. [Special Issue on Web Search.]. *Information Sciences, 179*(12), 1881–1892. doi:10.1016/j.ins.2009.01.029

Lovász, L. (1993). Random walks on graphs: A survey. *Combinatorics, Paul Erd\"os is Eighty, 2,* 1-46.

Luo, P., Xiong, H., Zhan, G., Wu, J., & Shi, Z. (2009). Information-theoretic distances for cluster validation: generalization and normalization. *IEEE Transactions on Knowledge and Data Engineering, 21*(9), 1249–1262. doi:10.1109/TKDE.2008.200

MacQueen, J. (1967). Some methods for classification and analysis of multivariate observations. In LeCam, L. & Neyman, J. (Eds.), *Proceedings of the Fifth Berkeley Symposium on Mathematical Statistics and Probability Vol. 1* (pp. 281-297). University of California Press, Berkeley.

Magatti, D., Calegari, S., Ciucci, D., & Stella, F. (2009b). Automatic labeling of topics. ISDA09 *Proceedings of the 2009 Ninth International Conference on Intelligent Systems Design and Applications* (pp. 1227-1232). IEEE Computer Society, Washington, DC, USA.

Magatti, D., Stella, F., & Faini, M. (2009). A Software System for Topic Extraction and Document Classification. *Proceeding of 2009 IEEE/WIC/ACM International Joint Conference on Web Intelligence and Intelligent Agent Technology Vol. 1* (pp. 283-286). IEEE Computer Society, Los Alamitos, CA, USA.

Maglio, P. P., Barrett, R., Campbell, C. S., & Selker, T. (2000). *SUITOR: an attentive information system.* In Proceedings of the 5th international conference on intelligent user interfaces (pp. 169–176). New York: ACM Press.

Maguitman, A. G., Cecchini, R. L., Lorenzetti, C. M., & Menczer, F. (2010). *Using Topic Ontologies and Semantic Similarity Data to Evaluate Topical Search.* To appear in CLEI 2010. Asuncion, Paraguay.

Maguitman, A. G., Menczer, F., Roinestad, H., & Vespignani, A. (2005b). *Algorithmic Detection of Semantic Similarity.* In WWW '05: Proceedings of the 14th International Conference on World Wide Web (pp. 107–116). New York: ACM Press.

Maguitman, A., Leake, D., & Reichherzer, T. (2005a). *Suggesting novel but related topics: towards context-based support for knowledge model extension.* In IUI '05: Proceedings of the 10th International Conference on Intelligent User Interfaces (pp. 207–214). New York ACM Press.

Maguitman, A., Leake, D., Reichherzer, T., & Menczer, F. (2004). *Dynamic extraction of topic descriptors and discriminators: Towards automatic context-based topic search.* In Proceedings of the thirteenth conference on information and knowledge management (CIKM) (pp. 463—472). Washington, DC: ACM Press.

Makagonov, P. (1997). Evaluating the performance of city government: an analysis of letters by citizens to the Mayor by means of the Expert Assistant System. *Automatic Control and Computer Sciences: Vol. 31. N. 3* (pp. 11–19). New York: Allerton Press.

Makagonov, P., & Reyes, E. C. (2008). *Applying the Document Search Image from a Museum Site Digital Library to Simplify the Document Retrieval on the Internet. Fifteenth Jubilee international Conference.* Crimea, Russia: Libraries and Information Resources in the Modern World of Science, Culture, Education and Business.

Makagonov, P., & Ruiz, F. A. (2005). A Method of Rapid Prototyping of Evolving Ontologies. [Springer-Verlag.]. *Lecture Notes in Computer Science,* N3406.

Makagonov, P., & Sánchez, P. Liliana, E. (2008) Simple applications of data mining and system approach to urban and regional problems analysis. *A Research Report in the Electronic Proceedings of International Workshop SoNet-08 Social Networks and Application Tools* (pp. 16-30).

Makagonov, P., & Sbochakov, K. (2004). Software for creating domain-oriented dictionaries and document clustering in full text database. In A. Gelbukh (Ed.), *Computational linguistics and intelligent text processing* (pp. 454-456). *Springer 2001. LNCS 2004.*

Makagonov, P., Alexandrov, M., & Gelbukh, A. (2004). Clustering Abstracts Instead of Full Texts. Text, *Speech, Dialog.* (pp. 129-135). *LNAI 3206, Springer*.

Makagonov, P., Ruiz, F. A., & Gelbukh, A. (2006). Studying Evolution of a Branch of Knowledge by Constructing and Analyzing Its Ontology. *Lecture Notes in Computer Science Volume 3999, Natural Language Processing and Information Systems: 11th International Conference on Applications of Natural Language to Information Systems* (pp. 37–45). NLDB. Klagenfurt, Austria.

Makagonov, P., Sboychakov, K., & Sánchez, P. Liliana E. (2007). Método y herramienta computacional para medir y mejorar la armonía de proyectos arquitectónicos. *Vitrubio. Creatividad, ciencia: Volumen 1 Número 1.* (pp. 31-37). Facultad de arquitectura, diseño y urbanismo de la Universidad Autónoma de Tamaulipas, México.

Manning, C. D., Raghavan, P., & Schtze, H. (2008). *Introduction to Information Retrieval*. New York: Cambridge University Press.

Markines, B., Cattuto, C., Menczer, F., Benz, D., Hotho, A., & Stumme, G. (2009) *Evaluating similarity measures for emergent semantics of social tagging.* In WWW '09: Proceedings of the 18th international conference on World Wide Web (pp. 641–650) New York: ACM Press.

Markov, A., Last, M., & Kandel, A. (2007). Fast categorization of web documents represented by graphs. In *WEB-KDD: Proceedings of Advances in Web Mining and Web Usage Analysis.* LNCS 4811, (pp 56-71). Springer Verlag.

Matsuo, Y., Sakaki, T., Uchiyama, K. o., & Ishizuka, M. (2006). Graph-based word clustering using a web search engine. *EMNLP '06: Proceedings of the 2006 Conference on Empirical Methods in Natural Language Processing* (pp. 542-550). Sydney, Australia: Association for Computational Linguistics.

McCarthy, D. & J. Carroll. (2006). Disambiguating Nouns, Verbs, and Adjectives Using Automatically Acquired Selectional Preferences. *Computational Linguistics 29-4*, 639–654.

McCarthy, D., Koeling, R., Weeds, J., & Carroll, J. (2004). *Finding predominant senses in untagged text*. Procs 42nd meeting of the ACL, 280–287.

Mccrickard, C. S., Mccrickard, D. S., & Kehoe, C. M. (2007). Visualizing search results using sqwid. In *WWW06: Proceedings of the sixth International World Wide Web Conference.* (pp. 65-77).

Mei, Q., Shen, X., & Zhai, C. (2007). Automatic labeling of multinomial topic models. KDD07 *Proceedings of the 13th ACM SIGKDD international conference on Knowledge discovery and data mining.* (pp. 490-499). San Jose, CA: ACM.

Mei, Q., Xin, D., Cheng, H., Han, J., & Zhai, C. (2006, August). *Generating semantic annotations for frequent patterns with context analysis*. Paper presented at the 2006 ACM SIGKDD international conference on knowledge discovery in databases (KDD'06), Philadelphia, USA.

Menczer, F. (2004). Correlated Topologies in Citation Networks and the Web. *The European Physical Journal B, 38*(2), 211–221. doi:10.1140/epjb/e2004-00114-1

Menczer, F. (2001). *Links tell us about lexical and semantic Web content*. Arxiv preprint cs/0108004.

Merlo, P., & Van Der Plas, L. (2009). Abstraction and Generalisation in Semantic Role Labels: PropBank, VerbNet or both? *Procs. 47th Annual Meeting of the ACL and the 4th IJCNLP of the AFNLP*, pp. 288–296.

Miao, D., Wang, G., & Liu, Q. (2007). *Granular Computing: Past, Present and future*. Beijing, China: Science Publisher.

Mihalcea, R. (2004) Graph-based ranking algorithms for sentence extraction, applied to text summarization. In *ACL 2004: Proceedings of the Interactive poster and demonstration sessions,* (pp 20). Association for Computational Linguistics.

Miller, G., & Charles, W. (1991). Contextual correlates of semantic similarity. *Language and Cognitive Processes, 1*(6), 1–28. doi:10.1080/01690969108406936

Miller, G. A. (1995). WordNet: a lexical database for English. *Communications of the ACM, 38*(11), 39–41. doi:10.1145/219717.219748

Milligan, G. W., & Cooper, M. C. (1985). An examination procedures for determining the number of clusters in a data set. *Psychometrika, 50*(2), 159–179. doi:10.1007/BF02294245

Milne, D., & Witten, I. H. (2008). *An effective, low-cost measure of semantic relatedness obtained from Wikipedia links*. Paper presented at the Wikipedia and Artificial Intelligence: An Evolving Synergy Workshop at the Twenty-third AAAI conference on Artificial Intelligence (AAAI-08).

Miyamoto S., Nakayama, K., (1986) Similarity measures based on a fuzzy set model and applications to hierarechical clustering, *IEEE Trans. on Systems, Man and Cybernetics*, SMC-16, 3, (pp. 479-482).

Modha, D., & Spangler, W. (2003). *Clustering hypertext with applications to Web searching*. US Patent App 10/660,242.

Mojena, R. (1977). Hierarchical grouping methods and stopping rules an evaluation. *The Computer Journal, 20*(4), 359–363. doi:10.1093/comjnl/20.4.359

Montiel Soto, R., García-Hernández, R. A., Ledeneva, Y., & Cruz Reyes, R. (2009). Comparación de Tres Modelos de Texto para la Generación Automática de Resúmenes. [Sociedad Española para el Procesamiento del Lenguaje Natural.]. *Revista de Procesamiento del Lenguaje Natural, 43*, 303–311.

Müller, C., & Gurevych, I. (2009). Using Wikipedia and Wiktionary in domain-specific information retrieval, *CLEF'08: Proceedings of the 9th Cross-language evaluation forum conference on Evaluating systems for multilingual and multimodal information access* (pp. 219-226). Aarhus, Denmark: Springer-Verlag.

Newman, M. (2003). The structure and function of complex networks. *SIAM Review, 45*, 167–256. doi:10.1137/S003614450342480

Newman, D., Asuncion, A., Smyth, P., & Welling, M. (2007). Distributed inference for latent dirichlet allocation. In *Advances in neural information processing systems* (Vol. 20).

Nie, Z., Zhang, Y., Wen, J., & Ma, W. (2005). Object-level ranking: bringing order to Web objects. *WWW '05: Proceedings of the 14th international conference on World Wide Web* (pp. 567-574). Chiba, Japan: ACM.

Ortega-Mendoza, R. M., Villaseñor-Pineda, L., & Montes-y-Gómez, M. (2007). *Using Lexical Patterns For Extracting Hyponyms from the Web*. 6th Mexican International Conference on Artificial Intelligence (MICAI 2007), LNAI4827, Springer-Verlag.

Osinski, S., & Weiss, D. (2005). A concept-driven algorithm for clustering search results. *IEEE Intelligent Systems, 20*, 48–54. doi:10.1109/MIS.2005.38

Ounis, I., Lioma, C., Macdonald, C., & Plachouras, V. (2008). *Research directions in Terrier*. Novatica/UPGRADE Special Issue on Web Information Access, Ricardo Baeza-Yates et al. (Eds), Invited Paper.

Padó, S.& M. Lapata, (2007). Dependency-Based Construction of Semantic Space Models. *Computational Linguistics* 33-2, 161–199.

Padó, U. M. Crocker, & F. Keller, (2006). *Modeling Semantic Role Plausibility in Human Sentence Processing*. Procs. EACL.

Pan, J., Yang, H., Faloutos, C., & Duygulu, P. (2007). Crossmodal correlation mining using graph algorithms. In Zhu, X., Zhu, X., & Davidson, I. (Eds.), *Knowledge Discovery and Data Mining: Challenges and Realities with Real World Data* (pp. 274–294). Hershey, PA: IGI Global. doi:10.4018/978-1-59904-252-7.ch004

Papadimitriou, S., & Sun, J. (2008). Disco: Distributed co-clustering with map-reduce: A case study towards petabyte-scale end-to-end mining. In *ICDM '08: Proceedings of the 2008 eighth ieee international conference on data mining* (pp. 512–521). Washington, DC: IEEE Computer Society.

Parton, K., et al. (2009). *Who, What, When, Where, Why? Comparing Multiple Approaches to the Cross-Lingual 5W Task*. Procs. 47ᵗʰ Annual Meeting of the ACL and the 4ᵗʰ IJCNLP of the AFNLP, pp. 423–431.

Pawlak, Z. (1991). *Rough Sets: Theoretical Aspects of Reasoning about Data*. Dordrecht: Kluwer Academic publisher.

Pearson, K. (1905). The Problem of the Random Walk. *Nature, 72*(1867).

Pedersen, T., Patwardhan, S., & Michelizzo, J. (2004). *Wordnet: similarity – measuring the relatedness of concepts*. In Proceedings of the Nineteenth National Conference on Artificial Intelligence (AAAI-04), pages 1024–1025, 2004.

Pei, J., Han, J., Mortazavi-Asl, B., Wang, J., Pinto, H., & Chen, Q. (2004). Mining sequential patterns by pattern-growth: the prefixspan approach. *Transactions on Knowledge and Data Engineering, 16*(11), 1424–1440. doi:10.1109/TKDE.2004.77

Pei, J., Han, J., Asl, M. B., Pinto, H., Chen, Q., Dayal, U., & Hsu, M. C. (2001). *Prefixspan mining sequential patterns efficiently by prefix projected pattern growth*. Paper presented at 17th International Conference on Data Engineering, Heidelberg, Germany.

Pereira, F., Tishby, N., & Lee, L. (1993). Distributional clustering of english words. In *In proceedings of the 31st annual meeting of the association for computational linguistics* (pp. 183–190).

Piotrovsky, M. (1975). *Text, computer, human being.* Nauka.

Pirolli, P., Pitkow, J., & Rao, R. (1996). Silk from a sow's ear: extracting usable structures from the Web. In *Proceedings of the SIGCHI Conference on Human factors in computing systems: common ground*, pp.118–125. New York: ACM.

Ponzetto, P. S., & Strube, M. (2006). *Exploiting Semantic Role Labeling, WordNet and Wikipedia for Coreference Resolution*. Procs. Human Language Technology Conference, NAACL, 192–199.

Porteous, I., Newman, D., Ihler, A., Asuncion, A., Smyth, P., & Welling, M. (2008). Fast collapsed gibbs sampling for latent dirichlet allocation. In *Kdd '08: Proceeding of the 14th acm sigkdd international conference on knowledge discovery and data mining* (pp. 569–577). New York: ACM.

Puig-Centelles, A., Ripolles, O., & Chover, M. (2007). Identifying communities in social networks: a survey. In *Proceedings of the IADIS International Conference Web Based Communities*, pp. 350–354.

Puppin, D., & Silvestri, F. (2006). The query-vector document model. In *Cikm '06: Proceedings of the 15th acm international conference on information and knowledge management* (pp. 880–881). New York: ACM.

Puppin, D., Silvestri, F., & Laforenza, D. (2006). Query-driven document partitioning and collection selection. In *Infoscale '06: Proceedings of the 1st international conference on scalable information systems* (p. 34). New York: ACM.

Rada, R., Mili, H., Bicknell, E., & Blettner, M. (1989). Development and application of a metric on semantic nets. *IEEE Transactions on Systems, Man, and Cybernetics, 19*(1), 17–30. doi:10.1109/21.24528

Radicchi, F., Castellano, C., Cecconi, F., Loreto, V., & Parisi, D. (2004). Defining and identifying communities in networks. *Proceedings of the National Academy of Sciences of the United States of America, 101*(9), 2658–2663. doi:10.1073/pnas.0400054101

Ramirez, E. H., & Brena, R. (2009). An Information-Theoretic Approach for Unsupervised Topic Mining in Large Text Collections. In *Proceedings of the 2009 IEEE/WIC/ACM International Joint Conference on Web Intelligence and Intelligent Agent Technology.* (pp. 331 – 334). Milan, Italy

Ramirez, E. H., & Brena, R. F. (2006). *Semantic Contexts in the Internet.* LA-WEB'06: Proceedings of the Fourth Latin American Web Congress, 74–81, Washington, DC, USA. IEEE Computer Society.

Ramirez, E. H., Brena, R., Magatti, D., & Stella, F. (2010). Probabilistic Metrics for Soft-Clustering and Topic Model Validation. In *Proceedings of the 2010 IEEE/WIC/ACM International Joint Conference on Web Intelligence and Intelligent Agent Technology.* (pp. 406 – 412). Toronto, Ontario.

Reisinger, J & Marius Paşca. (2009). Latent Variable Models of Concept-Attribute Attachment. *Procs. 47th Annual Meeting of the ACL and the 4th IJCNLP of the AFNLP*, pp. 620–628.

Resnik, P. (1996). Selectional Constraints: An Information-Theoretic Model and its Computational Realization. *Cognition, 61*, 127–159. doi:10.1016/S0010-0277(96)00722-6

Resnik, P. (1995). *Using information content to evaluate semantic similarity in a taxonomy* (pp. 448–453). In IJCAI.

Resnik, P. (1995a). Disambiguating noun groupings with respect to WordNet senses, *Proceedings of the 3th Workshop on Very Large Corpora* (pp. 54-68). ACL.

Resnik, P. (1995b). Using Information Content to Evaluate Semantic Similarity in a Taxonomy, *Proceedings of the 14th International Joint Conference on Artificial Intelligence* (pp. 448-453). Boston: Morgan Kaufmann.

Rhodes, B., & Starner, T. (1996). *The remembrance agent: A continuously running automated information retrieval system.* In The proceedings of the first international conference on the practical application of intelligent agents and multi agent technology (PAAM '96) (pp. 487–495). London, UK.

Ritter, A. Mausam & Oren Etzioni. (2010). A Latent Dirichlet Allocation method for Selectional Preferences, *Proceedings of the 48th Annual Meeting of the Association for Computational Linguistics,* 424–434.

Rocchio, J. J. (1971). Relevance feedback in information retrieval. In Salton, G. (Ed.), *The Smart retrieval system—Experiments in automatic document processing* (pp. 313–323). Englewood Cliffs, NJ: Prentice-Hall.

Rosenfeld, R. (2000). Two decades of statistical language modeling: where do we go from here? *Proceedings of the IEEE, 88*(8), 1270–1278. doi:10.1109/5.880083

Rubenstein, H., & Goodenough, J. B. (1965). Contextual correlates of synonymy. *Communications of the ACM, 8*(10), 627–633. doi:10.1145/365628.365657

Ruiz-Shulclóper, J., Guzman-Arenas, A., & Martinez-Trinidad, F. (1999). *Logical combinatorial approach to Pattern Recognition: supervised classification.* Valencia, Spain: Editorial Politécnica.

Sahami, M., & Heilman, T. D. (2006). A web-based kernel function for measuring the similarity of short text snippets, *WWW '06: Proceedings of the 15th international conference on World Wide Web* (pp. 377-386). Edinburgh, Scotland: ACM.

Salgueiro, P., Alexandre, T., Marcu, D., & Volpe Nunes, M. (2006). Unsupervised Learning of Verb Argument Structures. *Springer LNCS, 3878*, 2006.

Salton, G. (1991). Developments in automatic text retrieval. *Science, 253*, 974–979. doi:10.1126/science.253.5023.974

Salton, G., Wong, A., & Yang, C. S. (1975). A Vector Space Model for Automatic Indexing. *Communications of the ACM, 18*(11), 613–620. doi:10.1145/361219.361220

Salton, G. (1989). *Automatic text processing: The transformation, analysis, and retrieval of information by computer.* Reading, MA: Addison-Wesley.

Salton, G. (1986). Recent trends in automatic information retrieval. In *SIGIR '86: Proceedings of the 9th Annual International ACM SIGIR Conference on Research and Development in Information Retrieval,* (pp.1-10). ACM press.

Schaeffer, S. (2005). Stochastic local clustering for massive graphs. *Advances in Knowledge Discovery and Data Mining, 3518*, 354–360. doi:10.1007/11430919_42

Schenker, A., Last, M., Bunke, H., & Kandel, A. (2003). Graph representations for web document clustering. In *IbPRIA03: Proceedings of the first Iberian Conference on Pattern Recognition and Image Analysis,* LNCS 2652. (pp. 935-942). Springer Verlag.

Scholer, F., & Williams, H. E. (2002). *Query Association for Effective Retrieval.* In Proceedings of the Eleventh International Conference on Information and Knowledge Management (pp. 324–331). New York: ACM Press.

Schönhofen, P. (2006). Identifying document topics using the Wikipedia category network. In *Proceedings of the 2006 IEEE/WIC/ACM International Conference on Web Intelligence*, IEEE Computer Society Washington, DC, USA, pp. 456–462.

Schwartz, R., Sista, S., & Leek, T. (2001). Unsupervised topic discovery. In *Proceedings of workshop on language modeling and information retrieval*, pp. 72–77.

Scott, J. (2000). *Social Network Analysis: a handbook* (2nd ed.). Thousand Oaks, CA: SAGE Publications.

Séaghdha, Ó. D. (2010). Latent variable models of selectional preference. *Proceedings of the 48th Annual Meeting of the Association of Computational Linguistics*, pp. 435–444.

Shafer, G. (1976). *A Mathematical Theory of Evidence*. Princeton, NJ: Princeton UniversityPress.

Shan, H., & Banerjee, A. (2008). Bayesian co-clustering. In *ICDM '08: Proceedings of the 2008 eighth ieee international conference on data mining* (pp. 530–539). Washington, DC: IEEE Computer Society.

Shen, Q., & Zhao, R. (2011). A credibilistic approach to assumption-based truth maintenance. *IEEE Transactions on Systems, Man and Cybernetics. Part A, 41*(2), 85–95.

Sista, S., Schwartz, R., Leek, T. R., & Makhoul, J. (2002). An algorithm for unsupervised topic discovery from broadcast news stories. In *Proceedings of the second international conference on Human Language Technology Research, pp. 110-114.* San Francisco: Morgan Kaufmann Publishers Inc.

Slonim, N., & Tishby, N. (1999). *Agglomerative information bottleneck* (pp. 617–623). Cambridge, MA: MIT Press.

Slonim, N., & Tishby, N. (2000). Document clustering using word clusters via the information bottleneck method. In *In acm sigir 2000* (pp. 208–215). ACM press. doi:10.1145/345508.345578

Slonim, N., Friedman, N., & Tishby, N. (2002). Unsupervised document classification using sequential information maximization. In *Sigir '02: Proceedings of the 25th annual international acm sigir conference on research and development in information retrieval* (pp. 129–136). New York: ACM.

Smith, G. (2008). *Tagging: People-powered Metadata for the Social Web*. Berkeley, CA: New Rider Press.

Spearman, C. (1987). *The American Journal of Psychology; The Proof and Measurement of Association between Two Things. 100*(3/4), 441-471.

Srikant, R., & Agrawal, R. (1996). Mining sequential patterns: Generalizations and performance improvements. In P. M. G. Apers, M. Bouzeghoub, & G. Gardarin (Eds). *Intl. Conf. Extending Database Technology, 1057*, 3–17. Springer-Verlag.

Srivastava, J., Cooley, R., Deshpande, M., & Tan, P. N. (2000). Web usage mining: discovery and applications of usage patterns from web data. *SIGKDD Explorations Newletters, 1*(2), 12–23. doi:10.1145/846183.846188

Stein, B., & Zu-Eissen, S. (2004). Topic identification: Framework and application. In *Proceedings International Conference on Knowledge Management, 399*, pp. 522–531.

Steinbach, M., Karypis, G., & Kumar, V. (2000). *A Comparison of document clustering techniques. Technical Report #00-034*. Dept. of Computer Science and Engineering, University of Minnesota, USA.

Steyvers, M., & Griffiths, T. (2007). Probabilistic topic models. In Landauer, T., Mcnamara, D., Dennis, S., & Kintsch, W. (Eds.), *Handbook of latent semantic analysis*. Mahwah, NJ: Lawrence Erlbaum Associates.

Stone, M. (1977). Asymptotics for and against cross-validation. *Biometrika, 64*(1), 29–35. doi:10.1093/biomet/64.1.29

Strube, M., & Ponzetto, S. P. (2006). WikiRelate! Computing Semantic Relatedness Using Wikipedia, *Proceedings of The Twenty-First National Conference on Artificial Intelligence and the Eighteenth Innovative Applications of Artificial Intelligence Conference* (pp. 1419-1424). AAAI Press.

Suchanek, F., Kasneci, G., & Weikum, G. (2008). Yago: A large ontology from Wikipedia and Wordnet Web. *Semantics: Science. Services and Agents on the World Wide Web, 6*(3), 203–217. doi:10.1016/j.websem.2008.06.001

TextAnalyst Microsystems, Ltd. (2010). Retrieved from http://www.analyst.ru/

The Economist. (2010). *A special report on managing information Data, data everywhere.* http//www.economist.com/opinion/displaystory.cfm?story_id=15557443.

Theobald, M., Siddharth, J., & Paepcke, A. (2008). Spotsigs: robust and efficient near duplicate detection in large web collections. In *Sigir '08: Proceedings of the 31st annual international acm sigir conference on research and development in information retrieval* (pp. 563–570). New York: ACM.

Thiel, K., Dill, F., Kotter, T., & Berthold, M. R. (2007). Towards visual exploration of topic shifts. Systems, *ISIC2007: Proceedings of the IEEE International Conference on Man and Cybernetics.* (pp.522-527).

Tishby, N., Pereira, F. C., & Bialek, W. (1999). The information bottleneck method. In (pp. 368–377).

Treese, W. (2006). Web 20: is it really different? *netWorker, 10*(2), 15–17. doi:10.1145/1138096.1138106

Turchi, M., Mammone, A., & Cristianini, N. (2009). Analysis of text patterns using kernel methods. In Srivastava, A. N., & Sahami, M. (Eds.), *Text Mining Theory and Applications* (pp. 1–25). Taylor and Francis Publisher.

Turdakov, D., & Velikhov, P. (2008). Semantic Relatedness Metric for Wikipedia Concepts Based on Link Analysis and its Application to Word Sense Disambiguation, *SYRCoDIS* (Vol. 355). CEUR-WS.org.

Van Rijsbergen, C. J. (1979). *Information Retrieval.* London: Butterworths.

Virtanen, S. (2003). Clustering the Chilean Web. In *Proceedings of the 2003 First Latin American Web Congress*, pp. 229–231.

Voorhees, E. M., & Harman, D. K. (2005). *Experiment and Evaluation in Information Retrieval.* Cambridge, MA: MIT Press.

Wallach, H., Murray, I., Salakhutdinov, R., & D. (2009). Evaluation methods for topic models. In *Proceedings of the 26th Annual International Conference on Machine Learning ICML 09* (pp. 1-8).

Wan, X. (2008). An exploration of document impact on graph-based multi-document summarization. In *EMNLP '08: Proceedings of the Conference on Empirical Methods in Natural Language Processing,* (pp. 755-762). Association for Computational Linguistics.

Wang, P., Domeniconi, C., & Laskey, K. B. (2009). Latent dirichlet bayesian co-clustering. In *Ecml pkdd '09: Proceedings of the european conference on machine learning and knowledge discovery in databases* (pp. 522–537). Berlin, Heidelberg: Springer-Verlag.

Wartena, C., & Brussee, R. (2008). *Topic detection by clustering keywords.* In DEXA 2008: 19th International Conference On Database & Expert Systems Applications Proceedings.

Wasserman, S., & Faust, K. (1994). *Social Network Analysis: Methods and Applications.* New York: Cambridge University Press.

Weale, T., Brew, C., & Fosler-Lussier, E. (2009). Using the Wiktionary Graph Structure for Synonym Detection, *Proceedings of the 2009 Workshop on The People's Web Meets NLP: Collaboratively Constructed Semantic Resources* (pp. 28-31). Suntec, Singapore: Association for Computational Linguistics.

Weeds, J.& D. Weir. (2003). A General Framework for Distributional Similarity, *Procs. conf on EMNLP*, 10,81-88.

Wei, X., & Croft, W. B. (2006). LDA-based document models for ad-hoc retrieval. In E. N. Efthimiadis (Ed.), *Proceedings of the 29th ACM SIGIR Conference on Research and Development in IR.* 178-185, August 2006, Seattle, Washington, USA.

Wei, Z. (2010). *The research on Chinese text multi-label classification.* Unpublished doctoral dissertation, University of Tongji, China.

Weikum, G., & Theobald, M. (2010). From information to knowledge: harvesting entities and relationships from web sources. *In Proceedings of the twenty-ninth ACM SIGMOD-SIGACT-SIGART symposium on Principles of database systems of data* (p. 65–76). ACM.

Worring, M., de Rooij, O., & van Rijn, T. (2007). Browsing visual collections using graphs. In *MIR '07: Proceedings of the international workshop on Workshop on multimedia information retrieval* (pp.307-312). ACM press.

Wu, J., Xiong, H., & Chen, J. (2009). Adapting the right measures for k-means clustering. In *Kdd '09: Proceedings of the 15th acm sigkdd international conference on knowledge discovery and data mining* (pp. 877–886). New York: ACM.

Wu, Z., & Palmer, M. (1994). Verbs semantics and lexical selection, *Proceedings of the 32nd annual meeting on Association for Computational Linguistics* (pp. 133-138). Las Cruces, New Mexico: Association for Computational Linguistics.

Yamada, I., Torisawa, K., Kazama, J., Kuroda, K., Murata, M., de Saeger, S., et al. (2009). Hypernym Discovery Based on Distributional Similarity and Hierarchical Structures. *Procs. 2009 Conf. on Empirical Methods in Natural Language Processing*, pp. 929–937.

Yin, X., Han, J., & Fu, P. S. (2008). Truth Discovery with multiple conflicting information providers on the Web. *IEEE Trans. KDE*, *20*(6), 796–808.

Zaki, M. J. (2000, November). *Sequence mining in categorical domains: incorporating constraints.* Paper presented at 9th international conference on Information and knowledge management, McLean, Virginia, USA.

Zesch, T., Müller, C., & Gurevych, I. (2008a). *Extracting Lexical Semantic Knowledge from Wikipedia and Wiktionary.* Paper presented at the Proceedings of the Sixth International Language Resources and Evaluation (LREC'08), Marrakech, Morocco.

Zesch, T., Müller, C., & Gurevych, I. (2008b). Using Wiktionary for Computing Semantic Relatedness, *Proceedings of the Twenty-Third AAAI Conference on Artificial Intelligence, AAAI 2008* (pp. 861-866). AAAI Press.

Zhai, C., & Lafferty, J. (2001a). A Study of Smoothing Methods for Language Models Applied to Ad hoc Information Retrieval. In W. B. Croft et al. (Ed.), *Proceedings of the 24th ACM SIGIR Conference on Research and Development in IR*. 334-342, September 2001, New Orleans, Louisiana, USA.

Zhai, C., & Lafferty, J. (2001b). Model-based feedback in the KL-divergence retrieval model. *In 10th International Conference on Information and Knowledge Management, CIKM2001*. 403-410, November, 2001, Atlanta, Georgia, USA.

Zhai, C., & Lafferty, J. (2002). Two-Stage Language Models for Information Retrieval, In M. Beaulieu (Ed.), *Proceeding of ACM SIGIR 2002 Conference on Research and Development in Information Retrieval*. 49-56, August 2002, Tampere, Finland.

Zhang, Q., & Segall, R. S. (2009). Web mining: a survey of current research, techniques, and software. [IJITDM]. *International Journal of Information Technology & Decision Making*, *7*(4), 683–720. doi:10.1142/S0219622008003150

Zhang, X., Zhou, X., & Hu, X. (2006). Semantic Smoothing for Model-based Document Clustering. *In Proceedings of the 6th IEEE International Conference on Data Mining (ICDM 2006)*. 1193-1198, December 2006, Hong Kong, China.

Zhang, Z., Gentile, A. L., Xia, L., Iria, J., & Chapman, S. (2010). A Random Graph Walk based Approach to Computing Semantic Relatedness Using Knowledge from Wikipedia, *Proceedings of the Seventh conference on International Language Resources and Evaluation (LREC'10)* (pp. 1394-1401). European Language Resources Association (ELRA).

Zhou, X., Hu, X., Zhang, X., Lin, X., & Song, I. Y. Context-sensitive Semantic Smoothing for Language Modeling Approach to Genomic Information Retrieval, In E. N. Efthimiadis (Ed.), *Proceedings of the 29th ACM SIGIR Conference on Research and Development in IR*. 170-177, August 2006, Seattle, Washington, USA.

Zhou, X., Zhang, X., & Hu, X. (2008). Semantic Smoothing for Bayesian Text Classification with Small Training Data. In M. J. Zaki & K. Wang (Ed.), *Proceedings of the SIAM International Conference on Data Mining, SDM 2008*. 289-300, April 2008, Atlanta, Georgia, USA.

Ziarko, W. (1993). Variable precision rough set model. *Journal of Computer and System Sciences*, *46*(1), 39–59. doi:10.1016/0022-0000(93)90048-2

About the Contributors

Ramon F. Brena is full professor at the Tecnologico de Monterrey, Mexico, since 1990, where he is head of a research group in Distributed Knowledge and Multiagent Systems. Dr Brena is the head of the Master level graduate programs in Computer Science and Artificial Intelligence. Dr. Brena holds a PhD from the INPG, Grenoble, France, where he presented a doctoral Thesis related to Knowledge in Program Synthesis. His current research and publication areas include Intelligent Agents and Multiagent Systems, Ubiquitous computing and Ambient Intelligence, Formal Methods in Software Engineering, Knowledge representation and reasoning, Semantic Web, and Artificial Intelligence in general. He has been visiting professor at the U. of Texas at Dallas and the Université de Montréal. Dr Brena is member of the ACM, and is recognized as an established researcher by the official Mexican research agency, CONACyT (SNI level I).

Adolfo Guzmán-Arenas is a Computer Science professor at Centro de Investigación en Computación, Instituto Politécnico Nacional, Mexico City, of which he was Founding Director. He holds a B. Sc. in Electronics from ESIME-IPN, and a Ph. D. from MIT. He is an ACM Fellow, IEEE Life Fellow Member, member of MIT Educational Council, member of the Academia de Ingeniería and the Academia Nacional de Ciencias (Mexico). From the President of Mexico, he has received (1996) the National Prize in Science and Technology and (2006) the Premio Nacional a la Excelencia "Jaime Torres Bodet." He works in semantic information processing and AI techniques, often mixed with distributed information systems. More at http://alum.mit.edu/www/aguzman.

***

Gloria Bordogna holds the position of senior researcher at the National Research Council Institute for the Dynamics of Environmental Processes. She received a laurea degree in Physics from the University of Milano. Her research interests concern soft computing in the area of information retrieval, flexible query languages and Geographic Information Systems. She was involved in several European projects such as Ecourt, PENG and IDE-Univers, edited three volumes and a special issue of JASIST in her research area, participated to the organization of several events among which the 2009 IEEE/WIC/ACM International Conferences on Web Intelligence (WI'09) and Intelligent Agent Technology (IAT'09) and in the program committee of several conferences such as FUZZ-IEEE, ACM SIGIR, ECIR, FQAS, CIKM, IEEE-ACM WI/IAT, WWW.

Hiram Calvo obtained his Master degree in Computer Science in 2002 from National Autonomous University of Mexico, with a thesis on mathematical modeling, and his PhD degree in Computer Science with honors in 2006 from the Computing Research Center of the National Polytechnic Institute, Mexico, with a thesis on natural language processing. Since 2006 he is a lecturer at the Computing Research Center of the National Polytechnic Institute. He was awarded with the Lázaro Cárdenas Medal given by the president of Mexico in 2006 as the best Ph. D. student of IPN in the area of physics and mathematics. Currently he is a visiting researcher at the Nara Institute of Science and Technology, Japan. His interests are automatic common sense knowledge acquisition, and unsupervised methods for pattern recognition and machine learning.

Alessandro Campi is a researcher at the Politecnico di Milano. His works exploit the possibility of extending XQuery in several directions, more precisely, the possibility to add active rules, to execute fuzzy queries, to mine data and to draw the query without writing directly XQuery. Other research activities are related to investigating automatic construction and verification of data intensive Web site and on methodologies and tools for e-learning. He taught Programming languages, Data Structures and Algorithms, Database and Software Engineering at the Politecnico di Milano.

Rocío L. Cecchini is a Teaching Assistant at the Computer Science and Engineering Department at Universidad Nacional del Sur in Argentina and an Assistant Researcher at CONICET. In 2006 she obtained an Engineering degree in Computer Science at Universidad Nacional del Sur. Since then she has been conducting research in the areas of multi-objective evolutionary algorithms, knowledge discovery, datamining and more recently, biocomputing. She has obtained a PhD degree in Computer Science in May 2010 funded by fellowships from Universidad Nacional del Sur and CONICET. Email: rlc@cs.uns.edu.ar.

Fabio Ciravegna is Full Professor of Language and Knowledge Technologies at the University of Sheffield where he coordinates the Organisations, Information and Knowledge (OAK) Group. His research field concerns methodologies and technologies for the Intelligent and Semantic Web, with focus on Knowledge Management applications. He has considerable engagement with industry and user communities with projects funded by Rolls Royce, Kodak Eastman, Lycos, and the Environment Agency. He is part of the editorial board of the International Journal on ''Web Semantics'' and of the International Journal of Human Computer Studies. He is director of research of K-Now, a spin-off company of the University of Sheffield focusing on supporting dynamic distributed communities in large organizations. He holds a PhD from the University of East Anglia and a doctorship from the University of Torino, Italy

Celia Bertha Reyes Espinoza obtained her Master of Science degree in Electronics and Computer Science from "Mixtec Technological University" in Huajuapan de León; Oaxaca; Mexico in 2008. She is currently a full professor researcher of the Mixtec Technological University, author of 10 scientific publications. Her research interests include computational linguistics and information retrieval from Internet.

René Arnulfo García Hernández is Professor at the University of the State of Mexico in the Software Engineering Department. He received the B.Sc degree as Computational System Engineering in 2001 and received the M.Sc degree in computer science from National Center for Technological Research and Development in 2003. He obtained a Ph.D. in computer science from National Institute of Astrophysics Optics and Electronics in 2007. He is member of the National System of Researchers. His research interests include text and data mining, and natural language processing.

Kentaro Inui gain his Doctor of Engineering in 1995, Tokyo Institute of Technology. Has been Associate Profesor at the Kyushu Institute of Technology, and then Associate Professor at Nara Institute of Science and Technology from 2002 to 2010. Currently he is Professor at Tohoku University, Japan. He has received the Best Asian NLP Paper award in COLING/ACL-2006, the Best Paper Award at the 10th Annual Meeting of the Association of Natural Language Processing in 2004 and 2003. He is currently developing a system for evaluating credibility of web information. His interests are paraphrasing, text simplification, question answering, text-based knowledge acquisition, dialogue processing, co-reference resolution, and affective text understanding.

Carlos M. Lorenzetti is a Teaching Assistant and a Postdoctoral fellow at the Computer Science and Engineering Department at Universidad Nacional del Sur in Argentina. In 2005 he obtained an Engineering degree in Computer Science at Universidad Nacional del Sur. In April 2006 he started his doctoral thesis research with a fellowship granted by CONICET, and obtained a PhD degree in Computer Science in March 2011. His research interests include datamining, knowledge discovery and information retrieval. Email: cml@cs.uns.edu.ar.

Ana G. Maguitman is an Adjunct Professor at the Computer Science and Engineering Department at Universidad Nacional del Sur in Argentina and an Adjunct Researcher at CONICET. She obtained a Ph.D. in Computer Science from Indiana University in 2004 and has been a Visiting Researcher at the School of Informatics of that Institution until 2006. She heads the Knowledge Capture and Information Retrieval Group at the Universidad Nacional del Sur and is currently pursuing research in the areas of knowledge capture, recommendation systems, context-based search, and web mining. She is the author of more than 70 scientific publications in these areas. Email: agm@cs.uns.edu.ar.

Davide Magatti graduated in 2007 in Compuer Science at Università degli studi di Milano – Bicocca and received the Ph.D in Computer Science in 2011 at Università degli studi di Milano – Bicocca with a thesis on "Graphical Models for Text Mining: knowledge extraction and performance estimation". He works in the "Models and Algorithms for Data and Text Mining Laboratory (M.A.D)" at Department of Informatics Systems and communications (DISCo) of Milano-Bicocca university. His research area is Text Mining and in particular document clustering and supervised models for information extraction. He mainly works with probabilistic graphical models for topic extraction and information extraction models. He is also interested in the interplays between Text Mining and document management systems and in the development of solutions that integrate semantic web with text mining and machine learning.

Pavel Makagonov is D.Sc from 1978. He is currently a professor researcher of the Mixtec Technological University in Huajuapan de León; Oaxaca; Mexico. Dr. Pavel Makagonov is author of more than 100 scientific publications, including 6 monographs. His research interests include computational linguistics, natural language processing, system analysis and urban computing.

Yuji Matsumoto is currently a Professor of Information Science, Nara Institute of Science and Technology, head of the Computational Linguistics Laboratory. He received his M.Sc. and Ph.D. degrees in information science from Kyoto University in 1979 and in 1989. He joined Machine Inference Section of Electrotechnical Laboratory in 1979. He has then experienced an academic visit at Imperial College of Science and Technology, London; a deputy chief of First Laboratory at ICOT, and an associate professor at Kyoto University. His main research interests are natural language understanding, knowledge representation, linguistic knowledge acquisition and machine learning. He is author of more than 200 publications on these subjects.

Duoqian Miao received the Ph.D degree in 1997 from Institute of Automation, Chinese Academy of Science. He is currently a professor and vice dean of the school of Electronics and Information Engineering at Tongji University, P.R. China. His research interests include: Rough Sets, Granular Computing, Principal Curve, Machine learning, Web Intelligence, Data Mining etc. He has published 3 academic books and over 140 scientific papers in international journals and conferences. He has been honored with the Award of Scientific and Technological Progress of Ministry of Education (1st class) in China in 2007. He is a senior member of the China Computer Federation (CCF), a committee member of the CCF Artificial Intelligence and Pattern Recognition, the CCF Machine Learning; a committee member of the Chinese Association for Artificial Intelligence (CAAI), a vice chair of the Chinese Association for Artificial Intelligence (CAAI) Rough Set and Soft Computing Society, a committee member of the CAAI Machine Learning; a committee member of the Chinese Association of Automation(CAA) Intelligent Automation; a committee member and chair of Shanghai Computer Society (SCA) Computing Theory and Artificial Intelligence, is also a committee member of International Rough Sets Society.

Jesús-Ariel Carrasco-Ochoa received his PhD in Computer Science from the Center for Computing Research of the National Polytechnic Institute (CIC-IPN), Mexico, in 2001. He works as fulltime researcher at Computer Science Department of the National Institute for Astrophysics, Optics and Electronics (INAOE) of Mexico. His current research interests include Logical Combinatorial Pattern Recognition, Data Mining, Feature and Prototype Selection, Document Analysis, Fast Nearest Neighbor Classifiers and Clustering.

Giuseppe Psaila is assistant professor at the Faculty of Engineering at University of Bergamo. He obtained the degree in Electronic Engineering from Politecnico di Milano, and the Ph.D. in Computer Engineering from Politecnico di Torino. His research interests are in the field of databases, in particular database models and languages, data mining, XML and workflow systems. He participated to several European funded research projects in the database field, such as the IDEA Project (development of an active, deductive and object oriented database system), Mietta (on Multilingual Information Extraction) and cInq (consortium on knowledge discovery by Inductive Queries).

Eduardo H. Ramirez Rangel holds a Ph.D. on Intelligent Systems from the Tecnologico de Monterrey, Mexico where he has worked on Large Scale Topic Modeling technologies. During the course of his studies he had interned with companies like Microsoft Research and Yahoo! Research working in areas related to search-spam, search quality measurement and personalized search. Before joining the Ph.D. program he was co-founder and software architect of Ensitech de Mexico, a startup company specializing on e-Commerce and Internet Marketing software. He has also performed consultancy on topics like XML standards, software engineering, website performance and information architecture. His research interests include unsupervised learning, data mining, cloud computing, Internet economics and contextual advertising.

Alma Delia Cuevas Rasgado holds a degree in computer science from Instituto Tecnologico del Istmo located in Mexico. She currently holds a position in the University of Computing at the Instituto Politécnico Nacional as professor, Escuela Superior de Computo. Her area of research is ontology fusion with recent developments in Information System to Assurance quality in the Centralized Technological Institutes, Book about Process Orientes Information Systems at <u>ITComplements</u> company (writer).

Stefania Ronchi graduated cum laude in Computer Science Engineering, curriculum Information Systems, at the University of Bergamo in February 2008. She participated in the Italian regional research project ''Dote Ricercatore'' for the development of research projects in the technical-scientific area. She won a PhD grant in Information Engineering at the Department of Electronics and Information of Politecnico di Milano, where she currently carries out her research activity in the database area, dealing mainly with Web search, IR and Semantic Web. She authored two publications on her research topics in the proceedings of international conferences.

Grigori Sidorov obtained his PhD in Computational and Structural Linguistics from "Lomonosov" Moscow State University, Russia, in 1996. He is currently a full professor of the Natural Language Processing Laboratory, Center for Computing Research, Instituto Politecnico Nacional in Mexico City, Mexico. Dr. Sidorov is National Researcher of Mexico level 3 (highest level), member of Mexican Academy of Sciences, Editor-in-Chief of the research journal "Polibits", author of more than 150 scientific publications. His research interests include computational linguistics, natural language processing and application of machine learning techniques to NLP tasks.

Fabio Stella graduated in Computer Sciences in February 1991 at the Università degli Studi di Milano. From 1991 to 1994 he worked as research assistant for the EEC IMPROD project on semiconductors failure diagnosis, analysis and quality improvement. In January 1994 he became Assistant Professor of Operations Research at the Università degli Studi di Milano. He received the Ph.D. in Computatioonal Mathematics and Operations Research in 1995. In 2001 he became Associate Professor of Operations Research at the Università degli Studi di Milano-Bicocca. He directs the Models and Algorithms for Data and Text Mining Laboratory and actively collaborates with many Italian SMEs in the area of document management, financial risk management, and analysis of clinical and microarray data. He has been advisor of several Ph.D. students in Computer Science at the Università degli Studi di Milano-Bicocca. His main research interests include; continuous time Bayesian networks, data mining, text mining with specific reference to topic models, and computational finance with specific reference to on-line algorithms for portfolio selection.

José Francisco Martínez-Trinidad received his B.S. degree in Computer Science from Physics and Mathematics School of the Autonomous University of Puebla (BUAP), Mexico, in 1995, his M.Sc. degree in Computer Science from the faculty of Computers Science of the Autonomous University of Puebla, Mexico, in 1997 and his Ph.D. degree in the Center for Computing Research of the National Polytechnic Institute (CIC, IPN), Mexico, in 2000. Professor Martinez-Trinidad edited/authored six books and over one hundred journal and conference papers, on subjects related to Pattern Recognition.

Zhihua Wei received the Ph.D degree in 2010 from Department of Computer Science and Technology, Tongji University, China. She is currently a lecturer at Tongji University. Her research interests include Text mining, Machine Learning and Natural Language Processing.

Ruizhi Wang received the Ph.D degree in 2008 from Department of Computer Science and Technology, Tongji University, China. She is currently a lecturer at Tongji University. Her research interests include Clustering Analysis, Granular Computing and Data Mining

Zhifei Zhang He received the B.E degree in 2008 from Department of Computer Science and Technology, Tongji University. He is currently a Ph.D candidate at Tongji University, China. His research interests include Text Mining, Machine Learing, and Natural Language Processing.

Ziqi Zhang is a Research Associate at the University of Sheffield. He is a member of the Organisations, Information and Knowledge (OAK) Group. His research field concerns Human Language related technologies with focus on Information Extraction, text mining and Natural Language Processing. He has worked on a number of Information Extraction and Knowledge Management related projects and produced a number of relevant publications in some major conference venues such as Knowledge Engineering and Knowledge Management by the Masses (EKAW) and Language Resources Evaluation Conference (LREC). He currently holds a Master degree from the University of Birmingham, and is pursuing his PhD in the field of Information Extraction.

Index